Excursions with Thoreau

Excursions with Thoreau

Philosophy, Poetry, Religion

Edward F. Mooney

Bloomsbury Academic
An imprint of Bloomsbury Publishing Inc

B L O O M S B U R Y
NEW YORK • LONDON • NEW DELHI • SYDNEY

Bloomsbury Academic
An imprint of Bloomsbury Publishing Inc

1385 Broadway	50 Bedford Square
New York	London
NY 10018	WC1B 3DP
USA	UK

www.bloomsbury.com

BLOOMSBURY and the Diana logo are trademarks of Bloomsbury Publishing Plc

First published 2015

© Edward F. Mooney, 2015

All rights reserved. No part of this publication may be reproduced or transmitted in any form or by any means, electronic or mechanical, including photocopying, recording, or any information storage or retrieval system, without prior permission in writing from the publishers.

No responsibility for loss caused to any individual or organization acting on or refraining from action as a result of the material in this publication can be accepted by Bloomsbury or the author.

Library of Congress Cataloging-in-Publication Data
A catalog record for this book is available from the Library of Congress.

ISBN: HB: 978-1-5013-0565-8
PB: 978-1-5013-0564-1
ePub: 978-1-5013-0566-5
ePDF: 978-1-5013-0567-2

Typeset by Fakenham Prepress Solutions, Fakenham, Norfolk NR21 8NN

[I would] go before the mast and on the deck of the world, for there I could best see the moonlight amid the mountains.
—Walden, "Conclusion"

Suppose I try to describe faithfully the prospect which a strain of music exhibits to me. The field of my life becomes a boundless plain, glorious to tread, with no death nor disappointment at the end of it. All meanness and trivialness disappear. I become adequate to any deed. No particulars survive this expansion; persons do not survive it. In the light of this strain there is no thou nor I. We are actually lifted above ourselves.
—*Journal*, January 15, 1857

[O]ur prospects brighten on the influx of better thoughts. We should be blessed if we lived in the present always, and took advantage of every accident that befell us.
—Walden, "Spring"

[G]ratitude for life having been given at all is the spring of remembrance, for a life is cherished even in misery ... What ultimately stills the fear of death is not hope or desire [for outcomes], but remembrance and gratitude
—Hannah Arendt, *Love and St. Augustine**

---

* **Epigraphs:** *Walden; or Life in the Woods*, Jeffrey Cramer (ed.) (New Haven: Yale University Press, 2004), "Conclusion" p. 133 [para 4]; I give paragraph numbers in brackets after chapter titles for *Walden*. *Journal* January 15, 1857, p. 222; *Journal* citations will be from *The Journal of Henry D. Thoreau*, Bradford Torrey (ed.) (Boston: Houghton Mifflin, 2006) Vols I–XIV, available on-line: *The Writings of Henry David Thoreau: The Digital Collection*. *Walden*, "Spring," p. 303 [para 19]. Hannah Arendt, *Love and St. Augustine* (Chicago: University Press, 1996), p. 52.

Contents

Acknowledgments		ix
Note on Abbreviations		xi
Preface		xiii
1	Overture	1
2	Celebration and Lamentation	17
3	Sympathy with Intelligence	37
4	Concord Reflections	59
5	Transforming Perceptions	81
6	Ethics and the Wild	97
7	Expressive Bones	111
8	Child of the Mist	119
9	Deaths and Rebirths	135
10	Affliction and Affinity	147
11	John Brown	165
12	Souls in Infinite Culture	179
13	Currents of Time	191
14	Grounding Poetry	203
15	Face of the River	223
Closing Thoughts		239
Closing Images, Reveries, Prayers		241
Closing Passions		243
Chronology		253
Works Cited		255
Credits		263
Index		265

Acknowledgments

Writing is invitational and conversational. Whether we are rational, knowing or political animals, whether we are wounded, grieving or laughing animals, whether our primary capacity is language-use, cultural-construction, tool-use, or reverencing, each of these distinctively human activities and sufferings emerges in the nexus of our being passionately conversational. We are beings who negotiate the truths of our condition through earnest, playful, practical, tragical, comical, and stoical improvisations. This conversing seems destined to invite ever-wider circles of participants who listen often cross-generationally and over centuries to ongoing and emerging flows, adding to (and subtracting from) the mutuality of address that gives direction and depth to human existence.

Jim Hatley invited my thoughts on Thoreau and Levinas; I invited Lyman Mower to join in for it was he who first made the startling suggestion that the two might converse fruitfully. Clark West invited me to think of Thoreau's narration of Hannah Duston's capture and her revenge killings as the Fall of America, and prompted me to think twice about Levinas' story of the woman with bread and a brick. Some women and men are islands but luckily not all, or not all the time, and become partners in conversing. I've learned from Carson Webb, Rob Reuhl, and Andrew Corsa of Syracuse, from Kristen Case and Brendan Mahoney, of Maine and Vermont, from Sandy and Emily Budick and Milette Shamir, of Jerusalem and Tel Aviv. Ada Jaarsma of the Canadian colds got me to speak about warm passions. Tzachi and Orit Zamir welcomed my wandering ways and aimed me toward aspects of yoga and Lear's fury I otherwise would have missed. William Day put me on the track of Virgil's Aeneas contemplating war and seeing a world where "things weep," and thanks to Dan Conway who years ago pushed me along toward Thoreau long before the Concord saunterer really took hold.

I've taken heart and learned from the inspiring Branka Arsić, and from Kelly Jolley, who invited me to Auburn; they've been nothing but encouraging. Tami Yaguri has been at my side throughout and helpful on the anomaly of becoming young through aging. I've learned from William Eaton, editor of *Zeteo*, from Haaris Naqvi my editor, from Steve Webb, a friend who knows Henry Bugbee and Thoreau's *Journal* inside out, from Gary Whited, a brother and poet in Boston, from Rick Furtak, my long-time Colorado friend who showed how to shift gears from Kierkegaard to Thoreau, and from my friend Andrew Brown, a Unitarian Pastor in Cambridge England, musician, photographer, thinker, and Thoreauvian walker.

Note on Abbreviations

"Journal", unless otherwise noted, will refer to *The Journal of Henry D. Thoreau*, Bradford Torrey (ed.) (Boston: Houghton Mifflin, 2006) Vols I–XIV, available on-line: *The Writings of Henry David Thoreau: The Digital Collection*.

"Week": *A Week on the Concord and Merrimack Rivers*, Carl F. Hove, William L. Howarth, and Elizabeth Hall Witherell (eds) (Princeton: Princeton University Press, 1980).

"Walden": *Walden; or Life in the Woods*, Jeffrey Cramer (ed.) (New Haven: Yale University Press, 2004).

Preface

My absorption in Thoreau and his infiltration of my interests have never been narrowly academic but always straightforwardly a matter of fellow feeling, even love. The essays that follow mark way stations where particular questions have arisen of their own accord, as it were—not because I ever had a project laid out in advance that aimed explicitly to explore them. I came to Thoreau—or he came to me—quite unexpectedly, a mere half-dozen years ago. Quite fortuitously, it was in circumstances that allowed me time to think freely, with and about him. These essays thus have a personal bent that does not disguise my getting caught up in a theme or tension and being drawn along.

I open by taking up Thoreau's words to Lucy Brown delivered before his writing career was fully launched while he was still in convalescence from his brother John's sudden death, and from the equally sudden shock, just ten days later, of the death of little Waldo Emerson. I tread through this opening catastrophe and proceed through more pleasant, if sometimes tumultuous, terrain in an amble with Thoreau. Along the way I recall how in my experience of him Thoreau became, quite to my surprise, so much more than the counterculture icon I had embraced earlier. Having all but finished my present writing, I was startled to come across a short polemic that I wrote for a newspaper in the midst of student turmoil in California in 1968. As I staged him, Thoreau spoke for two counterculture options: seeking bliss by a pond or pursuing militant activism. Yet for me, by the mid-1970s, Thoreau had slipped into the shadows—only to be revived forty years later in the alternative terms I fill out here. The outspoken hero protesting social injustice and the self-reliant outdoorsman and yogi awakening on the shores of Walden Pond are now upstaged by a miraculous writer, an artist and religious adept whose métier is keen naturalist observation and sympathy with all in his ken. Thoreau's dialogues with the worlds he inhabits now leapt from the page with a beauty and gentle authority that pulled me to share his excursions and reveries.

In his meditations Thoreau enters a woodlot or ascends a river or meanders toward a cliffy overlook. These are exercises for regaining paradise and sanity. His pedestrian pace and perceptions uncover ripples of illumination that unfold like sublime musical effects. Thoreau doesn't write travel literature or tourist guides to special spots around Concord, nor does he write simple self-help books, nor programs for becoming Green. His writing speaks from unexpected moments of aesthetic-religious transformation, rendered with resonance and tremor that steal our composure. These moments work like the invasive pathos of a late Schubert sonata or of a Bach cello suite. In my case, they did not descend on a susceptible youth. They arrived after decades teaching humanities and philosophy—but, strange to say, not *Thoreau*.

In my early years teaching philosophy and literature, I lived easily with the reigning opinion among philosophers that he was a grab bag of good quotes and a courageous political activist but, like Emerson, a philosophical lightweight. He was more an outdoorsman and talented writer than a thinker. To shed these prejudices has been both humbling and exhilarating. My discovery of a philosopher through-and-through coincided with adopting a wider vision of philosophy. I now align a large segment of philosophy with poetic prose, unfinished essays, and writing dedicated to personal transformation. I abandoned the restrictive philosophical commitments in vogue since Descartes that privilege an intense focus on propositional certainty achieved through argumentative rigor. This focus, of course, rules out a literary or poetic lilt to philosophy and rules out philosophy aimed at self-transformation. It rules out the possibility of Thoreau as philosopher.

The Cartesian heritage leaves a debilitating gap between consciousness and body, and between mind and social or natural worlds. Flourishing in counterpoint to the Cartesian tradition is an alternative heritage, a tradition of great literary philosophers—Montaigne, Goethe, Kierkegaard, and many others—that refuses these dualities. For one thing, a mind–matter dualism has no place for *living* beings—their growth or maturation, their social and environmental interdependencies, and their embodied passions and commitments. A literary-philosopher more often than not embraces embodied expressiveness, and is unafraid to sing praises or laments of life, and of life among others and in nature. A great virtue of Thoreau as a philosopher is his willingness to expose the soul in its setting and embodiment in ways that avoid mind–body or mind–world standoffs. For instance Thoreau finds even bones—say, the bones he finds at shipwrecks on Cape Cod or Fire Island—to be infinitely expressive. I've come to see repeatedly that Thoreau rejuvenates philosophy as he brings eloquence to the business and pleasures of living.

Before setting out, let me fill in a bit of background and what to expect. Thoreau writes before sharp lines are etched separating natural science, social science, the study of religions, literature, environmental policy, cultural studies, philosophy, and so forth—each separated from all others and further subdivided. Thoreau belongs in all these niches, which in an age of required specialized disciplinary credentials amounts to making him homeless. We can't code or corral him as this or that.

Having warned against narrow branding, I nevertheless proceed to locate Thoreau as a poet-philosopher. I realize that in proposing this, I distance myself from his other identities—say as one of the early pioneers of comparative world religions, or as a father of the Green movement, or as a disciplined ecologist of the first order—not to mention his claim to honors outside the academy as a political activist, or as a yogi or holy man towing along a composite this-worldly religion without name.[1]

I opt for Thoreau the poet-*philosopher* rather than poet-only. I want to find more than tropes, symbols, repeated images, metaphors, synecdoche, irony, and so forth, and the messages these convey. The poetic-philosophy this writer bequeaths is in part Socratic, and in part a model of *askesis*—an ascetic way of life practiced by early Greek philosophers and by the early Desert Fathers of Christianity, and found in the *Bhagavad-Gita*, a classic Thoreau loved. His poetic-philosophy is also in part the sort of naturalist spiritual vision we find in Goethe or Coleridge. Associating Thoreau with any of these legacies makes him by dominant twentieth-century standards at best a marginal philosopher. Desert Fathers and Coleridge are not top-drawer thinkers by current standards. He positions himself in the world of the here and now and against objective systems that would align philosophy only with the style of detached scientific inquiry—a clinical style that puts poetry aside. Lucretius writes a long philosophical poem on nature that is fairly systematic and at times seems to adopt a cosmic perspective, what Thomas Nagel calls "the view from nowhere."[2] Thoreau writes something like philosophical poetry on nature, too, but unlike Lucretius, he stays away from any explicit system. He refuses the seductive "view from nowhere," the stance where one is set to capture all time and eternity in a pellucid overview.

To say that Thoreau avoids the systematic unity of formal philosophy is not to say that his writing lacks unity. The unity and coherence we find is like the unfolding temporal unity of an extended musical composition, or the spatially distributed unity of a multi-paneled mural, each panel expressing facets of a complex and changing reality, or the unity of a variegated prismatic display of colors like a mobile of Alexander Calder. Those who expect the unity of a tightly argued essay are quickly thrown off by Thoreau's capacity to move from scene to scene, motif to motif, sometimes

---

[1] Paul Friedrich, *The Gita in Walden* (Albany: SUNY Press, 2008); Andrea Nightingale, "Auto-Hagiography: Augustine, Thoreau," *Arion*, Fall 2008, pp. 111–48; "Henry David Thoreau: The Asian Thread," Robert Kuhn McGregor, *Thoreau's Importance for Philosophy*, Rick Anthony Furtak, Jonathon Ellsworth, and James D. Reid (eds) (New York: Fordham University Press, 2012) Ch. 12; Branka.
[2] Thomas Nagel, *The View from Nowhere* (New York: Oxford University Press, 1986).

whimsically it seems, presenting varying and often opposing moods and points of view. Of course if we stick to Thoreau's polemical, political essays, we find brilliant, single-focused arguments. But in works like *Walden* or *A Week on the Concord and Merrimack Rivers*, or in his masterful late essays "Walking," or "Wild Apples," we find argument fragments linked aesthetically, like figures in motion in the landscape of a Brueghel village painting, or like motifs in a contemplative medieval chant, not unlike the music box tunes Thoreau loved so much—tunes heard in a resonant, timeless and to us sad, uncanny, yet joyful place.

1

Overture

Standing on distant hills you see the heavens reflected, the evening sky, in some low lake or river in the valley ...—Does it not prove how intimate heaven is with earth?
—*Journal*, August 31, 1851

Each ball of the button-bush reflected in the silvery water by the riverside appears to me as distinct and important as a star in the heavens viewed through "optic glass." This, too, deserves its Kepler and Galileo.
—*Journal*, October 16, 1859[1]

1.

Thoreau is a philosophical poet *en route*, walking, pulling oars, gliding on rivers or ponds. He is also a religious poet, a kind of Eastern ascetic, and a scientific field researcher to boot. And he knows how to live with heaven and hell, praise and outrage.

Thoreau reveals shifting, complex and sometimes clashing realities. He shares what the world looks like to a sensitive observer in passing, a poetic reporter who files his story episode by episode. Of course, the world doesn't sit still for these reports from the field. It flows like a stream or wind— though occasionally it sits *relatively* still, like the bottom of Walden or the top of Mt. Saddle-back.[2] But if neither the world nor I can exhibit a stable anchor, how do I find, in the here and now, an intelligible sense of things?

Though philosophers have wrestled with this question from the very beginning, no *obvious* general answer has turned up, aside from challenging the legitimacy of raising the anxious question in the first place. Everyday relative stability of perspective and footing does not eliminate the possibility of a disorienting whirl of appearances opening frighteningly before us, prompting a general skeptical panic. Thoreau experienced

---

[1] Epigraphs: *Journal*, August 31, 1851, p. 438; October 16, 1859, pp. 395–6.
[2] "Mt. Saddle-back" is now Mt. Greylock. *A Week on the Concord and Merrimack Rivers*, pp. 182–8 (hereafter, *Week*); *Walden; or Life in the Woods*, Jeffrey Cramer (ed.), "Conclusion," p. 133 [para 4] (hereafter, *Walden*; for ease in using alternative editions, I give paragraph numbers in brackets after chapter titles).

something like this in the clouds atop Mt. Ktaadn.[3] He reflects playfully (and seriously) in *Walden*, on what it's like to seek ultimate foundations for reality. He searches for the pond's bottom.[4] He notes a positive aspect to our search: our deep need of "the unfathomable" that adds mystery and unfinished surprises to ventures in living.[5] He relishes the tale of the man on horseback who asks if the swamp that he has a yen to cross has a firm bottom. The man receives a laconic "Yes"—only to sink in up to his saddle, forgetting to ask how deep that bottom is.[6] Yet in the course of things, in our own lives and for Thoreau, bouts of skeptical panic disappear, or at least subside, one way or another. In nearly every case, for a good-enough span of time, we rediscover good-enough footing and perspective. And we recover, one way or another, without recourse to a philosophical self-help manual of procedures specifying *how* to alleviate doubt and get on with our lives.

We return to solid ground—or it returns to us. We grasp patterns in an ever-changing reality willy-nilly, even as we lack a strict formula or argument that explicates how this is possible.[7] The impulse to skepticism often remains, but that impulse is itself open to skepticism. Why trust the legitimacy of every instance of our recursive doubting? The trick is to forgo *wanton* self-questioning, to embrace, as Thoreau has it, a trusting availability to moments of intelligibility, luminosity, and abundance, as these arrive, as they strike. He shows openness to "the influx of better thoughts," an influx that lets life and our living go on.[8]

2.

To essay is to try, to undertake, and this captures the spirit of my efforts. The essays included here are excursions, conversational walking adventures,

---

[3] See *The Maine Woods*, "Ktaadn," Joseph J. Moldenhauer (ed.) (Princeton, NJ: Princeton University Press, 1972), pp. 69–71 (hereafter, "Ktaadn"). Also available in *Princeton Classics* paper edn and in annotated edition, Jeffrey Cramer (ed.) (New Haven: Yale University Press, 2009), pp. 62–5.

[4] *Walden*, "The Pond in Winter," p. 277 [para 16]. On Thoreau's search for foundations, see Stanley Cavell, *The Senses of Walden* (New York: Viking Press, 1972), pp. 74f.

[5] *Walden*, "Spring," p. 306 [para 23].

[6] *Walden*, "Conclusion," p. 321 [para 14].

[7] Rick Anthony Furtak, "Skepticism and Perceptual Faith: Henry David Thoreau and Stanley Cavell on Seeing and Believing", *Transactions of the Charles S. Peirce Society*, 43 (3) (2007): 542–61; Lee Braver, *Groundless Grounds: A Study of Wittgenstein and Heidegger* (Cambridge, MA: MIT University Press, 2012).

[8] *Walden*, "Spring," p. 303 [para 19].

each, including this opening venture, more than sufficient for a day.[9] It's only fitting that the emphasis is on what *Thoreau* has to say. There's a fair amount of discursive exposition of his views. I call these excursions *conversational* in light of Thoreau's being ever alert to his reader, as if awaiting a response, often uncannily anticipating it. It's as if he modulates his pace and words to keep his listeners alive to him as he utters. He is not merely passing on objective reports or unilateral polemics. My accounts are arraigned not as an orderly treatise but nevertheless in an order, with a fair amount of recurrence in motif and theme. They are episodic—as Thoreau's thinking is itself episodic and of the moment. He is not remembering a journey taken long ago, recollected in tranquility, and recounted in an orderly, single narrative. He wants to convey the excitement of *discovery-here-and-now*, living in the present. I try to pass on that sense of mobile and resonant presence.

Though not connected by a single plot, these ventures are nonetheless related. The same paths and their prospects reappear, now and again, first to last. They are related also because the conversational participants are more or less stable perceivers and raconteurs. Of course, there are subtle changes in sensibility—that's the point of the walks—but neither Thoreau nor I undergo radical personality shifts, even as the terrain can surprise us along the way. What I bring to these ventures—and what he brings to them—varies. The outcome is a loose network of prospects as we approach a pond, a mountain, or sight fish in the shallows, startle at the sound of screeching loons, or become soothed by gentle rain on the roof.

After this preliminary overture, I catch stride with Thoreau in the second chapter, taking up the theme of loss and mourning. In the third, I'm in pace with his late masterpiece "Walking." This is an exploratory meditation that culminates with what Thoreau calls "Sympathy with Intelligence." In the fourth chapter, I pursue the importance of living out a philosophy—rather than spelling it out in "subtle thoughts," and leaving it at that. Then I pause in chapter five with passages from *Walden* that exhibit at close quarters the transforming work of perception. In six I take up the many strands of Thoreau's wild ethics, coming to rest with the motif of preservative care. The seventh is an interlude, a meditation on the lively beauty of bird skeletons— of expressive bones.

In chapter eight, I take up Thoreau's proposal that at our best we are "children of the mist," seeing things lost in the glare of adult necessities. In chapters nine and ten, I consider oscillations between wonder and affliction

---

[9] For an introduction to walking as philosophical meditation see Dan Conway, "Answering the Call of the Wild: Walking with Bugbee and Thoreau," *Wilderness and the Heart: Henry Bugbee's Philosophy of Place, Presence, and Memory,* Edward F. Mooney (ed.), forward by Alasdair MacIntyre (Athens, GA: University of Georgia Press, 1999), pp. 3–17.

in Thoreau's writing, between Dionysian and less tumultuous outlooks. Then in eleven and twelve I bring together Thoreau's appreciations of the natural wild and his piercing political engagements, considering especially the case of John Brown. And I take up Thoreau's measures of valor, and the notions of infinite culture and porous souls. Chapter thirteen follows the course of Concord River, especially the opening passages of *A Week on the Concord and Merrimack Rivers*, while fourteen explores giving weight to the poetic in the light of Kantian perspectives suggested by Stanley Cavell. I want to explore what it would be to *ground* the poetic. Chapter fifteen closes out these excursions letting a major continental thinker of the last century, Emmanuel Levinas, join Thoreau in addressing the face of the river. I listen as each calls on the resources of fable and reverie.

3.

Thoreau's "befitting reveries," as I call them, are thoughts half way between philosophy and poetry, half way between factual reports and imaginative constructions, half way between what is and what would be. His most captivating and transporting passages are often moments of reverie—not "*just* a day dream" or "*just* a fantasy," as if they were things to dismiss once we awake. Sharon Cameron calls them "mesmeric ruminations."[10] They awaken us to more reality than we'd otherwise have, and to realities we hardly dreamed we *could* have.

These befitting reveries exemplify a particular feature of language that Rowan Williams describes this way:

> The connectedness of language to what is not language is a shifting pattern of correlation, not an index-like relation of cause and effect. We cannot easily imagine human speaking without the risk of metaphor, without the possibility of error and misprision, without the possibility of fiction, whether simple lying or cooperative fantasy.... [The] environment is there not as a fixed object for describing and managing but as a tantalizing set of invitations, material offered for reworking and enlarging.... [Its] intelligibility [is found] in its capacity to generate fresh schemata and fresh ways of expressing one identity through another.[11]

---

[10] Sharon Cameron, *Writing Nature: Henry Thoreau's Journal* (Chicago: University of Chicago Press, 1989), p. 67.

[11] Williams continues: "As speakers, we make things other than themselves: so far from constructing a definitively demarcated territory ... we constantly re-draw boundaries—or rather, perhaps, introduce migrants into different territories and make them speak new

Reveries are invitational. There's an ecstatic moment in *Walden*'s "Spring" when Thoreau spies a small hawk soaring, then falling, then remounting towards the clouds—a moment he elaborates in soaring, falling sentences.[12] It's not a moment to dismiss because dream-like but to cradle, one among others, like a moment in his chapter "The Ponds." He gazes into the pond— her waters reflecting skies above, and showing his face, and showing even intimations of the face of a Maker.[13] These moments are reveries marvelously befitting a condition we can share. They move us gently, effortlessly, through new sympathies with the world. Beyond any pretense of verisimilitude to a stripped-down object, they unabashedly show up a truth we can live for, a truth that exposes what we can cherish—the truth, say, that existence is as bounteous as imagination:

> The geologist has discovered that the figures of serpents, griffins, flying dragons ... "indicate a faint and shadowy [human] knowledge of a previous state of ... existence" ... I am partial to these wild fancies ... They are the sublimest recreation of the intellect.[14]

Such truths might come in walking, or in meditation by the pond: "I sat in my sunny doorway from sunrise till noon, rapt in a reverie ..."[15] Or he'd take his boat to the pond's middle, "lying on my back across the seats, ... dreaming awake."[16] And of course their significance might not be granted by everyone.[17]

> The frog had eyed the heavens from his marsh, until his mind was filled with visions, and he saw more than belongs to this fenny earth. He mistrusted [feared] that he was become a dreamer.[18]

---

dialects and wear new clothes. The unceasing effort to re-work perceptions as our means of exploring what it is for something to be 'there' for us is both free, in the sense that it is never accounted for by an energy-exchange model, and deeply constrained, in the sense that we are always trying to allow what is there to show itself—an ethical and not only an epistemological point, as it requires a systematic questioning of our starting point, our own interest. Mistakes, the capacity to recognize and build on mistakes, fictions and projections, all these tell us more about language than any dyadic interpretation." Rowan Williams, *The Edge of Words: God and the Habits of Language* (London: Bloomsbury, 2014), pp. 58–61.

[12] *Walden*, "Spring," p. 305 [para 22].
[13] *Walden*, "The Ponds," p. 187 [para 26].
[14] "Walking," *Collected Essays and Poems of Thoreau*, Elizabeth Hall Witherell (ed.) (New York: Library of America, 2001), p. 245 [para 56] (hereafter, "Walking"). The count of paragraphs from the start is bracketed to assist location in other editions: e.g. *Henry D. Thoreau: Essays: Fully Annotated*, Jeffrey S. Cramer (ed.) (New Haven: Yale University Press, 2013).
[15] *Walden*, "Sounds," p. 108 [para 2].
[16] *Walden*, "The Ponds," p. 185 [para 21].
[17] Art can be true to reality insofar as it reveals or exposes something we hadn't noticed in routine perception. If a new interpretive possibility is revealed, art can be true to such things revealed, claiming universal assent even as such assent is only partial actually.
[18] *Journal*, May 21, 1851, p. 207.

I return to these befitting reveries often—the soaring hawk, the "child of the mist," the appearance, in "Walking," of gods at Spaulding's Farm.[19] "Reverie" is the best word for that vivid moment in *Walden* where Thoreau considers devouring a woodchuck alive ("Higher Laws"), or for that moment (in "Reading") when he would have the villagers read all the classics in their original languages.[20] We also have befitting reverie as he sees the "Maker" of Walden in shore-side waters ("The Ponds") or conjures that "old dame" mother nature ("Solitude").[21]

If playful, such reverie is also deeply serious. It is full of Socratic provocation. It stirs imagination and upsets, for the better, our adjustments to the world around us. Befitting reverie is not an idle pastime. It can get us closer to reality. I return to the question of "grounding" such reverie in my all-but-last excursion. We could say that the Michelangelo David is both a likeness and a reverie of what he should really look like, or what we could be. Thoreau's reveries bring us toward what we might be, if only we had ears and eyes more lyrical. "If you have built castles in the air ... that is where they should be. Now put the foundations under them."[22] The foundations we might provide are in part the new perceptions that bring us in flow with these reveries—do we pause to hear frogs differently now? A reverie can be grounded by a way of being in the world responsive to it. A reverie of a Mozart melody is grounded as we seek out a concert that will contain it. And we can put foundations under these castle-like reveries in meditative, improvisatory elaborative responses—the sort of recreations that our present excursions with Thoreau will model. Our improvisations generously back up the befitting flights that Thoreau repeatedly initiates.

4.

Thoreau was unafraid of reverie and was also a first-rate naturalist. His meticulous field notes are still valuable to those who study the ecology of Eastern Massachusetts, especially those who want regional historical time-lines.[23] In addition, he advanced a number of worthy ecological and

---

[19] *mist* "Walking," p. 250 [para 73]; *Spaulding* "Walking," p. 252 [para 78].
[20] *woodchuck* "Higher Laws" p. 202 [para 1]; *classics* "Reading" p. 104 [para 9].
[21] *Maker* "Ponds" p. 187 [para 26]; *old dame* "Solitude" p. 133 [para 16].
[22] *Walden*, "Conclusion" p. 315 [para 5].
[23] Richard B. Primack and Abraham J. Miller-Rushing, "Uncovering, Collecting, and Analyzing Records to Investigate the Ecological Impacts of Climate Change: A Template from Thoreau's Concord," *BioScience* 62.2 (2012): 170–81.

geological hypotheses.[24] He speculated astutely about "the succession of forest trees." Why, after a fire, is the new growth not just a replacement of the old-growth species?[25] But Thoreau knew that gathering knowledge was only a small part of his life in nature and amongst others.

We are cognitive creatures, juggling networks of theories that promise to capture the flow of atoms or money, of social power or discourse, of child development or ecological interdependence, of political revolutions or mob behavior, of split brains or neural processing, of repressions or sublimations. We are creatures who gather data, and focus theories and make new ones, bent on improving scientific understandings. But we are not only that. Scientists love or are stoical or defensive about their work and their place in the world. They wake up, as all of us do, in foul or cloudy or buoyant moods, with aches in their limbs or hearts, with a sense of attachment to or alienation from close others. And they work, sometimes attuned to natural splendors, sometimes not. All this colors the way they—and we—are in the world. Consciously or unconsciously such mood, disposition, and attunement colors how we think and act, whether we're scientists or artists or bureaucrats or taxi-drivers. We live with a pre-theoretical, pre-cognitive largely tacit openness to (or rejection of) others, worlds, and ourselves. I call this *registering the presence of things*—their allure or repulsiveness, banality or splendor, gentle lilting or stark forbiddingness.

Thoreau takes up the philosophical task of refiguring these pre-theoretical, more or less poetic attachments or alienations, using his own sensibilities as his canvas and subject as he reveals unexpected worlds. This refiguring uncovers a vibrant, exuberant, and strangely serene way of living. He delights in what lies *mixed in* with scientific practices—without depleting their purity a bit. Observing and theorizing the natural world is paired with evoking its mobile presence. These aspects of awareness are parallel and not *necessarily* competitive. Thoreau accentuates both. He might sense that science has a mysterious aura even as he practices it flawlessly. He might sense the dark horror of an Indian attack even as he studies it with impeccable historical discipline and detachment. He might laugh at the lunacy of a loon even as he listened for the exact pitch of its cry. He might smell paradise in a lily even as he uncovered its ecological niche.

In "Walking," one of his last and most powerful essays, Thoreau names the twin to his more celebrated, naturalist's pursuit of knowledge. Musing on an invitation from a society for the propagation of useful knowledge,

---

[24] Robert M. Thorson, *Walden's Shore: Henry David Thoreau and Nineteenth-Century Science* (Cambridge, MA: Harvard University Press, 2014).

[25] See "The Succession of Forest Trees," *Collected Essays and Poems of Thoreau*, Elizabeth Hall Witherell (ed.) (New York: Library of America, 2001), pp. 429–43.

he quips that he would *only* join a Society for the Diffusion of Useful Ignorance.[26] Then he remarks that he prefers "Beautiful Knowledge," and a page later he leaves Knowledge behind and says his more constant desire is to have "Sympathy with Intelligence."[27] Let me delay for a moment the title he accords this alternative interest or vocation—the meaning of her tag is not immediately transparent. I'll focus on the idea that Knowledge is not his *exclusive* interest.

Throughout his musings, Thoreau knows that he can, and *does*, have both disciplined knowledge *and* its twin, a sympathetic alertness to what I'll call presence. Thoreau doesn't use this term, but flies with other idioms: "Beautiful Knowledge," or yet again, an alert *unknowing* that seems close to stunned, speechless ignorance before a rich presence. I think it's clear that he has no intention of *denying* Knowledge to make room for its alternative.

I can prefer cappuccino to the croissant that accompanies it while securely appreciating both immensely. Our ideological wars notwithstanding, science and a sensibility that is poetic, ethical, or religious, and receptive to "presence" are by no means *by their nature* in a competitive stand-off. Thoreau is wonderful witness to a capacity to be filled with both love of science and with what surpasses science. Openness to presence, to the wonder and beauty of things, is muffled, to be sure, as one adopts the lean objectivity required in preparing scientific reports. And there is a deep cultural obstacle to overcome—the supposition (surely false) that science *alone* can disclose or reveal reality—even the reality of a child's smile. Thoreau takes reality to be complex. It can deliver observational data and it can equally deliver the lunacy of a loon, the lilt of flowing grass, the gentle budding of the button-bush. Lunacy, lilt, and gentle budding are real.

5.

As a naturalist, philosopher, and voracious reader, we might assume that Thoreau is a devotee of Knowledge *exclusively*. He will enjoy the shock-value of overturning this expectation. But on second thought, it's not at all unusual for philosophers to place something other than knowledge at the apex of things one should strive for. Love might be more important than knowledge even as love and knowledge overlap. Honor or power might be primary, or

---

[26] Louis Menand reports that in the 1840s, a mass paperback series was launched on the east coast called *The American Library of Useful Knowledge*. See his essay "Pulp's Big Moment," *The New Yorker*, Jan 5, 2015. Thoreau's quip about useful ignorance is almost certainly a response to this series.

[27] "Walking," p. 250 [para 72].

perhaps friendship, serenity, or artistic creativity. Knowledge might be at best only a *means* to love, power, creativity, or honor.

Philosophers sometimes curb the majesty of Knowledge to make room for something else of supreme importance, say faith. This was Kant's aim, it seems. Stressing the limits of knowledge can also promote a salutary humility. But this is not *Thoreau*'s motivation. Thoreau has a guest share a place with Knowledge at his table, but not because he discovers that knowledge can't be total. He turns from Knowledge to "Sympathy with Intelligence" because he exults in the non-egocentric unknowing that comes with recognizing splendors all about—because he can enjoy revelations that make him happy to be alive amidst so much that is not him. There is nothing second best about embracing a world saturated by revelations. Having *Sympathy with Intelligence* (as he puts it in "Walking") will by no means *close down* knowledge. He can sip his cappuccino, nibble his croissant, and be entranced by both. He merely says the desire for one is constant, while his desire for the other is intermittent. There are not two worlds, the cognitive and the wondrous, between which we have to pick.

6.

Just out of college and a village schoolmaster, on December 7, 1838, Thoreau notes a striking philosophical desire: "Could we for a moment drop this by-play—and simply wonder—without reference or inference!"[28] He wants to avoid seeking *nothing but* "reference or inference." He wants space for wonder. Attaching a "reference" to something would be providing a kind of file-identity for an object. To proceed with an "inference" would be to try out a causal explanation of the indexed object. Much of Thoreau's late *Journal* could belong to the annals of science, for it meticulously indexes facts and assigns explanations. The desire to "simply wonder" may be less dominant there, but Thoreau always has wonder at the ready, nevertheless, it seems.

After the opening startle or gentle presence of something wondrous, words can tumble out—or sometimes we're silenced. What tumbles out may be a simple "Wow!" or perhaps an extended reverie, befitting the occasion, constructed on the spot or (if you're Thoreau) the next day in a *Journal*. In any case, wonder- or presence-launched words deliver much more than "reference or inference." They are revelations, and revelations of what

---

[28] *Journal*, December 7, 1838, p. 61.

Thoreau, rather enigmatically, calls "Intelligence"—a sort of divine "news," or "transmission," perhaps.

When seasoned scientists exit their technical papers, they can, and often do, expose the poetic side of their endeavors. They show their capacity to behold wonders even as they produce objective studies. In her study of Thoreau's *Journal*, Sharon Cameron concludes that for Thoreau, "man is in the natural world as its witness or *beholder*, not as its *explicator*."[29] He beholds the poetry of life, expressed and witnessed in befitting poetic response. To value "Sympathy with Intelligence" is not to sympathize *intelligently* or *prudently*. It's to behold the eloquent poetry and aura of plant life, animal life, even the life of rocks and stars, as these appear through radiant presence.[30] We open to sites of radiant animation, flowing toward us like star dust in moments of wonder.

7.

Thoreau improvises an implicit, impressionistic, or episodic metaphysics (or quasi-theology) that can seem esoteric at first. On reflection it's quite graspable though we might take it to be "over the top."[31] In *Walden*, Thoreau cites a line from the *Vedas*: "All intelligences awake with the morning."[32] To awake to intelligences is to awake to the revelation of each thing arising at dawn, glowing—a god-like packet of divine energy. In moments of revelation, routine perception is overridden. The *prose* of perception—say, data collection—can easily dumb-down and imprison. It can operate on only *muted* awareness. In Thoreau's account it leans toward sloth, despondency, and senselessness. To be struck by *Intelligence*, by the *poetry* of things, brings one instantly alive. To be bathed in Intelligence is to *behold*. In a passage that predates a more refined formulation, Thoreau writes: "My desire for knowledge is intermittent, but my desire to commune with the spirit of the universe, to be intoxicated even with the fumes, call it, of that divine nectar,

---

[29] Cameron, p. 75 (my emphasis).
[30] On auras, see Eli Friedlander, *Walter Benjamin, A Philosophical Portrait* (Cambridge, MA: Harvard University Press, 2012), pp. 147–50. On presence, see Alva Noë, *Varieties of Presence* (Cambridge, MA: Harvard University Press, 2012).
[31] See Howard Wettstein on "impressionistic theology" and improvisatory metaphysics in *The Significance of Religious Experience* (Oxford: Oxford University Press, 2012). I came across this marvelous study too late to fully weave into my explorations.
[32] *Walden*, "Where I lived," p. 87 [para 14].

... is perennial and constant."[33] What he calls "divine nectar" here, later on, in "Walking," he'll call "Intelligence."[34]

I resort to various idioms to capture the spirit of "Intelligence." There is an *ocular* idiom: intelligence *radiates* and *illuminates*, giving work to the eyes. There is an *aural* idiom: intelligence speaks *eloquently* and *musically*, giving work to the ears. There is a *tactile* idiom: Thoreau lets intelligence *touch* us. Intelligence can also address us through *odor* and *taste*, and can shimmer ontologically as *mood* or *climate*, as *allure*, *beauty*, and as *wonder*.[35] This proliferation of idioms underlines the conceptual elusiveness of the sort of address Thoreau singles out with the nametag "Intelligence." This divine "output" eludes any *single* model of delivery to the senses. Such moments arise in ecstatic surprise. We are, as it were, driven outside ourselves. We are absorbed in the delivery of a *wondrous presence*. Intelligence is *naturally here-and-now*.

8.

Receptivity to a variety of elusive presences is central to our sense of being alive. It's not so obviously essential when collecting data or writing up science. Knowledge *about* something requires that we stand apart as dispassionate observers. Thoreau seeks that, but also communion or intimacy. In his footsteps as a natural scientist, I might take in the river's objective girth, depth, or rate of flow. But if I take in the river's sleekness, laziness or roar, I'm not a dispassionate observer of facts. To be open to sleekness or to tremulous roars does not erase the importance of observational knowledge. It's to be open to more than explicit knowledge. To wonder at a child or a crab going sideways is to be ecstatically, sympathetically lost in them.

What is "Sympathy"? The Viola d'Amore is a predecessor to the modern violin and viola. It has a fingerboard and its strings are rigged roughly the way modern string instruments are. But it also has extra strings rigged under the fingerboard that vibrate sympathetically with the strings above. The player sets the top-level strings in motion by the stroke of a bow, as any player of the modern violin would. But there's a special resonance to the sound produced because the top-level strings set in motion the strings rigged below the fingerboard. A shower stall vibrates sympathetically with a

---

[33] *Journal*, February 9, 1851, pp. 150–1.
[34] I return to "Sympathy with Intelligence" in Ch. 3, p. 37–58 and Ch. 14, p. 219f., 241f.
[35] See Rick Anthony Furtak, "The Value of Being: On Appreciating the Beauty of the World," Furtak, Ellsworth, and Reid (eds), *Thoreau's Importance for Philosophy* (New York: Fordham University Press, 2012), pp. 112–26.

certain pitch sounded by my voice. Thoreau's aspiration is to vibrate sympathetically with the tones of things of the world, as they address him. Perhaps the world is God's musical instrument.

> These single strains, these melodious cadences which plainly proceed out of a very deep meaning and a sustained soul, are the interjections of God ... . God must be very rich, who ... can pour out such melody on me.[36]

We sense a flowing luminosity—even a melodic grace—in the scamper of a crab or a toddler, and we tremble gently in sympathy. These are not moments of Knowledge. Thoreau responds to the pond as he kneels before it, in befitting receptivity and responsiveness, "without reference or inference." Here, for a moment, he can "simply wonder."

> Nature always possesses a certain sonorousness, as in the hum of insects, the booming of ice, the crowing of cocks in the morning, and the barking of dogs in the night, which indicates her sound state. God's voice is but a clear bell sound.[37]

Some eight months before Thoreau's entry on wonder, on April 1, 1838 and across the Atlantic, Søren Kierkegaard reports a befitting reverie in *his* Journal: "This morning I saw half a score of geese fly away in crisp cool air... . They divided into two flocks arched like a pair of eyebrows above my eyes, which were now gazing into the land of poetry."[38]

9.

The conversations with Thoreau that follow might be heard simply as interpretations of his texts, or of passages in them, but this leaves something essential out. I don't work simply to interpret, or paraphrase, a passage. I work to deliver its presence and mood, the way it touches and envelopes me, the way it effects changes in mood and attunement directly through intimate contact. So beyond interpreting strings of words, I want to convey the touch and release of certain phrases and sentences. If intimate contact—*sympathy*—with them transmits a sense of place or event— ominous or welcoming, lucid or misting, foul- or sweet-smelling, wafting

---

[36] *Journal,* January 8, 1842, p. 317.
[37] *Journal,* March 3, 1841, p. 227.
[38] Søren Kierkegaard, *Papers and Journals,* Vol. 5, Howard V. and Edna H. Hong (ed. and trans.) (Bloomington, IN: Indiana University Press, 1978), April 1, 1838, p. 116.

or still—then words pass on surrounding woods or meadows or weather not just as bare things but as things *radiating presence, addressing us through presence.*

A particular thing over there strikes my eye (my ear, my touch) as if I received a sound, vibration or coloration. It's as if the thing-sensed—perhaps already well wrapped in words (perhaps not)—activates a membrane, like the membrane of the ear, or stimulates an array of receptors in response to a light, or starts the strings of the viol in motion. Viscerally, the thing gives a touch or sound that has bodily resonance. I'm brushed by a meadow's presence as it's brushed by the wind. Its allure or reserve or shimmering light forces a step back as would a quick and unexpected embrace. The allure might extend beyond a momentary incursion. It might bud toward an unanticipated reverie. This initial budding is a presence well before interpretation. Amazement can trigger words but *predate* them, as gasps, tears, or smiles predate any follow-up thoughts, sentences or phrases. Geese—their *presence*—flash above. They morph toward a pair of welcoming, beckoning *eyebrows*. Thus we are addressed—the skies strike us thus—well before we might retreat to wonder *how it is* that skies suspend geese—or *how it is* that geese suspend eyebrows—or *how it is* that eyebrows float invitingly into the land of poetry. It is never "interpretation all the way down," but always interpretation floating on surprise, startle, shimmer, allure, or a smile.

My job in writing about writing is to let membranes be aroused in startle or allure as the address of the place and its things emerge—as their startle or allure arise from the words Thoreau provides. I don't test a book's purported representations against something else I awkwardly or despairingly call "reality," nor do I set out immediately to interpret these moments (that some hear only as representations). I don't set out the deep roots of these striking moments in personal or cultural history. To let the impact of Thoreau's words register will sometimes mean dwelling on some aspect of his life in Concord. But my distinctive task is to evoke the music, shimmer, and surprise of a text-delivered array of animate, resonate things—including resonant persons, say, the meteor that is John Brown. I want to share something of the meadow and maples by letting their moods and climates address me (address us) as somber or lilting, as discretely inviting or coolly foreboding. To access presence or radiance is to let words invade and work on us, the way we let music invade and work on us. In the first instance, this is not actively *interpreting* the song, singer, or world, but letting their presence suffuse us. We become *abandoned* to them.

A venture in responsiveness and abandonment is suspect in an administrative, instrumental, production- and income-oriented culture. Those in academic settings are pressured to produce knowledge (rather than to evoke presence) and to train students for job-markets (not to expand their sensibilities). If I value the address of the world, if I think that dwelling with Thoreau's languid days, gentle rains, or cavorting gods becomes and abets a richer life, then insofar as business, social status, production, and common pleasures command *exhaustive* attention, then I disattend the business—and it returns the favor. There is no quantifiable outcome of my work. Yet it is incontestable that my life is more gratifyingly complete as I welcome Thoreau's passages as texts and companions—not to mention a Thoreauvian world delivered by them. Each site of revelation delivers wonder, reverie, and complexity otherwise missing. Not a few among my students sense this might be true for them, as well. This fact informs a deep conviction about pedagogy: let texts and art works sing beyond all the reductive categories we invent to place and master them: let them be; let them bloom.

10.

Art works and texts shape our cultural milieu, suffusing memory, refining present perceptions, cushioning or sharpening a sense of the future. We need to relearn over and over what to cherish in texts and objects of worth. We learn by exposure and reflection that supersedes that sort of critical thinking that only deflates, demotes, or translates into something else. Having the "right categories" for analysis or contextual placement falls short of establishing *why we should bother* to value the thing we ardently contextualize or scrutinize.

Values emerge in art, literature, and life from many, many sources. Prominent for Thoreau is the emergence of values through exposures to moments of radiance or eloquence. He pauses beside the lilt of moving waters, the smile of a child, the laughter of gods, the smell of a lily. Debunking what needs debunking is no substitute for relearning what's really before us as our redemption—what can redeem us from a debilitating sense of dullness, ingratitude, or despair. Eliminating the bad or unsavory, or identifying blindness, or a half-life does not guarantee preservation of worthy things. That preservative instinct is the curator's passion and sensibility. Teachers are the curators of their times, curators of a common trust

Dismantling the bad is no substitute for mantling or reviving the fine. Reviving the good honors and restores. In bringing a phrase, passage, text, or work of art—or the lives of persons or groups or epochs—to their fullest eloquent potential, we praise and preserve things of immense value. In the decay of these times, restoration and praise call us to affirmative labors.

Reviving the good, magnificent, or simply alluring, calls for ventures of poetic reverie and improvisation as response to presence—as well as to all that is factual. This is to preserve in all we attend to what's best—and yes, to acknowledge that what we attend to is so often distressingly fragile.

2

Celebration and Lamentation

Soon after John's death I listened to a music-box, and if, at any time, that event had seemed inconsistent with the beauty and harmony of the universe, it was then gently constrained into the placid course of nature by those steady notes, in mild and unoffended tone echoing far and wide under the heavens. But I find these things more strange than sad to me.
—Thoreau, to Mrs. Lucy Brown, March 2, 1842

[L]ife, as if itself mourning, recovers losses by distributing them into other animated beings.
—Branka Arsić, "Thoreau and Benjamin on Mourning"

Surely joy is the condition of life.
—Thoreau, "Natural History of Massachusetts"[1]

1.

There is a tension in Thoreau between celebration and lamentation. He laments the state of his society yet refuses, as he says in *Walden*, to produce an "ode to dejection." Even when he faces the most despairing of circumstances, he sidesteps a descent into protracted melancholy. There is a dark or tragic Thoreau, at odds with the cultural icon of a happy woodsman. You don't have to excavate far to find it. And you can't be misled by the generously upbeat. A striking case of his refusal of hopelessness—or helplessness—is chronicled in his essay, "Slavery in Massachusetts."[2] The Fugitive Slave Law of 1850 forced the return of former slaves who had been de facto freedmen. As it began to take hold in Boston and around Concord, Thoreau wrote: "I cannot persuade myself that I do not dwell *wholly within* hell."[3] Seeking to throw off despair, he takes a walk near a swamp he knows well. Suddenly he senses a lily rooted

---

[1] Epigraphs: *Correspondence*, p. 62; http://backdoorbroadcasting.net/2012/05/branka-Arsic-memorial-life-thoreau-and-benjamin-on-nature-in-mourning/; *Essays*, "The Natural History of Massachusetts," p. 22.
[2] "Slavery in Massachusetts," *Collected Essays and Poems of Thoreau*, Elizabeth Hall Witherell (ed.) (Princeton, NJ: Princeton University Press, 2001), pp. 333–47 (hereafter, "Slavery").
[3] *Essays*, "Slavery," p. 345.

in the muck of history, but rising up as a tiny flower of paradise, sweet in its smell. His despair is modulated.

> What confirmation of our hopes is in the fragrance of this flower! I shall not so soon despair of the world for it, notwithstanding slavery, and the cowardice and want of principle of Northern men. It suggests what kind of laws have prevailed longest and widest, and still prevail, and that the time may come when man's deeds will smell as sweet. Such is the odor which the plant emits. If Nature can compound this fragrance still annually, I shall believe her still young and full of vigor, her integrity and genius unimpaired, and that there is virtue even in man, too, who is fitted to perceive and love it. It reminds me that Nature has been partner to no Missouri Compromise. I scent no compromise in the fragrance of the water-lily.[4]

A near-tragic melancholy undergoes a catharsis, a transmutation toward affirmation and exultation. A century and a half after Thoreau's death we think and create under the shadow of the Shoah, of the AIDS epidemic, the assassinations of the 1960s, the war on terror that is its own terror. By my count, in the 70-odd years since Pearl Harbor, the US has been at war somewhere in the globe in every year but one. It's sobering to realize how many of the afflictions of Thoreau's times—genocide, racism, religious buffoonery, social and political alienation, environmental devastations—continue, unchecked, to this day. Thoreau suffers the afflictions of his times, and, as important, suffers pains of a much more personal nature. His brother John dies a grotesque death from lockjaw, writhing in spasms in Henry's arms. A few days later Henry displays identical jerking symptoms.[5] John's death seems to have pulled or invited Henry into an identical hell. Henry's body reenacts his brother's death. It wasn't long before his body shed the symptoms, but they continued to feed his writing. *A Week on the Concord and Merrimack Rivers* especially should be read as an act of mourning, as a soft-pedaled elegy to John.

2.

I propose an amble with Thoreau, keeping him usually in sight (and not reined in), and letting him be sometimes conjured rather than the subject of

---

[4] Ibid. p. 346.
[5] On the symbiosis of the brothers and on porous souls, see Wai-Chee Dimock, "Global Civil Society: Thoreau on Three Continents," *Through Other Continents: American Literature Across Deep Time* (Princeton, NJ: Princeton University Press, 2006), pp. 7–22.

an exclusively scholarly, investigative report. There will be some polemic, a reverie or two, and thoughts on how we might teach others, our students or neighbors, what our walking companion has taught us. I don't write solely from a place of expertise, but from one of long acquaintance. This amble should dispel some preconceptions about Thoreau, and free me from the barriers that exclusively disciplinary and scholarly investigations so easily throw up around him. If I am out to de-familiarize him, that's in part because the Thoreau I had known over the years has slipped into shadow, as a new, less familiar Thoreau comes to light. My old Thoreau had become too easy and familiar—too tamed and domestic. Now I've come to know two new faces, both wild: Thoreau as "child of the mist" and Thoreau as an ancient weather-beaten Bristlecone Pine.

Neither of these fall among half a dozen more familiar faces: Thoreau the environmentalist; Thoreau the antislavery activist; Thoreau the naturalist who sets a still-respected standard for biological and archaeological fieldwork; Thoreau an associate of The Transcendentalist Club, and much later, of the Occupy movement, and in between, the partisan of nonviolent resistance. His night in jail for refusing to pay taxes for an unjust imperialist land-grab was replicated, disseminated, and expanded in the eloquent disobedience first of Gandhi against the British, and then of Martin Luther King against the murderous customs of Jim Crow. Thoreau's "Resistance to Civil Government" even had a 2011 cameo appearance in Tel Aviv and Jerusalem where the moral legitimacy of illegal action in protest of West Bank conditions was framed in its terms.[6] Then there is the folk hero Thoreau, the tiller of beans who raised a cabin by the pond from recycled lumber. Since 1900 an estimated two million tourists have visited the replica of Thoreau's cabin at Walden. There was a time you could mail order a replica to place in your back yard. His face is on posters, and in blue states is still required high-school reading.

I amble with a somewhat hidden Thoreau, one who undergoes tragic loss and then recovers as a youthful "child of the mist," finding delight, finding his voice in an enigmatic upbeat lament. The Bristlecone Pine, an unimaginably old tree of the Sierra Nevada, is tragic in its weathered, twisted isolation, yet happy with its face to the breeze, and taking in incredible vistas that make the heart sing. I taught for decades within reach of California's Sierra Nevada. No doubt this feeds a recurrent dream in which Thoreau attains apotheosis as a Bristlecone Pine—that most gnarled, ancient and lonely of trees.

---

[6] Israeli women (2012) cited Thoreau in defense of illegally ferrying Arab women in disguise through military checkpoints for a day with their children at the seashore.

As if in anticipation of this reverie, we find Thoreau writing to Blake,

I am trying to wring slumber out of my pores;—For, generally, I take events as unconcernedly as a fence post,— absorb wet and cold alike, and am pleasantly tickled with lichens slowly spreading over me. Could I not be content then to be a cedar post, which lasts 25 years?[7]

The Bristlecone—not the cedar post—has the wildness and musically wind-wrought twists to make it for me Thoreau's totem plant, his vital being. Thoreau would have enjoyed being farther west, especially a century and a half past his death—a little more out of reach, a little more lost and mysterious.

The *New York Times* reports (October 6, 2014) that Gary Snyder and a number of other writers and poets hiked into the John Muir Wilderness in the High Sierra that September to name a peak "Mt. Thoreau." Fittingly, this was an act of minor civil disobedience: the National Wilderness Act forbids any new peak christenings. Thoreau would like the craggy wild. He'd not be pleased that he'd become as iconic as the legions of Mt. Washington hut boys, or as recognizable as the Boston Pops, nestled in the hills around Lenox. I prefer to think he'd appear as a Bristlecone, strikingly strange, self-sufficient, and austere.

3.

"I thank God that the cheapness which appears in time and the world, the trivialness of the whole scheme of things, is in my own cheap and trivial moment." Thoreau wrote this in his journal for March 26, 1842, a few months after his brother died.[8] He seems to make cheapness and triviality—and why not cruelty or injustice?—a feature of his cheap mood of the moment. The correlate seems to be that the beauty or delight of things is likewise a feature of his mood—of his moment, as he says, even if that moment is no longer trivial but filled with awe. Is the implication that a change of mood would change the world?

I take the drift of Thoreau's journal remark to be a quick aside, muttered under his breath of a morning when he is especially "down." Of course a better mood can indeed make a difference on many—not all—days when the

---

[7] I'd have his fence post morph toward the Bristlecone while he fancies himself morph from fence post "into a living tree, put forth leaves & flowers & have fruit." *Correspondence,* December 6, 1856, pp. 443–4.
[8] *Journal,* March 26, 1842, p. 349.

world is blue. But whatever the case with regard to the triviality of the world, when the issue is injustice, the matter runs deeper than any mood.

Remember Thoreau's approach to the sweet-smelling lily in his antislavery essay. He had been in a terrible mood—for good reason. The infamous Dred Scott decision encouraged slave catchers to roam Concord's woods, Thoreau's back yard, in pursuit of escaped property listing toward Canadian freedom—in pursuit of men and women suddenly deprived of their relative freedom that life around Boston afforded those who at one time were slaves. Thoreau makes it clear that it's not his bad mood but the facts of the matter, the raw injustice of it all, that makes his paradise revert to a living hell.

As he encounters the lily, it gives him a scent of paradise. Heaven has a sweet odor as well as a sweet sound, and taste, and look. Thoreau declares near the end of *A Week*: "We need pray for no higher heaven than the pure senses can furnish."[9] The odor and glimpse of beauty amid ugliness redeems a moment of paradise amid hell. The hegemony of hell is broken. A lily, not a mood, makes the difference.[10] The reality of injustice and cruelty is not erased, but for a moment it is not the only reality. If all we had were inescapable, bottomless, all-pervasive injustice, then Concord would in fact be utter desolation. Outrageous moral facts are not all that obtrude. Injustice is neither all-pervasive nor fully triumphant in its reign. The lily brings Thoreau's heart alive—even as Dred Scott breaks it.

Political worlds are not without bright moments, but there are also the prominently cruel ones where injustice seems to be a brute and inexpugnable fact. Injustice is a cause for outrage in a way that the world's "cheapness" and "triviality" aren't. We needn't be deflected by the metaphysical puzzle of how the world screams out injustices with an impact that is every bit as real as the impact of the table that I kick in irritation. Both are brute facts. The salient question is how, if injustice is real and seems inexpugnable, does Thoreau go on? It's not just habit that keeps him moving, nor is it that he abides injustice—he doesn't. How does he live out, simultaneously, his deep outrage and deep delight? Can it be just a matter of sequencing: now outrage, now delight? Or of sequestering one while the other roams free?

We are given arresting pictures of a dynamic and somewhat stable way of abiding despite discord. Thoreau cultivates latent delight as he refuses an inundating dark. He lets moments of joy forestall any crushing dominance

---

[9] *Week*, p. 382.
[10] On beauty being more than an ornamental touch we add to the world, when we're "in the mood," as it were, see Rick Furtak's incisive essay, "The Value of Being: On Appreciating the Beauty of the World," Furtak, Ellsworth, and Reid (eds), *Thoreau's Importance for Philosophy* (New York: Fordham University Press, 2012), pp. 112–26.

of cruelty or suffering. *That* there is suffering, cruelty, and decay is one thing. Whether it grinds the soul to dust is another.

4.

Here is Thoreau at his most upbeat in an 1856 letter to his devoted follower Harrison Blake: "I am grateful for what I am & have." He goes on: "My thanksgiving is perpetual. It is surprising how contented one can be with nothing definite ... . O how I laugh when I think of my vague and indefinite riches."[11] This mood seems far from the tragic, far from all that might lead him to mourn. Thoreau is not just victim of his moods, contentment descending one day, anguish or outrage the next. Celebration and contentment are his achieved answer to real grounds for sorrow. He had no lack of reasons to fall into abysmal grief. A focused and fertile imagination prevented grief from taking over.

As a result of a small cut to his finger, John Thoreau died in his younger brother's arms, violently. Thoreau then developed the symptoms. A doctor was called, but could do nothing and the family prepared itself for a second grotesque death. The very same month Thoreau suffered another loss. Emerson's son Waldo, a boy Thoreau had helped raise. Waldo died at age five of scarlet fever.

On a political level, Thoreau went to jail in protest of the United States' imperialist war and subsequent seizure of the northern half of Mexico.[12] Over decades, in a kind of ongoing grieving, he gathered Indian artifacts, preserving the memory of a vanquished people. Thoreau speaks ruefully in *A Week* of their eradication.

> Some spring the white man came, built him a house, and made a clearing here, letting in the sun, dried up a farm, piled up the old gray stones in fences, cut down the pines around his dwelling, planted orchard seeds brought from the old country, and persuaded the civil apple-tree to blossom next to the wild pine and the juniper, shedding its perfume in the wilderness. Their old stocks still remain. He culled the graceful elm from out the woods and from the river-side, and so refined and smoothed his village plot. He rudely bridged the stream, and drove his team afield into the river meadows, cut the wild grass, and laid bare the homes of beaver, otter, muskrat, and with the whetting of his scythe

[11] *Correspondence*, December 6, 1856, p. 444.
[12] Most of present-day New Mexico, Utah, Nevada, Arizona, California, and western Colorado was seized. Texas was assimilated by more roundabout means.

scared off the deer and bear. He set up a mill, and fields of English grain sprang in the virgin soil. And with his grain he scattered the seeds of the dandelion and the wild trefoil over the meadows, mingling his English flowers with the wild native ones. The bristling burdock, the sweet-scented catnip, and the humble yarrow planted themselves along his woodland road, they too seeking "freedom to worship God" in their way. And thus he plants a town. The white man's mullein soon reigned in Indian cornfields, and sweet-scented English grasses clothed the new soil. Where, then, could the Red Man set his foot? The honey-bee hummed through the Massachusetts woods, and sipped the wild-flowers round the Indian's wigwam, perchance unnoticed, when, with prophetic warning, it stung the Red child's hand, forerunner of that industrious tribe that was to come and pluck the wild-flower of his race up by the root.[13]

To pull up by the root is to eradicate.

At public meetings Thoreau gave a ringing defense of John Brown, who had dared to act on his revulsion at slavery. "Slavery in Massachusetts" appeared in 1854. In 1857 he meets John Brown. In 1859, he delivers "A Plea for John Brown" to an audience of 2,000 in Boston. Frederick Douglass was to have spoken, but after Brown's capture, he fled toward Canada. After Thoreau and others arranged a memorial service in Concord on the day of his hanging, outraged Concord citizens hung Brown in effigy. Thoreau places Brown, the rebel who would be hanged, as the defender of a freedom that Washington and Franklin had failed to defend. He had reason to grieve for his country.

Thoreau had plenty to unnerve his courage, plenty to trigger the deepest disconsolations. Yet his outstanding achievement, in my view, is avoiding overweening lamentation or jeremiad. While keeping alive to the evil around him, by dint of hard poetic labor, he managed to filter his personal grief through an impersonal bloom, through a matrix of impersonal grief—the infinite grief of Nature herself.[14] He is absorbed by infinite patterns of Nature in loss—in unending process of decay, death, and disintegration—and in regeneration. Nature can't but grieve limitlessly at her interminable losses, yet she simultaneously gains new life from death. New roots sprout from warm earth, from last year's decay—even from the decay of human remains.

---

[13] *Week*, pp. 52–3.
[14] Branka Arsić, *Bird Relics*, and "Magical Life: Thoreau and Benjamin on Nature in Mourning," http://backdoorbroadcasting.net/2012/05/branka-Arsic?-memorial-life-thoreau-and-benjamin-on-nature-in-mourning/

Thoreau helps construct a shallow pond in the cemetery where John is buried: his remains will feed life in the emerging swamp.[15]

Two months after John and Waldo died, Thoreau responds by letter to his friend Lucy Brown's sympathetic inquiry. His words (quoted also in one of the epigraphs to this venture) can seem austere and remote, far from heartbreak or lamentation. They weave Waldo's departure into impersonal grief.

> As for Waldo, he died as the mist rises from the brook, which the sun will soon dart his rays through. Do not the flowers die every autumn? He had not even taken root here. I was not startled to hear that he was dead; it seemed the most natural event that could happen. His fine organization demanded it, and nature gently yielded its request. It would have been strange if he had lived. Neither will nature manifest any sorrow at his death, but soon the note of the lark will be heard down in the meadow, and fresh dandelions will spring from the old stocks where he plucked them last summer.[16]

Waldo dies "as the mist rises from the brook, which the sun will soon dart his rays through." Ten years later, in his essay "Walking," Thoreau writes that when it comes to knowledge, "we are all children of the mist." It is as if he casts Waldo as an innocent child dispersed into nature even as the sun burns through the mist, dispersing it. Later he casts *himself* as a child, not dispersed but peering *through* mist, through a darkling glass. Finally, he proposes more generally that you and I are as children who see life-and-death only through mist, as we wonder at first and last things. With respect to knowledge of these so-significant infinities, we are none of us better placed to size up their significance than Waldo. Our knowledge but also our lives come and go like a mist, or like the ephemeral song of the lark.

And why should Waldo's "fine organization," his perfection, "demand" an early death? Well, why should the sound of a perfect orchestral cadence *demand* that no note follow thereafter? Why, when we experience perfection, do we so naturally feel that, "Then, I could die!"? Perhaps in its perfection, the moment can lose nothing through subsequent silence or death? Of course, we readily say of so many good things that it's better that they continue (rather than cease). Better that the grand oak or granite wall not crumple or rot.

But consider a clap of thunder, a sudden cloudburst, the ring of a bell, the brush of a kiss, the fall of the sun into the sea. Waldo's parting is the dispersal

---

[15] See Branka Arsić's account, *Bird Relics: Grief and Vitalism in Thoreau* (Cambridge, MA: Harvard University Press, 2015), pp. 385–7.
[16] *Correspondence*, p. 63.

of the mist, as wonderful and necessary as the falling sun, or the refusal of sunrise to linger. So why begrudge Thoreau's rendering the sudden death this way? Of course, we distinguish early death from death at great age, and distinguish both from death arriving in between. To think of a death at five rather than twenty-five or eighty-five is to invoke a measure external to the life-lived. Given his flawless constitution, Waldo was a perfect specimen at five and his death did not mar that perfection. The date of his death is extraneous to the life lived up to that time. In its unfolding, that life had no flaw.

I sense Thoreau merges with Waldo here, as he merged just weeks earlier with John, at John's death. That capacity to undergo multiple deaths can make him seem austere and ancient, like the Bristlecone. It takes a steely courage to enter the underworld with those we love. But that capacity also makes him young, for he emerges each time, renewed. And as he descends with Waldo, he descends as a child of the mist and will share the child's awakening.

Thoreau lives under the prerogatives of the seer or poet to evoke the anomalous, to bend imagination, to reveal and revel in wild time, wild place, and morphing embodiment. He confides in his Journal (March 27, 1842): "I am as old—as old as the Alleghenies." Or—*old as a Bristlecone*. Then he plays with the alternative: "I was going to say [Mt.] Wachusett, but it excites a youthful feeling—as I were but too happy to be so young."[17] If he owns that he's old as the Alleghenies, doesn't he disown being young and happy? But he takes himself to be young and happy, a child of the mist, and *simultaneously* old and austere. Time and embodiment are anomalous.

Thoreau has a capacity we all share, to see life-and-death, youth and age, under two aspects. I can see my identity intimately, my youth or age shaped and shattered by deaths of those close to me, or by loss of a talent or friendship, by longing for lost youth or fear of age. I can take my life *personally* as a site for loss and recovery, and also for prides and shames and the affronts of betrayal and injustice. Alternatively, I can also see my life-and-death under the aspect of deep time or eternity, and under the aspect of all of Nature. Thereupon, life seems to come and go like the rising and setting of the sun, quite indifferent to the details of my hopes and fears. Seeing our lives as we would if we were as old as the Bristlecone or the Alleghenies is to see our lives *impersonally*. From that prospect, there is no place for my thwarted desires or my magnificent aspirations or my crippling grief at the loss of a child.

---

[17] *Journal*, March 27, 1842, p. 352. Wachusett is the highest mountain east of the Berkshires. See Thoreau's early "A Walk to Wachusett," *Essays*, pp. 42–56.

5.

Thoreau can seem neighborly and contemporary, and simultaneously removed and distant. That he *eludes* us—while also being overwhelmingly present—mirrors his sense that he is lost to his neighbors (they can't quite make him out), while he is also overwhelmingly present to them. I discovered his stark remoteness only recently. Earlier he was not lost to me (so I thought), and it never would have occurred to me that he was lost to himself, that he yearned or mourned. I presumed too close an acquaintance.

Thoreau was nothing if not strong and self-sufficient—just what an adolescent needs. He had the answers; they were simple. I swelled with pride as he taunted Emerson standing there outside the jail, while Thoreau, on principle, sat within. I knew he was a neighbor from a few towns over who knew the Concord as I knew the Charles. We would both rather be rowing Sunday morning than be tame, observant Christians. And I knew he liked—how shall I say—camping! In my flawless wisdom he was a known quantity. I approved, and had nothing to learn.

Through college and then many years teaching college, things changed, but not radically. There was a striking moment of relevance during the student uprisings of the 1960s, when I could figure him as pointing simultaneously to solitary salvation in the woods and to engaged salvation in disruptive city activism. But by the late 1970s, Thoreau, in my consciousness, had entered a nostalgic dream world. He became a first love, fondly remembered, a kid's fantasy. I had moved on to more "challenging" figures. Thoreau was a wordsmith, but "not a real thinker"—so my philosophy professors made clear. He was OK for Sierra Club posters and summer reading at the beach, but frankly he was not a first-rate, exact, and un-fuzzy thinker. Neither my teachers nor I knew the high esteem Thoreau held for George Eliot and Virginia Woolf, for Gaston Bachelard, Michel Foucault, and Pierre Hadot. Philosophers in America in those years were tilting toward a scientific positivism. They scoffed at the provincial, rambling inelegance of William James. Emerson and Thoreau were not even on the map.

My condescension was shaken when I heard Stanley Cavell, surely a first-rate philosopher, lecture on *Walden* in the 1970s. But I took Cavell's interest to be quirky, an extravagant side-interest that only an aristocratic Harvard Professor could indulge. A grad student or young professor had better stay clear.

Quite by accident, and several decades later, I reopened Cavell's *The Senses of Walden*. I began reading *A Week on the Concord, Maine Woods,* and *Cape Cod*—in growing excitement that became a devouring rush.

Leafing almost randomly through Thoreau's *Journal*, I could pause with this:

> There is something more than [atoms in] association at the bottom of the excitement which the roar of a cataract produces. It is allied to the circulation in our veins. We have a waterfall which corresponds even to Niagara somewhere within us. It is astonishing what a rush and tumult a slight inclination will produce in a swollen brook. How it proclaims its glee, its boisterousness, rushing headlong in its prodigal course as if it would exhaust itself in half an hour! How it spends itself! I would say to the orator and poet, Flow freely and lavishly as a brook that is full—without stint.[18]

This lavish tumult was answer—or at least promise—even if I would be at a loss to say fully what answer or promise had arrived. I found an earlier *persona*—my mask as a critic-only, a detached refutation machine—quietly depart. A freer-thinking poet-Thoreau waited in the wings.[19] I could hear his exaltation: "Live free, child of the mist — and with respect to knowledge we are all children of the mist."[20] Our salvation, he seemed to say, lay with an alert openness to life that he labels, in his essay "Walking," a revelation-receptive "Sympathy with Intelligence." This was a notion I found as baffling as it was seductive. But with such promise beckoning, I read lavishly on, renewed again and again, page by singing page.

6.

We write elegies to those we've lost. Thoreau's little-read masterpiece *A Week on the Concord and Merrimack Rivers* was written while he was living at Walden Pond. It is a memorial to his brother John.[21] In 1839 the brothers had taken a river trip down the Concord and up the Merrimack to the base of the White Mountains in New Hampshire. They had sought the seat of the gods, as it were, and the source of local waters, of ice-melts flowing down to the sea.

A Week can seem anything but an elegy. It doesn't seem to harrow grief. It's been taken as little more than a piece of travel writing, inelegantly linked to a commonplace book, a compendium of paragraphs collected over time by a diligent reader responding to all he read. There are notes on literature,

---

[18] *Journal*, February 12, 1851, p. 155.
[19] My rediscovery of Thoreau was prepared by years with Henry Bugbee's classic, *The Inward Morning; a Philosophical Exploration in Journal Form* (Athens, GA: University of Georgia Press, 1999).
[20] "Walking," p. 250 [para 73].
[21] *A Week* was first published in 1852, *Walden* in 1854.

followed by Thoreau's poems, New England history, comments on friendship, the church, "Eastern wisdom" (the *Bhagavad-Gita*), and so forth. Apart from a broad hint before the writing-proper begins, one wouldn't guess that the mate of his life is dead. The dedication pleads: "Be thou my muse, oh brother."

Thoreau doesn't write to "work through" or "get over" his pain. His writing weaves grief in and out of all natural life. It is not something to leave behind any more than life is something to work through and leave behind.[22] All Nature is in a state of unending grief, registered in weeping leaves, in the stoic sadness of rotting stumps, in the somber quiet of night before the burst of new light—even in dawn's newness, for it *too* will pass. Impersonal grief courses through all we encounter. In *Walden*'s "Spring," Thoreau comes on the stench of a dead horse. The corpse that stores death stores provision for scavengers, and so is a site for new life.

> We need to witness our own limits transgressed, and some life pasturing freely where we never wander. We are cheered when we observe the vulture feeding on the carrion which disgusts and disheartens us and deriving health and strength from the repast. There was a dead horse in the hollow by the path to my house, which compelled me sometimes to go out of my way, especially in the night when the air was heavy, but the assurance it gave me of the strong appetite and inviolable health of Nature was my compensation for this. I love to see that Nature is so rife with life that myriads can be afforded to be sacrificed and suffered to prey on one another: that tender organizations can be so serenely squashed out of existence like pulp,— tadpoles which herons gobble up, and tortoises and toads run over in the road; and that sometimes it has rained flesh and blood! ... The impression made on a wise man is that of universal innocence.[23]

There's no little irony afoot here, I think—a bit of fun as Thoreau relishes what will seem shocking and uncouth to a strait-laced aunt shopping for Sunday dinner. (But his neighbor just west, Emily Dickinson, would smile appreciatively I'd guess.)

In one of his earliest *Journal* entries jotted down over a decade before the passage from *Walden*, in the year he graduated from Harvard and a few years before his brother's death, Thoreau wrote out a theme that would absorb him throughout his adult life:

> Every part of nature teaches that the passing away of one life is the making room for another. The oak dies down to the ground, leaving

---

[22] Arsić unravels the ontology of impersonal mourning in *Bird Relics*, pp. 338–56, 369–84.
[23] *Walden*, "Spring," p. 307 [para 24]; see also p. 303 [para 19].

within its rind a rich virgin mould, which will impart a vigorous life to an infant forest. The pine leaves a sandy and sterile soil, the harder woods a strong and fruitful mould. So this constant abrasion and decay makes the soil of my future growth.[24]

And he continues:

> As I live now so shall I reap. If I grow pines and birches, my virgin mould will not sustain the oak; but pines and birches, or, perchance, weeds and brambles, will constitute my second growth.[25]

Thoreau lets us see that episodic loss and decay pervade nature through and through as a prelude to new growth. Thus even loss is to be celebrated. To thus affirm and memorialize loss is to mourn. When focused on one's *personal* affliction, grief is self-centered. Metaphysically and religiously the proper course is to see death, the "raining of flesh and blood," as *innocent—beyond* good and evil. It is not part of a cosmic vendetta. They are not aimed at harming any one creature or corner of life as against all others. Death, viewed impersonally (rather than as the outcome of human cruelty), is not aimed at *me*. From this wider prospect, my personal grief hardly registers. Considering the *full extent* of the real, my *personal* losses diminish in significance.

Life itself—not just grieving—can be seen either personally or impersonally.[26] It is the site of my personal memories, accomplishments, shames, commitments, sensibilities, talents, selfishness or unselfishness—all strands of my intimate identity. But life is also the site of oxygen flowing in and out of my lungs, of vegetable matter flowing in and out of my digestive systems—akin to what Thoreau calls "my virgin mould." It is the site of my corpse feeding other animals and plants (if I'm buried properly). Broadly speaking, all this is surely part of my life (if not part of my personal, *intimate* identity).

This second angle on life accentuates its *impersonality*. Under the shock of immediate, *intimate* loss, we expect, permit, and excuse intimate, personal grief. Extended, it is liable to betray a *selfish* sense of my having been cheated out of a *possession* to which I have a *right*. Yet Thoreau will adopt a wider *impersonal* perspective. He will ask "*Am I not partly leaves and vegetable mould myself?*"[27] Under the perspective of my life as an inflow and outflow of vegetable matter and oxygen, heat and cold, my life will come and go

---

[24] *Journal*, October 24, 1837, p. 3.
[25] Ibid.
[26] I've learned much here from Tzachi Zamir, "Talking Trees," *New Literary History*, 42 (2011): 443.
[27] *Walden*, "Solitude" p. 134 [para 18].

impersonally over long spans of time. A leaf is not *personally* aggrieved as it dies (it has no intimate life-story). My breath is my life, but it is not *personally* aggrieved if it is not eternally replenished.

Thoreau mourns unselfishly, impersonally. He won't think he has been picked out for suffering or betrayal or that he has been deprived of a possession. Nature cares nothing for his intimate life, and as fused with nature, he will care nothing for it either. He mourns as participant in a largely unnoticed *impersonal* life and *its* grieving. This is impersonal grief, and it is permitted and pervasive. Geese grieve the loss of their goslings. The oak grieves the loss of her fall colors, and a corpse grieves her disintegration into mould. Perhaps he would count the chillingly somber quiet after a massive rockslide as a moment of Nature mourning. If we agree to these losses as occasions of grief, they are nothing if not impersonal.

Thoreau might be deflecting unbearable loss in adopting the notion of nature's impersonal grieving. Nevertheless, he sketches an ontological mourning that is of interest independently of its genesis in his personal suffering. (And why, we might ask, should its serving to deflect be a reason to dismiss it? Good theories can protect.) Impersonal grief can be acknowledged quite apart from any shield it might provide. At times, it seems that an all-pervasive goodness colors creation. At times it seems that an all-pervasive sadness cloaks mountains and seas. In Thoreau's *Cape Cod* we find calm ocean rollers calling out with a sigh to a drowned and shore-tossed Margaret Fuller.[28]

Thoreau is fascinated by a cut for the rail tracks in the bluff just up from the pond. He sees the sand as matter alive, organic, excreting and also weeping with the spring thaw. Trees sorrow in wind, skies weep, rocks cry out as they split from a wall. Is this personification gone mad? Yet Thoreau expects of us, and exemplifies in his own case, a radical conversion *away from fear of a pathetic fallacy*—attributing pathos to things that have none. Rather than bowing to the authority of pathos-police nabbing those guilty of fallacy, he suggests civil resistance: we accuse the courts of enforcing a spiritually invidious *apathetic* fallacy.

It's easy enough to burden Thoreau with the charge of projecting human grief onto flat, unfeeling surfaces of cold-steel stuff. Galileo gives us dead matter (the atom or the billiard ball). Such matter neither grieves nor disowns grief. His inanimate cosmos is gloriously free of vitality or pathos. It's a spinning whirl of dead stuff without meanings to share. In contrast,

---

[28] Thoreau hedges: he is uncertain that the bones are Fuller's in early reports (see *Journal* 3, p. 127). Yet his later *Cape Cod* account is clearly her memorial. *Cape Cod* (Boston: Thomas Y. Crowell Company, 1961), p. 123.

Thoreau awakens to days that inspire, instruct, hearten. He abjures dead matter, finding flint-chips become fruits, and sand-cuts become alive.[29] He embraces swirling, fining fish, and works to join these totem creatures. If my muse hears his, if Thoreau's revelations become ours, we together are shattered. As the old world falls away, we behold what we had hitherto only peered at, scanned, or scrutinized in a squint. Revelations crush, and restore. Something gets altered. These are moments to revel in.

Thoreau would have us behold familiar human grief as glancing participation in a deeper, more extensive phenomenon— a mourning that courses throughout Nature, that inheres ontologically in every crack and cranny of everything. We behold Nature always and forever living, moving and being in perfect animation in its rising cycles—and perfect mourning in its falling. For every new bud a leaf falls. Nature mourns her losses. Branka Arsić pursues this thought as a lynchpin in Thoreau's thought. She is surely right.[30] Thoreau beholds Nature's renewals and also her incessant mourning.

Thoreau has the germs of his view of impersonal mourning earlier than the deaths of Waldo and John. It falls into place on the occasion of catastrophe. We get no intimate, personal account of his loss. "Wouldn't we love to also have the manuscript Thoreau never wrote: the book about his feelings for his brother? And what a different person he would have been if he had been able to write that book!"[31] But are we unhappy with the austere, delightful, and prophetic young man who writes nothing personal—but "only" *A Week on the Concord and Merrimack* or *Walden*?

Imagine a writer, perhaps a counter-Plato, who delivers a version of Socrates' death quite other than the one we are familiar with. Would we want a quite different Socrates who grieves personally at his imminent demise and joins in with his friends' weeping and welcomes his distraught wife's presence? Instead of dwelling on his personal feelings, he turns to an abstract and dialectical discussion. Yet this deflection of pathos (if that's what it is) is integral to Plato's magnificent vision of immortality. Thoreau makes the deflection of private pathos (if that's what it is) integral to a magnificent ontology—a vision of Nature in mourning. If either Plato-Socrates or Thoreau had single-mindedly opened up in only personal grief, we would not have the writers we know and celebrate.[32] The world would be less for

---

[29] *Arrow-heads as stone fruit—Journal,* March 28, 1859, p. 90; *the live sand-cut—*"Spring," pp. 295f. [para 7, 8].

[30] Arsić, *Bird Relics,* see note 22, above.

[31] William Eaton (personal correspondence).

[32] Socrates' "greatness of soul" appears to Aristotle as "indifference to fortune" (*Posterior Analytics*). At the death-scene Plato has friends but not Socrates submit to grief—but

that, and have less truth for that. Thoreau loved Hamlet's wild thinking. Perhaps we should love Thoreau's thinking for its wild affirmation of Nature mourning.

7.

Sensing and studying an emerging industrial and administrative era, Marx, Thoreau, Weber, and any number of Romantics will accentuate the loss of a world-view that can celebrate life itself, that acknowledges the vibrant core of living things. Living trees become board-feet to sell; meadows in bloom become sites for new housing; scrub-covered mountains become obstacles to throughways and railways; oceans hold harvests of profitable fish, and provide sites for deep-water drilling or wind power. Nature increasingly becomes a resource for exploitation. The ever-spreading disenchantments of nature have become all too familiar in our time. We can lament this loss quite apart from the withering of belief in divine creation. Apart from theistic commitments, we can lament the loss of Creation, a plenum infused with value all its own. There is nothing intrinsically wondrous or terrible about the world of atoms Galileo bequeaths. In itself, such a world has nothing of its own to say. Yet the world of our lives is a plenum of things wondrous and terrible and quite ordinary, and in any case there-for-themselves, declaring a glory and power not of our making. Landscapes become disenchanted, denatured, "available resource," and persons too have been "human resources," instruments in organizations that instrumentalize themselves. As Thoreau put it, "Men have become the tools of their tools."[33] In academia, we corral texts, push them through chutes to be tranquilized by "theory" and packaged as jargon. Thank God Thoreau is so much more than a research niche. He's a Bristlecone Pine, or a race across pond ice in stride with a fox.[34]

In "Wild Apples" Thoreau situates his growing disenchantment with the modern world in the emergence of orchards replacing random scatterings of wild apple trees. Clearing land and planting in rows regiments the apples and the apple harvest. Crews walk straight-and-narrow corridors, collecting by the bushel. Trees aren't variously mixed in mosaics, with other sorts here and there, in their own disordered place and wild patterns. Confining apples in

---

also to laughter! Phaedo: "I was pleased, and I was also pained, because I knew that he was soon to die, and this strange mixture of feeling was shared by us all; we were laughing and weeping by turns." Andrew Corsa asks, "Isn't this interweaving of grief, humor, joy, and loss what we find in Thoreau?"

[33] *Walden*, "Economy," p. 36 [para 53].
[34] *Journal*, January 30, 1841, p. 186.

orchards provides an easy supply of a single kind or two. The profusion of wild apples will disappear. Kids will grow up thinking apples are of two kinds (and grown on Styrofoam trays). Thoreau could name dozens of varieties around Concord alone and found even more when he traveled to Minnesota for his health later on. He gets quite ecstatic describing the taste of an "ice apple"—an apple that doesn't fall but freezes on the branch.[35] Then "the usual January thaw" unfreezes the middle, its juice now fermented. You can drink a little hard cider fresh from the tree. He liked the "buzz" (my word, not his) and laughed at the Puritan disapproval of all drink. Each tree produced apples spiked slightly differently. You could sample, like wine tasting, except it was free, in the open. And it was free from snobbery. There is enchantment in wild apples.

8.

Let me say more of the disenchanted, gray halls of academe. There we find industrial alienations, not everywhere but prevalent enough to dwell on. I embrace the possibilities offered by these halls and regret all that stands in the way of bringing life to them. With a bit of hyperbole, we find cubicles squared up for specialized research: thoughts and texts chopped into bits; feelings for the living whole of things, cognitive and affective, sidelined or gently mocked; feelings partitioned from thinking, and thinking from feeling. We rule out of bounds sensing a text or phenomenon as a revelation or marvel—and what is Thoreau but marvelous revelations! He gives us things to behold, words that will burrow and transform if we heed them.

We read poetic narrative in and out of class, narratives that can—and should—be transformative. There's more to pass on than gray analysis or content:

> ... one cannot simply extract the analytic content from the story; the story has to be told, experienced, undergone, in order for its force to be felt. So philosophic song is not something to be mined for what its content might tell us about the spirit of the age. Rather, *philosophic song is a mode of critical thought because it forces its readers to undergo the very thing it is describing.*[36]

Do we have a place in administrative flow charts for teaching philosophical song, and for guiding transformations through texts? The influx of passion

---

[35] *Essays*, "Wild Apples"—"the frozen-thawed apple," p. 465.
[36] Colin Jager, quoted in James K. A. Smith, *How (Not) to Be Secular* (Grand Rapids: Wm. B. Eerdmans Publishing Company, 2014), p. 133 (my emphasis).

and of the transformative power attached to words should be at the heart of teaching in the humanities. There, "philosophical songs" and "transformative revelations" should be quite at home. There, we note, in texts and in teaching, the sort of "passionate speech" that Cavell defends.[37] When we opt for detached, clinical analysis only, we needlessly abandon to Church or Synagogue, to family, entertainment, or the streets, all revelations of wonder or value.

To float love of wonder, openness to surprise, the enigmatic and mysterious is *unavoidable* in treating literary texts and art works with care. In the writing of Thoreau, Wittgenstein, Cavell, and so many others, we find non-argumentative but nonetheless philosophical thought. This way of thinking

> does not lead the reader on an "intellectual forced march" demanding disciplined focus, but rather works by "implied meanings" conceived as "inherently in motion." Miming this motion, the reader is "to float along" in a state of receptivity, [in] a "relaxed" or associative approach to the text.[38]

The upshot is that song, poetry, and what I've called reverie and episodic improvisation, can, and often should, upstage analysis and deflationary, or lawyerly critique. Then we'll find room for Basho's fish to cry, or Thoreau's creeks to whisper, Lear's voice to roar, or fools to laugh. But all this remains undercover while the official academic mission is to maximize the acquisition and distribution of useful knowledge.[39]

Thoreau will pointedly refuse to rank useful knowledge over appreciations of beauty or what he calls "Sympathy with Intelligence". His writing is good for the soul, and for preserving wide acres of insight, wonder, and delight. In place of a narrow band of instrumental knowledge and reason he gives us expansive *exuberant* knowledge, or gives us *unknowing*. (We return to the admixture of exuberance and openness to beauty ever and again in the next excursions.) He gives *befitting reveries* and sympathy with revelations.

---

[37] For more on Cavell on passionate speech, see "Closing Passions" below. It's not irrelevant that Cavell, in his application for tenure at Harvard, barely survived an attack from two prestigious philosophers from another prestigious institution who went out of their way to warn that his mixing of literary and philosophical interests was "deleterious to the future of philosophy." See *Little Did I Know*, p. 442.

[38] See Ross Postnock, "'Don't think, but look!': W. G. Sebald, Wittgenstein, and Cosmopolitan Poverty," *Representations*, 112 (1) (Fall 2010): 114. In this passage, quotation marks signal Postnock's citing Adorno on non-argumentative thought.

[39] To find detached, scholastic analytic thought deficient, as Nietzsche, Thoreau, and Kierkegaard do, is perfectly compatible with harnessing meticulous analytical scholarship to the service of larger transformative aims.

We follow the sounds and rhythms of sentences miming the music of texts and things. Thoreau finds the vibrancy of things echoing through the night into morning, free from the moorings of abstract theory or institutional utility. He is ready—and readies us—for redemptive revelations. We are to be as ready as the lily rising up through the muck.

9.

"I long ago lost a hound, a bay horse and a turtle dove," Thoreau wrote in the first chapter of *Walden*, and the line has often been read as a scholarly riddle to be solved.[40] What might hound, horse, and turtle dove represent? Rather than being a code for specific objects lost, however, that line might be read as an evocation of a pervasive existential condition of abandonment and loss.[41] It might evoke Thoreau's burdens of separation and loss—of a brother, a child, or a friend (think of his break with the elder Emerson)—or of a lost innocence regarding the land that would claim his allegiance. Of the latter, he writes: "The remembrance of my country spoils my walk. My thoughts are murder to the State, and involuntarily go plotting against her."[42] He has lost friend, child, brother, and country, and is in danger—as anyone would be—of losing to despair his capacity to affirm or celebrate.

Of that enigmatic line, Thoreau writes to Benjamin Wiley in 1857:

> If others have their losses, which they are busy repairing, so have I mine, & their hound & their horse may perhaps be the symbols of some of them. But also I have lost, or am in danger of losing, a far finer & more ethereal treasure.[43]

Might that "more ethereal treasure" be the treasure of pure morning joy? "I long ago lost a hound, a bay horse and a turtle dove." If we speak that sentence slowly, musically, the vowels will fall in the rhythms of sighs, sighs of lament: Ah *la* ta ta *la* [I *long* ago *lost*]. And "turtle dove" is "turtle" not because of a hard shell, but because it softly sings "tu tu, tu tu," that is, "coo coo, coo coo," or in French, "tor*tue*."[44] The coos of love can be coos of

---

[40] *Walden*, "Economy," p. 16 [para 24].
[41] For Cavell, these words evoke inescapable existential abandonment: *Senses*, pp. 49–51.
[42] *Essays*, "Slavery," p. 346.
[43] *Correspondence*, Letter to Benjamin Wiley, April 26, 1857, p. 478. Another clue is in Thoreau's quote from Mencius: "If one loses a fowl or a dog, he knows well how to seek them again; if one loses the sentiments of his heart, he does not know how to seek them again ... The duties of practical philosophy consist only in seeking after those sentiments of the heart which we have lost." *Week*, p. 264.
[44] The resonance of "tu" with "turtle" is clearer in the French: "*tortue*."

greeting, but also the coos of lament and love lost, the dove calling grievingly for its love. This is the materiality, the body-mediated delivery, of verse, of the text. It's the grittiness of non-angelic voice.[45]

Thoreau is bound to the things of the earth. Sometimes child of the mist, sometimes Bristlecone Pine, he is neither diaphanous angel nor hard as a rock but a creature of loss, and of recovery, a grateful and joyous recipient. "Where is [the singer] who can excite in us a pure morning joy?" He is *here*.

> The merit of this bird's strain is in its freedom from all plaintiveness. The singer can easily move us to tears or to laughter, but where is he who can excite in us a pure morning joy? When in doleful dumps, breaking the awful stillness of our wooden sidewalk on a Sunday, or, perchance, a watcher in the house of mourning, I hear a cockerel crow far or near, I think to myself, "There is one of us well, at any rate,"—and with a sudden gush return to my senses.[46]

That creature of loss and recovery is ours if we dare undergo his impersonal yearning, mourning, and youthful exuberance. We share a sigh, let's say, not just of sadness but of delight as we part with night.

---

[45] See Branka Arsić, "What Music Shall we Have? Thoreau on the Aesthetics and Politics of Listening," *American Impersonal: Essays with Sharon Cameron,* Branka Arsić (ed.) (New York: Bloomsbury, 2014).

[46] "Walking," p. 254 [para 83].

3

Sympathy with Intelligence

I suppose that this value [in walking], in my case, is equivalent to what others get by churchgoing and prayer. I come home to my solitary woodland walk as the homesick go home. I thus dispose of the superfluous and see things as they are, grand and beautiful. I have told many that I walk every day about half the daylight, but I think they do not believe it. I wish to get the Concord, the Massachusetts, the America, out of my head and be sane a part of every day.
—*Journal*, January 7, 1857

Having nothing to do but walk makes it possible to recover the pure sensation of being, to rediscover the simple joy of existing
—Frédéric Gros[1]

Thoreau's late essay "Walking" meanders along like a conversation or brook; his aim is to leave the politics, markets, and gossip of the village behind as he sets out on his woodland rambles.[2] Through the linked arts of walking and writing, he will refine perceptions and regain sanity and freedom. Walking a path and unwinding a sentence are exercises for body and soul. Thoreau practices a religious ethics of *askesis*, a Greek, monastic, and Yogic practice that undoes restlessness, sloth, and desperation. The mass of men live lives of "quiet desperation," and he would not be one of them.[3]

1.

By adopting daily purifying routines like prayer, writing, or walking, *askesis* aims to improve one's life by focusing on essentials. Thoreau chides would-be philosophers of his time with the quip that there are plenty of professors of

---

[1] Epigraphs: *Journal*, January 7, 1857, p. 208; Gros, p. 83.
[2] See "Walking," *Essays* pp. 225-55. (Henceforth, "Walking." Paragraph numbers are given in brackets.) Thoreau's essay began as a lecture, delivered at the Concord Lyceum on April 23, 1851 and many times at various sites thereafter. He alternated a talk called "Walking" with one called "The Wild." Eventually they evolved into the single essay we know as "Walking." Published in the *Atlantic Monthly*, 1862, the year of his death, it is perhaps his greatest non-political essay.
[3] *Walden*, "Economy," p. 7 [para 9].

philosophy around Boston, but no true philosophers.[4] A true philosopher takes beliefs and their elaborations, in discourse or comportment, as part of the weave of living wisely, day in and day out. If Thoreau takes the things of the world to be radiant with significance, that thought is no stronger than his daily perceptual immersion in that significance.

Thoreau found *askesis* in classical Greek Stoic and Cynic traditions, say in the lives of Socrates or Diogenes—questioning, non-conformist, unconcerned with luxury—and he could encounter it in monastic and mendicant Christian traditions.[5] St. Francis or the Desert Fathers worked to purify body and soul of desire for wealth, status, or personal power in anticipation of an ecstatic afterlife. Thoreau purifies body and soul of worldly status-seeking or pleasures (as the village would define these), all in anticipation of an ecstatic present life here and now in Nature.

Thoreau knew these Western traditions of renunciation, and more intriguing, he was one of the first in America to absorb the asceticism of the Eastern Vedic scriptures.[6] To a friend, he speaks of being a yogi, one who scorns worldly desire, hones self-discipline through dietary rules, and adopts intellectual exercises for clearing and centering the mind.[7] His walking is a spiritual exercise akin to Zen's "walking meditations" and his writing is akin to the Protestant tradition of writing out the detail of one's daily spiritual wins and losses in a kind of confession that requires no priest.[8] Village life is a distraction from both ways of access to a sacred or redemptive reality. His pilgrimages, he writes, are akin "… to what others get by churchgoing and prayer."[9] He adds: "I come home to my solitary woodland walk as the homesick go home."[10] Note that home is a walk, not a place. Leaving his village home is coming home to the unfolding household of Nature, where communion with the mobile residents restores him to himself. Thoreau takes us to the paths around Concord to come home to himself. If we join him in

---

[4] *Walden*, "Economy," p. 14 [para 19].
[5] Nightingale presents Thoreau in pursuit of self-sanctification: Andrea Nightingale, "Auto-Hagiography: Augustine, Thoreau," *Arion* (Fall 2008): 111–48.
[6] See Friedrich, *The Gita within Walden*; Alan D. Hodder, *Thoreau's Ecstatic Vision* (New Haven: Yale University Press, 2001); and Branka Arsić, *Bird Relics*.
[7] For Thoreau's self-identification as a "yogin," see Letter to Blake, November 20, 184, *Correspondence*, p. 251; also, "I sat in my sunny doorway from sunrise till noon, rapt in a revery," *Walden*, "Sounds" p. 108 [para 2]; and Alan D. Hodder, *Thoreau's Ecstatic Vision*, (New Haven: Yale University Press, 2001).
[8] See Malcolm Clemens Young, *The Spiritual Journey of Henry David Thoreau* (Macon, GA: Mercer University Press, 2009).
[9] *Journal*, January 7, 1857, p. 208.
[10] Ibid.

spirit, we will see things "… as they are, grand and beautiful."[11] A contemporary French philosopher of walking has this to say:

> having nothing to do but walk makes it possible to recover the pure sensation of being, to rediscover the simple joy of existing, the joy that permeates the whole of childhood.[12]

To partake of the joy of existence among wondrous things Thoreau would return to childhood. He would become a "child of the mist" and have us join him. Getting only routine workaday sensory input doesn't grant things as grand and beautiful wonders. What we take in when half-awake carries no charge of the wondrous. And to be snapped alert by the wondrous—or the terrible—is only the start of absorbing something grand and beautiful. What I absorb marinates and stews over hours and evenings. Thoreau typically serves up the full effect of exposure to wondrous experience in writing a day or so after first impact. His encounters bud and flower over time and at his desk. Experience happens *here and now*, but it also flows into tomorrow and a year from now.

Thoreau says his walking is solitary, but that's a relative matter. Friends often accompanied him, and he befriends animals and plants, birds and trees, meadows and valley prospects as he encounters them along the way. There is an element of solitude, and also of the social. Apart from his companions, persons and pines, he also senses us reading over his shoulder, listening and walking with him as he brings his glancing encounters to their fresher and truer expressions.

He contrasts the liveliness of walking to drab, life-sapping village life. However that's a relative matter, too. He figures the village as burdensome custom, empty etiquette, and constraining mutual expectation. This is true and also hyperbole. After all, Thoreau knew the village as the site of family visits and playing with kids. But fit hyperbole provides impact, startling us awake—in this case, to reconsider how village ways in fact can sap life. The verve of his writing heightens our alertness. To paint Concord in boring dull monochrome heightens the contrast with everything wild beyond its pale. Lyman Mower puts it this way: "Hyperbole is the fundamental character of the wild. We experience the new hyperbolically, as plenitude or excess."[13] In an early essay Thoreau writes: "He who cannot exaggerate is not qualified

---

[11] Ibid.
[12] Frédéric Gros, *A Philosophy of Walking* (London: Verso, 2014), p. 83. Gros contrasts the nature ramble with the pilgrimage, and both to the promenade and protest march.
[13] Lyman Mower (personal correspondence).

to utter truth. ... Moreover, you must speak loud to those who are hard of hearing, and so you acquire a habit of shouting to those who are not."[14]

The plenitude or excess of incoming reality brings us new perceptions. A startle throws me outside myself but that is only the beginning. Experience buds. I knew a pleasant tune, yet it begins to change in my ear as I hear and remember it today and tomorrow. I hadn't heard—*now I do!* Thoreau seeks more subtle perceptions. He renews his walks daily. The scenery doesn't hold still day-to-day, and neither does the alertness of his seeing, smelling, or hearing. His ambles are wild because his senses become wildly alert, shocked or prodded into new receptivities—say, to the sudden rush of wings as a bird by the path is flushed. And after the moment of startled ecstasy, we let our perceptions bloom.

> [O]ur ecstatic states, which appear to yield so little fruit, have this value at least: though in the seasons when our genius reigns we may be powerless for expression, yet, in calmer seasons, when our talent is active, the memory of those rarer moods comes to color our picture and is the permanent paint-pot, as it were, into which we dip our brush. Thus no life or experience goes unreported at last; but if it be not solid gold it is gold-leaf, which gilds the furniture of the mind. It is an experience of infinite beauty on which we unfailingly draw.[15]

Beauty is infinite because we are never done with absorbing and renewing it. And the talent for review is as crucial as the genius for initial reception. If the village freights us with dullness and unhealthy labor, Thoreau asks us to surrender to the shock and refinement of beauty. Toward the end of "Walking," he confides that with luck, his walks culminate "with a sudden gush, [that] return[s me] to my senses."[16] Exposure to "infinite beauty" is not new knowledge but revelations that startle and bloom. Revelation doesn't advance natural science but restores the self to the world and the world to the self through the medium of awakened senses. It's rebirth.

2.

Thoreau's renunciation of village worldliness clears space for attaining contact with things sacred, things touched by Nature, by the hand of God, or

---

[14] *Essays*, "Thomas Carlyle and his Works," p. 200.
[15] *Journal*, September 7, 1851, pp. 468–9.
[16] "Walking," p. 254 [para 83]. For an elegant annotated copy, see *Henry D Thoreau, Essays*, Jeffrey S. Cramer (ed.) (New Haven: Yale University Press, 2013).

the gods. Poetic perception provides a fruitful communion that transforms one's place in the world, and one's place in time—one's relative age or youth.

Youth is a time before village protocols fence in imagination. As we've seen, Thoreau is devastated by his brother John's death, and then by the death of young Waldo. Yet within a month of these deaths, quite astonishingly, he refers to his recovery as retrieving his youth. "I am as old as old as the Alleghanies—but it excites a youthful feeling—as I were but too happy to be so young."[17] He is immensely old, as the dead are—and strangely young, ready to start life anew. Old and young, Bristlecone Pine and "child of the mist," he inhabits an anomalous zone, embracing contraries rather than fleeing toward village simplifications and exclusions. It would have him be young *or* old—not both.

Being stopped by the "beautiful and grand" is being stopped transcendentally.[18] A pilgrimage in and to paradise is no less than openness to innocent surprises, say, peering child-like through mists. Of course Nature is not uniformly beneficent, and in some sense, not beneficent in a *personal* sense at all. It can seem cruel, say, as Thoreau encounters piles of bodies—corpses—on the beach.[19] There is the death of his brother, and the stench of slavery. Coming home from the village he avoids the foul smell of a rotting horse.[20] But the terrain of "Walking" turns out for the most part to be impersonally nurturing, supporting him without doing him any special favors (or for that matter, harms). Worlds change with the subtlety of one's imaginative appreciation and grasp. For transformation toward the sacred and delight to happen, Thoreau needs special freedom.

3.

In his first words, Thoreau speaks up for Nature. The capitalization indicates if not reverence at least exceptional respect. To speak up for Nature is not to praise an abstraction but to nominate particular plants and animals, rains, rocks, and winds for special attention. They are singled out in recognition of a radiance blocked by village protocols of business, boxed-up religion, or politics. Village protocols smother access to Nature's dense and illuminating particulars. Those protocols aim for mastery over commodities, mastery over materials for impersonal factory and shop production, mastery over

---

[17] *Journal,* March 27, 1842, p. 352.
[18] *Journal,* January 13, 1857, p. 218.
[19] *Cape Cod* (Boston: Thomas Crowell, 1961) p. 123.
[20] *Walden,* "Spring," p. 307 [para 24].

social and individual behavior. Despite blemishes from crews harvesting ice or timber, or from a cut through a hillock for a railroad right-of-way, Thoreau can imagine Nature as a domain more or less free of human control. Her goodness and beauty are not yet fully subservient to human projects, or rampant commodification. Thoreau speaks up for Nature as a site of Absolute Freedom.[21]

The village sponsors a variety of *relative* freedoms—civic ones that protect rights to shop, vote, travel, and work, and that minimize palpable harm from others. Life in its confines rests on prohibitions. I can't drive on the wrong side of the road. Freedom outside the village is another matter. It descends as an invitation to joy and delight, to move by whim, instinct, or inner promptings, to follow the allure of wild things and places. To be free from village restraints is to be free to be as I wish (so long as I avoid harming others). I can walk at my pace, slow or fast. I can summersault or skip, sing or say not a word. The village thrives on protocols of mastery. In the wild, these are set aside. Loosened from such constrictions, the world is set free: "in wildness is preservation of the world."[22]

Relative freedom dances in the gaps between restrictions. Thoreau pictures *absolute* freedom as a dance with a divine lawgiver reigning above any village law. "The man who takes the liberty to live is superior to all the laws, by virtue of his relation to the law-maker."[23] A divine lawmaker is free to do as he pleases—that is God's genius. He gives the law to Nature and to the village.[24] The genius of the walker is a vibrant creativity and initiative that predates all village law. Civil freedom lets me into a concert (if I pay), but it is not the ravishing freedom of falling in love, or becoming one with the genius of music. When we fall for the sweep of a hawk, perception is as free as the call of things perceived. This freedom is absolute.

4.

Despite abandoning village ways, Thoreau is not misanthropic or anti-social. He walks with a friend. They are "Knights Errant," he tells us. To be errant is to stray from the usual path, wander from social expectations. ("Error" comes from the same root.) These knights stray from what the village would

---

[21] "The traveller must be born again on the road." *Week*, p. 306. Jack Kerouac underlined this sentence in his copy of *A Week*, before finishing *On the Road*.
[22] "Walking," p. 239 [para 37].
[23] "Walking," p. 250 [para 73].
[24] Compare Kant's view that the literary genius does not follow aesthetic conventions, but *gives* the law to nature.

take to be proper or holy service, but they do not utterly abandon sociality.[25] The town gossip is that Thoreau's walking is loafing. He's unmarried, underemployed and contributes nothing to society. So they say. But his sociality takes different forms, and unnoticed forms. He worked as a highly skilled land-surveyor, and labored in his father's pencil factory (his mechanical inventiveness led to a breakthrough in pencil making).[26] He was a paid lecturer on speaking circuits, and for a short time served as a schoolteacher. He worked assiduously at a trade—the writer's trade.

No slouch, throughout his adult life Thoreau devoted endless hours to reading, revising manuscripts, and adding daily to his *Journal*. In pursuit of his trade, he devoured literary texts, ancient and modern, and texts of the world's religions. He absorbed books of natural history, geology, and the anthropology of Native Americans. He's a keen observer of human nature, politics and the media. He made meticulous observations and kept detailed records of plant and animal life in and around Concord. They are considered even today to be expert work in field biology and ecology. His scientific expertise was remarkable.[27]

Thoreau made notable contributions to his society, not least through his radical politics. He refused to pay taxes to support the country's war against Mexico.[28] His night in jail was the occasion for the essay "On Resistance to Civil Government," an inspiration for Gandhi's resistance to British rule and for Martin Luther King's resistance to Jim Crow laws in the United States. As the Civil War approached, he supported the insurrectionist, John Brown, gave fiery anti-slavery lectures, and was one of the most active participants in Concord's underground railroad. His literary and scientific endeavors, his activism, and his work at pencil making and surveying refute the dismissive image of a man escaping social responsibilities. And he is congenial:

> Every day or two I strolled to the village, to hear some of the gossip which is incessantly going on there, circulating either from mouth to

---

[25] A selfish recluse would not have written, "Even the tired laborers I meet on the road, I really meet as travelling gods." *Journal*, August 15, 1845, p. 383.

[26] He refined the graphite used in pencils, permitting a trimmer pencil that took over the market. Later his father switched from making pencils to making the graphite sold to pencil makers all over New England.

[27] See Richard B. Primack and Abraham J. Miller-Rushing, "Uncovering, Collecting, and Analyzing Records to Investigate the Ecological Impacts of Climate Change: A Template from Thoreau's Concord," *BioScience* 62.2 (2012): 170–81; and Robert M. Thorson, *Walden's Shore: Henry David Thoreau and Nineteenth-Century Science* (Cambridge, MA: Harvard University Press, 2014).

[28] The war amounted to a giant 'land-grab' of Mexican territory, appropriating what became the states of Arizona, New Mexico, California, Colorado, and Nevada. The acquisition of Texas was more complicated.

mouth, or from newspaper to newspaper, and which, taken in homeopathic doses, was really as refreshing in its way as the rustle of leaves and the peeping of frogs.[29]

Walkers of genius, Knights Errant tilting toward Jerusalem, are not made but are born (*Ambulator nascitur, non fit*).[30] Their genius is a bit of God's grace. Not everyone can carry a tune, or pray. Not everyone can find the rhythms of true walking and listening, or the knack for wildness or lawlessness that it demands. Thoreau inserts in his essay a poem featuring Robin Hood, but it's not there to honor robbery in the name of helping the poor. It's there to underscore forest freedom. In the woods, Thoreau can disregard etiquette. If we lived on "the marrow of koodoos [and other antelopes] devoured raw," we'd show "a wildness whose glance no civilization could endure."[31] In politics, he brings wildness to town. It's a duty to be disobedient when the state wants your support in capturing half of Mexico at gunpoint. He makes the point in a *Journal* entry:

> I wish my neighbors were wilder. He ... who does not obey the law but whom the law obeys—reclines on pillows of down and is wafted at will whither he pleases—for man is superior to all laws both of heaven & earth—when he takes his liberty.[32]

And makes the same point defending freedom in "Walking":

> There is something servile in the habit of seeking after a law which we may obey.... a successful life knows no law.... The man who takes the liberty to live is superior to all the laws, by virtue of his relation to the law-maker.[33]

Walking is a God-given talent, and God is free, in obedience to no law. We are free when we follow the divine as an exemplar of freedom rather than follow a law than constrains or directs. No "how to" books exist for the acquisition of freedom.

Thoreau gives us a slogan in defense of wildness: "in wildness is the preservation of the world." But National Parks will not save us.[34] No law shows us how to walk in the right spirit through wildness. Even Thoreau can fail. "I have walked a mile into the woods bodily, without getting there

---

[29] *Walden*, "The Village" p. 162 [para 1].
[30] "Walking," p. 226 [para 5].
[31] "Walking," p. 240 [para 38].
[32] *Journal*, February 27, 1851, p. 171.
[33] "Walking," p. 250 [para 73].
[34] "Walking," p. 239 [para 37].

in spirit".³⁵ Learning to see and commune in the woods with wild cycles of birth, death, and rebirth—only that will preserve the world.

5.

Thoreau says only one or two persons have acquired the art of walking, of sauntering, of pilgrimage. By osmosis, we might have some of that art rub off, as we accompany him. "Saunter" might come from the French *sans terre* (without home), as Thoreau has it, or it might come from *a la sainte terre* (on the way to the holy land), moving toward a sacred site. One who saunters in the first sense (without home) will have a home nowhere in particular and thus can be at home anywhere in Nature. But there's a puzzle here. To be at home anywhere in Nature is already to be in a holy place. Yet to be on pilgrimage *to* a holy place is not yet to have arrived. The holy land, Nature, is both near at hand (we already inhabit it) and just around the bend (we're not there yet). Paradox is linguistically wild and true to reality, jolting us *into* the wild and real to absorb its shifting shapes.

Think of "paradise" not as a spot on the map but more like a river, both a specific place of satisfactions and a promise of future ones. While distant from a river's spill into the sea, I can be in its pleasures, and on the way to its further pleasurable prospects just out of sight. Thoreau seeks paradise (a temple just ahead) and enjoys paradise (a temple he inhabits in the moment). The holy place is here and just around the bend in the beauty of hills. Thoreau also says, rather ominously, that pilgrimage is a retrieval of "the Holy Land from the Infidels."³⁶ But the "infidel" is my inattentive self—unfaithful and dull to the present, and dull to what's next. The task, Thoreau says, is to get "*nearer to here.*"³⁷

Getting "nearer to here," true walking, is "never ending" and "undying".³⁸ Our walking is undying because Nature holds all changing things, living and dying, and hence is inexhaustible, making our walks of discovery unending. Second, ideals, or moments of their discovery, endlessly beckon, even while we are immersed in their present realizations. We live with undying adjustments between satisfactions of the moment and satisfactions awaiting just ahead. Walking is undying, third, because we let ourselves down, or the world lets us down. "[I]t sometimes happens that that I cannot easily shake

---

³⁵ "Walking," p. 229 [para 14].
³⁶ "Walking," p. 33 [para 2].
³⁷ *Journal,* November 1, 1858, p. 275. Also see Young, pp. 193–4.
³⁸ "Walking," p. 225 [para 3].

off the village. The thought of some work will run in my head and I am not where my body is."[39] Unholy desecration can intrude from the world. The recapture in Boston of an ex-slave, Anthony Burns, smothers Thoreau's capacity to enjoy the restorative present. He longs for a place where "Man and his affairs, church and state and school, trade and commerce, and manufacture and agriculture even politics ... [will have] little space ... in the landscape."[40]

The "unendingness" of walking appears in yet a fourth mode with the dissolution of clock-time. If I look at my watch when there's singing, I'm not in the presence of singing. Thoreau can scribble a note to date when the first robin arrives, but the presence of her arrival can seem as undying, "un-datable," as her song. Yet this timelessness, endlessness, co-exists with repetition. Any given dawn has an eternal presence compatible with its rising again and again.

> the air was ... so warm and serene that nothing was wanting to make a paradise of that meadow. When we reflected that this was not a solitary phenomenon, never to happen again, but that it would happen forever and ever, an infinite number of evenings, and cheer and reassure the latest child that walked there, it was more glorious still.[41]

The presence of song delivers us to "an undying adventure."[42] Love, too, seems to be an "undying adventure." It can be fully present yet always beckoning, here-yet-there-ahead. That's a feature too of music, or of the cry of the loon, or even of justice—present, yet around the bend.

As if undying adventure weren't complex enough already, we must add a fifth complication. To live under ideals—say of 'true walking"—is to suffer both happiness and unhappiness. We enjoy the presence of satisfactions in a here-now yet ache in their resistance to full assimilation. Too much stress on a satisfaction "here-now" creates the illusion of no tomorrow. Yet we know perfectly well, don't we, that we'll be hurt as tomorrow arrives? At the least, we will have lost the freshness of what is now. If we reverse emphasis, we know that to put too much stress on tomorrow's good news depletes resistance to disappointments here and now. This oscillation is unending.

Finally, to embark on an undying adventure means bracing ourselves for a journey from which we may never return. It is not going out and coming back, but leaving everything behind, continuously, unendingly, enacting abandonment. The Gospel, Thoreau reminds us, prompts us to abandon

---

[39] "Walking," p. 229 [para 14].
[40] "Walking," p. 230 [para 17].
[41] "Walking," p. 255 [para 85].
[42] "Walking," p. 226 [para 3].

"father and mother, brother and sister, and wife and child and friends."[43] Sensing heaven in birdsong leaves mothers and husbands behind—consigned to the village. Thoreau ends the third paragraph of his essay—so full of surprise—asking if we are prepared for a walk, that is, prepared to leave village and family behind, having "paid your debts, made your will, and settled all your affairs."[44] Only with accounts settled can we enjoy grasses and skies. It's obvious why only one or two have learned to walk.

6.

The absolute freedom gained in exposure to the wild comes with a kind of ignorance or unknowing. It's a Socratic, philosophical openness linked to acknowledging the limits of knowing. Thoreau is an observer, a naturalist who knows plants and fish, who knows that nature is thus and so. He is also full of know-how. He knows how to survey land and to hoe beans. He "knows," that is, he's familiar and at home with, an immense cultural background. He reads Greek and Hindu literature, Chaucer and Shakespeare, and immerses himself in Native American languages and cultures. But he comes to herald a "wild" knowledge that is, more accurately, a non-knowledge. It is neither "knowing that," "knowing how" nor "being familiar with," but a sort of ignorance, a luxuriant bathing in the unknown:

> My desire for knowledge is intermittent but my desire to bathe my head in atmospheres unknown to my feet is perennial and constant. The highest we can attain to is not Knowledge but Sympathy with Intelligence. I do not know that Knowledge amounts to anything more definite than a novel & grand surprise on a sudden revelation of the insufficiency of all that we had called knowledge before—a discovery that there are more things in heaven and earth than are dreamed of in our philosophy. It is the lighting up of the mist by the sun.[45]

---

[43] "Walking," p. 226 [para 3] Matthew 19.29. Luke 14.25–27 has a harsher version: "If anyone comes to me and does not hate his father and mother, his wife and children, his brothers and sisters—yes, even his own life—he cannot be my disciple." Thoreau doesn't ask us to *hate* family, and he doesn't say "leave and don't return." Perhaps you are to leave *as if* you will never return—you don't look back!

[44] Ibid. Some have linked Thoreau's love of walking and wildness to the nation's westward expansion. After all, he does gaze toward the Ohio and Mississippi in thinking of the wild. Yet we've seen that the aim is to arrive "here-and-now," not to the wilds of Colorado or California. "Civil Disobedience" *protests* western expansion. Emerson arrived in Yosemite; Thoreau didn't.

[45] "Walking" p. 250 [para 72]. Thoreau gently alters Hamlet: "there are more things in heaven and earth than are dreamed of in your philosophy."

Thoreau confides,

> At the same time that we are earnest to explore and learn all things, we require that all things be mysterious and unexplorable, that land and sea be infinitely wild, unsurveyed and unfathomed by us because unfathomable.[46]

We know that Socrates is ignorant. This is partly a ploy to get questions out in the open. But he's also ignorant in that he doesn't fathom the basis for Diotima's allure, or the wonder of her vision, or the deep trust he has in Athenian ways, or his trust in the words of an oracle. Socrates is ignorant, yet has sympathy with these sources of intelligence—sites of divine intelligence, we might say.

There are different registers of unknowing. On a wave lashed beach or at the summit of Mt. Ktaadn, Thoreau encounters a forbiddingly unknown sublime. This is not the benign atmosphere he could "desire to bathe my head in." Alternatively, he can find the unknown in simple things. "The shallowest still water is unfathomable."[47] The child can wonder endlessly at her simple reflection. In the essay in hand, he privileges gentle moments when the sun dissolves the mist, revealing wonders. We become "a child of the mist," with access to "more things than are dreamed of" in village life. He exclaims, in a kind of ecstasy, "Live free, child of the mist—and with respect to knowledge we are all children of the mist".[48] In the essay's final cadences, he visits Spaulding's Farm, where he allows reverie to set in. He hears gods at play, laughing and humming. He has a kind of "wild vision" or reverie. In all this, we have wandered away from the town commons of knowledge. We are in a space of unknowing and revelation. On foot, we have recovered "the pure sensation of being, ... the simple joy of existing, the joy that permeates the whole of childhood."[49] As Thoreau puts it in one of his earliest essays, "surely joy is the condition of life."[50] We seek the singer "... who can excite in us a pure morning joy."[51]

The link between child-like innocence and saving vision has a biblical source: "Except as you become as little children, you will not enter the kingdom of heaven."[52] For Nietzsche, too, one can do no better than become a child playing by the sea.[53] Children can evoke and embody a pervasive

---

[46] *Walden*, "Spring," p. 306 [para 24].
[47] *Week*, p. 48.
[48] "Walking," p. 250 [para 73].
[49] Gros, p. 83.
[50] *Essays*, "The Natural History of Massachusetts," p. 22.
[51] "Walking," p. 254 [para 83].
[52] Matt. 18.3.
[53] Friedrich Nietzsche, *Thus Spoke Zarathustra*, Graham Parkes (trans.) (Oxford: Oxford University Press, 2005): "Of the Three Transformations," p. 24.

sense of surprise. They can live in enchantment and remind us how little we know.

> I trust that we will be more imaginative, that our thoughts will be clearer, fresher, more ethereal, as our sky [is]—our understanding, more comprehensive and broader, like our plains—our intellect generally on a grander scale, like our thunder and lightning, our rivers and mountains and forests—and our hearts shall even correspond in breadth and depth and grandeur to our inland seas.[54]

I may *possess, take hold of,* common knowledge, but in contrast I am happily *possessed by* revelations and beckoning enchantments. They *overtake* me—sweep me from the safe haven of my insularity, individuation, and detachment. I acknowledge what I've been given—a piece of radiance emanating from *this thing* from the world. And I also see what I *haven't* been given. I have no clue about, am utterly ignorant about, how that gift arrived, and about what is transpiring in the giving, and what has happened to my pedestrian sense of myself as autonomous and secure.

I am ecstatic, beside myself. The sweep and wonder of the snow accosts me, throwing me, unknowing, into its resonance and allure. Any bit of knowledge, say the snow's depth, can be a portal to wonder, but the wonder isn't an extra bit of knowledge. Revelations can merge into what I've called "befitting reveries"—moments when the transcendent is nowhere but immanent, the enchanted nowhere but in the ordinary, and the sacred always here in what is close at hand.

Paradoxically, Thoreau claims that even over seventy years of a life, and never straying far from home, one still would not know one's surroundings.[55] "Nature is a personality so vast and universal that we have never seen one of her features."[56] *Not even one?* Each feature hides infinite reserves. The unfamiliar remains because enchantments never cease, and it's questionable whether one should even want to see Nature fully unenchanted. Moses is refused a sight of Yahweh. To wish to see Nature unveiled might be reckless and indecent. In any case, it's forbidden. We abide with the forever unfathomable, and need its reservoirs of wonder and surprise.

If I see the near side of the apple, I don't see the back or the inside. Like the edge of paradise, more knowledge lies just out of sight; and the wonder of its taste is *never* in sight. The meteorologist gives me the fact that a tornado

---

[54] "Walking," p. 238 [para 32].
[55] "Walking," p. 229 [para 15].
[56] "Walking," p. 251 [para 77].

approaches. I look, I isolate this bit and that: two yellow funnel clouds.[57] Given this data, a vast remainder lies in darkness, and more data may be irrelevant, for the darkness isn't just about missing data. What is to be done? Should I be this frightened? What is this riveting majesty? Nature (and my place in it) is too big, multiplex, and scintillating to nail down, piece by piece, as common knowledge. And perhaps it's hubris to want it otherwise.

7.

Thoreau yields to a kind of unknowing. Whether knowing is having data or theory, having know-how or familiarity, to seek full Knowledge is to know failure. Yet to be "unknowing" is not just to acknowledge this failure. It can be an occasion for access to something *other* than Knowledge. A priceless alertness and rapport can survive amidst unknowing, and Thoreau calls it "Sympathy with Intelligence." In a *Journal* entry it's clear that this is not a recommendation about *how* to pursue sympathy with all things (intelligently). It's a recommendation about *what* to pursue. We are to pursue a particular *kind* of experience, a "divine nectar":

> My desire for knowledge is intermittent; but my desire to commune with the spirit of the universe, to be intoxicated even with the fumes, call it, of that divine nectar, ... is perennial and constant.[58]

By the time "Walking" takes shape, some years after this entry, Thoreau drops any reference to "intoxication" with "the fumes" of the divine. But he retains the idea of communion with something more or less divine. Here we have no straightforward explication, so we have to reconstruct what Thoreau means by "intelligence" as the focal point of our communing or sympathizing.

Risking repetition of notes from earlier ambles, I find three leads to pursue. First, this aspiration appears immediately before his reverie at Spaulding's Farm, where he encounters the hum of gods thinking and their gentle laughing. Perhaps they are the Intelligence or Intelligences, the "divine nectar" that absorbs his communing sympathy. Presences, or gods, overflow mere physical objecthood. The presence of something is not an object, not a property, and not a "mere subjective projection." Presences—the voice of the river, the craziness of the loon, the power of sunset, the nectar of the

---

[57] Thoreau gets more and more immersed in factual notations in his late writing, especially in the *Journal*. This needn't conflict with revelation.
[58] *Journal*, February 9, 1851, pp. 150–1.

gods—are illuminations emanating from things and animating them. A second lead to what Thoreau means by this "less-intermittent" aspiration is his mention, in *Walden,* of a *Vedic* saying, "All intelligences awake with the morning."[59] The gods or intelligences residing on Spaulding's hill enchant the place. They waft through the mist to lift the world's burdens, and awake especially at dawn.

Why would intelligences awake with dawn if not to awaken the land with the swagger of a sunrise rooster? Thoreau celebrates the enchantments the gods provide, the radiance of stars and hawks above, the refulgence of organic earth and plants, of "vegetable life" and his own placement with such life. This provides a third access to his initially obscure honoring of "Intelligence" as the focus of sympathy. He asks, "Shall I not have intelligence with the earth? Am I not partly leaves and vegetable mould myself?"[60] To have intelligence with the earth is to partake of its radiant power to speak, to enchant. Though it is partially mould, my body *speaks*; it partakes of and bespeaks intelligence.

Concord becomes tarnished, losing enchantments it would have had for Lucretius, who could give us cosmology in verse, or for Homer, whose gods animated seas and plains and everyday home life, or for any who recited the *Gita*, where gods could be animals and animals, gods, and where gods saturated daily life. Concord abandons glories enjoyed by its earliest, now extinct, inhabitants, who found spirits in skies and birds. Even the biotic community lacks enchantment as berries go to market, or trees are continuously felled. He shares this reverie of the gods at Spaulding's Farm in compensation for these losses.

Galileo's science stripped Nature of purpose or magic, even of life: a well-designed, well-oiled machine is not alive. For Galileo, earth, plants, and mould are moribund atoms in motion. Christian theology banished pagan gods from the hills and streams where they had played and plotted. Emerging capitalism transforms Nature into a resource available for exploitation and markets. Ordinary people in an increasingly administrative and bureaucratic culture lose a sense of a "god within." They are increasingly little more than their file-identities, computer passwords, and Twitter accounts. In a manufacturing milieu, as Thoreau puts it, people "become tools of their tools."[61] You don't have to be wildly romantic, dreamily nostalgic, or a rampant pan-psychic to think that the loss of enchantments has disastrous consequences, not just for our habitat but also for we who inhabit it.

---

[59] *Walden*, "Where I lived," p. 87 [para 14].
[60] *Walden*, "Solitude," p. 134 [para 18].
[61] "Economy," p. 36 [para 53].

To right the balance a bit, Thoreau treads lightly, playfully, unveiling a Nature where gods might appear and disappear in early mist, and where an old "Maker" might gently scoop out Walden with the cup of a hand.[62] (The heavy equipment stays in the shop.) In Nature sandbanks are alive and organic, and a hawk offers an ethereal moment, mounting, then falling, then remounting.[63] It is born from an egg nestled in a crevice in a cloud. Re-enchantment means fanning the embers of imagination.

Both knowledge and imagination are essential to a full life. Each focuses different aspects of the world. Knowledge is a powerful technique of detached observation, experimental control, and the generation and use of abstract theory. The world is objects, their properties, and laws describing their motion. Imagination allows presence and enchantment into the world. We get to hear whispering trees; we tremble with the enchantments of Spaulding's Farm; we come to see Walden's Maker, or a hawk who nests in a "cliffy cloud." When it comes to Knowledge, Thoreau confides, we are all "children of the mist." Mists conceal and reveal, and we can't trace the difference with the confidence of knowing it. They slightly conceal the buildings and botany of Spaulding's place, but they reveal the presence of its myth-laden enchantments to imagination.

To sympathize with the animating songs of life is to refuse to hold life at a distance in theory. It is to sing resonantly *with* Nature. It's to affirm, by joining, a philosophical song.[64] To have Sympathy with Intelligence, in the case at hand, is to be in a holy communion with the gods at the farm and their music. It is to restore the music of one's life in writing and living. "To write great music," Bach is alleged to have said, "the musician must make his life a great song." This might as well be Thoreau. And making one's life a great song is not just whistling the tunes one likes. Bach goes on, again in a spirit Thoreau would take in: "... ceaseless work, analysis, reflection, writing much, endless self-correction, that is my secret."[65] Yet sometimes letting one's life be a song is less a matter of effort and work than of letting music play through one, apart from one's bidding or direction. Thoreau dreamed

> [I] was a musical instrument ... . My body was the organ and channel of melody, as a flute is of the music that is breathed through it. My flesh sounded and vibrated still to the strain, and my nerves were the chords of the lyre.[66]

---

[62] "The Ponds," p. 187 [para 26].
[63] sand-cut—"Spring," pp. 295f. [para 7, 8]; hawk—"Spring," p. 305 [para 22].
[64] See Ch. 2, note 32.
[65] These sentences are widely cited on record jackets—I have not been able to authenticate them.
[66] *Journal*, October 26, 1851, p. 81.

In a passage written well before "Walking," Thoreau tells us what it's like to hear the song of the world and to sing with it. The picture complements our image of the sympathetic strings of the Viola d'Amore. As if to reassure any who would frown at the idea of gods roaming Nature, here he leaves out "intelligences awakening at dawn."

> There is something more than [atoms in] association at the bottom of the excitement that the roar of a cataract produces. It is allied to the circulation in our veins. We have a waterfall that corresponds even to Niagara somewhere within us... . How it spends itself! I would say to the orator and poet, Flow freely and lavishly as a brook that is full—without stint.[67]

This is communion with Nature, sympathy with the radiant "intelligence" of falling water. Bare facts blossom and flower. The mechanics of falling water yield a cataract that sets in motion a Niagara in our veins. Thoreau promises that a slight increase in the flow of my blood will precipitate a rush of imagination that in turn will release lavish poetry.

Thoreau's writing becomes such ravishing and lavish flow. The genius of poetry is the genius of particular things. Their dense radiance is "a light which makes the darkness visible, like the lightning's flash, which perchance shatters the temple of knowledge itself."[68] Poetic intelligence bursts *from the world*, from a lily, from a child's smile. It radiates and illuminates; speaks eloquently; resonates musically; touches and addresses through odor, taste, mood, and climate. A map that records only objects-and-properties leaves out the presence of things. Sympathy with Intelligence is sympathy with presences throughout all of creation. "All intelligences awake with the morning."[69] Thoreau awakens with the winds and swaying trees. Snowdrifts sparkle with genius.

The *poet's* genius rests on exercising receptivity to *incoming* genius. We know eyes target things, and forget that things target us with their looks. It's the gaze of the mother that the infant first sees. The scholar sees books looking back from her shelf—full of majesty, intelligence, and humor. We stand in a garden to bask in a flower's greeting or stand under the moon to gather its blessing. If things look at us, or radiate wonder, Galileo won't say so, and thus cuts down our picture. In an age of mechanics, computers, and brain science, it's hard to hold onto the insight that the world looks on us, offering its poetry or address. Common sense (in our day or Thoreau's)

---

[67] *Journal*, February 12, 1851, p. 155.
[68] "Walking," p. 244 [para 50].
[69] *Walden*, "Where I lived," p. 87 [para 14].

favors deflation. Stars don't shine; they emit quanta of energy. Gardens have nothing to say, only poets and sentimentalists do. Things don't awaken at dawn. Eyes don't sparkle or laugh. But let's reverse the flow of significance.

The look of things is more than artificial, pasted ornament. The poet is adept at letting the look and sound of things bloom. He lets things speak and finds their primitive utterance fit for posting. There's reciprocity between finding the language of winds and streams and finding words that nail down that language of primitive utterance.

> He would be a poet who could impress the winds and streams into his service, to speak for him; who nailed words to their primitive senses ... whose words were so true and fresh and natural that they would appear to expand like the buds at the approach of spring ... to bloom and bear fruit ... for the faithful reader, in sympathy with surrounding Nature.[70]

When trees whisper, there's bloom. When the waters of Walden look back at Thoreau, there's bloom. We accept "the language which all things and events speak without metaphor."[71] Letting things speak attends their address.[72]

Of course there are times to set the primitive language of things aside, or to qualify the dominance of the poetic address of particulars. If I value my life I hear the mountainous terrain and its weather as brute fact apart from its bloom—I focus full attention on whether dangerous lightning or rockslides are near. In settings that test me materially I set aside a full openness to the genius, or allure of mountains. Yet as danger retreats I cherish, love, or am awed by these massifs. A full life demands love and wonder as we walk. The world has an excess of allure in the intelligence and bud of trees and the pond. We applaud with Isaiah:

> You will go out in joy, and be led forth in peace;
> the mountains and hills will burst into song before you,
> and all the trees of the field will clap their hands.[73]

---

[70] "Walking," p. 244 [para 53].
[71] "Sounds," p. 108 [para 1].
[72] There is a surface resemblance to Heidegger here. Although I can't argue the case, I think Thoreau is much closer to the truth of the matter than the author of *The Essence of Poetry*. See my discussion: https://edmooneyblog.wordpress.com/2014/12/17/heidegger-on-poetic-thinking/
[73] Isaiah 55.12 NIV

8.

In closing his essay, as he faces the hillock and woods of Spaulding's Farm, Thoreau offers a fable or reverie. There he finds the holy not transcendently out of this world, but amidst ordinary and pedestrian things. The farm appears in a wonderful dream-like moment to an ever-youthful, flute-playing Pan, the god of meadows and woods. The lighthearted farm reciprocates Thoreau's fanciful steps. Early on he conveyed a paradise unveiled as he sauntered toward the holy land. For this new revelation at the Farm to spread, he asks for "A people who would begin by burning the fences and let the forest stand."[74] His is a plea for *unfenced perceptions*—not for forest reclamation. Burning the fences allows gods to appear. The burning must be thorough.

> I saw the fences half consumed, their ends lost in the middle of the prairie, and some worldly miser with his surveyor looking after his bounds, while heaven had taken place around him, and he did not see the angels going to and fro, but was looking for an old post-hole in the midst of paradise.[75]

Paradise is when the scales fall off.

What does Thoreau see? He leaves the prairie aside and looks now on the tall trees of the Farm. Through the mist, on the hillcrest a "great hall" appears. Its residents he has never met. Yet they seem to be an "altogether admirable and shining family." No one has arrived from the village to pay them a call (or constrain them). They are Noble Spirits or Gods. "If it were not for such families as this, I think I would move out of Concord." "Nothing can equal the serenity of their lives." "Their attics are in the tops of the trees." Perhaps he heard "a suppressed hilarity." Nietzsche wanted unsomber gods who could laugh and dance.[76] The inhabitants "... are of no politics. There is no noise of labor." Yet they are not empty-headed idlers. One can "detect the finest imaginable sweet musical hum"—the "sound of their thinking".[77]

Spaulding himself is oblivious and drives his muddy cart right through the hall, hearing or seeing not a thing. The godly inhabitants hum on unperturbed. For them, the mud is no more than a puddle reflecting heavens.[78] So

---

[74] "Walking," p. 230 [para 16].
[75] Ibid.
[76] *Zarathustra*, 1, "On Reading and Writing": "I would only believe in a god who could dance," p. 36.
[77] "Walking," p. 252 [para 78].
[78] Thoreau sees heaven and mud simultaneously when the lily rises out of mud (*Essays*, "Slavery" p. 346), and when he sees mud through clear water, and heavens on its surface in *Week*, p. 48, and in *Walden*, "Pond," p. 187 [para 26].

we too might see heavens in pools even as mud lies beneath. What Thoreau sees is mirage-like, yet transforming—seen through a glass darkly.

Thoreau admits later that he has trouble recollecting his thoughts, recollecting himself. This removes him from responsibility for any outright assertion that gods inhabit the hill. After the fact, he's not quite sure. This later thought is his moment not of new knowledge but of sanity and revelation. Revelation is a moment of unknowing. His world is fuller, more vibrant, for having Sympathy with Intelligence, for having eyes to see the Great Hall, and for having ears to hear the gods' music and laughter and the hum of their thinking. Thoreau preaches "a newer testament—the gospel according to this moment."[79] And reveries are of this moment, and reveal more than we know.

Our "best thoughts" or perceptions—say, visions of the gods—can cohabit with humdrum ones, either one transparently overlaying the other. With double vision we see both Spaulding's Farm and the Gods' Great Hall. To bring paradise into the meadow or to bring the gods into the Farm is to refuse an ontological split between heaven and earth. We let each penetrate and inform the other. The possibility of increasing our vision, doubling it, as it were, in absorbing the gods at Spaulding's Farm, is repeated from a different angle in this marvelous *Journal* entry:

> I would not forget that I deal with infinite and divine qualities in my fellow. All men, indeed, are divine in their core of light, but that is indistinct and distant to me, like the stars of the least magnitude, or the galaxy itself, but my kindred planets show their round disks and even their attendant moons to my eye. Even the tired laborers I meet on the road, I really meet as travelling gods, but it is as yet, and must be for a long season, without speech.[80]

The "season without speech" will be a season for pilgrimage, and that season "is as yet"—not yet arrived. For lack of wild thoughts, freedom, and subtle perceptions, villagers and laborers will miss this temple and its inhabitants, and miss the travelling gods they might be if they sauntered. Benighted, this wild paradise and its divine inhabitants pass them by. The long season is a season of waiting without speech, either their speech or the speech of things all about.[81]

Speaking elsewhere of different reveries or fables, Thoreau comments:

---

[79] "Walking," p. 254 [para 82].
[80] *Journal*, August 15, 1845, p. 383.
[81] "Ours is the long journey of the Saturday, between suffering, aloneness, unutterable waste, on the one hand, and the dream of liberation or rebirth, on the other." George Steiner, *Real Presences* (Chicago, IL: University of Chicago Press, 1989), p. 231.

The hidden significance ... [of these fables is] not so remarkable as the readiness with which they may be made to express a variety of truths ... [A] superhuman intelligence uses the unconscious thoughts and dreams of men as its hieroglyphics to address men unborn ... [T]hese glowing and ruddy fables precede the noon-day thoughts of men ... The matutine [early morning] intellect of the poet [keeps] in advance of the glare of philosophy.[82]

A matutine intellect rises at dawn, before mists have cleared. It offers reveries open to express a variety of truths to those yet unborn—childlike: those *awaiting* to be born.

---

[82] *Week*, p. 61.

4

Concord Reflections

To be a philosopher is not merely to have subtle thoughts ... but so to love wisdom as to live according to its dictates, a life of simplicity, independence, magnanimity, and trust. It is to solve the problems of life, not only theoretically, but practically.

—*Walden*, "Economy"

There is nothing so sanative, so poetic, as a walk in the woods and fields ... I come to myself, I once more feel myself grandly related. It is as if I always met in those places some grand, serene, immortal, infinitely encouraging though invisible companion, and walked with him. There at last my nerves are steadied, my senses and my mind do their office ... I love and celebrate nature.

—*Journal*, January 7, 1857[1]

1.

In his essay "Walking," Thoreau speaks of Nature as paradise. Elsewhere, thinking of slave catchers in his woods, he speaks of his natural landscape as Hell. Nature is for Thoreau what others would call Creation, the landscape within which our living and dying, our growing and decaying, and our walking amidst bounteous particulars unfolds. In some sense, it's a divine gift. These omnibus terms "Nature" and "Creation" play a framing role. They are the canvas on which everything of interest is painted—or the field within which everything of interest happens. They are the sea within which we all play or swim, even as we are children of creation or nature. Thoreau's focus, we learn, is not on subtle thoughts (abstract considerations about nature or creation), but on philosophical *living*. He slips past theoretical questions about primal Origins, about defining 'Nature," about "Creation," about how a Creator creates, or about how we'd prove a Creator exists. "Nature" and "Creation" are prime examples of metaphysical or theological concepts. What kind of box, or boxes, does the world arrive in? Thoreau ducks away from *those* questions, leaving aside, as much as possible, metaphysical or

[1] Epigraphs: *Walden*, "Economy," p. 14 [para 19]; *Journal*, January 7, 1857, p. 208.

theological baggage. To my ear, this is part of Thoreau's practical wisdom: to avoid largely abstract and most likely unresolvable metaphysical conundrums in the interest of living out—and expressing experientially—what it means to be immersed in creation or nature, divinity or paradise, nature rejoicing or nature grieving (for example).[2]

Thoreau finds us already in place among the things of creation or nature. It's a place of address and response that stokes our capacity for joy and delight. More darkly, it's a place from which hellish things speak. Whatever the oscillation between heaven and hell, Thoreau harkens us to the world's address rather than prying open questions of causal genesis or final end-points. A hawk's flight quickens our sense of life quite apart from knowing its pedigree or telos or the mechanics of bird-flight. My sense of life is quickened as I follow Odysseus' return to Penelope, and this quickening occurs quite apart from my prying open other conundra, say questions about the creator of those Homeric passages, their transmission through time, or their ultimate purpose for humanity. Thoreau has a place for God and the gods in the big picture, but that place isn't examined abstractly nor is it his starting place. He awakens us to things he beholds, that bespeak the creation or nature we behold all about. Nature is *naturing*. I hone my receptivity to dispersed centers of animation and address and find myself in reciprocal resonance with them.

Words arrive strewn like seeds in the wind, finding multiple fields to take root. In some instances they bloom over years and around the world. Think of the global flowering of his essay on Civil Resistance. Other of his words feed my own strange reverie. I imagine him coming out of retirement to walk through a door in the rear of an academic lecture hall in Southern California. Here he is in the midst of a conference on his enduring standing. He's attentive, but academic discussion is not his cup of tea. He'd rather not wallow in the bad news of eco-catastrophes. In his time he lamented the shrinking of the salmon population in Concord River (salmon are no longer there). But he would not have traveled to Boston to lobby against dams or for limits on the catch. Not that he was a quietist. He just wasn't a *full-time* lobbyist or campaigner. He spent a night in jail in protest of the nation's military policy, worked for the Underground Railroad, and rang the village bell to rally citizens for John Brown. But he tried to limit his intake of life-sapping bad news.

Where would Thoreau fit on a university campus? He's a literary philosopher who keeps company with Goethe, and the *Gita*, with Diogenes, Epicurus, Milton, and Hamlet. What sort of philosopher is that? If analytic philosophy is non-literary, does that make him continental? Pierre Hadot,

---

[2] Bruce V. Foltz takes up the metaphysics of Creation in *The Noetics of Nature: Environmental Philosophy and the Holy Beauty of the Visible* (New York: Fordham, 2014).

the French philosopher, writes an essay on Thoreau in the 1970s and taught some of Thoreau's lessons to Foucault—the lessons that philosophy is a spiritual exercise and a way of life, that it can critique stifling institutions.[3] But Thoreau is closer to Kierkegaard than to continental post-structuralists.

Thoreau writes clarion sentences as clear as chanticleer's cry. Some continentals produce jargon-free sentences, and some let their writing mix with a non-scholarly life—I think of Sartre and Camus. Subtle thought and subtle living can merge for writers in the continental tradition. A colleague from the continental camp of philosophy writes digestible rural ethics and plows meadows. A friend from Los Angeles writes clearly on Thoreauvian virtues and climbs rocks in the Sierra Nevada. We can find a mix of good living and good writing here. Thoreau absorbed plenty of what we'd call academic knowledge—the histories of peoples, the classifications of plants, the natural history of Cape Cod. But beyond knowledge or critique he tried to live a philosophical life, a life that finds sympathy with living things, finds sympathy with intelligences bursting in the beauty of an ordinary or *petite* sublime.

2.

For Thoreau, earth is a holy place for pilgrimage, for writing prayerful meditations, and for prophetic condemnations—of slavery, for instance. The divine doesn't lie elsewhere in a realm beyond the furthest star. It appears in the radiant things of creation. The illuminations and songs of things elicit religious, philosophical, and poetic response that weave into the fabric of Thoreau's living as such. Thinking without living is empty; living without thinking, blind. For Thoreau, love of wisdom is not love of knowledge. Wisdom is tied to moments of wonder that percolate free of discursive identifications, classifications, or explanations. It lives with the unanswerable. Perceptual *affiliation* with things all about is *philia*, love for them. Affiliation *enables* a philosopher's virtue. Seeing with a sympathy for things fuels the virtue of simplicity. In *Walden*, we learn that a philosopher's love and wisdom will embody "simplicity, independence, magnanimity, and trust."[4]

I remember a simple this-worldly moment of wisdom at a philosophy meeting at a college not far from where Concord River meets the Merrimack,

---

[3] See Pierre Hadot, *Philosophy as a Way of Life* (London: Blackwell, 1995), and "There Are Nowadays Professors of Philosophy, but not Philosophers," Aaron Simmons (trans.), *Journal of Speculative Philosophy*, 19 (3) (2005).

[4] *Walden*, "Economy," p. 14 [para 19]. For a helpful overview, see Philip Cafaro, *Thoreau's Living Ethics: Walden and the Pursuit of Virtue* (Athens, GA: University of Georgia Press, 2004).

and the Merrimack goes down to the sea. It was evening, the end of a full day, and a few of us left unfinished beers to head for second- and third-floor rooms. There was a slight pause at the elevator, as if a collective decision were impending. Then in an instant, all turned for the stairs and bounded up in a salute to minimizing energy consumption. That was independence. The bounding was not herd instinct, and it takes an independent mind to notice the cost of elevator ascensions. It had simplicity. There was nothing sophisticated or ornate about the response. The day's common ventures had established mutual magnanimity and trust.

Thoreau is not rigid about his list of virtues. We have just heard his *Walden* list. From an earlier list we find the addition of truth, faith, and innocence. He writes, "I will not plant beans another summer, but [will plant] sincerity, truth, simplicity, faith, trust, innocence."[5] Perhaps his master virtue was attaining "Sympathy with Intelligence." At the start of *A Week on the Concord and Merrimack Rivers,* Thoreau gives us the *place* he would pursue a virtuous life:

> The Musketaquid, or Grass-ground River, though probably as old as the Nile or Euphrates, did not begin to have a place in civilized history until the fame of its grassy meadows and its fish attracted settlers out of England in 1635, when it received the other but kindred name of CONCORD from the first plantation on its banks, which appears to have been commenced in a spirit of peace and harmony. It will be Grass-ground River as long as grass grows and water runs here; it will be Concord River only while men lead peaceable lives on its bank

At other times Thoreau places himself at Walden, or on the way to Maine's highest peak, Ktaadn, or on Cape Cod. Accompanying him, we become residents-at-one-remove. Traversing his landscapes with him, even at one remove, is to abide and reside with him. He finds himself in place; we are invited in; we can join him if we will.

3.

A hallowed tradition, founded in Augustine's Confessions, continued in Descartes, and proceeding triumphantly through the Enlightenment, fixes personal identity in *inward* things. I am—quite obviously—my "inner self," or my soul (also hidden within). For my "sense-of-self" I'd look to my thoughts, memories, dreams, aspirations, shames. Thoreau doesn't deny

---

[5] *Journal,* August 15, 1845, p. 382.

that there's some glimmer of truth in this idea of a precious inner realm, but as we've seen, he also identifies his life with more impersonal things—his breathing, or "virgin mould." On this more impersonal side of selfhood it helps to hear his early mentor. Emerson says of a person, succinctly, "He is place"—*place,* nothing more, nothing less![6] Emerson takes the stance of an observer, but nevertheless the view is striking. The heart of a person is not a hidden interior, not a transcendental something rigged up to heaven. It is a way of finding oneself outside oneself. Then I am not an inner something but *the place I inhabit.* The stress shifts to "outer things" and the "inner I" shrinks to conceptual and phenomenological invisibility. Of course Emerson says other things, elsewhere, but like Thoreau, he doesn't apologize for thinking simultaneously in multiple directions. Both are improvisatory thinkers, unafraid of high-wire acts, experiments at the extremities of thought. To say we are place is a startling extremity. It seems to erase everything "inner," "private," or "hidden" that we have been taught to cherish as our own.

Yet in Emerson's favor, we at least sometimes value ecstasy, which etymologically, is standing (*stasis*) outside (*ec*) oneself. So perhaps we value being relocated, becoming place, a place outside. I can be "beside myself" in outrage or with joy. Then I seem to shed my interior. But there are more commonplace occasions when we can be tempted to say we become place, become our emplacement. Entering a room, I may be overcome by "inner anxiety," but I may just as likely feel my interior drop away. The room has a presence (lively or dull) and I may be shunted into that exterior, becoming lively or dull because I *am* that place. At the height of stadium fervor, I abandon myself to that fervor, becoming the place of the crowd. When soft light enters a room I become its luminous shaft. I greet a friend sitting there, the room receives my voice—I am, for the moment, a voice resonating out there in roomy space. From the crest of a hill, the valley welcomes my gaze and absorbs me. During coffee, the cup receives my sagging spirit and it lingers there outside me. To myself, what another sees as my eyes, body, and personal being, falls away, and what remains is a voice-filled room, a landscape, a coffee mug, each a welcoming and absorbing presence.[7] At those moments (it seems, to myself), I am place—and in big or little ways, ecstatic.

Thoreau is place as the presence of the pond overwhelms the presence, to him, of his viewing. An "inner self" disappears as he abandons himself to the rustle of sky or the darting of fish. In step with him losing himself in Nature, as readers, we find Thoreau's interior diminish in salience, and his

---

[6] Emerson, *Early Lectures: 1838-1842* (Cambridge, MA: Harvard University Press, 1972), p. 29: "that which is with him constitutes place. He is place and whatsoever is not with him in spirit is abroad and vagabond."
[7] This is part of what Cameron calls "the impersonal" in Thoreau. See *Writing Nature.*

presence as author diminishes, too. The name on the cover disappears as we read, absorbed by the pond. Thoreau becomes no more (and no less) than *the place and particulars he sings of*. The "I" of the singer is an indexing device receding before the wondrous detail that unfolds page after page. It's a virtue of trust and magnanimity to find oneself lost in his presence, in the presence of *this* place that for the moment he becomes.

4.

Thoreau follows the habits of birds and muskrats and he dates the honeysuckle bloom. He disappears as locus of inner things as he offers detached observation and diligent scholarship. Yet it's also clear that he values sympathy, a tilt of the heart or soul. So the moment of ecstasy or dispassionate observation gives only part of the picture. Sympathy can be a prelude to his disciplined counting or theorizing, isolating for him something *worthy* of study. Or he might sympathize with a corner of the plant kingdom for no special reason at all—just because it's *there*. Sympathy focused on large patterns might isolate *why it matters* to count just *these* blooms or to subsume them under a theory. But strictly speaking, *sympathy* for a particular is unnecessary to scientific practice—yet is perfectly compatible with it. Sympathy might precede or accompany detached measurement or classification and it might follow *after* counting or categorizing. We look appreciatively at our display-box of pressed blooms months after they were first picked. Or we look at our newly printed article, long ago finished, now singing nicely when laid out in fresh print.

More generally, sympathy with the living *enhances* the living—or at least doesn't participate personally in destroying it. We want to protect and sustain what draws on our sympathy, whether plant or fish, tree or the sick and abandoned. And sympathy with the dying can bring them *new life*—as with Thoreau's writing about John Thoreau, or his scooping out a small pond near his grave, that extended the 'mould' of John's life. Sympathy with nature's sounds can extend a dog's noise toward the music of braying. Not completely tongue-in-cheek, Thoreau has sympathy for otherwise abandoned local swamps and the singing of their gnats.

> I can fancy that it would be a luxury to stand up to one's chin in some retired swamp a whole summer day, scenting the wild honeysuckle and bilberry blows, and lulled by the minstrelsy of gnats and mosquitoes![8]

---

[8] *Week*, p. 300.

He wryly continues this sympathetic regard for the neglected:

> Hope and the future for me are not in lawns and cultivated fields, nor in towns and cities, but in the impervious and quaking swamps.[9]

Some will think that taste in these matters—lawns vs. swamps—is surely an utterly personal matter, not a matter of seeing infinite beauty "out there" in unexpected places. Going fast-forward a century and a half, we can hear neighbors cry defensively: "Thoreau can have his swamp—we'll take the mall!" But he would persuade us otherwise. When it comes to living, not all options for appreciation are born equal. "To devote your life to the mystery of divinity in Nature or to the eating of oysters: would they not be attended with very different results?"[10] He is frank about his own vocational convictions: "My profession is to be always on the alert to find God in nature—to know his lurking places, to attend all the oratorios, the operas, in nature."[11]

Thoreau would bring us there to the swamp for a sense of the ambient foot-slosh, the mushy alternative to a preference for the mall's metallic escalator precision. Landscapes and swamp-sites are best perceived from immersion, letting their presence sink in. The swamp teems with life in all sizes and shapes. Mall life is not wet and squishy and is for the most part restricted to other shoppers, sales attendants, and security guards. It sizes me up relentlessly by the measure of my wallet, of my looks, fashionable or unfashionable, of my taste in accessorizing. This mechanical un-living steel and glass box is engineered to make me spend, scoop up merchandise, consume. How unlike the swamp! There we find life in all sizes and shapes—lilies, frogs, fish, weeds, decomposing leaves, singing mosquitoes, tree roots, grassy hummocks. It's life, and life close enough to my own that with a dose of imagination sympathy will bloom! How can I *not* love a mud bath for toes?

Thoreau shows us what he can do *here* that is impossible at the mall. To feel comfortable with *life* (or not) can't be just a matter of *taste*. He sinks in (at least in reverie) with resonant things that eat, breathe, bloom, and die, that procreate—that are wet and smell, that move, swim, stand, and sway. Such is the wild we inhabit. It's a place that reciprocally arouses *our* life. The mall's metallic or plastic clank or snap, its inane shopping chatter, just can't bring out the raw life in you—beyond an ache to buy. At the swamp, nothing is priced; everything is priceless. It yields a palette of presences

---

[9] "Walking," p. 241 [para 43].
[10] *Journal*, September 7, 1851, pp. 471f.
[11] *Journal*, September 7, 1851, p. 472.

we can live with. Our body comes alive with the wet, the leaves—fish and floating feathers.

Can we *prove* that an hour in the swamp is preferable to a day at the mall? Thoreau had little use for abstract debate, and *wouldn't* have debated the issue. Ecstatic hours watching seals at play will do more for appreciation of life than all the arguments one might muster for the conviction that life is exuberant and precious. Hours by the sand-cut at Walden thawing in spring will do more for sensing the ubiquity of organic life than hours of argument mustering demonstrations that earth is alive and well.

5.

Thoreau's overarching aim is to bring readers to *sympathy with the resonances of life*. This aim is frustrated by entrenched cultural constellations. We have alluded over and again to the fact that Thoreau is fighting an uphill battle. He doesn't lay out in a sustained exposition the shape of forces he has to neutralize if his voice and his life are to come through. He scatters his critical remarks, saying *what* he wants, the *way* he wants, *when* he wants. So we are left to reconstruct the cultural presuppositions definitive of post-Medieval European culture that he so adamantly resists. This cultural gestalt emerges with Descartes, Hobbes, and Galileo and gets consolidated in the Enlightenment and Idealism. Its powerful "self-evidence" stands in the way of fully grasping—let alone accepting and living out—Thoreau's way: *flowing unstintingly with the resonances of life*. This way has religious and prophetic depth. It is the key to redemption of spirit, his own and his neighbor's.

Sympathy with the resonances of life is my shorthand for his more daunting phrase, "Sympathy with Intelligence." It means walking as pilgrimage, becoming exquisitely alert to the echoing presence, atmosphere, and diverse illuminations of things; it means regarding creation as a place of brilliance and resonance, and invites our absorption into this place. Living from this center will jostle and bother the structural shibboleths of the modern world. Here are five targets of Thoreau's often mocking and satirical critique:

- the presumption of a *Galilean mechanical science* that posits reality as self-evidently no more than dead atoms in motion, and privileges the human stance of detached measurement and theory;
- the presumption of *Cartesian dualism* that a) posits denatured selves (primal 'consciousness') facing off against denatured, non-living objects (bare matter), that b) covers up the primacy of embodied persons in

continuous mutual communicative exchanges, and that c) refuses the thought of an address or voice coming from things of creation;
- the presumption that *epistemology* is paramount in serious thinking, a Cartesian epistemology that places the ideal of indubitable *knowledge* at the apex of philosophical and scientific aspiration;
- the presumption of *market economies* that determine value as always market and instrumental value; every object, talent, or product, from berries to river-rapids, becomes packaged and priced, stripped of inherent value;
- the presumption of secularization and "the death of God," a factor mixed in with the quartet of forces just mentioned. Thoreau indeed has an uphill battle in a world that has cast everything he deemed sacred or religious under the bus.[12]

It is serious business to question these presumptions. It's even more daring to allow alternatives to speak. It can seem idle or feckless to proffer presences streaming from an unknown world that address our sympathy. Who today can seriously herald illumination and song bursting from the core of things, attesting to magnificent plentitudes?

6.

Let me dwell longer on the Cartesian and nowadays nearly universal presumption that in serious thinking and writing, *epistemology*—a theory of *knowledge*—is paramount. Apart from a few mavericks like Nietzsche, Kierkegaard, or Thoreau, it's taken for granted that a philosopher must lay out the dynamics of knowing. What else can vouchsafe our connections with the world? We may seek to connect through affections (say, love of a child) or through virtues (taking courageous political stands). But these ways can seem sentimental or second-rate; we unthinkingly accord primacy to knowledge.

---

[12] In his magisterial study of the historical emergence of secular society Charles Taylor finds gaps in that emergence for a loyalty to the immanent that simultaneously acknowledges *transformative practices*. These qualify as transcendent moments of "the religious"—moments not necessarily aligned with creedal or institutional affiliations. See the helpful commentary on Taylor's *A Secular Age* (Cambridge, MA: Harvard University Press, 2009) found in James K. A. Smith, *How (Not) to Be Secular* (Grand Rapids: Wm. B. Eerdmans Publishing Company, 2014). I find Taylor's discussion opening a place for the sort of religious but earthy and absolutely non-institutional perspective Thoreau elaborates.

A related presumption is that education as well as simple conversation concerns *information-transfer*:

> Utilitarian ideologies ... have convinced us that the main purpose of talking is to convey useful information. Thus we now value terse communication that conveys practical knowledge, and consider anything else a frivolous waste of time. [P]eople have become almost unable to talk to each other outside of narrow topics of immediate interest and specialization. [But] the main function of conversation is not to get things accomplished, but to improve the quality of experience.[13]

And to improve the quality of experience in hearing others is not to improve the quality of information *about* experience. Thoreau reports,

> My friends [make a] mistake when they communicate facts to me with so much pains. Their presence, even their exaggerations and loose statements are equally good facts for me.[14]

He values the *presence* of his friends, not merely the facts they may report or pass on.

But surely, we reply, to connect we must *know* the child we cherish; we must *know* what moral stands to take. Yet to circle back to *knowing* hides what is *not-knowing*. Love or commitment or courage begin to play second fiddle to deploying objective facts in managing the world. If I seek power, it too must be fed by knowledge; if I seek common pleasures, I gather knowledge about attaining them, and about which ones won't betray me, or land me in decrepitude, jail, or worse. Knowledge, we presume, is power, power rooted in *epistemological* premises, not in weak-kneed premises of sympathy, wonder, or love. Yet Thoreau marches to a different drummer. Sympathy and rapport give access to the realities that count, and whatever the importance of power or honor or knowledge, things of wonder and beauty matter, too. And they begin where knowledge leaves off.[15]

7.

Knowledge, of course, is multiplex, of at least four distinct kinds. There is *knowing that*—knowing that rain is essential to crops, and second, there is

---

[13] Mihaly Csikszentmihalyi, *Flow* (New York: HarperCollins, 2009), p. 129.
[14] *Week*, p. 363.
[15] See Furtak, "The Value of Being: On Appreciating the Beauty of the World," *Thoreau's Importance for Philosophy*.

knowing how—knowing how to plow, to harvest, to price and deliver things to markets. Yet as we walk with the rhythm and feel of meadow, sunlight, and rain, we can resonate with so much more than is delivered by "knowing that" or "knowing how." The world is more bounteous than whatever these sorts of knowledge deliver.

In his *Journal*, Thoreau mentions a candidate for a third kind of knowledge. In addition to "knowing that" and "knowing how" he recommends facts that are "warm, moist, incarnated." And he adds, "A man has not seen a thing who has not felt it."[16] This sub-division of knowing suggests an *immediate familiarity* or recognition, as when we *know* the feel of sand or the taste of blue cheese. Perhaps it also includes proprioceptic knowledge—say, our knowing that our feet are crossed under the chair. We know these latter tastes, feels, and placements without a bit of observation or scrutiny.

Here's a fourth kind of knowledge, one suggested by Paul J. Griffiths. Call it *knowledge as reciprocal participation*.[17] I know my violin in playing it, participating in its reality. By the same token, the violin comes to know me as it triggers my response in turn. Griffiths puts it this way:

> As knower, you gain from the creature known a property you could not have had without the known's being what it is which is not merely your delightedly reflexive intimacy with it, but also your awareness of yourself as delightedly intimate in just that way. Your knowledge of any creature is therefore a kind of participation in it, as its being known by you a participation of it in you.[18]

When knowledge is praised, it's helpful to remember which of its several instantiations is praised. In academic settings, for instance, pursuing knowledge seldom means valuing knowing-as-familiarity (the raw taste or feel of something), or knowledge-as-reciprocal, delightfully intimate-participation. In the academy we are to maintain proper distance and reserve. For all its promise Griffiths' ideal of participative-knowledge doesn't quite capture the sort of access to the world that Thoreau values so highly.

In that crucial passage from "Walking," Thoreau honors "Sympathy with Intelligence." This is not plain knowledge but a kind of *unknowing*. It's not unlike Socratic knowledge of ignorance. It does not denigrate ordinary knowledge (in its several incarnations) but it recommends an openness to a standing Socratic ignorance that technical research won't dislodge. And Sympathy with Intelligence leaves room for "uncanny knowledge," say the

---

[16] *Journal*, February 23, 1860, p. 160.
[17] Paul J. Griffiths, Intellectual Appetite (Catholic University of America Press, 2009), p. 131.
[18] Ibid.

knowledge that Socrates accords to his daemon—that uncanny inner voice that is always with him, an intelligence he sympathizes with, a daemon ready to tell him what not to do. But that's a difference: Thoreau's inner voice is affirmative, not negative. It silently but surely guides not with a "No!" but with a "Yes!"

Sympathy with Intelligence is Thoreau's preferred portal to the world and his watchword or guide while in it. It is not Knowledge of the four kinds we have catalogued but an access that is simply life-instilling. Life-instilling sympathy is not Griffiths' knowledge-as-participation, and seeing why will be illuminating. Griffiths holds that "As knower, you gain from the creature known a property you could not have had [otherwise]." There are two places where this parts company with Thoreau's vision. We participate via sympathy, but the object of our sympathy is not "a creature known." What appears for sympathetic attention is uncanny, mesmerizing, more or less *unknown* centers of radiance. These "unknown non-objects" are the divine intelligences of the *Vedas*. These intelligences are crucial to Thoreau's rough-hewn poetic-metaphysical sensibility. Note that intelligence, in this context, is not a mental capacity. It's an originating site of radiance, sublimity, and plenitude. Originating sites of beauty, presence, sound, and mood deliver what Thoreau calls "intelligence." My violin and the songbird that addresses me at sunrise are not "objects-known" but divine sites of plenitude and inspiration.

In addition, what arrives in an address to me is not, as Griffiths has it, "a property [I] could not have had [otherwise]." Something arrives to steal my breath away. What arrives are not *properties* or *attributes* of an object. I receive *presence*. A thing's presence is not an attribute like an object's weight or color or size. A thing's lilt, slant, or delight, its uplift or foreboding, is no more a property than the weather is a property of the sky. Thoreau's world is a precious place, full of wonder, not just the site of objects-with-properties. Griffiths is on target in saying that beyond detached knowledge or know-how I seek a "delightedly reflexive intimacy with [the world]," and have a wonderful "awareness of [myself] as delightedly intimate" with the things of the world. But Thoreau would insist that reflexive intimacy is not a function of *knowing*. Knowledge is not to be abandoned but it's not everything by any means. Resonating sympathetically with things leaves us richer in awe, beauty, and even love—but not richer in knowledge.

It's a widespread presumption that a serious thinker must have an epistemology. This is a disposable Cartesian presumption. Thoreau reflects indirectly on the Cartesian problem of knowledge, but he is not obsessed with it. It's more important to live well than to seek justification for claims to knowledge or models of scientific method. At most he makes glancing remarks on the defeat of skepticism, or on the issue whether values can be objectively known, or whether God exists, or posses this or that divine attribute. To the chagrin of some, Thoreau is not obsessed with justifying his claims at all. Argument is seldom found. "Befitting reveries," like dreams or theater productions, carry an aura of "take it or leave it." That doesn't make them philosophically without merit, or mean that they are ultimately beyond discussion any more than Pharaoh's dreams or Plato's myths or a great Dickinson poem are without merit or beyond discussion. Dream, myth, and poetry can be philosophical.

Sympathy with Intelligence or sites of radiance moves us beyond, or apart from knowledge. In "Walking," before Sympathy with Intelligence appears as a worthy alternative to Knowledge, he tosses off its precursor. *Beautiful Knowledge,* is an "unknowing-knowing," and a worthy focus of aspiration.[19] This is neither *useful* knowledge, nor is it know-how. It is "unknowing" because beauty seems to transcend ordinary observational knowing. You can't catch the *beauty* of a cock's crow through disciplined observation. Further, and distinct from disciplined knowing, the Beautiful overtakes us—we don't overtake it. To be overcome by the Beautiful is to yield to being touched by things we grant are beyond our ken. And yet, as Plato thought, the idea of Beautiful Knowledge is not entirely oxymoronic. The touch of the beautiful seems to expose a kind of *transcendent* knowledge, as when we assent to the vision, in the *Symposium,* of a ladder of love that leads up to a beautiful redeeming vision. Sympathy with Intelligence guides Thoreau toward redemptive communion with, and love of, the world, and a deep gratitude for its daily blessings. To follow one's loves and their infinite beauty is perhaps a knowing-unknowing.

8.

Wonder, or "Sympathy with Intelligence," is akin to the immediacy of love. Reflective, disciplined detachment resists such immediacy. Nietzsche has a place for love of things and the world. It's not enough for an intellectual to offer detached, clinical critique. Nor can the philosopher always be "dynamite," breaking apart all that's false and illusory.[20] Writing in the wake of Emerson, Nietzsche makes a plea for life-affirming re-evaluations. If we

---

[19] "Walking," p. 249 [para 70].
[20] "I am not a man, I am dynamite." Friedrich Nietzsche, *Ecce Homo,* "Why I am a Destiny," Duncan Large (trans.) (Oxford: Oxford University Press, 2007), p. 88.

assemble those things around us that we love we'll find things worthy of praise.

> What have you truly loved up to now, what has elevated your soul, what has mastered it and at the same time delighted it? Place these venerated objects before you in a row, and perhaps they will yield for you, through their nature and their sequence, a law, the fundamental law of your true self.[21]

On his walks Thoreau sought those things he could love, even those things that had slipped away or were lost—the fish under ice, the birds not yet returned from the south, the blossoms not quite ready to bud forth again. He was attentive to things present and to things absent. He attended to things lost, or leaving: the fox cavorting across the ice, the lost hound, dove, and bay horse.[22] The dove is lost, but still heard, and chanticleer, though absent in night, will crow at dawn. We need an unfashionable love of the world, even love for things lost. The absent or eclipsed world is not a permanent darkness but a phase of eclipse. The eclipse of the dove's 'coo', or of the presence of God or the good, is always partial, passing with the seasons, never permanent. Thoreau had a faithful conviction that despite losses—even catastrophes—joy and serenity have not reached their final hour.

Thoreau's abundant hope and good cheer were not based on an *estimate* that the future was rosy or that the past had been fine, or that on balance things were better than worse. Who would dare bet on happiness on the eve of that great uncivil slaughter? Thoreau's hope was not contingent on the realization of one sort of future rather than another. In that sense it was absolute. Relative hopes and faiths are contingent on outcomes. If you don't get what you hoped for, you're thrown into dismay or despair. By staying free of *explicit and specific* expectations, absolute hope or faith maintains poise. Outrage or sullen despair are not his predominate attunement.

Thoreau vows in *Walden* that he won't write an Ode to Dejection—despite all around him that already is, or threatens, disaster.[23] He survived the catastrophes of his brother's death, "little Waldo's" a month later, and John Brown's some years later still. He survived the shameful humiliation of the Black tradesman Anthony Burns, recaptured in Boston under the Fugitive Slave Law. He didn't *just then* preach serenity and joy. But serenity and joy had not reached their final hour. They were found under leaves, in a

---

[21] Friedrich Nietzsche, "*Schopenhauer as Educator*," in *Untimely Meditations*, Daniel Breazeale (ed.), R. G. Hollingdale (trans.) (Cambridge: Cambridge University Press, 1997), p. 129.
[22] *Walden*, "Economy," p. 16 [para 24].
[23] *Walden*, "What I lived for," p. 81 [para 7].

heron's flight, in the least meadow or the bobbing cranberry in the marsh. "I have never had a deeper and more memorable experience of life—its great serenity, than while listening to the trill of a tree-sparrow among the huckleberry bushes after a shower."[24]

Then there is Thoreau's extraordinary reflection on the capacity of music to draw him outside himself, outside personal grief and even outside the impersonality of *nature's* grieving. Uncharacteristically, it seems to draw him momentarily even beyond the radiance of bounteous particulars and his fellow creatures.

> Suppose I try to describe faithfully the prospect which a strain of music exhibits to me. The field of my life becomes a boundless plain, glorious to tread, with no death nor disappointment at the end of it. All meanness and trivialness disappear... No particulars survive this expansion; persons do not survive it. In the light of this strain there is no thou nor I. We are actually lifted above ourselves.[25]

The sound of his music box lifted him beyond his sadness at young Waldo's death. He arrived at a sense of strangeness in the world. But in this passage, Thoreau lets music lift him ecstatically beyond the uncanny, even beyond relationship to those he has lost—and even beyond relation to himself. It delivers him to an unknowing serenity. Yet in other passages he claims such serenity as his own. Here, in memorializing serenity, he pulls the "I" that he is into retirement. There is a to and fro to the self's presence or absence to itself.

Several years earlier than the passage just quoted Thoreau writes that although John died an agonizing death, John was also serene and grateful to have lived. Such is the anomalous region of the emotions. We can be serene in our agony, sing in the fires that extinguish us—that we are grateful to have lived.

Here is Hannah Arendt on love and gratitude:

> gratitude for life having been given at all is the spring of remembrance, for a life is cherished even in misery ... What ultimately stills the fear of death is not hope or desire [for specific outcomes], but remembrance and gratitude ...[26]

These words might have been Thoreau's. He had written to Blake in 1856, a decade and more after John's death and while embroiled in the catastrophes

---

[24] *Journal*, September 29, 1843, in *Writings of HDT*, J. Vol. 1, 1837–44, Elizabeth Witherell (ed.) (Princeton, NJ: Princeton University Press, 1981), p. 469.
[25] *Journal*, January 15, 1857, p. 222.
[26] Hannah Arendt, *Love and Saint Augustine* (Chicago, IL: University of Chicago Press, 1996), p. 52.

sliding toward civil war, "I am grateful for what I am & have. My thanksgiving is perpetual."[27]

Having surveyed the terrain and crisscrossed its features, we can jot down some upshots: that living philosophically is to embody the virtues of simplicity, independence, magnanimity, and trust, and to follow a daily practice of writing and walking to procure serenity, remembrance, love, and gratitude; that living philosophically is also embracing Sympathy with Intelligence, an embrace that instills life; that living philosophically is cultivating a knack for memorializing (and mourning) life.

9.

Classically, we're told that we are the rational animal, the language-using animal, and the political animal. We are also the mourning and wounded animal.[28] As we've seen, for Thoreau, to be mourning is not a momentary fix for sudden sorrow, nor is it a prescribed path to closure. It's interminable. And nature herself mourns. On this, we have St. Paul's authority: "the whole creation has been groaning as in the pains of childbirth right up to the present time."[29] Thunder shudders, trees crack as they fall, and muskrats suffer in traps. Yet these aren't moments one should *endlessly* mourn. "The poet will maintain serenity in spite of all disappointments. He is expected to preserve an unconcerned and healthy outlook over the world, while he lives."[30] Thoreau looks for the singer "... who can excite in us a pure morning joy."[31] Moments of loss have their moments of nobility to be noted. Nature *alone* is permitted *interminable* mourning (along with incessant joy).

Nature accepts deaths in due course. Accepting this releases Thoreau from the sense that his losses are uniquely his to endure or protest alone. "Every part of Nature teaches that the passing away of one life is the making room for another."[32] It's striking that Thoreau makes this entry on the first page of his newborn *Journal*. From the start, the crack of dawn cuts through lingering darks. There's nothing dejected in Thoreau's raising a cairn to Margaret Fuller by the surf off Fire Island where she drowned and was

---

[27] *Correspondence*, December 6, 1856, p. 444.
[28] See Steven Mulhall, *The Wounded Animal: J. M. Coetzee & the Difficulty of Reality in Literature & Philosophy* (Princeton, NJ: Princeton University Press, 2009).
[29] Romans 8.22.
[30] *Essays*, "Carlyle," p. 188.
[31] "Walking," p. 254 [para 83].
[32] *Journal*, October 24, 1837, p. 3.

ravaged by sharks. Here is the passage—I'd call it majestic in its affirmative mourning:

> I expected that I should have to look very narrowly at the sand to find so small an object, but so completely smooth and bare was the beach … that when I was half a mile distant the insignificant stick or sliver which marked the spot looked like a broken spar in the sand. There lay the relics in a certain state, rendered perfectly inoffensive to both bodily and spiritual eye by the surrounding scenery, a slight inequality in the sweep of the shore … It was as conspicuous on that sandy plain as if a generation had labored to pile up a cairn … It reigned over the shore. That dead body possessed the shore as no living one could.[33]

At first he sees only a sliver, a splinter that he sings into a spar, and then a stone cairn—bones become a saint's relics, and the bouldered tomb communes with the wash of the sea, the sea, we might say, that "rolls on as it rolled five thousand years ago."[34] Indeed, the sea can express an interminable longing, but as Thoreau presents the scene he has no place for personal tears or misery. In its dappled majesty it's a hymn to creation in sighs that are breaths of delight—delight at being alive to it all, alive even in memorial uttering.

Thoreau's writing effects communion with living and dying. His poetry, in this case, approaches liturgy. He celebrates Margaret Fuller and John Brown for their particular good, for all to acknowledge. He reminds a community that a forgotten corpse can commune with the sea. In writing obituaries for insignificant citizens of Concord, he reminds a community that there are no forgettable persons—no one so insignificant as to be forgettable.[35] From the dark of the pond, he drags up a giant snapper by the tail, to be examined and praised in full light. Thoreau mourns the great and the small, the anonymous Irish dead at an immigrant shipwreck, and the world-historical John Brown.[36] He grips telling detail that will make of the dead or forgotten or lost more than a scatter of bone or a muddy shell.

Thoreau even roughhouses with his own death, burial, and rebirth. He climbs Mt. Greylock to the ramshackle Williams College observatory to take in the expanse of three states below (Vermont, Massachusetts, New York). At night he configures loose boards scattered at the foot of the observatory into a makeshift coffin, and crawls in, securing the topmost plank with a rock, entombed until morning. He explores and commemorates

---

[33] *Cape Cod*, p. 123. The roots of this passage appear in *Journal*, October 31, 1850, p. 80.
[34] Melville, *Moby Dick*, concluding line (many editions).
[35] See obituary for Anna Jones, *Yeoman's Gazette*, 1837, discussed in Arsić, pp. 340–6.
[36] On Victor Hugo's plea for Brown's life, see "Addenda" to Ch. 12, below.

transitions and metamorphoses, from life to death to rebirth to death again. His writing-as-mourning is participation in ubiquitous, recurrent loss. As St. Paul put it, "creation has been groaning."[37] We find a ground bass mourning throughout the *Iliad*, where all men rage and weep. But Thoreau *refuses* to rage and weep.[38] He weaves a different register of mourning that lessens site-specific hurt by broad identification with nature's cycles of loss and regeneration.

There are important anti-Cartesian corollaries to note. In his account there are living, *embodied* persons in living *exchange* with others and the things of their worlds. The Thoreauvian self is not an isolated, asocial consciousness. Grief and celebration are not diaphanous inner states. They are expressed bodily and are socially embedded, and reverberate with things throughout nature. We have neither a monism nor a Cartesian dualism but a five-fold synergy—mutual inter-animations among psyche, soma, social others, things, and natural surrounds. These dissolve any metaphysics that would sequester mind from body, persons from others, or socially constituted persons from Nature and radiant things.

We remember that Thoreau's walks are pilgrimage to and in the domain of the holy or sacred. The holy interpenetrates the five-fold couplings we've just mapped—psyche, soma, social others, things, and natural surrounds. It flows in more concentrated form from dispersed Vedic divinities or intelligences and also from a more condensed divinity, say, the "Maker" of Walden Pond, or the divinity—beauty—that he addresses in *A Week*. "The eyes were not made for such groveling uses as they are now put to and worn out by, but to behold beauty now invisible. May we not see God?"[39] Early in his *Journal* he writes,

> From the summits I saw the heavens; from the vales I looked up to the heights again. In prosperity I remember God … ; in adversity I remember my own elevations, and only hope to see God again.[40]

The God at issue is one of radiance, beauty, and magnificence, a God of epiphany and aesthetic, sublime revelation. Nietzsche avers in *The Birth of Tragedy* that only art can redeem life in the face of the suffering and the destruction that all humans undergo. Classically, theodicy is the attempt to vindicate God against the evidence of massive evil. At issue is personal morale. If God's justice can't be vindicated, what is the point of faith or hope?

---

[37] Romans 8.22.
[38] Alice Oswald's remarkable *Memorial: An Excavation of the Iliad* (London: Faber & Faber, 2011) aims to bring Homer's dead alive.
[39] *Week*, p. 382.
[40] *Journal*, February 20, 1842, p. 320.

In classical theodicy the defense is lawyerly. Thoreau works to restore morale *aesthetically* rather than forensically, calling on arts of commemoration and evocation.

The arts of commemoration, gratitude, and delight redeem life for Thoreau without appealing to God's justice or injustice. In the classic staging of The Book of Job, Job loses all he has and in anger and despair questions God. *Why does He rain evils upon me?* Job assumes he suffers injustice—until his final reception of the Whirlwind as a force *beyond* justice or injustice. Thoreau doesn't assume that injustice has been done as he undergoes his Job-like loss of a brother and young Waldo. What sidetracks despair is a redeeming vision not unlike Job's received through the Whirlwind, melting his protest. Rather than bemoaning life for including suffering and death, Thoreau's mourning affirms it.

Job yields, melts away, before the magnificence of creation delivered in the song of the Whirlwind. He drops his earlier presumption that he should put God and existence on trial. In his protests, Job had assumed that divinity must bow before the bar of Justice, or that divinity must *embody* it. Now he abjures or retracts that view, acknowledging that he then "Spoke without wisdom."[41] Witnessing to the wonders of creation, and gratitude for being present to them, is enough to ask of a person. For the divine to be present with those wonders is enough to expect of the divine. All nature undergoes dying and affliction, none of it deserved, none of it judged as just or unjust—much of it majestic, some of it routine. Thoreau's writing energizes life-and-death beyond jurisdictions of Justice. In the long run, protest or complaint is uncalled for.

10.

Like much art and writing, religious and otherwise, Thoreau's is a rescue of things from irretrievable decay and dissolution.[42] Put another way, things otherwise destined for utter eradication from memory and presence are kept alive by his art. Such rescue ameliorates wounds living creatures endure. We are not simply rational, political, passionate, speaking, or ethical animals. We are that, and we are wounded animals who know and can't forget

---

[41] I take Job's final response to the Voice from the Whirlwind to indicate a "melting away" from his previous stance of presumption-to-know, not self-abhorrence or self-abasement.

[42] Along with art, we have ceremony: Good Friday gives us memories of death and resurrection; Passover lets us remember captivity and deliverance.

pain.[43] Yet if we follow Thoreau, despite wounds, we can sing all that's worth preserving in life—here and now, and in life around the bend, in life just eclipsed in loss,—say, in the loss of a brother. There's lyricism that makes his loss of a hound, bay horse and turtle dove, well *this* side of devastating.[44] Thoreau senses nature enduring interminable loss, and he mourns with her in a register of commemoration.

What's "interminable" in nature's mourning is not a pathological fixation on moments of trauma, a chilling repetition. Mourning includes awareness of nature's regenerations. Any site of mourning spills out temporally over previous and anticipated subsequent sites of loss and regeneration, and spills out transversally to contemporaneous sites, as well. Such reverberations fill memory and imagination, making up the fabric of life-and-death.

The unfurling of mourning-commemorations saturates Thoreau's writing and walking—the pitch of the voice, the register of the sentence, the rhythm of the walk, the melody of philosophical song and befitting reverie. The musical outcomes are episodes of fulfillment, sufficient unto the day. We do not get an all-time frozen position on suffering and delight to pocket as his simple creed. Thoreau takes the poet's prerogative, switching momentum, register, or mood as the world and words unfold in routine and then surprising sequences. This prerogative frees him from burdens of forced consistency or system.

At times an almost whimsical remark (on the flight of a bird or the stench of a horse) has inestimable value, freeing intelligibility and verve. His loose assemblage of "takes" on life and death, on mourning and celebration, on creatures and creation, on natural and civic life, hang together like motifs in a sonata or like elements in a Breughel portrait of village life. No one mood or element dominates all others—unless something as general and vulnerable to ridicule as "delighted openness to teeming life—including its declining toward death." The testimonies of life do not yield a single uniform narrative. Thoreau will appear distressingly full of contradiction or hodgepodge or unfortunate reversals only if one demands strict order and argument. He delivers not chaos but discrete and vibrant elements that can be unified and stalled in their motion and focused, first this way, then that—from this angle and that. And that's as good as it gets.

An *apercu* of the moment can carry great weight, even as *contrary* ones emerge in their time—and even as *converging* ones emerge in *their* time.

---

[43] J. M. Coetzee has his protagonist describe herself as a "wounded animal" in *Elizabeth Costello* (London: Penguin, 2004). See the extended discussion in *Philosophy and Animal Life*, Cavell, Diamond et al. (New York: Columbia University Press, 2009), and Mulhall, *The Wounded Animal*.

[44] *Walden*, "Economy," p. 16 [para 24].

So often Thoreau's artistry weaves them beautifully together to give a more truthful account of the difficult realities creatures face, and face creatively, than any more streamlined account could—say, one that privileges explicit order and cool objectivity. Moving at our own peril at some distance from details we're left with a near-platitude: difficult times exclude neither joy nor exuberance; preserving our best moments is a most worthy endeavor.

I return to these themes, following them further, at the close of the next excursion. There I find a focus, once more, in the sufferings, affirmations, and gratitudes found in the Book of Job.

5

Transforming Perceptions

I heard the dream of the toad—It sung thro' & filled all the air—[as] though I had not heard it once. & I turned my companion's attention to it—but he did not appear to perceive it as a new sound in the air.

—*Journal*

What is all nature and human life at this moment, what the scenery and vicinity of a human soul, but the song of an early sparrow from yonder fences, and the cackling hens in the barn?

—*Journal*[1]

A benefit of sauntering with Thoreau is the thorough congeniality of the setting. He would be uncomfortable at a departmental seminar: too indoors and confining. Plain walls do not speak the way meadows do. Just as restricting, once on campus, he belongs in no department. He writes literature, philosophy, ecology, and religion, but annoys the administrators. He doesn't fall comfortably in any of these cubicles. Philosophers shunt him to literature, literature shunts him to environmental rhetoric, and religion departments think he's only literary. He doesn't belong.

Of course I'll dismiss the image of Thoreau the happy camper, at home in his cabin by the lake. I also dismiss the cynic's jaded response, that Thoreau is a hypocrite because his mother brought him lunch. In any case, the main point is that living in a cabin is not Thoreau's essence. And I won't locate him within the rhetoric of environmentalism, nor within ideological struggles around individualism or civil rights—at another time, these would be fine sites to explore.

As I set out, I want to underline two things that I find quite striking. First, Thoreau brings us repeatedly to life's terrors and unpleasantness—not just to its comforting beauties and pastoral or rural consolations. As I sense it now, a key issue in Thoreau's life and writing is a struggle with disquietude, even with occasions of desolation that he manages to defuse.

Second, Thoreau doesn't just say, or argue that life has its upsides and downsides, pleasantness and unpleasantness. He immerses us in things pleasant and unpleasant. Viscerally, tactilely, musically, he catches us in currents that carry us from downside to upside, from fright to reassurance,

---

[1] Epigraph: *Journal*, October 26, 1853, p. 453; March 20, 1842, p. 341.

from disharmony to harmony. And just to keep us honest, he carries us in the opposite direction, from comfort to discomfort, from quiet to disquiet. Reality, it turns out, is shifting and multiple. It isn't just one thing or the other—it's anomalous and episodic.

He pulls us into these currents and crosscurrents by spinning phrases and paragraphs that shift the tenor of immersions from one mood to the next, in ongoing transformations. Words slip under our skin. Suddenly we're blushing, overtaken by unexpected beauty that flows over us, effectively deflecting shadows of terror or dullness. Thoreau spins words-phrases-sentences that nudge us from one reality to the next. His sentences do not depict change but create it. Sentences or phrases are actions aimed at our receptivities. Responsive to them as they arrive, pebble by pebble, sound by sound, image by image, we get an intimate grasp, by monitoring our changes, of how and why Thoreau becomes among the greatest of American writers—and among the world's great religious adepts, political polemicists, and subtle philosophers.

1.

Here's an exemplary passage that moves in a downward direction from unqualified ecstasy—to the unpleasant whiff of rotting flesh.[2] Listen for the way beauty can blot out humdrum awareness. And listen for the way Thoreau alters our sense of time and place, putting us in flow with radiant, mobile things. The passage begins with a specific date. Medieval mystics used this convention to precisely mark the occasion of divine visitation:

> On the 29th of April, as I was fishing from the bank of the river near the Nine-Acre-Corner bridge, standing on the quaking grass and willow roots, where the muskrats lurk, I heard a singular rattling sound, somewhat like that of the sticks which boys play with their fingers, when, ... looking up, ... I observed a very slight and graceful hawk, like a nighthawk, alternately soaring like a ripple and tumbling a rod or two over and over, showing the under side of its wings, which gleamed like a satin ribbon in the sun, or like the pearly inside of a shell ... . The Merlin it seemed to me it might be called: but I care not for its name. It was the most ethereal flight I had ever witnessed. It did not simply flutter like a butterfly, nor soar like the larger hawks, but it sported with proud reliance in the fields of air; mounting again and again with its strange

[2] *Walden,* "Spring," p. 307 [para 19].

chuckle, it repeated its free and beautiful fall, turning over and over like a kite, and then recovering from its lofty tumbling, as if it had never set its foot on terra firma.

It appeared to have no companion in the universe—sporting there alone—and to need none but the morning and the ether with which it played. It was not lonely, but made all the earth lonely beneath it.

Where was the parent which hatched it, its kindred, and its father in the heavens? The tenant of the air, it seemed related to the earth but by an egg hatched some time in the crevice of a crag;—or was its native nest made in the angle of a cloud, woven of the rainbow's trimmings and the sunset sky, and lined with some soft midsummer haze caught up from earth? Its eyry now some cliffy cloud.[3]

Thoreau plugs in our senses—the *sound* of the hawk, its *look* from beneath. And he places its tumbling falls and climbing up again in the ether half way between sun and stony cliff. He introduces space and also time. He wonders about the hawk's past, its father, and where its egg was placed at the start. And he refuses to let the mother remain too earth-bound. Thoreau has her place the egg up in a cloud. He takes out his paints to commemorate the place of birth: the nest in a crevice in the cloud is made not of twigs or grass but is "*woven of the rainbow's trimmings and the sunset sky.*"[4]

In the wider setting, Thoreau is fishing. He fishes for fish and his soul. He looks down at the stream, hears a cackle, looks up, and finds the hawk first fall, then remount. He thinks the egg down from a cloud to a nest on a cliff, and then transports the egg back up to the clouds. He finds the hawk unlonely. *He* feels lonely, abandoned to earth.

Give him a minute and Thoreau will look down at his fish again, skimming under water—as the Hawk floats high above. We move up and down through an anomalous zone, half-earth, half-sky. Here are Thoreau's last questions again:

Was its native nest made in the angle of a cloud, woven of the rainbow's trimmings and the sunset sky, and lined with some soft midsummer haze caught up from earth? Its eyry now some cliffy cloud?[5]

A blissful reverie of clouds, rainbow, sunset, midsummer haze, *the haze transported up* from earth … things can't get better than *that* ! Bliss is of the moment, however, and we enjoy it only for an instant—though like a kiss, it can seem like eternity.

---

[3] "Spring," p. 305 [para 22].
[4] "Spring," p. 306 [para 23], (my emphasis).
[5] "Spring," p. 306 [para 23].

Casually, almost lazily, Thoreau forgets the hawk and clouds, uttering a stray mumble about the fish he's caught. His thought slips its focus—breaking the spell. "Besides this, I got a rare mess of fish!" *Well!* He's just sung that he's seen "… the most ethereal flight I had ever witnessed." Then, as if the ethereal never happened, he mutters, "*Besides this*, I got a rare bunch of fish!"[6] As if it's typical to move from ecstasy to paying the phone bill. Do I exaggerate? The fish are not *quite* as drab as a phone bill. Though he has abandoned the ethereal, he has not abandoned a taste for aquatic beauty. "Besides this I got a rare mess of golden and silver and bright cupreous fishes, which looked like a string of jewels."

In his passage downward from heavens to streambed Thoreau alters his coordinates for locating this immersion—this site of befitting reverie. Now the axis of attention is no longer *up and down* from river bottom to sky, but sideways, this way and that, across the meadow. And the axis of *mobility and immobility* is altered, too. Thoreau is now not utterly immobile waiting for fish nor is he utterly immobile taking in the hawk in the sky. He reminds us that he's been alive and moving, bounding like a fox or a hound, and his skyward reverie is but a moment in an awakening, lively reality.[7]

> Ah! I have penetrated to those meadows on the morning of many a first spring day, jumping from hummock to hummock, from willow root to willow root, when the wild river valley and the woods were bathed in so pure and bright a light as would have waked the dead, if they had been slumbering in their graves, as some suppose. There needs no stronger proof of immortality. All things must live in such a light. O Death, where was thy sting? O Grave, where was thy victory, then?[8]

We descend from the clouds to the bridge and the fish—then scan sideways to the meadows, fading into river valley and woods. All bathe in radiance so pure—as to wake the dead. Joyful immortality is the counterpoint to incessant mourning.

Thoreau can't help making a parenthetical aside. The dead might not really be dead, but only asleep. He's kidding, of course. But in any case, it's pleasant to imagine the dead merely asleep, ready to awake at any moment! Thoreau ends his reverie and mini-oration with a ringing biblical affirmation. Although he scorns the church, he knows his New Testament. He triumphantly asks, "O Death, where was thy sting?" This invites the dead to rise up, with us—to rejoice and join paradise.

---

[6] Ibid.
[7] For his scampering after a fox, see *Journal*, January 30, 1841, p. 186.
[8] Ibid.

This is cheery Thoreau at his best, the world is redeemed, death, defanged, paradise alive and well. One wants to go home with him, arm in arm, infinitely happy. But ... the undersides of life don't just disappear. Where are John or Waldo's gruesome deaths, Margaret Fuller's shark-mangled flesh, or the shouts of slave catchers in his woods? His cheerful vision is legitimate—life does have its ecstatic moments. And these occupy *Walden* more that life's dismal moments. Although he will mention his night in jail and his work helping escaping slaves, terror and discomfort don't make extended appearances here.

And yet, Thoreau wouldn't let us remain *inordinately* happy. Just a few sentences after his ethereal vision—and out of the blue—he introduces rotting carrion. We see and smell "the vulture feeding on the carrion which disgusts and disheartens us, and deriving health and strength from the repast." And a few sentences further on he reflects:

> There was a dead horse in the hollow by the path to my house, which compelled me sometimes to go out of my way, especially in the night when the air was heavy.[9]

Ecstasy is soured by the stench of rotting flesh. Death now has a sting—or a stench.

There's a preface and follow up to the image of the feeding vulture. Restoring them adds new layers to his views. Thoreau doesn't say that there are upsides and downsides in life, or that for every heavenly bird there's a rotting horse. He says we should be *cheered* by the stench of a rotting horse. Why cheered?

> We are cheered when we observe the vulture feeding on the carrion which disgusts and disheartens us, and deriving health and strength from the repast ... I love to see that Nature is so rife with life that myriads can be afforded to be sacrificed and suffered to prey on one another; that tender organizations can be so serenely squashed out of existence like pulp—tadpoles which herons gobble up, and tortoises and toads run over in the road; and that sometimes it has rained flesh and blood! With the liability to accident, we must see how little account is to be made of it. The impression made on a wise man is that of universal innocence.[10]

We witness tortoises run over and rains of flesh and blood. This is not just a dark Thoreau, rubbing our nose in what we'd normally think is repugnant.

---

[9] "Spring," p. 307 [para 24].
[10] Ibid.

Everything is framed as something mysterious and complex. Not only sunrise, but also the stench of a horse can spread cheer! The vision is eccentric and religious.

As I hear him, Thoreau thinks that Nature—the Universe as a whole—is oblivious to matters of justice. Nature is innocent not because she has good will and commits no crimes. She is innocent because she has no ill will—*nor* does she have good will, for that matter. Human indifference to matters of justice can be cause for outrage. Thoreau knows this, and acts on it. But *Nature's* indifference to justice is no cause for complaint. Why should I expect Nature to care for me personally? She doesn't care personally about the destruction caused by floods or forest fires or the discomfort caused by the stench of a horse. We are cheered (when we "observe the vulture feeding on the carrion which disgusts and disheartens us") to the extent that we are cheered and thankful for being present to the drama of life-and-death. We cheer her blessing as we cheer sunrise and sunset, just for being. We cheer her for being what she is, sometimes glorious, sometimes terrible, and always, given some reflective distance, worth embracing. That is, worth embracing if only we're given reflective transfigurations of the sort delivered by a Whirlwind to Job, or by Thoreau's refiguring death's stench. It is a strange lesson. We must learn to embrace life even after irruptions of unspeakable horror.[11]

Thoreau transforms what would otherwise be the inexpungible fault of death's stench into a sense of the redeeming innocence of Nature. It was not Nature's malice that loosed vultures on horse carrion, nor was it Nature's malice that took John Thoreau or Emerson's son, whom Henry adored. Nature innocently—that is, non-maliciously—*dispenses* death, devouring her young and old with the erratic abandon of innocent children swatting at flies. This is not an occasion for melancholy, or outrage, but a scene Thoreau would have us take in—no doubt with some hyperbole—with good cheer.

I don't think this vision has a name. It's the opposite of our obsessive hankering after single-vector simple answers. There is no cosmic justice, nor is this the darkly mottled world of *Ecclesiastes*. We want plain answers: Life obviously tends toward evil—or life obviously tends toward good. We hanker after simple summations. God is obviously *just* (... always?). God is obviously *indifferent* (... always?). God is obviously heartlessly *cruel and unjust* (... always?). We want to assert conclusions. But Thoreau will not deliver those "obvious" conclusions that simplify and falsify experience. He prefers to leave us with a Nature that is anomalous, wild, and wondrous.

---

[11] "I have set before you life and death, blessing and cursing: therefore choose life, that both thou and thy seed may live." (KJV) Deuteronomy 30.19.

In *Cape Cod*, Thoreau points out crabs inhabiting a strip between sea and dry land, a strip lacking steady shape. It's constantly changing, neither here nor there, an anomalous zone. "*Nomos*" is law—or law-like. The law seeks sharp definitions and framings. It likes clear verdicts and justice in all things. The crabs inhabit a different reality. Thoreau is contrarian and antinomian. He likes to blur and dissolve boundaries, writing fables that gesture toward truths, and delivering oxymorons like a "cheering stench," or "mother Nature innocently devouring her young." The brute shock of these oxymorons diminishes with reflection, but their 'truth' remains.

And not all oxymorons shock: some appear gently. "Nothing so fair, so pure, and at the same time so large, as a lake, perchance, lies on the surface of the earth. *Sky water*."[12] When they are well chosen, they are revelations—say, that the world is anomalous and amorphous, wild and shape-shifting, a place of wonder rather than of strict order or justice. As Branka Arsić puts it, "Life, then, doesn't have its proper territory, but flourishes … in shifting terrestrial conditions."[13] We live in a metaphysical and religious wild. This is the vision from the Whirlwind in the Book of Job.

2.

Thoreau aspires to a spirited serenity that mitigates desolation. As we've mentioned, John Thoreau died writhing in Henry's arms. He had nicked his finger sharpening a shaving blade. Antibiotics were a century away. A few days later Henry came down with John's symptoms, though he hadn't been nicked. Henry's life was John's life, and John's death, Henry's death. We're used to contagious laughter or weeping, but this is a contagion more dramatic and profound. It's as if Henry was so fully absorbed in John's bodily spirit that he descended into the underworld with him.[14] Thoreau's ache for salvation is rooted in many things. High on the list is the pain of John's death. Writing philosophy or literature, or taking up religious walking or meditation might palliate trauma. But the range of pain in loss, and the range of joyful gratitude for having existed at all—these strangely overlap. The world is anomalous in its crosscurrents and flow, and so are our emotions, moods, and passions.

People in trouble often lurch for a handhold toward religion. For some, it appears in the form of a creed or belief or a church to cling to. This is not

---

[12] *Walden*, "The Ponds," p. 182 [para 17] (my emphasis).
[13] *Bird Relics*, p. 225.
[14] See Wai-Chee Dimock, "Global Civil Society: Thoreau on Three Continents," *Through Other Continents: American Literature Across Deep Time* (Princeton, NJ: Princeton University Press, 2006), pp. 7–22.

Thoreau. He deflects or mitigates troubles through daily meditation, through prayer-like writing-and-walking that takes the shape of communions with ponds and rivers, with fish, oaks, and meadows, with sky above and grass below. It's earth-and-sky, meadow-and-creek religion.

Occasionally, his down-to-earth communion with particulars is supplemented by an encompassing view from the heavens. He climbs high above rural woods, meadows and rivers to savor a God-like overview of creation. He takes in sweeping panoramas from Mt. Greylock, Mt. Washington or Maine's Mt. Ktaadn. He has a poet's eye for the detail of particulars, an ecologist's eye for life's interdependent circles and cycles, and a holy man's eye for the pervasive unknown and divine.

And the mood of these contemplations or reveries is complex. Joy is "the condition of life."[15] But it lies next to life's losses. Thoreau will say "The thrills of joy and thrills of pain are undistinguishable."[16] Such apparent paradox forces us to recalibrate our perception. Kierkegaard writes of a strange admixture of joy and terror in *Fear and Trembling*.[17] Rilke says beauty is the beginning of terror.[18] Nietzsche puts terror at the wellsprings of art. Thoreau's art exposes his faith that in this strange mix of pain and beauty, beauty or the sublime can prevail—and prevail not infrequently. His writing is working through minor and major hells through remembrance of and gratitude for minor and major heavens. Writing is a meditative assisting technique. It can't rescue him once for all—nothing can. Like cleaning house it's a process that is never complete.

Thoreau often leads us through a wildness at some mid-region between the terrible and ecstatic, a wildness that is a bracing tonic.

> Our village life would stagnate if it were not for the unexplored forests and meadows which surround it. We need the tonic of wildness ... At the same time that we are earnest to explore and learn all things, we require that all things be mysterious and unexplorable, that land

---

[15] *Essays*, "The Natural History of Massachusetts," p. 22.
[16] *Walden*, "The Ponds," p. 182 [para 17].
[17] Abraham finds joy on his terrible climb with Isaac to Mt. Moriah: see Mooney, *Knights of Faith and Resignation: Reading Kierkegaard's "Fear and Trembling"* (Albany: SUNY Press, 1991). For the mix of joy and suffering in Kierkegaard, see Carson Webb, *Attunements to the Good Life: Religious Joy and the Critique of Eudaemonism in the Writings of Søren Kierkegaard*, Ph.D. Dissertation, Syracuse University, 2014.
[18] Rilke: "For beauty is nothing / but the beginning of terror, which we still are just able to endure, / and we are so awed because it serenely disdains / to annihilate us. Every angel is terrifying." *Duino Elegies*, Stephen Mitchell (trans.) (New York: Vintage, 2014). Nietzsche: "[It is in] art in general, through which life is made both possible and worth living." *The Birth of Tragedy* (New York: Penguin, 1993), p.16.

and sea be infinitely wild, unsurveyed and unfathomed by us because unfathomable.[19]

Yet Thoreau also opens toward a wilder landscape than the pastoral woods and meadows around Concord. He paints a wild that is awesome and sublime:

> We must be refreshed by the sight of inexhaustible vigor, vast and titanic features, the sea-coast with its wrecks, the wilderness with its living and its decaying trees, the thunder-cloud, and the rain which lasts three weeks and produces freshets.[20]

Here is a foretaste of the scenes of wildness on a 'titanic' scale that he recounts in *Cape Cod* and in his account of chaos at the top of Mt. Ktaadn. "We need to witness our own limits transgressed, and some life pasturing freely where we never wander."[21] For the most part in *Walden*, he muffles the worst of Nature's wildness, and soft-pedals chaos.

3.

I want to recall that moment from Thoreau's late book, *Cape Cod*. Against the background of Nature's terrible blows we hear a gradual ameliorating of the worst. Carnage is changed by the poet's eye, the poet's alchemy, into something majestic and sublime.

Margaret Fuller was one of several extraordinary thinkers centered in Boston and Concord. She was an original, a genius, a young friend and equal of Emerson who walked with him regularly and edited the transcendentalist journal *The Dial* (to which Thoreau contributed). She was hired away from Concord by the *New York Herald Tribune* to be a section-editor—the first woman to win such an important post in an American newspaper. With the onset of the Italian Revolution of 1848, she traveled to Italy to report first hand on the struggle for liberty. There she met an Italian Count supporting the revolution. She had a child by him. The fighting grew too intense, and she sailed back to America with her infant son and her lover. An inexperienced ship's Captain misread coastal signals. In the middle of a storm he wreaked the ship in the dark on a reef off Fire Island, thinking he was heading into New York Harbor. Fuller and dozens of other passengers drowned in the breakers that tore the ship apart.

[19] *Walden*, "Spring," p. 306 [para 24].
[20] Ibid.
[21] Ibid.

The news of the disaster spread up to Boston, and Thoreau was commissioned by his Concord friends to travel down to Fire Island to search for the remains and retrieve her effects, including any writing that survived. I think his friends knew of his capacity to stare death in the face. He arrives on the scene nearly a week after the wreck. Scavengers have picked most that is of value. Bodies are unceremoniously piled up in carts. There is no sign of Fuller's, but Thoreau is directed some distance down the beach, where a shark-torn body has been buried in the sand, the place marked by a small stick.

Thoreau is never absolutely certain that the remains are those of Margaret Fuller. He writes up the episode in his *Journal*, and later transposes the scene into *Cape Cod*. Although he does not mention Fuller by name, the *Cape Cod* account is clearly her memorial. Artistry mitigates the disaster. This reverie bears hearing again.

> Once it was my business to go in search of the relics of a human body, mangled by sharks, which had just been cast up, a week after a wreck. I expected that I must look very narrowly to find so small an object, but the sandy beach was so perfectly smooth and bare that when I was half a mile distant the insignificant sliver which marked the spot looked like a bleached spar, and the relics were as conspicuous as if they lay in state on that sandy plain, or a generation had labored to pile up their cairn there. They were singularly inoffensive both to the senses and the imagination. That dead body had taken possession of the shore, and reigned over it as no living one could, in the name of a certain majesty that belonged to it. The bones were alone with the beach and the sea, whose hollow roar seemed to address them, as if there were an understanding between them and the ocean which necessarily left me out.[22]

What I find mesmerizing—like a passage from Schubert—is the ease with which Thoreau moves us from disaster to commemoration. You can hear funeral bells and heavy steps in Schubert's D946 Sonata. They toll sadly for the composer's early death, a death he was certainly aware was upon him. Yet these dark tolling passages are interspersed with phrases of pure joy. Schubert writes somberly of his death while he joyfully commemorates life—all within a page or minute. He moves from melancholy to rejoicing in pure majesty, on the go, bit by bit. Reality is responsive to Thoreau's pen and wish, too, stroke by stroke.

In the April 29 passage from *Walden*, Thoreau changes focus from a heavenly hawk to its nest on a cliff or a cloud, and then to a fish-filled

[22] *Cape Cod*, p. 123.

river. Here in painting—writing—the beach on Cape Cod or Fire Island, he alters focus from a corpse-strewn beach to a simple beach, and then to a sandy site of majesty. The tenor of place and time undergo transformation. We're moved from an ordinary beachcomber's sense of temporality to the resounding eternity of memorial address.

Thoreau manages the world-change for us seductively. The first sign of transformations is the word "relic." Saints leave relics, ship's passengers don't. Next are changes in what lies ahead. An anticipated sliver of wood—a mere twig—turns into a bleached spar (a good ten feet high, I'd imagine). The spar then becomes a stone memorial erected through generations. Time becomes deep time, and size becomes towering. Appropriately for the remains or relics of a saint the flesh is not rotted at all and is miraculously free of stench.[23] Fuller's remains are "singularly inoffensive both to the senses and the imagination." Ruling over the shore, she is a saintly regal majesty. Then, in benediction, we hear Fuller's ghost sing to the sea that gently answers her plaint. We hear that this is a sublime understanding between soul and sea that leaves Thoreau out.

Thoreau doesn't write novels, and his essays and especially *Walden* are full of fictions, fables, and reveries. These are not falsehoods. They animate soul and imagination to deliver us truths. "Some expressions of truth are reminiscent, — others merely sensible, as the phrase is, — others prophetic."[24] (The idea that some truths are "merely sensible" is, to his ears, a strange denigration of what are the highest truths: one *sees and tastes* the divine and significant.) His fables and reveries trigger truths and meanings, the best insights we can have, while in the making. He doesn't offer affidavits of true representation. He's simply not beholden to narrow-gauge physicalistic standards of stripped-down verisimilitude fit for a detective's fact-gathering report. "It is not every truth that recommends itself to the common sense. Nature has a place for the wild clematis as well as for the cabbage."[25]

Truth is fidelity to the best, whether in reports or in witness to value. Thoreau wants to be in the truth (and for us also to be in the truth—in the best). He wants us to live truly, in fidelity to what's best on the paths of this life-and-death. And we have some control over the slant we take on life-and-death, and hence have *some* say over the world that appears.

A single gentle rain makes the grass many shades greener. So our prospects brighten on the influx of better thoughts. We should be

---

[23] Dostoevsky has Zossima's corpse smell too early—creating a scandal. *The Brothers Karamazov*, Constance Garnett (trans.), L. Carr (ed.) (Heritage Illustrated Publishing), Book 7, Ch. 3, p. 377.
[24] "Walking," p. 245 [para 56].
[25] Ibid.

blessed if we lived in the present always, and took advantage of every accident that befell us, like the grass which confesses the influence of the slightest dew that falls on it; and did not spend our time in atoning for the neglect of past opportunities, which we call doing our duty. We loiter in winter while it is already spring. In a pleasant spring morning all men's sins are forgiven. Such a day is a truce to vice ... Through our own recovered innocence we discern the innocence of our neighbors. You may have known your neighbor yesterday for a thief, a drunkard, or a sensualist, and merely pitied or despised him, and despaired of the world; but the sun shines bright and warm this first spring morning, *recreating the world*, and you meet him at some serene work, and see how it is [that] exhausted and debauched veins expand with still joy and bless the new day, feel the spring influence with the innocence of infancy, and all his faults are forgotten. There is not only an atmosphere of good will about him, but even a savor of holiness groping for expression, blindly and ineffectually perhaps, like a new-born instinct, and for a short hour the south hill-side echoes to no vulgar jest. You see some innocent fair shoots preparing to burst from his gnarled rind and try another year's life, tender and fresh as the youngest plant. Even he has entered into the joy of his Lord.[26]

Unfortunately, the truths one can live with—that nature is innocent, that a neighbor can be forgiven—are not tame, domesticated, or simple truisms. These truths are wild and the truth one is faithful to is wild. The pursuit is difficult and ambiguous, for to be wild is to lack sharp edges of identification or place.

4.

We're rounding the bend to the end of this excursion. Nature is innocent. Consider the Whirlwind at the end of Job. It delivers wildness in a reverie befitting Job's condition. Just before the Whirlwind appears, Elihu, a forerunner of the Lord, reminds us that truth comes through suffering, songs, and dreams in the night.[27] Songs and dreams are relatives to reverie. Thoreau's art records trouble and is alert to redeeming beauty or sublimity. Here's a final passage, from *Walden*'s chapter "Solitude." The way it finds

---

[26] *Walden*, "Spring," p. 303 [para 19] (my emphasis).
[27] See the classic discussion by Herbert Fingarette, *Revisions: Changing Perspectives in Moral Philosophy*, Stanley Hauerwas and Alasdair MacIntyre (eds) (London: University of Notre Dame Press, 1983), pp. 249–86.

Nature or Godliness a response to an ache for salvation is almost an echo of the way Elihu and the Whirlwind respond to Job's ache.

> Such sympathy have [sun and wind and rain, summer and winter] ever with our race, that all Nature would be affected, and the sun's brightness fade, and the winds would sigh humanely, and the clouds rain tears, and the woods shed their leaves and put on mourning in midsummer, if any man should ever for a just cause grieve.[28]

Working backward, we hear that if a man grieves with good cause, Nature will be moved to grieve with him, to *comfort* him. Elihu and the Voice from the storm respond to Job's suffering, but they do not offer *comfort*. What can we make of this?

Let's say the wounded person is Job, grieving injustice. He's been stripped of all he loves, despite righteousness and fidelity. If that's the scenario, then Thoreau dreams that Nature will shower the just man with sympathy. The sun's inconsiderate brightness will fade, and winds will "sigh humanely." Nature will mourn with him. Nature winces in sympathy. Virgil has stones weep at the cruelties of war.[29] We are *stunned* by the folly of war, and to see stones weep is to have our grief confirmed. But there's a puzzle.

Granting, for the moment, the possibility that Nature can sympathize, how is that compatible with the other fact, that Nature can also be supremely indifferent (if not cruel)? Nature dashes bodies to the beach, and buckles John Thoreau in painful contortions. She refuses to disable slave catchers slinking after their prey. But which is it? Is Nature indifferent or sympathetic?

We'd like to see God, to interrogate Him. Like Job, we want to find out. In *A Week on the Concord* Thoreau asks directly if he might not see God. Of course, he already *has* caught sight of Him—there in the pond, in the light spread over the meadow. To see God is to see divine illuminations, intelligences, all around, just as the Whirlwind scatters holiness all around in sublime profusion. God, or Godliness, is innocent of malice, but hardly a figure of majestic *Justice*. Lacking malice, Nature is innocent. But if she's not closely concerned with my well being, how can she mourn *with* me—*sympathize* with my suffering?

One thought is that Nature is fickle—or if you prefer, wild. She is not one-phase or simple. She's shifting and anomalous. Beautiful mornings follow terrible nights; the first are comforting, the second, discomforting. Another thought is this. Nature mourns with us only when we suffer injustice at the hands of other persons. She will not mourn at John Thoreau's

---

[28] *Walden,* "Solitude," p. 133 [para 16].
[29] In tears Aeneas refers to "*lacrimae rerum,*" the tears of things. *Aeneid,* Book I, line 462.

death because that death was "innocent." Nature will mourn with us when we have "just cause," as Thoreau puts it. But Nature will not think of John's death, or the death of a horse left on the path to rot, as *just cause*—a good *reason*—for us to *plead* for special sympathy, or for sympathy to be *given*.

Thoreau's primary conviction is that Nature is innocent, in this sense: she is not intentionally cruel, *and is not intentionally beneficent, either*. She does not pick me out for special punishment or special sympathy. Perhaps Thoreau then adds another thought—what I'll call an ancillary or supplemental *reverie of reciprocity*. The sun's warmth touches me and I warm to its touch. Its warmth can console my grief. Nature grieves with me, but not with special attention. I think Thoreau's conviction is steady even as he allows reveries differently pitched. Dreams and songs don't all occur in the same register or mood.

Even so, quite apart from its alignment with Thoreau's conviction, this reverie of reciprocity is not free of ambiguity. Nature's mourning *with* me is anomalous, even when qualified as a reverie of reciprocity. To be warmed and consoled by morning light might be followed by burdensome or intolerable light. Then it has no gentle touch, and may seem to attack rather than comfort me. Warmth can become unbearable heat; or if not unbearable, then bittersweet, expressing a distant mourning. The bottom line is that shifting reveries and root convictions need not cohere in a pellucid straight-arrow narrative. In a non-systematic, poetic thinker, they won't.

Nevertheless: it's not exactly fickle to allow that the crab belongs now to the sea, now to the sand. A root conviction is that the crab remains a crab, an *innocent* crab, now of the sea, now of the sand. Thoreau asks that we stay open to "the influx of better thoughts." This means living with the anomaly that Nature is Innocent, and that innocence can scamper now over the sands of consolation, mourning *with* me, now over the a wash of indifference. The chance for "our prospects [to] brighten on the influx of better thoughts" is too valuable a chance to refuse.[30] And the possibility of nature mourning with me is just such a valuable "better thought."

The sea's majesty can console and terrify, but the consolation is in no way the sea's altruistic project. Schubert's last piano sonatas can console but they were not made to console me. Their boon is *impersonally* delivered even as I am *personally* awakened. In that sense Nature (or the Lord) is innocent of both beneficence and ill will. The dawn consoles but it does not arise in order to console. The Lord speaks to Job:

---

[30] *Walden*, "Spring," p. 303 [para 19].

> Canst thou command the dawn?
> The look of things is changed by it.
> They stand forth as if clothed in ornament.[31]

The Lord does not shout, bully, or demand self-abasement. He sings in the powerful voice of the sublime. He awakens profusions of magnificence with no message of moral good or lawful justice. He is even indifferent to whether Job is in fact touched or awed. He'd sing his song in any case, for its own sake. His task is not to win admirers or elicit bows acknowledging the nullity of the beholder before the all-powerful. These onslaughts of sublimity alter Job. But quite apart from whether a witness is altered, or whether others notice or are consoled, Nature will speak in upsurges and quiets, in flows and sudden stops, in consolidations and disintegrations, from a wild plenitude.

As I hear the great book, that is the Lord's final word. And as I hear the great book from Concord, that is Thoreau's final word, too—though not always sung as a majestic oratorio. Thoreau is a master of the grand sublime, and also of what I'd call the petite, ordinary, or diminutive sublime:

> I heard the dream of the toad—it sung thro' & filled all the air ... Loud & prevailing as it is—most men do not notice it at all— ... That afternoon the dream of the toads sang through the elms by Little River & affected the thought of men though they were not conscious that they heard it.[32]

---

[31] Job 38.12–15, from Herder's trans. *Dimensions of Job*, Nahum Glatzner (ed.) (New York: Schocken, 1969), p. 149.

[32] *Journal*, October 26, 1853, p. 453. Old English etymology links "dream" to joy and ecstasy. And if Thoreau mulls on the songs of dreaming toads, Jonathan Edwards will wonder "what sleeping rocks dream of." See James D. Lilley, "Being Singularly Impersonal: Jonathan Edwards and the Aesthetics of Consent," *American Impersonal: Essays with Sharon Cameron*, Branka Arsić (ed.) (New York: Bloomsbury, 2014).

6

Ethics and the Wild

I was unexpectedly struck with the beauty of an apple tree—
The perception of beauty is a moral test.

—*Journal*[1]

We find critiques of religion and affirmative delivery of religious revelations throughout Thoreau's writing. We also find political polemic and a naturalist's meticulous observations. Where does *ethics* fit in? He makes specific ethical appeals and exhortations, and models an ethical way of life, a path of *askesis,* the ascetic way.[2] His *Journal* observations can be assembled as an environmental ethics based on care for the wild, care for meadows, streams, and birds. But Thoreau is lyrical rather than systematic. He names virtues: simplicity, independence, magnanimity, and trust. He sketches an ascetic, meditative way of life, and might fall in step with the French philosopher, Emmanuel Levinas, who finds ethics in responsiveness to the face of a person. Perhaps Thoreau's ethics is that, and also is responsiveness to the face of a river or the face of Yosemite's Half Dome. We'll take up this possibility in our final excursion. For the moment we'll trace the wild orders and disorders that emerge as what we'll call Thoreau's ethics.

1.

From an everyday point of view, Thoreau obviously has an ethics, in that he has well-considered views on matters of ethical importance. He is courageously activist on the deeply divisive issue of slavery. For many, he is the first to make the environment an ethical concern. For some, his life becomes saintly, a model of meditative ascetic excellence. Yet professional philosophers would not necessarily welcome him as a *bone fide* member of their club. They'd rule out any connection between acting ethically and having ethical opinions, on the one hand, and on the other, making contributions to the technical research-field of ethics. Academic philosophers have their doubts, and Thoreau is dismissive in return. Early in *Walden* he tells us

---

[1] Epigraph: *Journal,* June 21, 1852, p. 126.
[2] See Branka Arsić's discussion of his search for "no-self," self-renunciation, or what Cameron calls "impersonality." *Bird Relics,* 253f.

that there are no *philosophers* in Massachusetts, only *teachers* of the subject. Yet he would have welcomed a walk with Socrates or Diogenes, those most 'unprofessional' of thinkers. Many continue, nevertheless, to dismiss Thoreau-the-thinker, taking him to be only a fashionable "man of letters," an essayist who could appear in *The New Yorker*.

Professors who resist this offhand dismissal will want to show he's really a Platonist, Transcendentalist, or Kantian, or they might attire him as a virtue theorist defending the cluster of excellences that make up an admirable life. Taking these options involves creative reconstructions of Thoreau's informally scattered ethical remarks. Early in his first book, *A Week on the Concord*, Thoreau considers the classic confrontation between Krishna and Arguna in the *Gita*. Is it obligatory, Arguna asks, to slaughter relatives if they belong to the opposing army? Writing under the gathering clouds of the American civil war, Thoreau asks, in effect, if it is right to go into battle against one's kith and kin. But he raises this issue without providing an answer, and with next to no ethical analysis.

I don't think Thoreau works out an ethical *theory*. He improvises, brilliantly, case by case. He listens attentively to a bittern call, and reminds us that *attention* is a moral virtue; as he enjoys fermented ice apples, he mocks Puritanical prohibitions against them. He can model serenity even in personal desolation, and can model ethical exuberance, crowing the arrival of morning light. Ethics, in part, is a guide to highest value. He finds it in unexpected places, not just in a bittern's call, but in ignorance or unknowing. He models Socrates in asking teasing questions while ducking answers. If we had to pick a centerpiece, it could be the simple injunctions "*Wake up! Pay attention!*" But then, pay attention to *what*, in what *mood*, from what *angle*, at what *distance*, to what *end*, in what *circumstance* or *locale*?

Stanley Bates places Thoreau in the broad ethical tradition of Nietzsche, Kierkegaard, and Carlyle, and earlier of Plato, the Stoics and Cynics.[3] This literary-philosophical tradition is dormant today, making it easy to say that Thoreau is not an ethical thinker. Academic philosophy becomes specialized in the twentieth century. The grand sweeping visions of William James or Schopenhauer are not in fashion. Many of the luminaries in this earlier tradition lived outside and mocked university life. They found its warrens stifling. For their part, professors of philosophy began to take scientific problem-solving as their model, dismissing the literary-philosophical improvisations of Nietzsche, for example.

---

[3] See Bates, "Stanley Cavell and Ethics," in *Stanley Cavell*, Richard Eldridge (ed.) (Cambridge: Cambridge University Press, 2003), p. 39.

In 1882 Josiah Royce, a California high school teacher, joined the Harvard philosophy faculty having impressed William James and Charles Peirce through letters carried by Pony Express. He was not hired on the basis of publications, competitive interviews, or because he was expert in a particular philosophical specialty that needed coverage. He had an indefinable but recognizable native philosophical talent. In 1937 Martin Buber immigrated to assume a position not in philosophy but in the sociology department at Hebrew University in Jerusalem. He was a philosopher whose reach included being a social theorist, a religious thinker, a psychologist, and a translator of the Hebrew bible into a modern, poetic and idiomatic German. Though he had held a Philosophy Professorship in Germany, he was not offered one in Jerusalem. I suspect the resident philosophers frowned on his sweeping vision and non-technical writing. He did not occupy a professional niche and sub-field of expertise, which ruled him out. Things had changed since 1882 when Royce got his job.

Contemporary professors may quietly feed from this older, non-professionalized tradition but most won't confess to sharing its aspirations. Of course there are notable contemporary exceptions—writers housed in the university who range imaginatively across otherwise narrow research niches. The danger of lists is their arbitrary exclusions, but I think of Richard Rorty, Martha Nussbaum, and Stanley Cavell as philosophers who transcend narrow philosophical specializations. As important, I find Robert Pogue Harrison, a Dante scholar, and his Stanford colleague from Classics, Andrea Nightingale, also to have burst out of their disciplines, writing "grand moral theory." We find Harrison's improvisations in essays on Heidegger, forests, death, and gardens, and Nightingale's in her commentaries on *Moby Dick, Walden,* and Augustine's *Confesssions*.[4] This broader tradition lives astride history, psychology, religion, natural philosophy, and world literature. It boasts what can seem grandiose aims. Nietzsche, Schopenhauer, Emerson, and James ask what it is to live (and die) well among others, what it is to undergo sublimity tempering all action and passion, what it is to be rooted in earth and her instincts, or to be poignantly aware of heritage, birth, and impending death, what it is to be finite creatures of infinite imagination and infinite desire. To make matters worse, they aspire to be *living exemplars* of all they celebrate in writing. This is the home of Thoreau's wild ethics.

---

[4] Among other works, see Robert Pogue Harrison, *Forests: The Shadow of Civilization* (Chicago, IL: University of Chicago Press, 1992), pp. 220–30; and Andrea Nightingale, "Auto-Hagiography: Augustine and Thoreau," *Arion* (Fall 2008): 111–48.

2.

Thoreau writes ethics from relatively untamed landscapes, among tangled plants and spirited animals, and from disasters, where things have gone wildly wrong. On Fire Island he approaches a shipwreck, the tumult where Margaret Fuller, her family, and countless others have drowned. Then there's the wreckage of John Brown's hanging after his wild insurrection. Thoreau's ethics is wild in yet another sense; it becomes characteristic of his consciousness. Repercussions of the disaster of John's death permeate his particular inwardness and play out over decades. And to complicate matters further, Thoreau doesn't just find the details of his life and experience to be wild. He intimates that our subjectivity *in its very constitution* is cleaved by wild, untamed gaps.

We carry within precarious tensions between aspirations not-yet-achieved and an actual place from which aspirations flow. We negotiate gaps that can become wild between where we are and where we might be. Wild gaps also arise between convictions in place, and doubts about our accuracy in assessing the strength of those convictions: we are subject to wild bouts of self-doubt. A soul is wild like a river's torrent or the mystery of a deep pond, terrain powerfully intimated but not well surveyed. The self or soul is always a moving target, day-by-day, mood-by-mood, word-by-word. If world and soul are reciprocally unruly, serenity may be just learning to live with that.

This many faceted wildness militates against ethical theories that are abstract and monocular, that seek simple focus through a minimum of rules or principles. In contrast, Thoreau provides a plurality of ethical angles and moods, a weave of multiple strands, only loosely interlaced. Against the systematics of School-taught ethics (Utilitarian or Kantian, Intuitionist or Aristotelian, Virtue-centered or Levinasian) Thoreau looks *merely* impressionistic, providing only a mosaic or medley. But is that a bad thing? The contemporary ethicist Charles Taylor also refuses a monocular vision. He figures ethics as corrals, meadows, and forests.[5]

3.

Ethics can be fenced in as an extended forensic or lawyerly debate about moral codes and law-constrained behaviors. It aims to clarify, revise, and facilitate conflict resolution—under law, as it were. Its regulatory principles

---

[5] See Charles Taylor, *Dilemmas and Connections* (Cambridge, MA: Harvard University Press, 2011), p. 11.

include justice and freedom. Taylor dubs this place of lawyerly argument and adjudication the *corrals* of ethics.[6] Arguments for expanding civil rights belong here.

As we move out of the fenced yards, we enter open fields, sites where virtues are cultivated and their absence is lamented. We describe and cultivate the growth of friendship, courage, or sympathy, and work to weed out greed or villainy. Thoreau cultivates "a life of simplicity, independence, magnanimity, and trust."[7] We work these fields to understand a saint's generosity or a demon's malice. We attend to pivots of excellence and corruption. Here we're offered orientation and sensibility rather than training in defining and defending principles of justice or respect.[8] We encourage imaginative roaming, taking note of particulars of scene, action, and character. Jane Austen, Martha Nussbaum, and so many others deliver sensitive portraits of virtue and its absence. They paint the allure of a way of being, and are unafraid to let religious and non-religious excellence mix. Generosity, for instance, can wear both the robes of the heavenly and the garments of the everyday.

Beyond corrals and meadows lie the forests. There we are exposed to the dark unknown intermittently broken by shafts of light. We are racked by tragedy and personal devastation, and also blessed by unexpected love, serenity, or delight. These are the ethico-religious forests of Job's exposure, of Dante's hell, of Sebald's haunting evocations of incinerated German cities toward the end of the Second World War.[9] This is not ethics as principles or prohibitions, and is not ethics as virtues and vices. It is not problem-solving: quite the reverse. It is a place of unsettling, of revelation, torment, despair, and redemption. We would welcome a saving hand, if one appeared and we could believe. Thoreau held his brother through horror and later welcomes the world. Ethics seems poised over an abyss—or, as Dickinson has it, plummeting through one:

> And then a Plank in Reason broke
> And I dropped down, and down—
> And hit a World at every plunge,
>   and Finished knowing—then—[10]

---

[6] Ibid. p. 5.
[7] *Walden*, "Economy," p. 14 [para 19].
[8] For an excellent study of Thoreau and the virtues, see Philip Cafaro, *Thoreau's Living Ethics: Walden and the Pursuit of Virtue* (Athens, GA: University of Georgia Press, 2004).
[9] For Sebald, see "Closing Passions," below.
[10] *The Complete Poems of Emily Dickinson*, Thomas H. Johnson (ed.) (Boston: Little, Brown, and Company, 1960), #280.

One can undergo swings of such amplitude that orientation totters or implodes. Ethical desires for deliberation from shared principles or for pictures of virtue now seem inept or alien. Yet we can also hope, as in Job, that radiant worlds wait in the wings ("I hit a World at every plunge").

This exposure to profound disorder and relief is easily cast in religious terms. To be vulnerable in forest ethics can be a "dark night of the soul," or it can harbor moments of redeeming light. Beyond the reach of law or commonplace excellence, the self (or soul) can seek a deep account of itself, and be open to change or conversion. A forest dark is the home of anxiety that we'd deflect by immersion in projects or vocations, seeking the path of a poet, a monk, a politician, or throwing oneself into consumption, family life, or business, or falling into dissipation. Vocations offer a grip on Whence, Why, and Wither. Yet we can be plunged into disorder, or worse, at every turn. These are Taylor's dark woods. Ethics can seem fragile as it shows a glimpse—*only* a glimpse—of the godly, good, beautiful, or true.

Thoreau takes up the forensic edge of argument or saunters in fields where virtues and failings stand out. And beyond argument and admiration he is alert to a wonder or terror that is nothing if not religious. On Ktaadn he finds dark chaos. He is seized and undone.[11] On Cape Cod, he finds sublime consolation as anxiety gives way to the luminous dark of the sea.[12]

4.

A threefold division of the ethical becomes blurred, especially in crisis. Thoreau faced the disaster of the extinction of Native Americans. Within the first sentences of his first book he speaks of the "extinct peoples" who once inhabited the land.[13] Here ethics (and its absence) speak from our prides and shames, our sense of excellence (in according persons their due) and of failure (in treating persons as sub-human). Memorializing earlier peoples is memorializing their virtues of resourcefulness, frugality, and respect for others. Evoking these excellences fuels shame as we accentuate our distance from theses ideals. And religious stains of radical evil obtrude.

The hanging of John Brown is another moral disaster. His execution as a militant abolitionist is a crucial point in the struggle leading to the Civil War. Thoreau's oration in Brown's defense appeals to laws, to virtue, and to the sacred—intermingled precariously and magnificently. Brown's insurrection,

---

[11] *Essays*, "Ktaadn," pp. 111–14.
[12] *Cape Cod*, p. 123.
[13] *Week*, p. 5.

rebellion, or act of war against the slave-holding South marks the start of the nation's plunge into carnage. Thoreau argues Brown's case forensically. Brown does not abide ordinary law when that law serves tyranny. In attacking the Federal arsenal at Harper's Ferry, he takes up arms against tyranny just as his forebears in Concord and elsewhere did. This brings out the tension between "laws on the books," and forest-located appeals to "higher laws" and displays the virtue of courage.

The appeal to Sacred Liberty is mythic-religious. Americans are born of Freedom's Stock; the Constitution is God-inspired. In mythic register, those who resisted tyranny in Concord pass the banner of Freedom forward to Brown, even as those Concord Revolutionaries inherited it from earlier Heroes. Victor Hugo reminds those about to hang Brown that they will thereby hang Spartacus, who led a slave revolt against Rome and was crucified.[14] Thoreau has John Brown carrying on a sacred tradition of resistance to tyrants, and then raises the ante by making Brown a crucified Christ. His wild ethics rings like a ship's bell in fog.

In his clarion attacks on slavery in Massachusetts and in his impassioned defense of John Brown, Thoreau speaks in registers that interweave principles, virtues, and the sacred. He asks whether those who martyr John Brown know their Gospel. Brown dies on a cross. Christ is crucified a thousand times over in slave states: each slave is a Christ.[15] Thoreau's essay on civil resistance, so important to Gandhi, Martin Luther King, and millions more, shows him matchless in forensic oration. Moving to virtue, he embodies and enacts his ethics, being a "conductor" at the Concord station of the Underground Railroad. Famously, he spends a night in jail in protest of the invasion of Mexico. He lives out his principles in speaking at mass anti-slavery rallies, ringing the church bell on the day of John Brown's execution, displaying courage, solidarity, and justice. Living from his overlook at Walden Pond, he exhibits yogic and pagan simplicity. He provides sketches of virtue and vice in *Cape Cod*, *A Week*, and *The Maine Woods*. His essays travel through Taylor's wild forests. There is religious prophecy as he rains down the wrath of the gods, and less harshly, there is hope for redemption of a village or soul now benighted. He can confide, "Even the tired laborers I meet on the road, I really meet as travelling gods."[16]

Thoreau's implicit environmental ethics appears in his attention to earth, its waters, its mountains, varied inhabitants and vegetative covers. It also appears in his devotion to natural history. He did not see his scientific

---

[14] See "Addenda," Ch. 12.
[15] Ibid.
[16] *Journal*, August 15, 1845, p. 383.

activity as irreligious or morally neutral. Local ecological patterns revealed importance and worth. In nature's patterns Thoreau discerns "Higher Laws" of growth, decline, and equilibrium. His image of life as a pilgrimage reveals a religious tenor to ethics, and his *Journal* is what Pierre Hadot calls spiritual exercise—a pious meditation. Beyond arguing forensically or evoking virtues, he witnesses to the wonder of a world that is holy.

5.

Thoreau writes literary masterpieces; he's a kind of philosophical poet. This puts him at odds with a contemporary conception of philosophy, and with an ancient tradition, as well. Plato exiles the poets from the just city—perhaps ironically. By retreating to the pond, perhaps Thoreau effects his own exile. Be that as it may, the tradition of "great moral philosophy" bypasses this warfare to celebrate a happy union of philosophy and poetry. Plato himself, among the first who *seems* to put philosophy and poetry at war, mixes philosophy with poetry, myth with religion, in his tales of love in *The Symposium*. He gives an intriguing drama of immortality in *The Myth of Er*. Plato depicts escape from imprisoning darkness in *The Myth of the Cave*, and praises inspired poetic madness in *Phaedrus*. In Thoreau "befitting reverie" can liberate and instruct. Among our contemporaries, Stanley Cavell has philosophy in a daring affiliation with literature and film.[17] In the 1970s he presents *Walden* as literature, as philosophy, and most radically, as scripture.[18]

Contemporary philosophers who look askance at these discipline-defiant weddings typically see their craft as a chapter in the history of science where unornamented argument and systematic exposition are one's ideal. This yanks Thoreau off the stage. But granting Thoreau status simultaneously in philosophy, letters, and non-institutional religion—not to mention natural history or science—is no one's *loss*. Allowing poetry, ethics, and religious sensibility to sing in the same choir not only amplifies Thoreau's or Plato's capacities, but Pascal's, Kierkegaard's, and Heidegger's.[19] This is

---

[17] Stanley Cavell, *Cities of Words, Pedagogical Letters on a Register of the Moral Life* (Cambridge, MA: Harvard University Press, 2008).

[18] See *The Senses of Walden*, and Brendan Mahoney's "The Echoes of *Walden*: Reading Thoreau's Inverted Scripture through Cavell," *The Concord Saunterer: A Journal of Thoreau Studies*, Vol. 21 (2013).

[19] Cavell cites a line from Wallace Stevens' *The Necessary Angel*: "One function of the poet at any time is to discover by his own thought and feeling what seems to him to be poetry at that time." Cavell adds, "What Stevens will not conceive is that the philosopher may have a comparable function of discovery, as if for Stevens philosophy, in its otherness, is

the non-professionalized way of ethics that Stanley Bates calls "great moral philosophy." It provides an "exploration of human living aimed at seeing and living it better."

> I think of Hegel, Kierkegaard, Emerson, Thoreau, Marx, Nietzsche, Freud, Dewey, Heidegger, Wittgenstein, and Sartre ... These thinkers tend either to produce narrative structures or to reflect on the narrative structure of human existence, not in order to provide a formula, or a template, of human existence, but to deny the possibility of such a formula.[20]

Whether on a walk, a river trip, or a climb up Ktaadn, Thoreau's traversals bring him through the corrals, meadows, and dark woods of ethical life. He is not out to retrieve a holy grail in the shape of a 'formula' for living well but instead he's out to give one way, his way, of seeing life better, and so living it better. His manner, of course, is suggestive and invitational: we can affirm or dismiss, in part or in whole. And achieving insight is not once-for-all. A step that shows growth in care for the soul opens new vistas whose contemplation ratchets up a capacity to act responsive to the revelations provided—the revelation, say, that all this *matters* ... within an always-unfinished ethical life.

Thoreau cultivates a sensibility and manner of living at once practical, moral, aesthetic, religious, and political. It relies on images, pictures, scenarios, aphorisms, and narratives that present the wild of our thoughts and worlds as untamed wonder—then as a glimpse of terror—then as a moment settling into serenity. Accepting the "new testament of the present moment" is learning to live with these shifting realities in troubled times.

6.

We've sketched corrals, meadows, and forests in Thoreau's ethics. Changing our template to one of recurring motifs, we can find five that appear and reappear: 1) The motif of the importance of angle and scale; 2) the motif of unending revisions in response to imperfections; 3) the importance of

---

a fixed, oracular structure and those who speak for it are in possession of an authority that goes beyond what they are able to articulate out of their own experience and practice and wit on each occasion of being stopped to think." *Artists, Intellectuals, and World War II: The Pontigny Encounters at Mount Holyoke College, 1942-1944*, Christopher Benfey and Karen Remmler (eds) (Amherst: University of Massachusetts Press: 2006).

[20] Bates: "Stanley Cavell and Ethics," in *Stanley Cavell*, Richard Eldridge (ed.) (Cambridge: Cambridge University Press, 2003), p. 39.

mobile, shifting surrounds that envelope and elicit our response; 4) the nimble dance between political activism and restorative solitude; and 5) the conviction that an ethico-religious sensibility is more than an intellectualist venture. I then end this excursion with a discussion of the great arc of preservative care.

First is the importance of scale of perception, whether close up or a vast panorama. There is a bittern's call and then the prospect from Mt. Greylock that brings four states into view. Exhilaration feeds on the scale of the prospect. The mountaintop prospect opens toward ethical nobility or sublimity, a prospect that fuels gratitude to have been given it. Less pleasant is the prospect from the crest of Ktaadn.[21] In this inhospitable and inhumane place he is stripped of dignity. He's been thrown into the workshop of chaos among monstrous deities. He might look out anywhere, but fogs hem him in. There are no principles or tablets of law to find here—only a terrifying dehumanizing space. There is no *human* scale, and he flees. Part of ethics is finding the appropriate measure of apprehension. On Ktaadn neither the world nor viewer can be sanely sensed. The place is impersonal, disorienting, disembodying, disemboweling. Thoreau's spirit escapes from between his ribs. He cries, "*Contact! Contact! Who are we? Where are we?*"[22]

Shifts in scale and angle mark Thoreau's narratives of domesticity (residing at Walden), of travel, pilgrimage, and commemoration (*Cape Cod, The Maine Woods, A Week on the Concord*), of living either well or poorly with others ("Slavery in Massachusetts", "A Plea for Captain John Brown", "Resistance to Civil Government"), and of living alone with oneself (parts of *Walden*, "Walking" and "Wild Apples").[23] The scale and angle of ethics makes the call of things audible, just as light makes the color and shape of things visible.

As we behold from apt angles of vision, we sense imperatives to respond. Such felt-imperatives do not derive from a theory or system "any rational mind" ought to accept. I see a child in danger and reach to protect her. I might think, "She's about to fall, about to be harmed." But that is not to enunciate or defend a principle. It is not to endorse the maxim "Always treat children well." It is to see things aptly, befittingly, from an angle of sympathy and care—the child *here at hand, this very moment*. Ethics is experiential and reflexive and presupposes scale and an angle of vision.

The importance of scale and angle are evident in Thoreau's walk toward bones on the sandy beach after a shipwreck. Having been sent down from

---

[21] *Essays*, "Ktaadn," pp. 111–14.
[22] Ibid. p. 113.
[23] See *Essays*.

Concord to retrieve Fuller's effects (and if possible, her body), Thoreau discovers unclaimed bones. The discovery is rattling. It prompts a distinctive and memorable response, an ethico-religious-poetic recoil and assimilation. He hoped to find Fuller's half-buried bones, but this was more than the angle of an investigator's search. And the scale of discovery and rendering becomes the vastness of the sea and the anonymity of the sand. He expands to become more than an observer gathering facts. If truth be told, in this case he just doesn't know *whose* bones he uncovers. But this invites imaginative rehabilitation.

Then and there, and later in the leisure of a *Journal* recollection, Thoreau raises a monument. To have seen only anonymous remains and leave it at that would be a failure of moral imagination. From meager materials he funds an angle of vision that bespeaks an ethical accomplishment. His angle transmutes bones to "relics" apt for commemoration. He then bequeaths them an uncanny understanding with the sea that earlier had tossed them cruelly aside as worthless remains. "[The] bones were alone with the beach and the sea, whose hollow roar seemed to address them … as if there were an understanding between them and the ocean."[24] He discovers an angle from which bones commune with the sea. The trudge toward the distant wooden sliver that marks the place of the bones facilitates "the influx of better thoughts." The calm of the sea makes this and its whispers possible. His perception of beauty amidst devastation makes his response a *moral* test: to make beauty is a preferred response—the moral response—to otherwise morale-killing ugliness.

The *second* recurrent motif in Thoreau's ethics is this. The ethical self is always under revision, always open to another day's demands for renewed ethical responsiveness. In his deliveries of Thoreau, Emerson, and others, Cavell articulates what he calls "moral perfectionism."[25] I'd call it moral *imperfectionism*, for it gives our aspirations as always only *imperfectly* realized. One's deepest values shift in and out of prominence, exposing the unfinished business that is *exactly* an ethical life. We don't know what new demands will devolve upon us, or what old ones will speak anew. Thoreau keeps listening, knowing inchoately that he is always incomplete and never beyond reproach.[26] A frozen self will be shattered and then revised. Wildness and unexpected demands are always around the bend. The old self shatters

---

[24] *Cape Cod*, p. 123.
[25] *Conditions Handsome and Unhandsome* (Chicago, IL: University of Chicago Press, 1990).
[26] To be "never beyond reproach" marks Cavell's "Perfectionism" (*Conditions*; *Cities of Words, Pedagogical Letters on a Register of the Moral Life* (Cambridge, MA: Harvard University Press, 2008).

in surprise, rapture, wonder, or outrage. There is no smooth sailing, yet there is more than turmoil.

Thoreau flexes, finding a next and better self. He undergoes the loss of his brother, of Emerson's young son, and the loss even of his mentor, the elder Emerson. Early on he has little success as a writer, and no faith in a government that coddles slavery and pursues imperial conquest. Each disappointment calls for a compensatory ethical response. Each disruption of yesterday's self mobilizes ethical reserves for shifts toward a better one. Thinking of Socrates, this is what Hadot calls care for the self.[27] It is a self forever doomed to fall short of what it would grasp.

A *third* motif is the interlocking of unfinished selves and unfinished surrounds. Thoreau gives us a Taoist sense that the flow of self and the flow of nature are seamlessly intertwined. In writers like Wendell Berry, Henry Bugbee, or Annie Dillard we find variations, sometimes expressed in the claim that humans are immersed in a wondrous surround, participants in its all-inclusive embrace. As a meadow or a river addresses Thoreau, he'll bear lyrical witness to its wonder. He raises the hearty sense that it is *there*—to be celebrated and preserved.

An attention that husbands and a preservative care are environmental virtues—perhaps the crowning and abiding ones. Our care is mobile, attuned, unfolding in natural surrounds. The world addresses Thoreau and he returns the favor. The mobility of the river is the mobility of the self attending it. Rivers, persons at risk, meadowlarks, are, in a sense, "primitive": we can delve no deeper than their presence, illumination, and call. And our increasingly attentive flow with them is "primitive," too: there is no deeper or better contact to be had. Thoreau's delivers thankful celebrations of this primal cohabitation. We startle in wonder and gratitude that such things appear, that this is the place of our moving and being.

A *fourth* motif in Thoreau's wild ethics is a dance between activism and solitude. These are not, let us concede, the best of times. Nor was Thoreau sailing under clear skies. Yet even in dark times, Thoreau insists that despair is not the end of the story. He is courageous in husbanding resistance and hope through ongoing poetic transfigurations of worlds and through direct action. Activism is a response to a dreadful state of things; so is the poetic elegy or oration even when born (if not delivered) in relative solitude. Raising a cairn to anonymous bones is transfiguring them and altering a gruesome death. The whisper of stones overheard in the endless listening of

---

[27] Pierre Hadot, "There are nowadays Professors of Philosophy, but not Philosophers," Aaron Simmons (trans.), *Journal of Speculative Philosophy*, 19 (3) (2005).

the sea transforms the site toward majesty. Imagination will release praise and hope. Spirit and body will converge in renewal.

A final, *fifth* motif is his insistence that ethical-religious sensibility is not solely an intellectual business. Thoreau holds that the *senses* are central to ethical self-culture (in its 'perfectionist' mode), and that virtues like friendship and courage, involving far more than naked cognition, are essential to "human living" and to "living life better." He seeks a flourishing life that he, and others, can at least partially realize. Simultaneously, injustice does not stem from failed intellect, nor does his rage spring from his intellect. Abominations make his blood curdle.

7.

As I've zigzagged through the terrain of Thoreau's ethical concerns, a recurrent focus is his *caring attention* to living things—trees, hawks, persons in distress or in bondage, and his caring attention to things less obviously living—rivers, plowed fields, or mists. This attentiveness might be a quasi-theological response to creatures, each a center of godly revelation. But in any case, life appears to Thoreau under *the great arc of preservative care*.

In the 1970s, Carol Gilligan contrasted an ethics of personal care with an ethics of impersonal rules and strict obligations or rights. Care speaks in a voice quieter than an assertive demand for rights or the shout of a moral injunction. Ethical solicitations and response can be warm and hospitable. Quite apart from rights or obligations, a life I can own with no shame will include cherishing children, hearth, and place, and attentiveness to the fragility of each. There are two striking corollaries that accompany centering Thoreau's ethics under an arc of preservative care. First, a caring response can be simultaneously an aesthetic, ethical, religious, and political response. Beauty can be a moral test in this sense: it can ask if I will work to preserve things of beauty. Second, the recipient of such care need not be a person. A beautiful old violin or magnolia bush calls for response in the register of aesthetic delight and simultaneously in the ethical register of preservative care. Think of the "heritage value" of an old house, its meadows, woodlot, and creek. To discern and protect that value are ethical activities.

To commemorate those places where Thoreau's ethics incontrovertibly shine, we'll honor flourishing life, offense at injustice, the itch of knowing ones inevitable imperfection, and expansions of care into ever-widening regions of attention. And we commemorate the way Thoreau lives out his cares and his steadfastness in adversity and loss. He gave attention to every passing moment, not letting a thing pass unnoticed. He could see more in a week of than most of us see in a year. And he had faith through enigmatic shifts, say from suffering and sadness to absolute delight—not won at the price of denying terrors or degradations, but by letting the lily or muskrat not escape notice. Like Goethe and perhaps Nietzsche, he knew how to see into the dark and yet sparkle with life. A rare knack: perhaps the heart of his genius, wild and unruly as it is.

7

Expressive Bones

Saw a shrike pecking to pieces a small bird, apparently a snowbird. At length he took him up in his bill, almost half as big as himself, and flew slowly off with his prey dangling from his beak. I find that I had not associated such actions with my idea of birds. It was not birdlike.

—*Journal*[1]

I hold in my lap a handsome book of drawings. I have always pictured birds in flight, singly or in flocks, or tending eggs, regal swans, slowly drifting, or birds swooping down for a fish or a mouse. But elegant drawings of birds *undressed*—bones picked dry, neither dead nor alive? I've never seen the likes of these— inhabitants of a nether land, comically stripped, shamelessly exposed.

Thoreau gives us pencil sketches in his *Journal*, but they are far from fine art. Katrina van Grouw's expert drawings give us specimens from all over the world. She's former curator of the ornithological wing of the London Museum of Natural History, the author of a book on the history of birds in art, and an accomplished artist. This is a coffee table book of impressive scope and accomplishment. Most of all, it gives an irresistible and disturbing parade of birds unattired, defrocked in ways one could never imagine. They're birds stripped of feathers and often of flesh, yet still avian beauties. Their bony structures are distressing to observe, but just try to avert your eyes!

No single frame catches the show. It's not just an anatomy lesson, not just a coroner's exhibit, not just a fashion runway of the half dead and sometimes grotesque. It is certainly not a desecration of majesty. It's a *celebration* of plumed majesty.[2]

The effect of van Grouw's drawings is to restore life—to give even a pile of bleached bones some measure of enchanted integrity. These birds are new creatures, born-again wonders of vibrant engineering and unmistakable soul, as alluring as any soaring hawk, or as any hectic hummingbird stopped a foot from my nose.

Penciled in sepia, here are four odd-shaped skulls, skulls with a protruding bump on top. The first displays the bare architecture of a beak, tenuously

---

[1] Epigraph: *Journal*, December 24, 1850, p. 129.
[2] Drawings are from Katrina van Grouw, *The Unfeathered Bird* (Princeton, NJ: Princeton University Press, 2013).

EUROPEAN ROBIN
Erithacus rubecula
Skeleton.

Katrina van Grouw. *The Unfeathered Bird* © 2013 Katrina van Grouw.
Reprinted by permission of Princeton University Press.

hung on the skull. I cannot recall which colored feathers belong back of the beak. I give the caption a furtive look. It's not the Polish Fowl, whose would-be adornment I can almost imagine. It's the Helmeted Curassow—Greek to me. I read that these four heads belong to the family "skulls with crests."

Here on the next page is a rounded basket weave of slender bones, most likely a tumbled-down rib cage. It's labeled "Ostrich." But it needs serious visual unscrambling. If that's a rib cage, where is the rest of this long-legged ostrich? Rechecking the caption, I learn that the legs are removed. In a flash, the eye of imagination provides phantom limbs, joined right *there*—to a pelvis.

Here is a Kiwi, a Dodo, a Swan. The illustrator steps aside to write charming introductions. Even the overall narrative has a sense of enchantment. The individual drawings show a quirky inquisitiveness and storytelling inventiveness, and the full narrative has a quirky arch as well. At the very end, after the index, come two familiar figures: a stripped-down robin on its back, quite dead, and a waddling mallard, quite alive. Death and resurrection?

For most readers and lookers, Robin and Mallard are as familiar as Bert and Ernie. Images can have a cultural saturation. Robin, feet stretched up, bones thoroughly picked—many of us have seen this as kids in the back yard. But why is it placed just here in the story? It cannot be deader than the rest of these pages of assembled bones—but it *seems* so. Other skeletons are poised for life and action. Lest I read too much angst or morbidity into this next-to-last drawing, consider the waddling Mallard bones, given the last word. Having grown up around Boston, I cannot help but think of the children's story, *Make Way for Ducklings*, a family of such birds, on the go. It's happiness and regeneration.

The Unfeathered Bird offers pleasing aesthetics, piques our scientific interests, and poses philosophical questions. Think of insides and outsides of bodies, or the outside of body and the inside of spirit or soul. And think of the anxieties that arise when I hold something living that I value, and dare to move from its outside to its inside.

Removing and disposing of the rind of a grapefruit, I happily prepare for the feast within. Pealing the bark from a tree, I feel more ambivalent. Matters get worse if I try to get to the inside of a whale by peeling its rind. Might I distract myself, like the crew of the *Pequod,* throwing myself into the raucous athleticism of skinning?

What is it to peel the feathered rind from a bird—or from bird after bird, of every shape and size, from Coot to Green Woodpecker to Dodo? I can't help asking this, leafing through van Grouw's book. Nevertheless, by now I'm completely assured that this book on my lap is a visual, tactile, and encyclopedic masterpiece. The chances seem meager that in one person we would find the knowledge of an expert ornithologist, the drafting skill of a great illustrator, the writing skill of an essayist, and imagination to bring these gifts together. The book beckons to more lands and skies than I could ever explore. As I turn from page to page it seems to always sense the greater whole even as it bathes in the detail of this skull, this foot and wing tip, this incredibly long snaking wind-pipe attached to an average-sized singer—this curve of neck, these vertebrae, one by one, the innards of just *this* curve-throated crane. A universe is no more interesting than its assembled and disassembled particulars.

Questions proliferate. If I see spirit, bones, flesh, or feathers, do I see them serially or simultaneously? Do I see them directly or does imagination quickly fill in what's missing? How do I see absent flesh and feather, or the

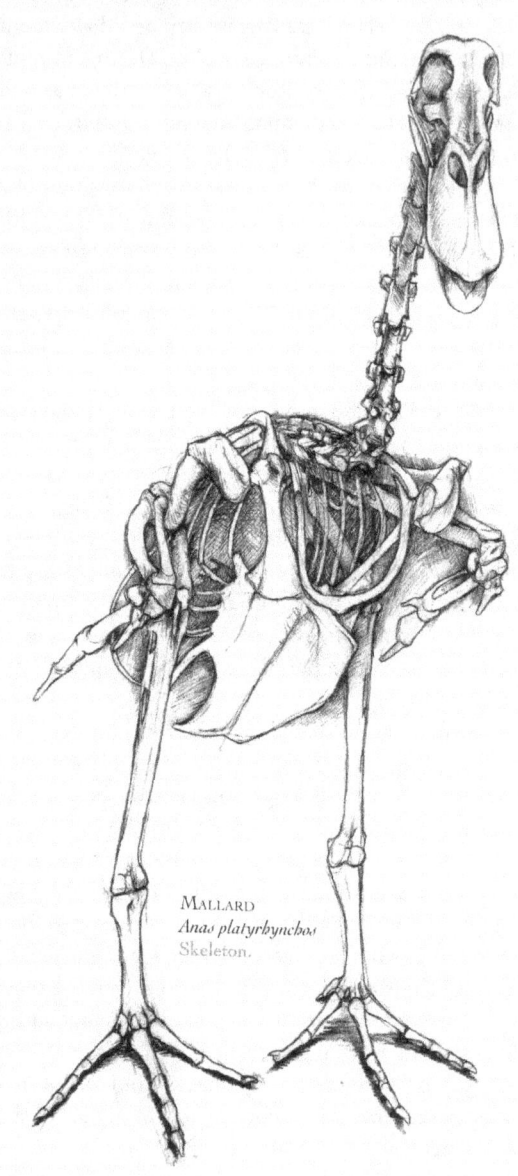

Katrina van Grouw. *The Unfeathered Bird* © 2013 Katrina van Grouw. Reprinted by permission of Princeton University Press.

bird alive when all I really have is an assemblage of bone—or lines on a page? How have I remained ignorant of beauty beneath skin, flesh and feathers, the beauty of cleaned bones and of their mechanics? I have no interest in the innards of my iPhone, beautiful as they may be to the geek, but I'm stopped dead in my tracks at a glimpse of *these*.

The unseen world is as lively and animated as the world at large: a rib cage, a ligament tying hip to foot, the architecture of a fisher's bill, the cross-stitching of a hen's ribcage, air tunnels opening down into lungs and up into songs! Aristotle says knowledge begins in wonder. Wonder can defy gravity; it can just float, neither seeking nor needing culmination in earthy knowledge.

Specialists in bird anatomy who have "been there, done that" might turn a blind eye to these renderings of the hidden. But I look and look away and look again. There are threatening undercurrents. I remember sixth grade when I resisted dissecting the frog. I don't feel that comfortable looking at Rembrandt's "Anatomy Lesson": fully clothed students peering at a professor peeling a corpse. I'm told that among first-year med students, it's not uncommon for several to pass out during their first dissection.

In the *Philosophical Investigations* Wittgenstein announces that the body is the best picture we have of the soul.[3] He doesn't investigate whether a corpse pictures a soul. Are the bodies displayed here alive or dead? Do they picture a soul? A bird's body, its voice box, can sound a soul. Mozart wept at the death of his nightingale. In the eye of a sparrow, Kant saw heaven. It takes a soul to call on a soul, or to be called by one.

The Unfeathered Bird can take philosophical wonder in yet a further direction, for it asks, *What, after all, is a body?* If it's bodies I see on these pages, how do they arise from unfeathered bones? And if what I'm looking at is *feather-deprived*, has it been stripped of the best of its body?

I think of *expressive* bodies, not ice cold things on the coroner's slab. I think of them performing—speaking, moving, gesturing, leaping, dressed for the part and the party. An un-fleshed human body must be something like the colored skeletal charts in a doctor's office showing various body-systems. Van Grouw's bodies don't look at all like doctor's office posters; they look alive. We don't have bony mechanical parts here but expressive bones. Some skeletons perch on a limb, resting for the moment, or plummet down from the sky for a watery dive. How does she convince us that bones alone, if only they are appropriately assembled, oriented, and drawn, picture life, and a soul?

---

[3] Ludwig Wittgenstein, *Philosophical Investigations* (London: Blackwell, 3rd edn, 2001), II, iv.

What are we to think of the discarded flesh and feathers—the bird's clothes, as it were? Thoreau worried about the divide between living and dead, and saw it as a shifting, anomalous zone. He nearly entered the underworld to join his brother, just dead, blurring the lines. Would he be alive with John, under the earth? He wondered what would count as being fully deceased, just as we wonder about whether bones of winged angels might be as alive as the flesh or feathers of their associates.

Thoreau also saw the Indian arrowheads he collected around Concord as bones—as relics to the dead. By memorializing them—as van Grow memorializes bony relics of birds—he keeps those apparently soul-less items alive. Here is a startling *Journal* entry: "[the arrow-head] is a stone fruit. Each one yields me a thought. I come nearer to the maker of it than if I found his bones."[4] These cavorting bird-bones yield thought. Bones are infinitely expressive.

Van Grouw's collection of unfeathered, un-fleshed birds is impressively extensive, especially when we remember that she didn't just collect birds, but had to reduce them to bones, and then render them with pen with great care. Thoreau had a penchant for archiving the remains of human life of earlier times through collecting local arrowheads. This was serious business, not an idle pastime:

> It is now high time to look for arrowheads, etc. I spend many hours every spring gathering the crop which the melting snow and rain have washed bare. It is one of the regular pursuits of the spring.

Yet he can also joke mildly about the business:

> I have not decided whether I had better publish my experience in searching for arrowheads in three volumes, with plates and an index, or try to compress it into one.[5]

Branka Arsić reports that Thoreau worried about corpses and clothes (bones and feathers?) and their living or dying:

> [Thoreau] was never certain about what ontological status to attribute to the clothes of the dead. Were they part of the living persons who wore them and, if so, could it be said that a person dies fully only when his clothes decay completely?[6]

She quotes Thoreau directly on the matter:

---

[4] *Journal,* March 28, 1859, p. 90.
[5] Ibid.
[6] Arsić, *Bird Relics,* p. 348. She reports on John Thoreau's little-known bird notebook, and Henry's use of it after John's death, 145f.

> My friend died long ago—why follow a body to the grave yard? ... There still remain his clothes—shall we have a third service when they are decayed?[7]

A Romantic can find religious sensibility under any rock or reef, yet I can't help believing that Katrina van Grouw gives us a religious sensibility. It's unromantic in a way that both disturbs and exults. She leads us to layered realities that never travel far from the spirit and soul of unfeathered *archly material* bones. I think here of a lyrical evocation from Thoreau's *Walden*:

> The night-hawk circled overhead in the sunny afternoons ... like a mote in the eye, or in heaven's eye, falling from time to time with a swoop and a sound as if the heavens were rent, torn at last to very rags and tatters, ... The hawk is aerial brother of the wave which he sails over and surveys, those his perfect air-inflated wings answering to the elemental unfledged pinions [wing tips] of the sea. Or sometimes I watched a pair of hen-hawks circling high in the sky, alternately soaring and descending, approaching and leaving one another, as if they were the embodiment of my own thoughts.[8]

Looking at van Grouw's drawings of birds, featherless and seldom in flight, and often verging on disenchanted cold, mechanical materiality—looking at these, I find them nevertheless morphing into astonishing carriers, as if they were angels or tiny gods in disguise. We have animated soft evocations of flight, breath, and cry—not to mention "falling from time to time with a swoop and a sound as if the heavens were rent, torn at last to very rags and tatters." These birds are surely earthbound, as far from aerial wizardry as imaginable. Yet though they don't quite sail over waves or swoop from the heavens, they nevertheless bespeak "the elemental unfledged pinions of the sea." Or so it seems.

---

[7] *Journal*, 3, 1848.
[8] *Walden*, "The Bean Field," p. 154 [para 6].

8

Child of the Mist

As for Waldo, he died as the mist rises from the brook, which the sun will soon dart his rays through.

—To Lucy Brown

Live free, child of the mist—and with respect to knowledge we are all children of the mist

—"Walking"

A new growth is rising all around, preparing another aspect for new infant eyes. Almost the same johnswort springs from the same perennial root in this pasture, and even I have at length helped to clothe that fabulous landscape of my infant dreams.

—*Walden*[1]

1.

Thoreau called himself a mystic, a transcendentalist, and a natural philosopher, but that doesn't tell us what these labels meant to him—or what they mean to us.[2] We have linguistic instability here, slippery titles, without effable *centers*—however effable their swirls may be. Can we give a rounded sense to these terms—transcendentalist, natural philosopher, mystic? Rather than start with abstractions, I'll take up a striking image. In several contexts Thoreau invokes the image of "a child of the mist." We've encountered that image in a letter we've noted before, from the spring of 1842. It appears just after the deaths of John Thoreau, and of Waldo Emerson, the young child Henry cared for. As we know, Thoreau suffered an attack that mimicked John's lockjaw. After convalescing roughly two weeks, in his first more or less public acknowledgment of his loss, he writes to Lucy Brown, "As for Waldo, he died as the mist rises from the brook, which the sun will soon dart his rays through."[3] But how can this be a way of memorializing a child? Isn't it all too blunt, too … offhand?

---

[1] Epigraphs: *Correspondence*, p. 62; "Walking," p. 250 [para 73]; *Walden*, "The Beanfield" p. 151 [para 2].
[2] *Journal*, March 5, 1853.
[3] *Correspondence*, p. 62.

Let me present more of the letter. Before speaking of Waldo's disappearing as "the mist rises from the brook," he tells Lucy Brown that he consoled himself with music:

> Soon after John's death I listened to a music-box, and if, at any time, that event had seemed inconsistent with the beauty and harmony of the universe, it was then gently constrained into the placid course of nature by those steady notes, in mild and unoffended tone echoing far and wide under the heavens. But I find these things more strange than sad to me.[4]

I think Thoreau lets fall a sudden downpour of thought in these two sentences. I can't help but unfold and amplify them, losing some of the compactness of his reverie but letting the sense shine through a bit easier. He says to Lucy Brown:

> The event of John's death might seem inconsistent with the beauty and harmony of the universe. But if at any time it seemed that way to me, this sense of dissonance or anomaly was reined in, gently constrained, by the steady notes of the music box. Those notes sent a mild and unoffended tone echoing far and wide under the heavens, dissolving any lingering sense of disharmony or inconsistency. Its steady tones returned me to the placid course of nature, and returned nature to herself. Under the sweep of such music, death seems less sad than strange. It's not *sad* to have music return to the listener the placid course of nature. It's *strange—a marvel*. It's a strange marvel that life yields to death, that music returns a world for a moment lost, and that the world, yes, is a wonder.[5]

It is against this preamble, this stage setting, condensed in Thoreau's letter and expanded in my paraphrase, that Thoreau can write "As for Waldo, he died as the mist rises from the brook, which the sun will soon dart his rays through." The sun darting his rays through the mist has all the wonder of musical strains—from Thoreau's music box but *also* from *nature's* "steady notes."[6]

---

[4] Ibid.
[5] Here Thoreau finds what he desperately needs, a serenity beyond anomaly or discord. But reality remains anomalous nevertheless, in the sense that neither serenity nor discord are "the last word."
[6] Nature speaks musically but in a way that brings it beyond dissonance or consonance, much as the Whirlwind speaks wildly beyond justice and injustice. See Arsić, "What Music Shall we Have?"

2.

Thoreau's response to Lucy Brown's sympathetic inquiry can seem austere and remote, but his distance from lamentation does not, in my view, show a lack of feeling—as if he were coldly indifferent to his loss. After all, he was in complete physical and spiritual collapse for two weeks. And he must have suffered much longer. His seeming remoteness reflects the outcome of a struggle for composure, for a balanced and not unhappy repose. Well before these deaths struck, he admired a kind of stoic serenity. Putting that serenity in play, however, can't have been easy. His *Journal* goes mute. He succumbs to John's symptoms, terrifying his family. In climbing out of the abyss he harnesses himself to an imperative that will bring joyful repose. The categorical imperative is this: *fall in love, with nature and the world and all they contain.* Devastation and collapse fall away as he tracks glimmers of light. He tends joyful signs until they shine as spring buds and birdsong. Lucy Brown is the first to know.

Thoreau writes, almost ecstatically—uncannily, poignantly—that "nature [does not] manifest any sorrow at [Waldo's] death, but soon the note of the lark will be heard down in the meadow, and fresh dandelions will spring from the old stocks where he plucked them last summer." He finds a love of the lark, and of fresh dandelions. Such tender attachment marks therapeutic renewal.

3.

Falling in love means coming to see someone, or something, under a special light of wonder and plenitude. Everything has an extra quota of meaning—though others will be blind to it. We all see a grassy meadow. Only you and I, as lovers, know it as the pool of waving grass that caressed our bare feet. For us, it tells a story of love. We recount that story, if we do, as a poetic reverie that befits our sense and reality of plenitude. Thoreau will place the child he knew, Waldo, in a story of love. Placing him as dispersing in the midst is bringing Waldo close in memory—not watching him disappear and longing for him. Thoreau is memorializing his love of Waldo in a reverie of the world that they both loved.

With this image and reverie, Thoreau does not disavow death. Death remains present as the underlay that gives poignancy to the child of the midst. Thoreau makes death an underlay or sustained tonality well short of inconsolable grief and tempered by its placement within a greater story.

Where Thoreau might have stalled indefinitely in the agony of loss, instead he moves decisively on. It's as if lost innocence—a necessary phase of human development, though a plunge into hell—will not become a permanent state of desolation for him. He does not exactly regain a lost innocence—far from it. But he can place himself in the present sunrise imagining the light coming through the mist, and imagining that Waldo, rather than suffering the clutch of death, is a "child of the mist" now with him. This transforms the past. Rather than these two nearly simultaneous deaths marking an indelible and agonizing sadness, they are now integrated into a wider love story, and that integration retrospectively alters their tenor. This recasting of an otherwise indelible hurt staunches the wound. The memory of these deaths is now evoked in a reverie that returns him to life.

Here is more of that befitting reverie:

> As for Waldo, he died as the mist rises from the brook, which the sun will soon dart his rays through. Do not the flowers die every autumn? He had not even taken root here. I was not startled to hear that he was dead; it seemed the most natural event that could happen. His fine organization demanded it, and nature gently yielded its request. It would have been strange if he had lived. Neither will nature manifest any sorrow at his death, but soon the note of the lark will be heard down in the meadow, and fresh dandelions will spring from the old stocks where he plucked them last summer.[7]

Imagination drives dreams of fuller life. Flying under the banner of "productive imagination," it is central to German and English romanticism, a force beyond reception of impressions or employment of Kantian categories like causality. The lesson transcendentalists and romantic poets take from Kant, in addition to his highlighting productive imagination, is his confession of philosophy's almost tragic limitations:

> Human reason has this peculiar fate that in one species of its knowledge it is burdened by questions which ... it not able to ignore, but which, as transcending all its powers, it is also not able to answer.[8]

---

[7] *Correspondence*, pp. 101–2.
[8] Kant, *Critique of Pure Reason*, Norman Kemp Smith (trans.) (New York: St. Martin's, 1965), a.vii. The role of imagination in romantic poetry is linked to Kant, but only suggestively, partly because Kant is so obscure. In the *Critique of Pure Reason* we learn that imagination is "a blind though indispensible function of the soul, without which we would have no cognition at all, but of which we are seldom even conscious" (B edition 103). His theory of the sublime is no doubt a better place to turn.

In Thoreau's hands, imaginative reverie opens a place beyond self-pitying grief, a place of *impersonal* mourning. This mourning is impersonal in that it shuns personal self-pity or selfish complaint—one's *own* person is not especially singled out for pain. Waldo's loss is of a piece with larger cycles of loss. It does not single out Thoreau. Ice departs in spring thaw, mists die with sunrise, leaves expire as winter paints them brown. Waldo's loss is "the most natural event that could happen."

And perhaps the perfection of certain aesthetic moments fully retire the "I" and "thou," retire the personal "life-and-death" we otherwise take to be framing features of human existence. I'm thinking of Thoreau later on adverting to a musical "strain" that, as he hears it, opens a prospect in which the "… field of my life becomes a boundless plain, glorious to tread, with no death nor disappointment at the end of it." And "In the light of this strain there is no thou nor I."[9] But Thoreau writes this *Journal* entry not in the immediate aftermath of catastrophe but fifteen years later.

Thoreau's reverie of Waldo dying "as the mist rises from the brook" soon to be dispersed by sunlight proceeds to cast every natural event as perfect—it is as it must be and will not be wished otherwise. "I was not startled to hear that he was dead; it seemed the most natural event that could happen. His fine organization demanded it, and nature gently yielded its request." As in great art or romantic love, each detail is as it must be, and is totally affirmed. The organization is fine. Within the passing of this reverie, each detail demands its place in the wondrous whole. And if the focus of our attraction must fall out of view, that's OK too. Waldo disperses in slanting light.

4.

Reverie displaces devastation. It realigns perception—in this case, around the figure of a child. This is Thoreau abandoning despair, resentment, rage, or numbing indifference. This is heroic the way great poetry is heroic, showing courage, imagination, and skill in precarious circumstance. A heroic blindness takes hold (like a hero's refusal to feel pain). Love's blindness is heroic. It refuses to take pain as a personal affront, and buries skulking or fiendish nihilism. Love's blindness lets the world go round.

In writing or living for love of the world we deflate customary self-importance. We fail to see the world as our personal adversary or personal opportunity. In seeing our smallness in the scheme of things, as we do under

---

[9] *Journal*, January 15, 1857, p. 222; see p. 73, above. John and Waldo died in 1842. The loss of both "thou" and "I" marks what Cameron calls the "impersonal" in Thoreau.

the shock of death, we are dropped down a peg. We "get out of the way," and grant to things their inestimable worth. They now can take on new color, new garments. In reverie, sparkling details of the world arrive unbidden, not as deserved or earned. The presumption that freedom from suffering or happiness is our special right triggers self-pity and resentment when happiness vanishes.

If we drop a *right* to happiness however—and drop the allied presumption of self-importance—then loss can take on quite a different meaning. It is freed from the sense that one has been singled out. Loss as a personal affront is replaced by a vision of impersonal loss-and-recovery in cyclical motion. Such cycles have a sublime allure and impersonal serenity. Personal score keeping of undeserved pain or well-deserved pleasure is nowhere to be found. The world's shining particulars enter and leave our purview as they must, in glorious disregard of our desires. All inclination to claim *rights* to happiness, fulfilled or violated, disappears. Falling in love with the world once more, we cherish things in a mood of pure attention that sets questions of self-importance and justice aside. Cavell allows that to fall in love with the world is a permissible form of blindness.[10]

Stripped of any claim to exemption from unhappiness, Thoreau's wanderings are again open to take in the multitude of things worthy of praise and affirmation, the plentitude of existence in loss and recovery. Reverie at this panorama is Thoreau's rebirth from rubble. If the response to catastrophe is elegiac, that's uplifting—only slightly tinged with mourning or melancholy. If it's lament, it's muted. A wonderfully embraceable world is the place of his being.

5.

Some two decades later, toward the end of his life in his essay "Walking," Thoreau again invokes the image of a "child of the mist." Now the occasion is not grief or loss. It's a celebration of a child's happy play in the world, before knowledge sets in to deflate innocence and claim precedence as the most worthy way of being in the world. We are *not* exhorted to pass through the world as an elder who has seen and knows everything. We are exhorted to pass through the world, *as a child*: "Live free, child of the mist—and with

---

[10] See Stanley Cavell, *The Claim of Reason: Wittgenstein, Skepticism, Morality, and Tragedy* (Oxford: Oxford University Press, 1979), p. 431. And see Furtak, "Skepticism and Perceptual Faith: Henry David Thoreau and Stanley Cavell on Seeing and Believing," *Transactions of the Charles S. Peirce Society*, 43 (3) (2007): 542–61.

respect to knowledge we are all children of the mist."[11] Here, being a 'child of the mist' is not a device deflecting the aftereffects of trauma. Here the image serves as a reminder of the insufficiency of knowledge. "Mere knowing," observational knowing, falls painfully short as a guide to death-and-life, to sorrow-and-delight. Being a 'child of the mist' is to be in the world in a mode of unknowing—full of sympathy, communion, and innocent wonder. If Thoreau is playful in his wanders and befitting reveries, he is acknowledging that we are as children when it comes to knowledge and that there is much to be said for an exuberant attunement to the world of the sort we can recognize in the unguarded delight of a child running and shouting in a meadow.

Roughly a decade after his letter to Lucy Brown, but years before he wrote "Walking," he speaks, in *Walden* of the "fabulous landscape of my infant dreams." Fabulous landscape is a fabled land, a mode of being in a story land that is more than a story, and that he shares in reverie:

> When I was four years old, as I well remember, I was brought from Boston to this my native town, through these very woods and this field to the pond ... And now tonight my flute has waked the echoes over that very water. The pines still stand here older than I ... a new growth is rising all around, preparing another aspect for new infant eyes. Almost the same johnswort springs from the same perennial root in this pasture, and even I have at length helped to clothe that fabulous landscape of my infant dreams.[12]

Reverie brings us to co-constructed, inter-animated space: the spring shoots of johnswort invite a reverie and the infant in reverie clothes them as marvels. The inviting open hand meets the hand offering vestments. The world is not there as a lump, targeted by hyperactive imagination. In the flow of our being in the world, a companionable partnership reigns. I am not in the world solo and the world is not solo impinging on me. Reverie affords a couples' dance or duet. The child's smile dances with mine; I dance with it. Direction of fit becomes immaterial and drops away.

The motif of a child of the mist becomes a sustaining talisman over the years. Matters of life-and-death, joy-and-affliction, heaven-and-earth, are only seen dappled, innocently through mist. None of us is better placed than Waldo or the young Thoreau. We come and go quite beyond knowledge, like the ephemeral song of a lark.

---

[11] "Walking," p. 250 [para 73].
[12] *Walden*, "The Beanfield," p. 151 [para 2].

6.

When it comes of age, Nietzsche's child laughs by the mist of the sea. We become a child—after being camel, then lion.[13] We are born as apprentices, carrying heavy burdens, dull but dutiful as a camel. Then, ideally, with the brio of a lion we break away from those burdens roaring. Finally we might become a child, all innocence, creativity, and play by the sea. The breakers come and go in advance and retreat with the tide. Jesus has us become as little children, innocent, unknowing, open to creative perception and reverie. Kierkegaard says that the abandonment of Knowledge, "Socratic ignorance … is maturity; is intellectually what rebirth is ethically and religiously; is what it is to be a child again."[14] Thoreau becomes a child, in reverie at Spaulding's Farm. Nietzsche, Jesus, and Thoreau beckon us back to childhood—or is it forward? They speak not of biological age, but a way of being open to a timeless back-and-ahead, like the mists over tides. "I too cherish vague & misty forms—vaguest when the cloud at which I gaze is dissipated quite & nought but the skyey depths are seen."[15]

I retrieve dreams that grow into new instants of experience. Reverie retrieves vaulting prospects of life-and-death. It lets us pass through the gateway Thoreau calls "Sympathy with Intelligence." At one point Thoreau writes, "Our truest life is when we are in dreams awake."[16] Even as he died he sparkled with a child's humor and wonder. He confided to a friend, who asked if he had thoughts of an afterlife, that he had no need of a world to come. He was in fruitful communion with the present world, and that was enough. He will, he tells his friend, take "one world at a time." Yet within this single bounteous world, he could see more than one thing at once.

Thoreau would gaze with John at the edge of the Merrimack and see sky on the river's surface or see sky on the quiet muddy bottom. The gossamer surface held cloud and tree while transparent to bottom. As he put it, the eye has more than one intention, seeing heavens and muddy bottoms at once, just as I might be adult and child at once.[17] I'm younger than I was at thirty wrestling career and family. Now, I can gather myself again by sleek rivers. Age is anomalous. When are we young? Why privilege public records? When Henry and John kneel by the waters, they see bottom and sky. I can fall into reverie remembering the fall of a pine shattering the banks of the Charles

---

[13] Friedrich Nietzsche. *Thus Spoke Zarathustra*, Graham Parkes (trans.) (Oxford: Oxford University Press, 2005): "Of the Three Transformations," p. 24.
[14] 1849 journal entry: JP, # 3567 (vol. 3, p. 637) / Pap. X-1 A 679.
[15] *Journal*, November 9, 1851, p. 99.
[16] *Week*, p. 297.
[17] *Week*, p. 48.

on a windless afternoon.[18] I can't resist quoting Bronson Alcott on Thoreau, lyric, and mist: "Thoreau is a walking Muse ... he comes amidst mists and exhalations, his locks dripping with more moisture in the sonorous rains of an ever-lyric day."[19]

7.

I wonder how to be with this figure of reverie, a child of the mist. I don't want to do anything to it—pigeonhole it, or take it apart. I want to tarry with it, let its unassertive presence shadow me; or perhaps I will let myself shadow it. Is that how an image, a picture, a reverie teaches? If we're captive, that's good. What is it to be captive in a way that releases rather than binds us?

Letting myself be shadowed by a mist's imponderables, and sharing the experience of being shadowed, is an essential part of my learning in literature, song, or philosophy. To be shadowed by imponderables is not sensing a limit, a stop sign, "Clarity ends here, no admittance!" Nor is it the dismal imperative, "Whereof one cannot speak, thereof one must be silent!"[20] To abide with reverie as "a child of the mist" is not to shun clarity but to let a door open, to let eyes gaze through a shadowed glass to see more than before.

Should a professor, mother, friend, or pastor become as a child, dwell in mist, and invite others to share its dappled light? What of the inevitable burn off? In the course of things, mist *will* burn off. But that needn't sidetrack tarrying with imponderables. To tarry is to be with—undistracted by worries of darkness down the road. Of course, a mist's partial veil may show only the banal—who knows? To tarry is to shadow the imponderables, not to master or disperse them, or to bank on the extraordinary.

8.

At this present, a juncture of two eternities, we are "children of the mist," happy with wondrous imponderables. Too bright a light will wash out the mystery of a face. You might think that in reverie we become shades,

---

[18] With apologies, ammending Dylan Thomas' *Fern Hill*: "When I was young and easy under the apple boughs, time held me green, *undying* ... and I sang through the *mist* like the sea."

[19] *The Journals of Bronson Alcott*, Odell Shepard (ed.) (New York: Little, Brown, 1938), pp. 193–4.

[20] Final sentence, Wittgenstein's *Tractatus Logicus Philosophicus* (London: Routledge, 1974).

insubstantial as mist, or as diaphanous as angels. But Thoreau has us full-bodied children.

Thoreau's walk by Spaulding's Farm, related in the last pages of "Walking," lets the house "appear dimly still as through a mist." Seeing through the mist reveals something through soft focus that would be lost using a harsh, sharp focus. What he finds looking up through the meadows comes out in reverie: "trees gradually come out of the mist—life looks like a dream—you are prepared to see visions."[21] As we know, he espies a "Great Hall" hovering among the pines on the ridge. It seems to overlay Spaulding's simple barn. He hears laughter and song from within. This is a place of playful gods.

We see this wonder with him, provided only that we're friendly with his readiness for the fabulous—his reverie. Then we are privy to wonders, the Farm's Hall, divinities within. We needn't deny others who don't see this, nor have we made up something artificial to paint over the Farm. I see what others see, yet my eye has a 'second intention.'[22] I see the river bottom and also the sky laid over that bottom; or see the barn, and also the Great Hall—as if superimposed on it. Neither intention of the eye—Great Hall or simple barn—refutes the other.

Looking at the bottom in doubled concentration we see the sky. Or we look up, away from the bottom, and see the sky. This single intention of the eye diminishes wonder for we then see the sky at the expense of the bottom. Heads raised, eyes drift over the pines, and the river is lost. But with a second intention, vision is doubled. We have sky and pine tops and river-bottom, simultaneously, each overlaying the other.

Thoreau wants sky and muddy bottom united in the medium of the river. He wants life to overlay death, and death to overlay life, age to overlay childhood, and innocent wonder to overlay age. To look at Spaulding's Farm blinkered in tunnel vision is easy enough. Seeing it with an eye's double intention is more difficult. Through reverie we have the Great Hall and the gods and Spaulding's Farm, each overlaying the other. Reverie lets this happen.

Thoreau pauses his row up the Merrimack to kneel by the river, John beside him. The reverie they share might be a scene taken from the book of Psalms. They "lay down by still waters." These are moving waters that they look into—but still enough to give them their faces, and the river bottom, a portion of earth, and the sky above reflected here below. Within these moving-still waters they see both clear sky *and* muddy bottom *and* themselves gazing as in prayer or contemplation or pure wonder. Unlike the reverie at Spaulding's Farm, they have separate access to river and its

---

[21] Cameron, p. 67.
[22] *Week*, p. 48.

muddy bottom apart from access to the open sky. They have merely to look up and away to be reminded that sky in its own right is distinct from the sky as reflection. Yet at Spaulding's Farm, there is no separate access to the gods or the holy apart from access to the meadow and trees of the Farm. When reverie affords Thoreau access to the gods, to their singing or laughter, that welcome access cannot be separated from the hill and its great trees—not in the way the sky *in* the Merrimack can be accessed as something distinct from the sky *above* the Merrimack. At Spaulding's, the gods are here-and-now on the crest of the hill or nowhere—here-and-now and inexpugnable as any paradise worth its salt would be.

Thoreau attains the land of reverie not by stripping down to disembodied spirit, or by rising from embodiment like angels to heaven.

> We notice that it required a separate intention of the eye, a more free and abstracted vision, to see the reflected trees and the sky, than to see the river bottom merely; and so are there manifold visions in the direction of every object, and even the most opaque reflect the heavens from their surface.[23]

This is an observation not unlike one reported by Lucretius:

> A puddle of water no deeper than a single finger-breadth, which lies between the stones on a paved street, offers us a view beneath the earth to a depth as vast as the high gaping mouth (hiatus) of heaven stretches above the earth, so that you seem to look down on the clouds and the heaven, and you discern bodies hidden in the sky beneath the earth, marvellously.[24]

Thoreau kneels by waters to see through their mist. In *Walden* he will peer into waters to find "... *fish in the sky, whose bottom is pebbly with stars.*"[25] He is vulnerable and full-bodied, neither ghost nor angel nor toiler. He tarries in dappled majesty absorbed in befitting reverie. As a "child of the mist" he is mystic, transcendentalist, and natural philosopher: *natural philosopher*, insofar as he philosophizes attentive to river, sky, and early birdsong; *transcendentalist* insofar as he lets poetic imagination clothe the meadows of his youth; and *mystic* as he lives beyond knowledge where he can join in a union of earth-and-heaven, death-and-life, self-and-nature. These meld in a flux where self-and-world become beside themselves, ecstatic.

Let me turn to a final instance of a union of heaven-and-earth, waters-and-sky, delivered this time in a page from *Walden*. It gives yet another

---

[23] *Week*, p. 48.
[24] *De Rerum Natura*, Frank O. Copley (trans.) (New York: W. W. Norton, 2011), Bk 4, p. 92. I thank Andrew Brown here.
[25] *Walden*, "Where I lived," p. 96 [final para].

instance of a child-like, dream-like reverie delivering wondrous access to the blessings of a living world.

9.

In Thoreau's magical voice, a child-like, dream-like reverie can be simultaneously delightful, funny, quirky, and wise—and full of revelatory transformations enacted in the very telling of the reverie. The one I have in mind begins simply and famously enough with a very quotable line: *"Time is but the stream I go a-fishing in."*[26] The philosophical wisdom is this—that to be alive as temporal creatures is not just to face death, as Heidegger would have it. More importantly, it's to find the time of our lives in the present (and deathless) delights of fishing. And fishing for *what*, pray tell?

Thoreau's delightful and quotable *aperçu* intimates the philosophical question to which he provides a simple answer. "What is time?" becomes "*What do you do with your time?*" He blurts out, half-playfully, an answer that *seems* to take us well out of philosophy: "I fish!" And we overhear an implicit injunction: "*Go and do likewise!*"

If we think that's the start and finish of this short *Walden* reverie, we quickly learn otherwise. The lyric has just begun. The words that immediately follow *"Time is but the stream I go a-fishing in,"* effect a subtle change. With no preparation Thoreau adds, "*I drink at it.*" Now we see that the sweep of time is for *fishing and drinking*, primal delights and blessings. Then our writer adds another down-to-earth fact: "*but while I drink I see the sandy bottom and detect how shallow it is.*" We have hardly begun to see, or detect, the beckoning depths of the present flow of things.

Now Thoreau seems to raise another metaphysical question: "*What is eternity?*" He notes that the stream's "*thin current slides away, but eternity remains.*" Time passes but eternity—the eternal present—remains. We drink and fish in time *and* eternity. Then Thoreau challenges himself: "*I would drink deeper.*" This disguises an injunction: *Don't be satisfied with life or understanding as you now have them: dig deeper.*

We can go back to the top to refresh our sense of the flow of this reverie: "Time is but the stream I go a-fishing in. I drink at it; but while I drink I see the sandy bottom and detect how shallow it is. Its thin current slides away, but eternity remains. I would drink deeper." And then we're carried further: "I would drink deeper; fish in the sky, whose bottom is pebbly with stars."[27]

[26] Ibid.
[27] Ibid.

The levels of allure are artfully unfurled: the allure of time and eternity, of fishing and drinking, of a sandy bottom "pebbly with stars." These strings of images, when carefully unfurled, have a certain poetic necessity. Reverie can be revelation—of reality. Then there's the mystery of having the stars above seen also below, here at the stream's shallow bottom. But the bottom can't be *that* shallow if it cradles the infinite depth of the heavens. And the art of this unfurling lingers in the ambiguity of the phrase, *"fish in the sky."* These four words say *"Look! There are fish in the sky!"*—blurted out as I look down into the stream. But those simple words also call me to action: *"Come! Let's fish in the starry skies!"* Great minds, and great writing, tell us two things at once—effortlessly—as it magically conjoins them.

Then without losing a beat, Thoreau interrupts. He gives us what at first sounds like nonsense: *"I cannot count one. I know not the first letter of the alphabet."* To my ear, this is what happens: we're struck by the wonder of fish in the sky and by the wonder of actively fishing among stars glittering on a pebbly bottom. Dumfounded in wonder, we can only utter a child-like gasp. We'll discover that we *"can't count even one"* star or fish or pebble. The simple reason is that we are overwhelmed by a multitude. Where to begin? Where would the counting end? The project of *counting* is just out of the question. But the *non sequitur* goes deeper.

"*I cannot count one*" marks an end of counting in this instance, and brings out a wider question—whether the very *capacity* to count has disappeared. In radical wonder or dumbfoundedness, I lose my one-two-threes—and not just in the sense of losing where to begin. In childhood, before I *knew* my one-two-threes, the starry heavens, fish, and pebbly bottoms threw me into wonder or awe utterly relieved of any imperative to assign numbers to everything, and to arrange things neatly in alphabetical order.

There could be a hint of regret or *angst* in his cry, "*I cannot count one.*" In any case, he quickly adds, *"I know not the first letter of the alphabet."* So he's cast into a world that predates the wisdom of numbers and letters. He adds wistfully, *"I have always been regretting that I was not as wise as the day I was born."* Exactly how early did his regretting begin? Be that as it may, the day he was born he possessed the wisdom of wonder—though he had not yet learned to count, read, or arrange alphabetically.

Getting beyond or before counting and labeling is not an *absolute* desideratum for Thoreau. It's not first in a rank ordering of things to cherish, as though wonder is first in importance and counting plants and knowing their Latin names is second. No such all-purpose ranking of varieties of experience, of the wildness and often anomalous disorder of experience, can be imposed. Thoreau promotes living in the present, and the present *at this moment* rewards him with otherwise overlooked plenitude beyond ranking, numbers, or names. The need to count and spell will kick in on its own when the time comes. We can count on that.

The genius of "E=MC²" is concision. Concision accompanies Thoreau's quirky, profound, and delightful wisdom. Having spent time chopping and sorting, it's good to hear his passage straight through, brought together in its concise, sweeping, and native rhythms.

> Time is but the stream I go a-fishing in. I drink at it; but while I drink I see the sandy bottom and detect how shallow it is. Its thin current slides away, but eternity remains. I would drink deeper; fish in the sky, whose bottom is pebbly with stars. I cannot count one. I know not the first letter of the alphabet. I have always been regretting that I was not as wise as the day I was born.[28]

10.

Thoreau links youth to good cheer, delight, and fancy attainable at any age. In his *Journal* October 1857, he reflects,

> This old man's cheeriness was worth a thousand of the church's sacraments and momento mori's. It was better than a prayerful mood. It proves [that] to be [in] old age [is] as tolerable, as happy, as infancy.[29]

Such joy only encourages happy imagining, resonating with sounds floating through mist at water's edge. Dreaming frogs snore, and are lifted joyfully in their dreams. The Old English etymology of "dream" links it to joy and ecstasy. Frogs do not just have "images" or "image-narrations" while asleep; they have befitting reveries. "The sound of the dreaming frogs prevails over the others."[30]

> The frog had eyed the heavens from his marsh, until his mind was filled with visions, & he saw more than belongs to this fenny earth—He mistrusted that he was become a dreamer & visionary—leaping across the swamp to his fellow what was his joy & consolation to find that he too had seen the same sights in the heavens—he too had dreamed the same dreams.
>
> From nature we turn astonished to this *near* but supernatural fact.[31]

---

[28] Ibid.
[29] *Journal*, October 20, 1857, p. 110.
[30] *Journal*, June 13, 1851, p. 253. As remarked above (Ch. 5, note 32) the old English etymology of "dream" links it to joy and ecstasy. Frogs do not just have image-narrations while asleep; they have befitting reveries.
[31] *Journal*, May 21, 1851, pp. 207–8.

What astonishes us as supernatural is that we can access realms beyond the merely routine and factual. We can marvel, as Thoreau has it, at the wonder that this world exists at all, and we in it. He can confess that *"... the existence of man in nature is the divinest and most startling of all facts."*[32] This is a "near"—that is, *immediate*—access to plenitude beyond measure. Then there is this marvelously affirmative witness:

> In youth before I lost any of my senses, I can remember that I was all alive and inhabited my body with inexpressible satisfaction, both its weariness and its refreshment were sweet to me. This earth was the most glorious and musical instrument, and I was the audience to its strains.[33]

The Book of James invokes a mist in a despairing register: *What is your life? For you are a mist that appears for a little while and then vanishes* (James 4:13–14). It is Thoreau's genius to make our communion with mist a moment of joy.

---

[32] Ibid. (my emphasis).
[33] *Journal*, July 16, 1851, p. 306. See Arsić, "What Music Shall we Have?"

9

Deaths and Rebirths

I saw an old bone in the woods covered with lichens, which looked like the bone of an old settler, which yet some little animal had recently gnawed, ... so indefatigable is Nature to strip the flesh from bones and return it to dust again.
—*Journal*, November 11, 1850

Every part of nature teaches that the passing away of one life is the making room for another.
—*Journal*, October 24, 1837[1]

Tragic undercurrents course through Thoreau's writing, especially in some of his lesser-read works, and prominently in his *Journal*. "If it is not a tragical life we live, then I know not what to call it," he writes.[2] Also from the *Journal*: "What a pity if the part of Hamlet be left out."[3] And this: "The whole of life is seen by some through this darker medium,—partakes of the tragic,—and its bright and splendid lights become thus lurid."[4] And finally, "It is the ... wild thinking in Hamlet—in the *Iliad*—and in all the scriptures and mythologies that delights us."[5]

Gloom is held at arm's length in his first book, *A Week on the Concord*, written as a memorial to his older brother who had died a tortured death in Henry's arms. A tragic strain also surfaces in a description, in *Cape Cod*, of approaching a decomposed corpse, a body we take to be Margaret Fuller's.[6] We find tragic pathos in his defense of the anti-slavery militant, John Brown.[7] Given these persistent tragic undertows, Thoreau's affirmations and avoidance of pessimism or depression attain a high pitch of accomplishment. They also give new angles on the theme of the wild. As we've seen in these excursions, Thoreau's wild is pluriform, and one of its dimensions relates to tragedy and to what Nietzsche calls the Dionysian.

---

[1] Epigraphs: *Journal*, November 11, 1850, p. 93; October 24, 1837, p. 3.
[2] *Week*, "Sunday" p. 67.
[3] *Journal*, March 21, 1840, p. 129.
[4] *Journal*, September 1, 1852, p. 335.
[5] *Journal*, November 16, 1850, p. 97.
[6] *Cape Cod*, pp. 123f.
[7] *Essays*, "A Plea for Captain John Brown" and "The Last Days of John Brown."

Nietzsche claims in *The Birth of Tragedy* that only art makes life sufferable. Thoreau writes to transmute tragedy as raw suffering into something we can affirm. Art opens from afflictions into the sublime and the sacred.[8] Just as Emerson should be read with Kant and Nietzsche, so Thoreau should be read with his forebears, say Aurelius or Socrates, and alongside his continental contemporaries, Kierkegaard or Nietzsche.

1.

In the first instance, tragedy is not theatrical performance or a literary genre, still less a philosophical image of the human condition. It is undergoing terrible suffering. The affliction of a person or persons spreads out in waves to afflict others who witness. Tragedy on stage feeds on our knowledge of off-stage tragedy. It gives us a culturally shared scenario of life at the limit. It is suffered viscerally, pressing the senses to the point of radical incapacity. We are struck dumb, blinded, even as the world impinges with intensity so explosive that it verges on blackout, a loss of self and world. We become less than ourselves, reduced to the pain of our affliction.

Oedipus rips out his eyes because he cannot bear what he has seen and done, but it is also true that there is no more left to see, given pain's saturation of his bodily consciousness. His world is suffering, and he doesn't need eyes to know that. He remains the intense living site of pain's demonic power even while suffering wipes out any other world. Yet Oedipus, Hamlet, or Lear are not stripped of speech, not utterly, mad though that speech may be. Here, tragic suffering merges with eloquent lament. Their expressive powers are resistance to the denaturing force of affliction. Through eloquence we hear dignity played out in circumstances that undermine it. "The need for dignity arises", Fred Beiser writes, "when tragic circumstances put a strain on our human nature, on the normal human constitution ... Dignity indeed arises because of the great weakness of human nature; but that weakness reveals itself only under tragic circumstances."[9]

---

[8] In "Silence and the Night" (unpublished), Lyman Mower presents Levinas' view: there is raw suffering from which there is no release, escape, or mitigation through art or any other means: it is pointless, useless, insufferable. Levinas calls this "the tragic." See *Time and The Other*, Richard A. Cohen (trans.) (Pittsburgh, PA: Duquesne University Press, 1990), p. 73.

[9] Frederick Beiser, "*Schiller as Philosopher*: A Reply to my Critics," *Inquiry*, 51 (1) (February 2008): 69. "The personal suffering or sacrifice involved in performing some moral actions is the result of tragic circumstances as much as the weakness of human nature. Gods, angels, or titans, which have much more robust constitutions, could do all their duties with grace simply because they are never prone to suffering."

Tragic dignity is not pessimistic or defeatist. To earn it is to defeat the so-called wisdom of Silenus: *better to die early, best never to have been born.*[10] Whatever tragedy Oedipus or Hamlet endures, and whatever tragic circumstance Thoreau endures, a measure of dignity supervenes. Thoreau comes close to embracing the *inversion* of Silenus, the wisdom of Achilles: *better to live long, but best never to die.*[11] The qualification is that Thoreau thinks that endless life, "never to die," is nowhere to be found in nature, and so, an impossible and irreverent aspiration. It is irreverent and vainglorious to place persons apart from creation or nature. Thoreau's wisdom is to live fully in the present knowing death will come in its season; it is to be celebrated as fully as life.

As Nietzsche has it, tragic drama has roots in Dionysian rites of suffering and sacrifice. Sacrifice forestalls annihilation by giving it an anticipatory, ceremonial voice. Rituals celebrate cycles of death and overlapping cycles of rebirth. Participants enact lives and deaths over and again, accompanied by music, dance, and intoxication. Dionysus is destroyed, then reborn. Celebrants reenact cruelty and its metamorphosis in ceremonial rebirth. A witness to tragic drama, or participant in Dionysian festivals, undergoes ceremonial suffering and survives.

Through the eloquence of words and taking steps, Thoreau lives out the ephemerality of pain and its transformations: death yields to life and life yields to death. He lives through a hell as John died, and through a hell before the coming war, yet in a swamp outside Concord he smells paradise in a lily.[12] Hell yields to a promise of heaven; death foretells life. He encounters Dionysian dismemberment—Margaret Fuller's fate. Thoreau was sent to find her body, yet he brings wonder and majesty to that desolate site.[13] If affliction is inescapable, there is also metamorphosis. It doesn't attain unmitigated dominance.[14]

In early tragic theater, the hero emerges suffering in eloquent resistance. But the Dionysian wildness at the archaic heart of tragic drama is wiped out, as Nietzsche has it, with the triumph of rationality, ascetic intellectualism, and a rage for order. Greek Platonism (or as he would call it, Socratic religiousness) is a stance that in promising that "the good man cannot be harmed" and promising immortality denies affliction and death. But the price is to deny Dionysian life. Wildness is a vital counterforce to orderly

---

[10] Nietzsche, *The Birth of Tragedy from the Spirit of Music*, Douglas Smith (ed. and trans.) (Oxford: Oxford University Press, 2000), p. 27 (henceforth, *Birth*).
[11] *Birth*, p. 28.
[12] See "Slavery," p. 345.
[13] *Journal*, October 31, 1850, p. 80; *Cape Cod*, pp. 123f.
[14] On tragic moments that are beyond redemption, see note 7 above.

Apollonian impulses. Thoreau and Nietzsche disavow detached theoretical on looking, a stance that sunders persons from immersion in the lively disorders of the senses and of mobile embodied life.

Dionysian undercurrents reflect Thoreau's affirmation of a *many-faceted* wildness. In a bio-centric view of life there is wildness in competition among trees and insects, salmon and hawks. There is the alien, even horrific wild that Thoreau finds atop Mt. Ktaadn and the lethal wild that takes Margaret Fuller, Emerson's young son, and John Thoreau. Then there is the woodland or forest wild celebrated by present day environmentalists. The banner "In wildness is the preservation of the world" comes from "Walking":

> The West of which I speak is but another name for the Wild, and what I have been preparing to say is, that in Wildness is the preservation of the World. Every tree sends its fibers forth in search of the Wild. The cities import it at any price. Men plow and sail for it. From the forest and wilderness come the tonics and barks which brace mankind.[15]

Here, the wild is something cities import and tree roots seek. And parenthetically, Thoreau advocates the wild without advocating westward expansion of the nation. "Civil Disobedience" protests western expansion, and walking occurs in and around Concord. It is an attempt to get nearer to *here*—not nearer to the far-off Rockies or the Pacific.

In *Walden*, Thoreau cites the Dionysian in contrast to the measured allure of the Apollonian:

> [I] find an instinct toward a higher … life and another toward a primitive rank and savage one, and I reverence them both. I love the wild not less than the good.[16]

The Dionysian is sensed in Thoreau's desire to devour a woodchuck in his path—in his joy in tasting fermented and frozen wild apples—in his rebellion against Apollonian stasis in business-as-usual Concord—in tracking cycles of death and rebirth in plants and all life—in his affinity for the wildness of John Brown (who, on Thoreau's rendering, dies and is reborn).[17] It is present in the sense of impending apocalyptic destruction, laid out at the biblical close of his essay "Wild Apples", and less catastrophically in his thoughts on

---

[15] "Walking," p. 239 [para 37].
[16] *Walden*, 'Higher Laws," p. 202 [para 1]. We are given a wildly comic picture—as if Thoreau's devouring a woodchuck would be ingesting wildness itself, making one *more* wild. Eating might also *tame* or *subdue* it. Further on in "Higher Laws," the wild seems in retreat. Thoreau plays out both instincts, the Dionysian and the Apollonian. This mirrors Nietzsche, who has tragic drama require the reign of *both* divinities.
[17] See "The Last Days of John Brown," *Essays*, and Ch. 11, below.

music: "there is something in a strain of music [which] reminds me of the cries emitted by wild beasts".[18] The Dionysian is found in "the wild thinking in Hamlet ... that delights us".[19] In *A Week on the Concord* Thoreau alludes to archaic Corybantic rites enacting deaths and rebirths.[20] Only half tongue-in-cheek, in "Walking," he says he might prefer that life be "a divine tragedy" rather than "this trivial comedy or farce."[21] His treasured fields become "a Dismal Swamp."[22]

The tragic feeds the outrage of his political essays and burns elsewhere. In *A Week on the Concord* there is a wild story quite unexpectedly inserted. Hannah Duston escapes in 1697 down the Merrimack after her capture in an Indian raid. Her still-nursing child is ripped from her arms and savagely killed. Later she kills and scalps her captors (and their children) in their sleep, bringing her bloody trophies downstream by canoe. This is not Apollonian orderliness, Christian Paradise, or the New World "City on a Hill."[23]

Plato says philosophy is a rehearsal for death.[24] Henry took John Thoreau's death as an occasion for his own rehearsal. As we know, he took on John's dying symptoms.[25] *A Week* became a rehearsal of death in the form of eulogy. Thoreau had translated for *The Dial* violence in Aeschylus and Homer. He would later be spiritually eviscerated high on Mt. Ktaadn.[26] Through the mist he sees the workshop of indifferent Gods; his spirit flies outward through a crack between his ribs.

Death's insistence calls us to moods that are counter to death: joy and exaltation at being alive among others. Philosophy can carry a recuperating sense of aliveness. It can rebound from grief or lamentation to affirmations of a wonder-saturated world. Thoreau presents a wry and exuberant resistance to grief lived out in walking, moving up river, skating, tasting fermented cold apples, writing through and over all of these. His walk into

---

[18] "Wild Apples," *Essays*, p. 312; "Walking," *Essays*, p. 168.
[19] "Walking," p. 166; also *Journal*, November 16, 1850, p. 97.
[20] *Week*, p. 337. The Corybantes were children of Apollo and Thalia (the rustic muse of comedy). Revelers enacted deaths and rebirths through non-linguistic vehicles not unlike the walking, tasting, beholding, and climbing that we find in Thoreau.
[21] "Walking," p. 173.
[22] Ibid. p. 164.
[23] For Duston's escape as a myth of American Fall from Innocence, see Linck C. Johnson's *Thoreau's Complex Weave: The Writing of A Week on the Concord and Merrimack Rivers* (University of Virginia Press, 1986), Ch. 4, pp. 122–62. John Winthrop's 1630 sermon warned that the world was watching their holy experiment, citing Matthew 5:14: "You are the light of the world. A city that is set on a hill ..."
[24] *Phaedo*, 64a–c.
[25] See Wai Chee Dimock on the "symbiosis" between brothers: "Global Civil Society: Thoreau on Three Continents," in *Through Other Continents* (Princeton, NJ: Princeton University Press, 2006), Ch. 1.
[26] "Ktaadn," pp. 69–71.

life reanimates limbs over land and pencil over his *Journal* in a crescendo acknowledging the musical pulse of life and death.

Searching for Fuller, Thoreau returned to Concord having found nothing but scraps of clothing. Bones in the sand, never precisely defined as hers, were still on his mind days later when he reports a "lurid" " blood-stained" sky. He also called that sunset "glorious."[27] Writing a monument to Fuller's majesty was an imaginative achievement.

A Week on the Concord is a liturgical week, starting on Saturday, the day Christ enters the underworld to rescue the dead.[28] Holy Saturday would bring John up from the dead. He would be more than a corpse or a body in death's spasm. Later, Henry assisted in creating a shallow depression or pond near John's burial site that would fill and become swampy, allowing John's remains to ravel back into natural life.[29]

2.

A glimpse of heaven is occasion for deep joy at just being alive. It is a renewable redemption from desperation. Thoreau's words of gratitude and attentive praise, his hymning love of the world, leave desolate circumstance aside—nearly aside—on the best days and when possible.[30] There's no denying his lively delight as he glides across a frozen pond in pursuit of a scampering fox. His exuberance finds him in heaven. We are redeemed from dark hours by joining his gliding pursuit. This joy does not spring from the luck of a cheerful disposition. He relishes his capacity to spot that fox, and glide with it as it curves through snow. At a different level of perception and response is his redemption of Margaret Fuller.

---

[27] "A glorious lurid sunset tonight, accompanied with many somber clouds ... Pale saffron skies with faint fishes of rosy clouds dissolving in them. A bloodstained sky." *Journal*, undated, 1850, p. 51.

[28] Holy Saturday commemorates the Harrowing of Hades, Christ's descent into Hell to raise those deserving better. Clark West suggests this possibility.

[29] See Arsić *Bird Relics*, pp. 385–7, and Thoreau, *Journal*, October 10, 1860, p. 109.

[30] "Falling in love with the world" is a "blindness" that is permissible in the face of dismal skepticism. See Stanley Cavell, *The Claim of Reason* (Oxford: Oxford University Press, 1979), p. 431. See also "Skepticism and Perceptual Faith: Henry David Thoreau and Stanley Cavell on Seeing and Believing," Rick Anthony Furtak, *Transactions of the Charles S. Peirce Society*, 43 (3) (2007): 542–61, and my "Stanley Cavell as Religious Continental Thinker," *Lost Intimacy in Western Thought: Personal Philosophy from Thoreau to Cavell* (New York: Continuum, 2009). For his "redemptive writing" and "a theology of reading" see William Day, "A Soteriology of Reading: Cavell's Excerpts from Memory," *Stanley Cavell: Philosophy, Literature and Criticism*, James Loxley and Andrew Taylor (eds) (Manchester: Manchester University Press, 2011), pp. 76–91.

A distant splinter marks the place he hopes holds Fuller's bones. This must be a place of grief. Yet as Thoreau approaches, as we know, he sees the inconsiderable stick become a ship's spar; and then become a rugged cairn, a monument holding the place of her reign. "That dead body had taken possession of the shore, and reigned over it as no living one could, in the name of a certain majesty that belonged to it."[31] This passage is imported from Thoreau's *Journal* (October 31, 1850), three months after he returned from Fire Island to Concord. On the beach he found spectators, scavengers, and those looking for friends or relatives. He learned of a body given a shallow burial five miles up the beach, marked by a stick. Thoreau wrote to Charles Sumner that there was such decomposition that his "poor knowledge of anatomy" left him not knowing if it were male or female.[32]

A spar displaces a stick, and a cairn displaces a spar. The wide sweep of the shore displaces any offense the remains might have held. This is metamorphosis in an anomalous world that doesn't hold still. The place of Fuller's majesty, as we know, becomes the place of her communion with endless surf, a rapport that leaves him out.

> [The] bones were alone with the beach and the sea, whose hollow roar seemed to address them ... as if there were an understanding between them and the ocean which necessarily left me out.[33]

Kierkegaard calls this sort of metamorphosis the transfiguration of experience: "All poetry is life's glorification (i.e. transfiguration) through its clarification (through being clarified, illuminated, 'unfolded', etc.)."[34]

Poetry and philosophy can deflect the cruelest of realities without becoming only illicit cover-up or avoidance. Deflection can be a healthy defense—say as we deflect a blow to the head. Thoreau's art deflects or sublimates, not as denial of trouble or affliction, but as activity that transfigures it in the service of life.[35] He writes to redeem tragic conditions in his "Plea

---

[31] *Cape Cod*, p. 123.
[32] Lacking a body, no grave was ever erected for Fuller or her husband. Their son's body was found. I thank Steve Webb for detective work.
[33] *Cape Cod*, p. 123.
[34] Søren Kierkegaard, *Papers and Journals: A Selection*, Alastair Hannay (ed. and trans.) (Harmondsworth: Penguin Books, 1996), February 5, 1839, p. 101. He raises a toast: "To genius, beauty, art, and the whole glorious world: ... May it live a transfigured life here or hereafter." *Early Polemical Writings*, Julia Watkin (ed. and trans.) (Princeton, NJ: Princeton University Press, 1990), pp. 66–7. See Joseph Westfall, *The Kierkegaardian Author: Authorship and Performance in Kierkegaard's Literary and Dramatic Criticism* (Berlin: Walter de Gruyter, 2007), p. 51, pp. 216f.
[35] Ian Hacking reminds us that deflection is not always an unhealthy defense. See *Philosophy and Animal Life*. Cavell sees philosophical skepticism about other minds as a deflection of deep, and often tragic, loneliness and separation.

for John Brown"—we witness an achievement of immortality for Brown.³⁶ He works to redeem Brown or Fuller and his own partial burial in the hurt of John's death, the death of Emerson's young son, the hell of an approaching civil war. He passes on the sense that his transforming resistance can be ours.

Thoreau's wisdom is a counter-weight to the dismal unwisdom of Silenus, best never to have been born. In "Slavery in Massachusetts," he sees hell along his meadows and ponds in the increasingly violent clashes over slavery and the approach of war. Yet walking the edge of a malodorous swamp, a fresh-smelling lily appears, a promise of purity, hope, and heaven that for the moment offsets political stench. There is a moment of paradise in *A Week*. Having slept the night at the top of Mt. Greylock in the make-do comfort of a ramshackle coffin, he awakens to look across three states, surveying a heavenly expanse of good earth.³⁷ Returning to the Merrimack, old hell obtrudes. The now and again turbulent river that the brothers take upward toward New Hampshire's White Mountains is the river that carried a desperate Hannah Duston back down by canoe with scalps, to her burned out home in Haverhill, her slaughtered infant fresh in mind.³⁸ Thoreau links the upstream Merrimack journey toward life-giving waters to the downstream memory of a fall for humankind in the scene of Duston's capture, forced march, retaliatory violence, and downriver escape. Some months after the recapture of Anthony Burns in Boston in 1854, Thoreau laments that his usual sojourns in meadows are bringing no relief. "I cannot persuade myself", he writes, "that I do not live wholly within Hell."³⁹ Then a lily gives a glimpse of paradise.

3.

Thoreau elicits imagined yet not unreal moments of the best, "befitting reveries" that forestall inundations of the worst. He asks for an increase of fragrance in the land—delivered by lilies, for instance. In a mock-Kantian twist, he gives his categorical imperative: "So behave that the odor of your actions may enhance the general sweetness of the atmosphere ..."⁴⁰

---

[36] See Ch. 11, below.
[37] *Week*, pp. 186–8.
[38] Porte sees the upriver trip as a search for the source of rivers and "of all seas and mountains, indeed of primal daylight." *Consciousness and Culture: Emerson and Thoreau Reviewed* (New Haven: Yale University Press, 2004), p. 131. He does not notice the downstream memory as one of tragic fall or travel through hell.
[39] *Essays*, "Slavery," p. 345.
[40] Ibid. (my emphasis). This mimics Kant's moral imperative: "So act that the maxim of your action can be made universal law."

A phoebe darts against the fragrance of a meadow, moist earth slippers our feet. These saving perceptions can be turned over in hindsight and memory, playing a role in the refinement of perception, and in expanding our capacity to meet more fragrant worlds. Reflective memory is the space where Thoreau's *Journal* takes shape, where his perceptions mature in a fertile marinate of imagination and reverie. Perception is *Philia*, a companionable relation, a communion and "Sympathy with Intelligence." It is affinity and affiliation. At its most animated, perception is an ongoing duet of perceiver and perceived, achieved and at risk. In the case at hand it works over hell and its stench for a glimpse of heaven, even as a harvest moon glimpses us, feet in the mud.

Heaven can appear in the wild of a woodlot, the wild of fermented apples, nectar of the gods, or the wild of all life—from leaves and flowing sands to the life of rivers and soaring hawks.[41] To say these are creation and heaven-like is to picture them unfolding under something like the glance of a divinity—as if a fine creator were appreciating the passing wonder of her work, always underway. Or it is to picture them as centers of resonance, radiance, or revelation—the 'intelligences" with which he has sympathy.

At the more desolate reaches of the wild, Thoreau shows us eloquent resistance. The very sea that kills Fuller sings to her undying spirit. Perceptual metamorphoses deliver saving moments. Eyes see the spar and the cairn that memorialize Fuller; ears overhear her whispered communion with the sea. Writing raises the dead through effecting sensory transformations of an ever-changing range of prompts fit for a modulation toward lyric perception. This ongoing pattern of three-way exchanges among incoming sources, perceiving, and writing, never abandons the senses. Near the end of *A Week*, Thoreau declares, "We need pray for no higher heaven than the pure senses can furnish …"[42]

It's not only a sentimentalist who can believe that senses can furnish a heaven. Even the rigorous Kant succumbs. As his friend Wasianski reports:

> [Kant's] face radiated [a] kind of grave charm when he told with intense delight how he had once held a Swallow in his hands, peered into its eyes, and felt as though he had looked into heaven.[43]

In a strange parallel, Thoreau imagines himself looking through the eye of a bittern, a bird contemplating water, who "may have wrested the whole of

---

[41] Thoreau finds that even flowing sand is alive—a complex organism. See *Walden*, "Spring," pp. 295f. [para 7, 8].

[42] *Week*, p. 382, (my emphasis).

[43] Wasianski: *Kant's Last Years,* quoted in W. R. Washington Sullivan, *Morality as a Religion* (BiblioBizaar, 2007 [orig. 1898]), p. 50.

her secret from Nature."[44] Despite Nature's mists, veils, and secrets, Thoreau would know her through a liquid eye attentive to waters. In *A Week*, he asks wistfully (and not altogether hopelessly) "May we not see God?"[45] Perhaps seeing through the eye of a bittern who sees and "wrests all her secrets from Nature" is the closest we'll come—and close enough—to seeing God seeing creation.

For Kant, mind is not an empiricist's passive, empty basket where impressions are scattered out for inspection, sorting, or joining. It is more like a construction or processing site where experience and judgments are shaped or produced. Kant asks what the mind must be like if the world is as it seems. Thoreau asks what the world can be. Can it be better—if we but attend to its influx of beauties and wonders?

Kant asks what makes ordinary perception of ships or spoons possible for us. Thoreau asks why perceptions sink so easily toward the dull and deadening. Kant wants to explain perceptions and experience while Thoreau wants to expand the range and depth of our experience and perception—the depth of evils, but also of heavens. He wants to reform waning capacities for tasting apples that the gods savor, for scenting heaven in lilies, for sounding ponds that can hardly be fathomed. We have hardly begun even to desire to perceive. And to fully perceive is to be lost in the things perceived, as in a transporting communion.

Kant can only hope to see heaven in the eye of a swallow. The official system of his *First Critique* does not allow glimpses of heaven. The *Third Critique* might do better. The theme of the sublime and the positing of aesthetic ideas can expand imagination to a world beyond the pale objecthood of ships or spoons. Aesthetic ideas include love, envy, fame, death, and vice.[46] If these open toward the sublime, in dramas of yearning, beholding, and despair, we might imagine them also to open toward a glimpse of heaven in the eye of a sparrow, or toward a glimpse of Hades in death's eye; toward a glimpse of love in the eye of a friend, or a glimpse of vice in the cold visage of a southern slave-catcher.

Kant does not linger with the role of affect, desire, or mood as affording access to beauty, vice, or revelations. Nor does he linger to consider educating senses and imagination, as these might afford better attunements to worlds perceived, and to better renderings of them, and to better voice in

---

[44] *Week*, pp. 235–6. Joel Porte notes this passage, and relates it to Bachelard's discussions of Thales (water) and Heraclitus (a hearth's fire). See Porte, *Consciousness in Concord*, p. 132. Among twentieth-century Parisian philosophers, Bachelard was a great reader of Thoreau, as was Pierre Hadot.

[45] *Week*, p. 382.

[46] See J. M. Bernstein, *The Fate of Art* (University Park: Penn State Press, 1992), p. 96.

rendering our placement in them.[47] In *Autumnal Tints* Thoreau sketches the discipline needed to *perceive* beauty:

> Why, it takes a sharp-shooter to bring down even trivial game ... ; he must take very particular aim, and know what he is aiming at ... And so it is with him that shoots at beauty; though he wait till sky falls, he will not bag any if he does not already know its seasons and haunts, and the color of its wing,— if he has not dreamed of it, so that he can *anticipate* it; then indeed he flushes it at every step ... He prays for it, and often sacrifices ... After due and long preparation, schooling his eye and hand, dreaming awake and asleep, ... he goes out ... and *therefore* gets them. He had them half way into his bag when he started.[48]

What goes for beauty, I'd think, goes for perceiving *goodness* or *divinity*. In a famous moment in the *First Critique*, Kant pauses to bask in awe under starry heavens. But this is an uncharacteristic break in an otherwise puritanical focus on justification and works. Thoreau wants to bask in every possible break from duty and to refuse unseemly scrambling for justification and legitimacy. Thus the joyful lilt of so much of his writing, despite undertones of pain.

---

[47] For an account of the education of the senses and perception in the never-ending achievements of moral sensibility, see Sabina Lovibond, *Ethical Formation* (Cambridge, MA: Harvard University Press, 2002).
[48] *Essays*, "Autumal Tints," p. 395.

10

Affliction and Affinity

What we are supplying are really remarks on the natural history of human beings.
      —Wittgenstein[1]

Thoreau doesn't give us an explicit theory of perception, but it's clear he would have rejected both the classical empiricist model of mind, a receptacle for impressions, and the Kantian model, a bustling multi-storied processing plant. He passes on a variety of perceptual attunements to the world across an expansive range of possibilities, and he notes our stubborn distance from attunements that could be liberating. I read him as roughly following a Stoic model. To perceive well is to acquire affinities—one's embodied actions meshing with others and with one's habitat and milieu. One learns adjustments—culturally, if one is a cultural animal—that attune one to needs, desires, physicality, sociality, place, family, politics, history.

1.

Oikeiosis is the Stoic term of art for the acquired fit between a fox and its world, for instance its capacity to bound naturally through snow; for the acquired fit between a bird and its capacity to find non-poisonous berries, or between a duck and its awareness of its speed, wing alignment, motion, and the look of the pond as it descends in an easy water landing that gracefully confirms its fit to its world. This perceptual fit of creature to itself and world is "*Oikeiosis*," a network of affiliations and affinities.

Such a network is also close to what in modern parlance we'd call, 'economy.'[2] We speak of an ongoing perceptual economy of connections, or more poetically of an unfolding dance of the senses—with others, with oneself, with things, with remembered previous perceptions, with anticipations of our next perceptions. Connectedness is self-evident in animal and vegetable worlds. For human animals, even when affiliation is admitted as a

---

[1] Epigraph: see Wittgenstein's *Philosophical Investigations* (London: Blackwell, 3rd edn, 2001), entries 25 and 415.
[2] See Wayne M. Martin, "Conscience and Confession in Rousseau's Naturalistic Moral Psychology," available at privatewww.essex.ac.uk/~wmartin/MartinRousseauPaper.pdf

goal, achieving it can often be excruciatingly difficult. Unlike snails or daisies, we become alienated and distraught. Nevertheless in our life-routines this flow of affiliation can be so easy we hardly notice—getting dressed, getting through a pleasant workday, attending to business, negotiating traffic.

When perceptual affinities are lost or damaged, we become misfits. We undergo estrangement, disenchantment, objectification. We suffer loss of meaning and morale. How can we picture, in more detail, a successful fit-to-world? My touch on your shoulder (as we move into a turn) gives a perception to you. And your shoulder touches me as I touch you, delivering a perception back to me in the instant I deliver one to you. Our successful attunement rests on a mutual fittingness of perceptions exchanged. We learn aptness of fit from response of the other. Perhaps your flinch tells me my perceptual delivery has misfired. I learn thereafter to better modulate my tactile communication—or abandon attempts.

My perception of you is modulated by your perception of me. You return a perception (a kind of gentle yielding, a kind of flinching). Such is our dance-like access to the world, and the world's dance-like access of us.[3] Thoreau imagines the roar of the sea addressing Margaret Fuller, calling to her scoured bones; they return the favor in kind. It's a simultaneous "give-and-take" with neither actor nor recipient—sea nor bones—taking a privileged seat of honor in the exchange. Her bones enter communion. They become ears (as it were)—alert to the endless whisper of waves. Her bones enter communion; so does the sea. Each become ears (as it were) for the other. The bones are alert to the endless whisper of waves, and the waves are alert to the plea of the bones. Thoreau addresses us through a concatenation of word-wrapped perceptions that are a moving communion between Fuller and the sea (an affinity that excludes him). We are warmed by, or we flinch at, these affinities and exclusion as they reach toward us (and we reach toward them).

The world and others advance and recede, even as we advance and recede. We hear better (or worse), feel more (or less) in a touch delivered. A sound has a pitch, extension, and rhythm evident but perhaps not fully registered—part of its presence is an unknown ambiance. We vary day by day in what we hear in a chord. A look has a density. How much of its measure is available, can we sense? The press of a hand has insistence or gentleness. Narratives emerge as my touch meets your shoulder, and your shoulder touches back, this way or that. The dance of mutual perceptions

---

[3] An echo endorses perceptual affinity: a call into nature is returned in kind. "Of what significance is any sound if Nature does not echo it"; and "woodland lungs ... seemed particularly sound to day," seeming "to mouth" their answer. *Journal*, after October 31, 1850, p. 81.

weaves into ever-expanding narratives of approach and avoidance, lordship and bondage, embrace and exile, love of the world and suffering its refusals.

Thoreau works to modulate his sight of and feel for the world. With the sight of a bounding fox, he bounds in response. Under a silent sky he's silently patient. As whippoorwills whistle from across the lake, he sings back. For him at his best, sensory input does not arrive unfit for a dance, inert like fields strewn with dust, or like manikins undressed, absent allure. Things of the world and their absence greet us, surprise or annoy us, pique our curiosity or raise our ire. They prompt a song or lament or a bounding, mimicking celebration. Learning to modulate perceptual affinities is an ongoing, educational affair: learning to hear and see better, catching promising affinities (and ducking unpromising ones).

Philia begins as a register of *Oikeiosis*, as part of our elemental perceptual fit-to-world. It can be as evident as the moves of a dance-couple on ice, or the moves of a sloop tacking into the wind—hearing (and seeing) the flowing warnings and invitations of a breeze and a chop. Alternatively, this perceptual fit can be easily overlooked. As I stride I'm given the sense that a mild unevenness in the floor threatens to upset my poise, and calls for correction. The bump calls for an adjustment from me, that I make effortlessly, thus restoring and maintaining filial exchange between my body and world. Through infancy and beyond, endlessly, perceptual fit is refined as part of initiations into aspects of physical and social life—an ability to balance in snow, an ability to apologize. Refinement in perception allows me to register burdens in my friend's halting glance.

Our best perceptions are founded on kinship, communion, on what Cavell calls love of the world and acknowledgment of others.[4] This is not to say that such love won't be crushed by the intrusion of evil or of indifference or of natural catastrophe—or by our own insufficiencies of heart. Thoreau figures our best perceptions as achieved—like a runner's perception of her degree of fatigue.[5] And often they are something yet to achieve, as our elemental natures develop toward more complex second natures.[6] Perceptions that are initially solely *Thoreau's* achievement infiltrate to tilt *my* developing perceptions.[7]

---

[4] Cavell, *The Claim of Reason*, p. 431, and my "Acknowledgement, Suffering and Praise: Stanley Cavell as Religious Continental Thinker," *Lost Intimacy*, Ch. 7. I consider Cavell's "passionate utterances" that "improvise in the disorders of desire" in *On Søren Kierkegaard* (Farnham: Ashgate, 2007), pp. 52–3. Also, see "Closing Passions," below.
[5] See the passage on achieving a perception of beauty in the selection from "Autumnal Tints" that I include below in "Closing Images, Reveries, Prayers."
[6] See Lovibond, *Ethical Formation*, on McDowell's and Aristotle's second nature.
[7] Lyman Mower points out that here Thoreau expands the Heidegger of *Being and Time*: things can appear as instruments-in-use ('at hand'), or as "mere occurrence" ('to hand', looked at with detachment), but also as things to enjoy, take delight in, or love.

With its generous inspirations, the world meets Thoreau's generously inspired eye and pen. Margaret Fuller delivers majesty and Thoreau's eye and pen receive and convey it to us. Thoreau's startling rendering of the beach is a imaginative achievement. This is not data-reception, but a dance full of potential stumbles and miscues and meaningless diversion—while also full of potential for wonder (or terror). Too often we regress from perception's wonders to insistently explicate or defend. This is to forego filial communion for the trappings of by-play. "Could we for a moment drop this by-play—and simply wonder—without reference or inference!"[8]

2.

Thoreau's genius for perceptual range, depth, and acuity is fueled by an inventive and keen imagination that modulates his affinities to the presence of things arriving through sound, sight, touch, taste, smell, and sense of balance. The fulfillment of this genius is his passing on his perceptions to *us*, and thus passing on the expressiveness of a world that delivers all that is worth perceiving. Thoreau opens a hand to a world that extends its hand to him. At its best an expression of self is completed, at least momentarily, in the unfolding reality of an expressive world, and an expressive world is completed, at least momentarily, in the dance of a self's expressiveness attuned to the expressiveness of the world.

Co-creation and communion are the mutual implication of self and world. In a romp with a fox, or a glide across ice, any gap between perceiver and perceived disappears. With the smoothest exchanges from self to world, or from world to self, causal directionality is absent. Take a famous passage from Rousseau's *Reveries of a Solitary Walker*. He recounts a moment of rebirth after having been felled by a racing Great Dane:

> Night was beginning to fall. I perceived the sky, some stars, and green leaves. This first sensation was a delicious moment. I was conscious of myself only through this. I was being born into life in that instant, and it seemed to me as if *all I perceived was filled with my frail existence*.[9]

Rousseau chooses the idiom of the perceiver flowing out, reaching out into the world to become part of it. But that moment might invite an idiom that reverses initiative.

---

[8] *Journal*, December 7, 1838, p. 61.
[9] See *Reveries of a Solitary Walker*, second walk (my emphasis).

Reversing directionality, the world would flow out from itself and flood the perceiving self. Drenched by a sense of "being born into life," the self being born falls away leaving only a sense of the animated world that sustains this "delicious moment." A falling away of directionality— our being completely satisfied neither with the idiom of "inside out" nor "outside in"—recommends a possible third perspective: seamlessness in mutual affinity. Cavell describes his mother letting her being flow with perfect intimacy into the notes her piano and score provide.[10] Her fingers deliver Brahms or Schubert leaving no room for interpretive gaps. We have ecstatic connection between text, reader-listener, and music (sound).[11] It's a gapless intimacy with the world. As Cavell puts it elsewhere, "our relation to the world's existence is somehow *closer* than the ideas of believing and knowing are made to convey."[12] In this case of sight reading, as in the case of Rousseau's "seamless affinity" with his surround, the model of an inner feeling opposed to an outer thing felt disappears. So there's nothing to invite a posit of directionality. My touch reaching yours is yours reaching mine.

Such moments of seamless intimacy may not be as rare as we suppose. They can mark ecstatic moments against which more mundane experience can be measured, or mark less momentous, more ordinary or banal occasions. The coldness of the stream into which I plunge my hand becomes the coldness of my hand. Before we launch into causal explanations, coldness, hand, and stream are an undifferentiated plenum. Dissolved are hallowed divisions between subject and object, consciousness and thing. Rousseau becomes the tree, flows into it, as its limbs and greenness, flooding out any Jean Jacques apart from its presence.

Thoreau is receptive to the movement and whisper of wind and to the gaze of stars; in turn, he is polyphonically expressive in his address to them. Each can be better or worse in attunement to the other. Blinding snow repels our walk and sight. Fetid scatterings of flesh repel a gaze and approach. A striking melody falls on deaf ears. Not hearing the sea address the shore,

---

[10] See Cavell's *Pitch of Philosophy*, p. 18. There are other possible ways of amplifying life besides losing one's subjectivity in intimacy with a world (of music or trees). Life might be amplified by my becoming an *object-among-others*: see Tzachi Zamir, *Acts: Theater, Philosophy, and the Performing Self* (Michigan: University of Michigan, 2014), pp. 106–7.

[11] Some aspects of Emerson's famous passage toward becoming a "transparent eyeball'— where he is what appears and what appears is he—can be understood along similar lines. See Barbara Packer, *Emerson's Fall* (New York: Continuum, 1982), pp. 79–82.

[12] *Senses*, p. 145.

debris will win out. Wonder-raising prose depends on wonder-flowing worlds, and on what Hamlet calls "wonder-wounded hearing."[13]

At its best the world has an erotic appeal addressed to our capacities for love. Yet *Eros, Philia,* and preservative love—dispositions linked to perceptions promising a yield of affiliation, or openness toward "the influx of better thoughts,"[14]—are always coupled with risk. Achieving "Sympathy with Intelligence" is far from easy. What lover walking the wreckage-strewn beach would not want to avert her eyes at the spot where Fuller's body is tossed and half-buried like old lunch? The bones must be more than discarded flesh. They must be what they can be, and other than trash. Thoreau's words and eyes yield a saint's relics, nestled inoffensively in the sand. To see only their brokenness is to be false to the friend who walked with him in Concord. Thoreau's cairn makes a place for her continuing life. He responds to her catastrophe in registers of friendship and love, mixed with grief. He responds to the catastrophe of slavery in registers of outraged integrity and of justice defiled. In less catastrophic troubles—someone in need of shelter and the warmth of companionship—he responds with hospitality. Welcome is perception-based.

In an underappreciated essay, perhaps best titled "The Inn Keeper", Thoreau elaborates a primal religious theme—unstinting welcome to the stranger and traveler. The Inn and its keeper offer a humane and convivial refuge and succor in answering the knock of all who travel from home, who list between homes, or are homeless. The Inn, its keeper, and his tavern answer pervasive estrangements, answer the sense of placeless *unheimlichkeit*. This generous host offers shelter to those of all faiths and walks of life.

> Methinks I see the thousand shrines erected to Hospitality shining afar in all countries, as well Mahometan and Jewish, as Christian, khans, and caravansaries, and inns, wither all pilgrims without distinction resort.[15]

His roof gathers in any who arrive to escape storms or the chill, giving haven to all to talk, eat, drink, and share in good cheer. The tavern keeper also presides, if not over full Dionysian revelry, then over mild inebriation. In "Wild Apples," Thoreau savors fermented apples, the very nectar of the gods.[16]

---

[13] *Hamlet*, III, i. Here, the stars themselves "stand as wonder-wounded hearers" before the wails of Laertes; but the irony is that his wails would not catch the interest of a toad. Hamlet is sarcastic.
[14] *Walden*, "Spring," p. 303.
[15] *Essays*, "The Landlord," p. 108.
[16] "The poet's body even is not fed like other men's, but he sometimes tastes the genuine nectar and ambrosia of the gods, and lives a divine life." *Week*, "Friday," p. 365.

Of course, the needs of those caught in tragedy exceed what simple hospitality can offer—though hospitality must always be welcome. They need more than shelter and good cheer. Calamity calls on our capacities for outrage and willingness to witness: *Philia* is betrayed. E. M. Forster's "only connect" sounds against a world bent on destruction. Rick Furtak observes that when our connections with life are severed, "... it is as if an erotic bond has been broken."[17] But what is broken might be mended, or made sufferable, and it is worth the try. Abandoned by love, Thoreau writes, "There is no remedy for love but to love more."[18] Achieving affinity is my opening to the world and the world opening to me.

3.

Philosophers who expect a preponderance of disciplined argumentation will be irked by those moments of quiet, or wondrous affinity, we encounter in Thoreau. As a "'literary philosopher" his experiential evocations have non-argumentative impact. If Thoreau bursts out "I want to devour the woodchuck live on the spot!" he might be revealing something about his desires, something that might be a premise in an argument. But he is also calling listeners to witness to an impulse they might have disowned or missed as their own.[19] Wonders and startles have a time of their own in philosophical writing other than being an occasion for argumentative response. Wonder—and less commonly, its shadows, say disgust, terror, or outrage—is woven seamlessly through Thoreau's most detailed descriptions, through his most arching overviews, through his most sober critiques. That presence calls us to behold. It awakens our passions. It is a fully philosophical moment—perhaps the most important and neglected one for Thoreau.

Stanley Cavell calls words whose force and effect is an intervention in "the disorders of desire" an instance of *passionate utterance*.[20] It activates that site of conflicted impulses, fantasies, aspirations, and despairs one could call the soul, the place where values are valued and revalued, one way or another.[21] As Cavell puts it, passionate utterance is "an invitation to improvisation in the disorders of desire." Thoreau's passionate, intimate words cannot effect

---

[17] "Skepticism and Perceptual Faith," Furtak, p. 552.
[18] *Journal*, July 25, 1839, p. 88.
[19] For moral thinking as engaging imagination beyond judgment and argumentation, see Alice Crary, *Beyond Moral Judgment* (Cambridge, MA: Harvard University Press, 2007).
[20] See my excursus on "Passionate Speech" below in "Closing Passions."
[21] Cavell, *Philosophy the Day After Tomorrow* (Cambridge, MA: Harvard University Press, 2005), p. 185.

change willy-nilly, but they can appeal movingly to our need for change, to our yearning or only half-acknowledged readiness for it. He alerts our sensitivities to the improvising poetry of his appeals. And perhaps we will respond in a way that shows we are changed, in small or bigger ways.

In his political essays especially, Thoreau makes extended and powerful argumentative appeals. But elsewhere, narrative is the stream that carries arguments along; they don't have automatic pride of place. Socrates is irritated at the boys squabbling at his feet because they don't grasp the larger aims and visions in whose service Socrates argues and interrogates. For them, philosophy means intellectual swordplay, an amusing diversion, a chance to hang out with a very interesting guy. All that by-play deflects from wondrous realities close by in the wings that Socrates jostles us toward conversationally, indirectly. Through the intimate and often hidden force of his words, Thoreau, like Socrates, aims to change listeners and readers and their immediate settings. Words have a public, "performative force" and can effect more intimate interventions as vehicles of the passions.[22]

There is a way of writing philosophically, for instance in Montaigne or Aurelius, which stalls or sidesteps the impulse toward smart rejoinder or counter-argument. What's being presented is not a striking premise or conclusion, or not only that, but wisdom or insight free and clear. Thoreau gives us philosophical showings—for instance of delight, affliction, wonder, farce, friendship. His sentences say something and also reveal and evoke. As they reveal or bring something wondrous to mind, they deflect—take the place of—the immediacy of that suffering that had been the mind's sole focus. The wondrous then opens space for what Cavell calls love of the world.[23]

Plato teaches by argument but also with drama, myth, images, and Eros. Each clears the mind (or soul) for something better. These benches and tools of word-craft are essential to his task.[24] Rousseau presents arguments in his prize essays. In *Reveries of a Solitary Walker* he gives us showings, evocative

---

[22] *Peformative vs. passionate speech*: If I announce my executive ruling at a business meeting, in announcing it I follow certain rules that let my words effect a change in the world in the very saying of them, as I would change it had I promised or apologized. These "speech-acts" illustrate what John Austin called the "performative force" of words. The force of Thoreau's lilting and lyrical writing has its effect at a more intimate level, and may or may not change the world. It is an *invitation* to change desire and passion.

[23] See Mooney, *Lost Intimacy*, especially Chs. 7, 11; and see Furtak, "Skepticism and Perceptual Faith."

[24] See Paul Friedlander, *Plato, An Introduction* (Princeton, NJ: Princeton University Press, 1958) for Plato's desire to have his *philosophical poetry* supersede the writing of the tragedians. In the final chapter of *Cities of Words,* Cavell suggests that Plato's aim (in *Republic*) is to let philosophical poetry show its claim to be heard and be *better* poetry.

settings, moods and flashes of light where insight appears.[25] In his *Critiques*, Kant gives us deductions but in his *Essays* he gives us his myth of (a part of) creation: animal instincts are *"that voice of God that all animals obey"*.[26] He gives no argument for this mysterious and unexpected claim. He knows that no argument could be given. Yet Kant is not just indulging a foolish whimsy. We get a specifically philosophical conceit, a moment of philosophical caprice and wonder, a kind of reverie we find all over in Thoreau. Creatures, Kant confides, have access to the voice of God. God accesses them, and they obey naturally, instinctually. So instinct is not a hard-wired mechanical response but a wonderful answering-to-a-call (or command).

Kant is figuring an animal's place in creation in an emphatically non-Cartesian framework. Expanding his abbreviated gesture toward myth, we could take an animal's *answer* to heaven's call (or command) as *itself* a form of speech—as when our physical comportment speaks. Hawks bespeak ease and power and grace in their flight. Thoreau alerts us to "the language in which all things and events speak."[27] Instinct is the way animals bespeak their affinity with their settings, and with the divine, taken as the benign downward look that tells us that this affinity has been made real, and is good.[28] The eye of a sparrow, in its luminous glimmer, bespeaks the eye of heaven, in its glory. This is co-creation, a dance of affinities between divinity and creature.

Of course logically speaking, these are loose, even flimsy, associations that *demonstrate* absolutely nothing. But Kant's minor myth, given with his glance at a small corner of creation, can provoke poetic-philosophical wonder that I would not want to censor or suppress. Such poetic-philosophical wonder is a recurrent theme in Thoreau, often conveyed in minor reveries not unlike Kant's myth of a sparrow's eye. We can also find the evocation of wonder in more recent thinkers of great repute.

Wittgenstein announced without elaboration, "if a lion could speak we would not understand him."[29] This oracular surprise and surmise belongs

---

[25] See Frederick Garber on resonances between Rousseau's fifth walk and Thoreau's seeking "immediate presentness": *Thoreau's Redemptive Imagination* (New York: New York University Press, 1977), pp. 153f.

[26] "Conjectures on the beginning of history," *Kant on History*, Louis White Beck (ed.) (Indianapolis: Bobbs Merrill, 1963), p. 55 (my emphasis). For Kant, instinctual responses of animals are expressions of obedience; their actions voice compliance. By extrapolation, we might conclude that creatures who can hear the will of another and voice their obedience are also creatures that *judge*: the cat judges that she has to run faster to catch her prey, or judges that instead, she should rest in the shade.

[27] *Walden*, "Sounds," p. 108 [para 1].

[28] In a similar vein Thoreau remarks that Nature is in a kind of unspoken obedience: "Nature puts no question and answers none which we mortals ask. She has long ago taken her resolution." *Walden*, "The Pond in Winter" p. 273 [para 1].

[29] Wittgenstein, *Investigations,* II, xi, p. 223.

with his picture of language as inescapably at play within forms of life. It's an image meant to displace the picture of language as a deracinated propositional system. Wittgenstein assumes that we share too little life with a lion to understand him—were the lion to speak. Whatever its worth, his point is uttered with no *argument* about animal speech or its failures. We're left with a picture, as if from a children's book, of a speaking lion who can't be understood.

The image of the lion is meant to persuade largely on its own—and on our willingness to improvise stories, as if to a listening child, stories that might (or might not) give the image more resonance. If such an offhand picture-remark *works*, Wittgenstein will have deposited a moment of philosophical wonder (with its inevitable undercurrents of philosophical doubts). This wonder can be amplified and reviewed after its initial strike, but it's clear that Wittgenstein is not offering a smart, doubt-stopping QED meant to cancel all further discussion. The remark works (or doesn't) like Kant's reverie of animals obedient to God either works (or doesn't). If the intrusion of these images or story-fragments in philosophy's cool sanctum doesn't work, we'll be left annoyed, exasperated. Re-reading Wittgenstein's gnomic aside, we'll just throw up our hands. What in the world are *lions* doing here!

Provoked (I admit, not entirely negatively), I'll add a philosophical trailer: "If a lion could talk, we wouldn't understand him *much more than we already do*!" This shift in the picture is a shift from a presumed *lack* of understanding across species to a plain (if partial) *sufficiency* of understanding. Thoreau can bound across snow with a fox because he understands it—quite apart from speech. I understand my dog's plea for a walk. We already understand the lion who (through instinct, as Kant would say) speaks, voices, gestures, roars: roars, "This turf is mine! Back off!" We bi-pedaled speaking-animals who read this page share ways of life with these felines, and so share understanding, in advance of what Wittgenstein conjures as a lion speaking and our *failure* to understand.[30] Not unlike lions, we too protect our food and our cubs and occasionally bask in the sun. Some, like Thoreau, will bound after a fox. He enacts, thereby, mutual understanding across species.

Now if these evocations of a shared form of life across species seem the least bit plausible, I've accomplished something philosophical with barely a shred of argumentation (though parts could be recast rather woodenly as an argument). Philosophical insight, if it's deepened at all, comes in this case, and in others like it, through little scenarios and fantasies and imaginative

---

[30] Perhaps the point is that lions don't have an *inaccessible* life, in the sense of an "inner life"—a life they could report on if only they had speech. In any case, let me add that my amendment doesn't entail that Wittgenstein has *made a mistake*. His claim is open-ended and *provokes* as much as declares: which may be enough for his purposes.

prods, meant to make a new aspect of things come to light. In writing like Thoreau's, or in this snippet from Wittgenstein, insight, if it arrives, will not have been secured by making an elaborate case, say for our affinities with animal life that is backed up by the argument that animals have rights or minds, or that they can reason or suffer. Insight will arrive (if it does) in a glance of surprise or recognition, followed by what we called philosophical song or befitting reverie.

These moments in Kant and Wittgenstein on animals, and my stab at amplifying them, illustrate a place in philosophy for wonder and its shadows. They mark a place for the unargued and perhaps the unarguable. They mark a place for the capacity of philosophy, well beyond argument alone, to reorient our perspectives and so let us see. And they also exhibit what I called toward the beginning of these excursions, the "episodic" character of philosophy as Thoreau unveils it: an insight here, an insight there. This provokes readers to try out schemes of partial and passing unification.

Thoreau gives us many pictorial and narrative philosophical visions or reveries. Their philosophical work can be exhibited by disassembling them carefully piece by piece—as we've disassembled his discovery of Walden's Maker, and paused to consider his dreaming frogs. We find a small-scale narrative excursion in Kant's remark on the access of animals to God, or in Rousseau's *Reveries,* where being felled by a speeding dog, his being exits his body, or in Wittgenstein's story of a lion, one among many stories in that strange assemblage of scenarios, questions without answers, images and anti-pictures called *The Philosophical Investigations*.[31] The upshot is that Thoreau cannot be excluded from the precincts of philosophy solely on the basis of his relative disinterest in elaborately sustained arguments.[32] Let me consider another instance of philosophy without much argument, the case of Hamlet.

When Hamlet asks, "to be or not to be", he is not—or not only—weighing impartial arguments on the merits of suicide. He is letting dark truths flare out with unrivaled eloquence. He exposes his exposure to a world not ordinarily acknowledged, exposing to us his exposure to what Cora

---

[31] Wittgenstein holds that thinking runs astray when "a picture holds us captive." We might think of pictures as playing a role in static representations, as in picture galleries, where we can take in the whole scene framed in a picture in a glance. Images, in contrast, might be seen as shifting, indefinite, "spectral" items in narrative or poetry, things inchoate and hard to pin down, even while having dreamlike power. On images, see Thoreau, *Essays,* "Autumnal Tints" p. 394. See also Bence Nannay, "Narrative Pictures," in *The Journal of Aesthetics and Art Criticism* (2009).

[32] He belongs shelved not only in literature, but with philosophy, as does Henry James, Dostoevsky, and Proust (to name just a few). Their identities are wider than any single disciplinary or cultural classification.

Diamond calls difficult realities.[33] The troubles we undergo are not only the work of a vagrant subjectivity but are all too often rooted in objectively troubling realities. When harsh realities afflict all my hopes for serenity, "objective" arguments meant to "explain" or assuage my suffering will be largely ineffectual, beside the point, irksome, or patronizing. Hamlet speaks to our vulnerabilities insofar as his speaking exposes his own vulnerabilities. Even if Hamlet scratches the surface of argumentation regarding suicide, at stake overall is the domain of his bitter afflictions, and my appreciation of them. These saturate the tonality of my reception of his eloquence.

Hamlet is witness to his troubles. He exposes his vulnerability to them, and so invites us to inhabit the world of our own difficult vulnerabilities. He is not a meticulous accountant keeping track of malfunctions in the world. The startle and wonder of it all, listening to his exposures, is that his words of dark exaltation fly wildly, elegantly, above and through, those troubles: "What a pity", Thoreau exclaims, "if the part of Hamlet be left out."[34] Hamlet's words ought to stop us in our tracks—awaken us to terror, yes, but *also* to the wonders of the human voice, its capacity to mitigate and modulate terror, despair, and lassitude. We are animals who bound through snow beautifully. And we are also animals who launch into boundless registers of eloquence.

Hamlet's voicing of melancholy, doubt, and wonder should not be lost for philosophy merely for lacking the armor of decisive argument. Over and over in Thoreau, there are moments of philosophical radiance, joy, and exaltation. They do not stand to be confirmed or refuted, but are exposed on their own to stand on their own, for what they are. In the moment, they quiet or arouse quite independently of supportive reasoning. Yet as responsive creatures, we're moved to speak in memoriam and celebration, in elaboration and repetition, continuing and renewing the moment of their life. We bring words again and again onto this meager stage where they can speak, can be heard, be exposed and seen, once again.

Here again is Thoreau at that place of mourning, transformed through his reverie of commemorative evocation.

> There lay the relics in a certain state, rendered perfectly inoffensive to both bodily and spiritual eye ... That dead body possessed the shore as no living one could. [The bones were] alone with the sea ... whose hollow roar seemed addressed to the ears of the departed.[35]

---

[33] *Philosophy and Animal Life*, Ch. 1.
[34] *Journal*, March 21, 1840, p. 129.
[35] *Cape Cod*, p. 123.

What Thoreau takes as Fuller's shark-scored bones yields to infinite communion with the sea's address. Sorrow and terrible loss are largely displaced.

4.

Consider another literary thinker, a Danish writer and walker as rich in philosophical insight as Nietzsche (with whom we began the present excursion). We'll remember that in December, 1838, Thoreau wrote out in his *Journal* a brief but striking philosophical desire:

> Could we for a moment drop this by-play—and simply wonder—without reference or inference![36]

Some eight months earlier, a literary philosopher from Copenhagen reported in his Journal:

> This morning I saw half a score of geese fly away in crisp cool air ... They divided into two flocks arched like a pair of eyebrows above my eyes, which were now gazing into the land of poetry.[37]

We might be surprised that Thoreau bears comparison to Kierkegaard (yet we can read just that in the marvelous entry on Thoreau in *The Stanford Encyclopedia of Philosophy*).[38] Of course once we think of it, there are intriguing parallels.

Each kept astounding journals, Thoreau starting his at age twenty, in 1837. Kierkegaard jotted his first entry at age twenty-one, in 1834. Both were poetic, ethical, political, and religious, and both skewered their fellow citizens with mordant wit. Both were philosophers of the place they inhabited. While their reading made them global and brought the past to their present, Kierkegaard left provincial Copenhagen as seldom as Thoreau left Concord. From the mid-1840s on, Kierkegaard exposed the sham of his city's Christendom. Thoreau found the freedom won at Lexington and Concord despoiled when Mexico was invaded and slavery was enforced in Concord and Boston, the latter in the case of Anthony Burns. Kierkegaard dies disowned by the elite of his city at forty-two, while Thoreau dies almost

---

[36] *Journal*, December 7, 1838, p. 61.
[37] Søren Kierkegaard, *Papers and Journals,* Howard V. and Edna H. Hong (ed. and trans.) (Bloomington, IN: Indiana University Press, 1978), April 1, 1838, p. 116.
[38] Rick Furtak first noted the proximity of Kierkegaard and Thoreau in his entry on Thoreau for *The Stanford Encyclopedia of Philosophy*.

uneventfully at age forty-four, his demise overshadowed by the Civil War. Yet he had his part in bringing on that cataclysm.[39]

There are differences, notably of temperament. Thoreau was not sentimental enough to have written this: "no turtle-dove builds its nest in my branches".[40] And lacking Thoreau's marvelous animal exuberance, Kierkegaard could not have given us this:

> I saw a fox ... making across to the hills on my left. As the snow lay five inches deep, he made but slow progress, but it was no impediment to me. So yielding to the instinct of the chase, I ... bounded away, snuffing the air like a ... hound.[41]

At a deeper level, there are a number of convergent philosophical motifs whose presence might surprise. In no special priority, these five stand out:

- Thoreau said one could find teachers of philosophy but no philosophers in and about Concord. He valued not just a conception of how to live. He valued its exemplary enactment in the detail of one's life. Kierkegaard mocked the strictly academic practice of professors of philosophy that had absolutely no bearing on living out one's convictions in daily life.
- Thoreau waits for new days to dawn, creation occurring ever and again bequeathed to those with "eyes to see"; Kierkegaard's poetic "young man" awaits a new world delivered in a thunderclap, given in an *Augenblick* that he calls "repetition."[42]

---

[39] Thoreau lived from 1817–62; Kierkegaard from 1813–55. Thoreau starts his journal in 1837; Kierkegaard starts his in 1834. Thoreau's first essay appears in 1842, the year of John's death. Kierkegaard publishes *Either/Or, Fear and Trembling*, and *Repetition* in 1843. In 1846, Thoreau writes "Ktaadn," and in 1849 "Civil Resistance" and *A Week on the Concord*. He retrieves Fuller's body in 1850. "Slavery in Massachusetts" appeared in 1854. In 1857 he meets John Brown. In 1859 he delivers "A Plea for John Brown" to an audience of 2,000 in Boston. Douglass was to have spoken, but after Brown's capture, fled toward Canada. After Thoreau and others arranged a memorial service in Concord on the day of his hanging, outraged Concord citizens hung Brown in effigy. Kierkegaard was not martyred, but church dignitaries shunned his funeral, and student supporters disrupted the graveside service, protesting church rites they were sure he would despise.

[40] Kierkegaard, *Papers and Journals, A Selection*, Alastair Hannay (ed. and trans.) (Penguin Books, 1996), July 9, 1837, p. 109.

[41] *Journals*, January 30, 1841, p. 186. Kierkegaard tried to get a taste, not of bounding after a fox, but of the park on horseback, but he failed. He lacked an athletic knack for saddles.

[42] See *Kierkegaard's Repetition and Philosophical Crumbs*, Edward F. Mooney (ed., intro and notes), Marilyn Piety (trans.) (Oxford: Oxford University Press, 2009, and my "*Repetition*: Getting the world back," *The Cambridge Companion to Kierkegaard*, Marino and Hannay (ed.) (Cambridge: Cambridge University Press, 1998).

- For both, the telos of awareness is an earnest openness, a moment for responsibility, not just a moment of cognitive success or of self-interested or rational satisfactions.[43] Kierkegaard calls this subjectivity; Thoreau has no single term to catch this fertile slant of attentiveness, though perhaps "Sympathy with Intelligence"—or perceptual resonance and communion—would do.
- Thoreau asks why George Washington, who never gave his life or word to rid the land of slavery, should be ranked higher than John Brown, who did. Kierkegaard asks why Abraham, who was ready to sacrifice another's life, should be ranked higher than a common murderer.
- Maine's Ktaadn, at the top, is an indifferent, even hostile mountain: spirit exits through a gap in one's ribs; a frighteningly 'raw existence' forces Thoreau to cry out in uncharacteristic dismay, "*Contact! Contact! Where are we? What are we?*"[44] Kierkegaard calls this onslaught and frightful flight of existence dizziness or anxiety, and places it, like Thoreau, in a dark before the world is born.[45]

We have more than enough here to improvise (on another day) any number of extended conversations.

5.

Thoreau belongs, as we've seen, to a tradition of moral philosophy flourishing in the work of Nietzsche and Kierkegaard, Hegel and Carlyle, and earlier in the work of Plato, Aristotle, and the Stoics. It's a tradition devoted to "an exploration of human living aimed at seeing and living it better," as Stanley Bates puts it.[46] Cultural commentators, psychologists, journalists, or students of literature may focus on how one should see and live life better,

---

[43] For the move from the epistemological goal of neutral cognition to the broadly ethical goal of "subjective" responsibility, see Charles Larmore, *The Romantic Legacy*, (New York: Columbia University Press, 1996).
[44] See *Essays*, "Ktaadn," p. 113.
[45] See *The Concept of Anxiety*, Reidar Thomte (ed. and trans.) (Princeton. NJ: Princeton University Press, 1980).
[46] Stanley Bates, "Stanley Cavell and Ethics," *Stanley Cavell*, Richard Eldridge, (ed.) (Cambridge: Cambridge University Press, 2003), p. 39. Bates notes the striking fact that since the latter part of the nineteenth century when academic philosophy divided itself into subdivisions and the specialty of moral philosophy was created, almost no one who has practiced that specialty has been among the century's "great" philosophers.

but these thinkers, Bates says, fall outside what has become the restricted twentieth-century academic rubric of "moral philosophy."[47]

> [Since the latter part of the nineteenth century], or a bit earlier, almost all of the philosophers who have been most significant in helping general readers to understand how to live their lives would not be classified as 'moral philosophers.'

These philosophers, as he puts it,

> ... tend either to produce narrative structures or to reflect on the narrative structure of human existence, not in order to provide a formula, or a template, of human existence, but to deny the possibility of such a formula.[48]

Thoreau gives us narratives of *domesticity* (through writing and residing at Walden Pond, establishing a home) and narratives of *travel, pilgrimage, or commemoration* (*Cape Cod, The Maine Woods, A Week on the Concord and Merrimack*). He delivers narratives of ways that others *refuse to live with others* and deny their freedom ("Slavery in Massachusetts", "A Plea for Captain John Brown", "Resistance to Civil Government"). And he delivers narratives of ways of *living with oneself* (parts of *Walden*, "Walking," and "Wild Apples"). Further, we find haunting undertones of tragedy that intimate the *impossibility of any simple formula* or template to guide seeing and living life, given its ample vicissitudes, swinging between moments of cruelty and moments of joy and gratitude.

Contemporary discussions of moral philosophy in colleges and universities aim to uncover "action guides," or clarity about basic principles or constraining and enabling rights, or the shape of specific virtues (and vices): courage, compassion, magnanimity and jealousy. But these efforts are seldom tied into larger understandings of the human, and they set aside questions of tragedy or comedy or the varied textures of ordinary life. They tend to duck altogether what Cora Diamond calls "the difficulty of reality"—its contingencies, interruptions, and doubleness. When we see a living room portrait of smiling young friends in uniform from years past, to use her example, do

---

[47] Philosophers have much to learn from Robert Pogue Harrison's *Forests: The Shadow of Civilization* (Chicago: University of Chicago Press, 1992), *The Dominion of the Dead* (Chicago: University of Chicago Press, 2003), and *Gardens: an Essay on the Human Condition* (Chicago: University of Chicago Press, 2008). These explorations in moral philosophy emerge from the academic precincts outside of philosophy; Harrison writes from Comparative Literature, which confirms Bates' thesis.

[48] Ibid.

we see the *over-flowing vitality* of innocent youth—or the tragedy of *life cut dreadfully short* by war.[49]

Bates finds Stanley Cavell's discussions of Emerson, Nietzsche, and others to be frankly affirming "what used to be called the state of one's soul" and "the possibility or necessity of the transforming of oneself and of one's society."[50] Even as Thoreau's goal becomes impersonal selflessness, his concern for the soul, his concern for relation to others, to the wild, and to one's society, secures his place as a "great moral philosopher." He's at home in the company of Kierkegaard, Nietzsche, or Marx. He marks a path through life—and that marking lights it for another. It's a path that skirts undue constrictions, corruptions, and quiet desperations, all for a *perceptual soaring and wisdom* that is the other side of dullness and affliction. It is a vision beyond irritation, outrage or despair, a vision of eloquent serenity and delight.

---

[49] Cavell, Diamond et al., *Philosophy and Animal Life*, pp. 74–8.
[50] Stanley Cavell, *Conditions Handsome and Unhandsome: The Constitution of Emersonian Perfectionism* (Chicago: University of Chicago Press, 1990), p. 2, discussed in Bates, p. 39.

11

John Brown

In the beauty of the lilies Christ was born across the sea, with a glory in his bosom that transfigures you and me.
—Julia Ward Howe, "John Brown's Body"

Let me propose a unifying impulse behind Thoreau's evocations of wildness and his piercing political essays. That impulse is *a love of the world as it addresses us* in the guise of Nature. That unifying impulse is challenged by naked cruelty and injustice. Thoreau's political essays can be seen as restorative, an attempt to correct for the disruption of love when cruelty and injustice obtrude. A love of the world is not lessened by the natural death of a brother or of a child, or by the death of a horse that begins to rot, or by the death of a sparrow carried aloft by a raptor. Falling leaves, forest fires, or floods that sweep away meadows do not diminish Thoreau's love of the world. The omnipresence of death and decay are not a radical impediment to love. They are part of the symphony that one loves, its minor and major keys part of an unfolding song. These acceptable losses do not spring from cruelty or crass injustice. Of course, when brute cruelty and injustice come on stage, Thoreau rises in protest.

1.

To perceive and celebrate a love of life is to see wonder and music in the rise and fall of the seasons, in the departure and burial of the old, and in the welcoming of a child or youth. It is to see wonder and hear music in the new generations of forests and in the moulding decay of roots or of an owl's carcass. To care for these cycles of birth and decay through commemorative writing and active hoeing and husbandry expresses love of the world. Thoreau abides death in life's cycles—even commemorates it. He does not abide cruelty or injustice.

He delivers the serenity of Walden Pond with one hand, and with the other, a defense of civil disobedience in protest of the invasion of Mexico. We share his climb up Maine's austere Ktaadn and then his "Slavery in Massachusetts," delivered at a rally after the re-enslavement of Anthony Burns. We may remember "Walking" or "Wild Apples," redolent of woods or meadow. We remember equally his impassioned "Plea for Captain John Brown." Thoreau's "nature essays" and his political essays often temporally overlap. He delivered "Wild Apples" in February 1860, less than three months after Brown was hanged. Thoreau died on May 6, 1862. "Wild Apples" was published in November of that year, so this pair might be considered his "Amen." Love of the things of the world—including respectful and affectionate relations among persons—ties these moments together.

Brown's raid on Harper's Ferry appears today as the opening skirmish of a bloody *uncivil* War, a skirmish won by the South who had him hanged. Thoreau's full-throated defense was as much against the local grain as his "retreat" to Walden. His vivid evocations issue from an impulse to save what's best in Brown and what's best in the land and terrain we inhabit together.

Through varied phases of his life, Thoreau sought fullness in becoming—recounted, composed, passed on to us in words. His songs articulate a passion to save what's worth saving. The eternal sound of the sea is saved for our serenity, the taste of wild apples is saved as the elixir of the gods,[1] the testament of John Brown is saved for our humanity,[2] the scent of a lily is saved as the hope of creation.[3] Sometimes this caring, preservative passion is expressed through engagement in an explicit public project speaking in defense of John Brown). Sometimes this caring, preservative passion is is expressed as a retreat from projects, as disengagement, as a giving way to radiant things, getting lost in the intake of bounteous gifts—say, gifts of infinite life. Singing an instinctive love is both a *giving up* (of any grasping possessiveness) and a *getting back* (of things now gifted).[4] It is both a doing and a doing nothing, a step forward and an absorption that is no step at all. In any case, such singing saves what's worth saving—sometimes by intervention, sometimes by getting out of the way (or at most disappearing in an effortless dance of perceptual communion).

---

[1] *Essays*, "Wild Apples," p. 448.
[2] *Essays*, "A Plea for Captain John Brown," p. 417.
[3] *Essays*, "Slavery," p. 346.
[4] In Kierkegaard's *Fear and Trembling*, Alastair Hannay (trans.) (New York: Penguin, 1985) faith is characterized as a giving up (of possessiveness) and getting back (what one had falsely tried to love through possession). See Mooney, *Knights of Faith and Resignation* (Albany: SUNY Press, 1991).

2.

Thoreau is a philosopher of the senses: "We need pray for no higher heaven than the pure senses can furnish ..."[5] Sensing the world from new angles brings it alive anew. His paths toward the rocky heights of Ktaadn cut through varied wilderness. He sees and takes note of the detail along the way, beholding a mobile, evanescent surround that alters as he moves and sees anew. There are lakes, dense forests, dangerous rapids, and the sense that few humans have marked the terrain—none will have marked it with the renderings he will distribute.

Approaching the summit, he's stopped dead in his tracks, for the top is invisible, shrouded in mist, unnerving, forbidding. There is no sense of the human or even of life—only boulders, precariously balanced, as if castaways randomly tossed and ready to plummet. A mile into clouds, he's struck down by the sight of "some undone extremity of the globe."[6] This is no longer a forested approach, and has none of the serenity of a pond or meadow. It seems to Thoreau that "some vital part" of him "escape[s] through the loose grating of his ribs."[7] Ktaadn gives him inhospitable, unfinished creation, quite unlike the dawns he recounts by Walden Pond. This sight doesn't so much bring the world alive as remind him that the world can be desolate and lost.

Worlds otherwise dull or drained can spring alive in Thoreau's ample poetic perceptions, in simple sentences or extended befitting reveries. He seeks the ship wrecked remains of his friend, Margaret Fuller. The place of Fuller's bones, as we've seen, is at first of dark mourning or grief; yet a sprig rises to become a ship's spar and then a rugged cairn, holding her reign and majesty. A place otherwise redolent of death is transformed toward radiance and dawn. "Her bones were alone with the beach and the sea, whose roar seemed to address them ... as if there were an understanding between them and the ocean that necessarily left me out."[8] So her communion with the endless surf lengthens the time she inhabits.

Thoreau witnesses communion too vast, long-lasting, and impersonal to include him. Nevertheless, the beach cradles Fuller, a fellow-writer and activist, and he has time to give witness to her majesty. On Ktaadn, in contrast, he is accosted by the impossibility of anything like communion, personal *or* impersonal, the impossibility *any* contact with the terrain. It

---

[5] *Week*, p. 382.
[6] "Ktaadn," p. 64.
[7] Ibid.
[8] *Cape Cod*, p. 123.

repels his presence, his view goes blank and spirit flees, as if before a terror that cannot afford to be seen.

3.

Sight is one path of access of the world. Taste of the world is another. Thoreau is wise in the taste of wild apples, the taste of a breeze. But even here, matters of angle, scale, and placement obtrude. The refreshing taste of wild apples expands toward the gods and eternal youth. Wild apples "pierce and sting and permeate us with their spirit," and hold the elixirs "that keep the gods forever young."[9] To taste is to know spirit, to enjoy an immediacy that brings moments of fulfillment.

At its best the world provides relish that answers desires for taste, for contact, for communion (that's relishing). "What a healthy out-of-door appetite it takes to relish the apple of life, the apple of the world!"[10] The life of the world is the life of our tastes for apples or sharp winds, for damp earth beneath our feet or a stream's curling eddy around blistered toes. The world's life is the flickering of our mobile senses and visceral responses, and also the life of our words. The contacts Thoreau transmits are conveyed through words that reenact his primordial contacts—with the world, but also with the words of the *Gita*, of the Gospels, of Milton, and of endless others.

Thoreau is a saunterer. Seeing, hearing, and tasting, and a sense of breath and body in motion, and then stilled, converge in his tramping. Walking is an art, he says, that very few have mastered. (A parallel thought is that very few know how to die.) To leave that provocation in mid-air—that I may not know how to walk—leaves his words strange, and the world strange, and wonderful, as it would be for a child in its best moments.

If we give our heart to that wonder, that we might yet learn to walk, we acknowledge the world as a holy place we inhabit yet have not quite entered. Henry Bugbee, a philosopher deeply indebted to Thoreau, characterizes philosophy as a "walking meditation of the place."[11] This fits Thoreau's practice exactly. He is a tramper living out a visceral communion with body, earth, and air that this wedding of walking and thinking so wonderfully affords. Sauntering, as we've heard, is a beholding-in-motion, a moving in and toward the wondrous, sacred, or intimate sublime. It beholds a

---

[9] *Essays*, "Wild Apples," p. 459; p. 448.
[10] Ibid., p. 461.
[11] See Henry Bugbee, *The Inward Morning, A Philosophical Exploration in Journal Form*, Alasdair MacIntyre (foreword), Edward F. Mooney (intro.) (Athens, GA: University of Georgia Press, 1999), p. 139.

place in motion even as its beholder is mobile. Both are in unending creation. Sauntering is pilgrimage through the ordinary-become-sacred, or the sacred-become-ordinary, the sacramental act of taking steps steeped in the wilds all around. The sacred is housed just over the horizon and right here underfoot. Wherever earth, sky, and waters, wherever blossom of trees, sounds of companions, and tastes of apples greet us under the aspect of wonder—there we have sacred sites. Their sacrality is their power to transform as we move therein.

Wondrous contact is not "raw data" but schooled and thought-seasoned toward the bounteous. As Thoreau has it, "We are comparatively deaf and dumb and blind, without smell or taste or feeling … What is it, then, to educate but to develop these divine germs [seeds] called the senses?"[12] We sense the taste of apples (gifts of the gods), the meteor flash that is John Brown, the communing of the sea with Fuller's bones.[13] These are achievements of sharpened eyes, ears, and tongues. At times Thoreau comes close to suggesting that the world is not primitively, in itself, either sacred or unsacred, but awaits its best advent through our tuned sensibilities. At other times he seems to intimate that the things of the world are already sacred, primitively, if only we become properly attuned. He hones our senses toward receiving the bounteous in its passing.

The poet-walker is also a singer and rower, matching breath, limbs, and motion to song. "We rowed by turns swiftly over the surface [of the lake], singing such boat songs as we could remember."[14] As all singers must, Thoreau listened—in expectation of answering evening songs. He awaited the "doleful trill" and "wailing hymns" of owls;[15] (or their "melodious hooting").[16] He hears the "thump" of the hares;[17] the thunder and first voice of the toad.[18] Linking the voice of thunder with the voice of the toad reminds us of Thoreau's refusal to cut off the grand sublime from little things equally arresting and elusive—the petite or ordinary sublime.[19]

In a college essay, Thoreau holds that the sublime is not triggered by fear or danger, as Burke and Kant would hold. "Contact with the infinite," he says, occurs through wonder and awe, and responds less to fear and death than delight and birth. Delight and rebirth are the marks of awakening with the

---

[12] *Week*, p. 382.
[13] "meteor flash," "Last Days," p. 427.
[14] "Ktaadn," p. 37.
[15] *Walden*, "Sounds," p. 121 [para 18].
[16] *Journal*, December 15, 1856, p. 182.
[17] *Walden*, "Winter Animals," p. 271 [para 14].
[18] April 17, 1856, p. 289.
[19] Kierkegaard speaks of finding the sublime in the pedestrian: *Fear and Trembling*, Alastair Hannay (trans.) (New York: Penguin, 1985), p. 70.

dawn, of the discovery of a "newer testament" that can palliate afflictions and dreads.[20] Greek gods are saved from fear of death, yet the thunder of Zeus could still bring them to awe, clearing heavens for dawn. We can think of the top of Ktaadn, or looking skyward in his boat, as moments of "the sublime" or "infinite." He'd take his boat to the pond's middle, "lying on my back across the seats ... *dreaming awake.*"[21] Rousseau, too, has a reverie, looking up from a boat's bottom finding above a glimpse of "the infinite."[22]

Thoreau awakens to the lusty herald of a cock at first light, and to the godly music of thunder, yet he would not slight the wonder of more diminutive sounds, the intimate sublime. He builds a cover affording a dry place for sleep. There he's serenaded "by the sound of raindrops on the cedar splints which covered the roof."[23]

4.

To have a love in and for the world is to be alive to its presence and preservation. Sight, taste, scent, and hearing are modalities that expand, close down, or transfigure—even as the world they contact expands, contracts, and transfigures. On Ktaadn Thoreau's sense of the world falls away. Somewhere between desperation and ecstasy, he shouts "rocks, trees, wind on our cheeks! The solid earth! The actual world! The common sense! Contact! Contact! Who are we? Where are we?"[24]

We get contact and orientation (we hope), and then turn to powers of articulation and conveyance. Sometimes a dumb stupor supervenes, or a speechless awe. But if we yearn for poetic translation, or if it descends unbidden, words then enact and rearticulate the mobility and evanescence of the world at hand. We take in importance from one angle to the next, from a lack of touch to vivid sight or hearing, from the corrupt to the redemptive. It's a poet's gift in which we all take part. When schooled toward the sacred, contact restores bounteous worlds.

Thoreau's pen and capacity for contact moves us from stench to sweet lilies, from bare bones to saint's relics, from a noose that kills to a hanging that launches a meteor, John Brown.[25] Thoreau casts the day of Brown's hanging as the day of his "translation." Brown is "translated" from a man having his last

---

[20] "Walking," p. 254 [para 82].
[21] *Walden*, "The Ponds," p. 185 [para 21], (my emphasis).
[22] Rousseau, *Reveries of a Solitary Walker* (New York: Penguin, 1979), 5th Walk, p. 85.
[23] "Ktaadn," p. 23.
[24] "Ktaadn," p. 113.
[25] "Last Days," p. 427.

meal with his wife to "a divine spark,"[26] and from a spark to "a meteor," making him "more alive than he ever was."[27] Brown earns "immortality," and is now "in the clearest light that shines on this land."[28] These metamorphoses parallel the shifting beach scene where Fuller's bones attain an apotheosis as she communes with the endless sea. Thoreau gives us life through words whose spring seems inevitable, compelling. They are companions to dawns or thunderclaps.

A single passion—*yearning for life's wellsprings*—makes Thoreau's political words of a piece with his sauntering or rowing. It's a passion for life that funds *protest* at its defilement by injustice, that *stiffens spirit* on a climb on Ktaadn, that *opens to soothing waters,* meadows, or woods. He opens to life's swirls to write them as he finds them (and as they find him).

The lives of words mingle the everyday with the wild. Tapping those lives, we share them with others. The untamed, unknown, or sublime are sources of life to which we have immediate experiential access and have mediate access through the lives of words. We can amplify such life linguistically for a natural flow through families, tribes, collectives, and our solitude. Language is not a private preserve. Thoreau brings us to fields of words (as we read). In turn these words sing the fields of Maine (and we hear). He keeps us among lustrous things and things austere, delivering us from shadow and collapse. For thunder to scrub my world clean with a bang, I must have ears attuned. (I can't be deaf, or too absorbed to notice), and the heavens must roaringly provide. Portals for thunder or the thump of frogs allow sheen or ornament to arrive from the world that obligingly delivers it. The ear gives power to thunder and thunder powerfully shapes the ear. Contacts transfigure bi-directionally. Thoreau is shaped by the arrival of birdsong, and the world is richer as his ear is shaped. In learning to listen the world is reborn.

Thoreau is not the same after writing *The Maine Woods* nor is Ktaadn, now misted in ghostly power. Fuller's bones are not the same after their poetic transfiguration. The body secreted from Harper's Ferry to Manhattan's Battery, and then by rail to North Elba for burial, is not the same after "A Plea for Captain John Brown" and "The Last Days of John Brown."

5.

It's not just the crow of a barnyard cock that transforms night to day, and not just a slender stick marking Fuller's bones that triggers the change from

---

[26] "A Plea," p. 415.
[27] "Last Days," p. 428.
[28] "Last Days," p. 428.

a site of unnecessary death to the raising of a cairn and a communion of bones with the lap of the sea. On occasion, at issue is the raising up of an entire polity, nation or region—not particulars but a world itself, gripped by desolation and demanding restoration, as he addresses the darkness of a nation under slavery. There is a coming apocalypse, and John Brown is its prophet and avenging angel. Corruption has left its inescapable olfactory stench. In "Slavery in Massachusetts," Thoreau recounts the unbearable odor of Daniel Webster's joining slavers in support of the fugitive slave act of 1850. The Massachusetts senator sponsored a bill that strengthened Southern power, and granted license to slavers infiltrating the North to hunt down blacks on the run.

Anthony Burns was the center of one of the more violent and celebrated cases of slave recapture and attempted rescue. "Slavery in Massachusetts" was Thoreau's exasperated, angry, even despairing, but ultimately affirming response to the Burns case, delivered July 4, 1854, at an abolitionist protest and rally in Framingham, Massachusetts. It was published in Garrison's *Liberator*, July 21.[29] We find Hell morphing toward the possibility of paradise in the wafting scent of a lily. Thomas Wentworth Higginson, a friend of Thoreau, was a leader in the attempted rescue of Burns, and was to become a member of "The Secret Six," a group who financially supported John Brown's Kansas paramilitary attack at Harper's Ferry. He was also an editorial confidant at *The Atlantic* of the young Emily Dickinson.

Burns was cornered by Southern hunters and jailed in the Boston courthouse, as the new federal law required. A crowd of several hundred abolitionists and free blacks joined for a rescue attempt, battering a hole in the doors. The crowd grew to at least two thousand. In the assault, shots were fired. A jailer was killed, apparently stabbed. Some gained entry, but Burns was held inaccessible on the third floor. Federal soldiers moved in, foreign soldiers, as it were—enforcers of a despised law, the work of an alien, power. Or so it was for Thoreau and a crowd of angry and humiliated New Englanders.

On his way to the ship that would return him to captivity, Burns was paraded as a trophy between columns of cavalry and foot soldiers in full military dress, rifles loaded, a horse-drawn cannon at the ready, should it be needed. The ceremony was a show of Federal power and of the nullity of a slave. Burns was made to endure a humiliatingly slow and shackled walk down to a Federal ship that would return him to the South. Fifty thousand citizens lined the streets shouting "shame!" at the spectacle. Cannon, rifles, four Federal companies in full regalia, two companies of Boston militia,

---

[29] William Lloyd Garrison, *The Liberator*, 1854, July 21.

and several artillery companies, ridiculed the Abolitionist cause and Burns himself. Soldiers were ordered to shoot into the crowd at any sign of "disturbance"—hence a restaging of the Boston Massacre. Southern slave-catchers gloated. The military was "teaching New Englanders a lesson." The headline in a Maine Abolitionist newspaper was "Rubbing it in! Man-Hunting in Boston."[30]

There was no New England spring that year for Thoreau. The fragrance of woods and meadows is lost. Everything offends his keen moral sense and blocks his sense of the woods. In place of sauntering he has only joyless slogs through stench. Yet at last, a sweet smell wafts from swampy waters. After walking us through pages of moral pollution, he comes upon a fragile lily, so slight it is almost overlooked. His keen nose opens this site of surviving heaven. This might be the wisdom of Staretz Silouan: "Keep your mind in hell, and despair not."[31] The sweet swamp-lily opens to the wondrous. The flower whose tendrils descend indecorously to a fouled anchorage gives off a fragrance rising from eons of accumulated grime. Mud feeds sweet bloom. Thoreau finds in this the hope of a world reborn.

Julia Ward Howe was the wife of one of the undercover Secret Six, men who at great risk provided financial support for John Brown's work. She invokes the lily in verses published in 1862, too late for Thoreau to have heard them. They were set to the tune we know as "John Brown's Body." We hear the lily's Gospel roots:

> In the beauty of the lilies Christ was born across the sea, with a glory in his bosom that transfigures you and me. As he died to make men holy, let us die to make men free.[32]

Thoreau had no doubt that John Brown died to make men free.

6.

We've heard of a transfiguration of apples and bones and of the stench of the woods and meadows, and a transfiguration of Ktaadn to dark Chaos. Thoreau transfigures the death—and life—of John Brown. Thoreau offers a new, transfiguring angle of hearing. On the day of Brown's death, he "heard that he was hung" but did not "hear that he was dead ..."—and Thoreau lets

---

[30] See Austin Willey (ed.), Maine's *Portland Inquiry*, June 1, 1854.
[31] Silouan is quoted on the frontispiece to Gillian Rose, *Love's Work* (Schocken, 1997).
[32] "John's Brown's Body" was already a popular military camp song, following the tune of the Battle Hymn of the Republic. Here, beauty, holiness, and freedom converge: see Furtak, "The Value of Being: On Appreciating the Beauty of the World."

the enigma linger.[33] If he had heard that Brown was hung, why, for heaven's sake, would he need to hear that Brown was dead? We must work with his words as he gives them—not slough them off as poetic acrobatics. He tests our imaginative patience in telling us that a life might not perish in hanging, and that hanging might not bring death.

Thoreau's refusal to hear that Brown is dead opens a door: Brown might live on as a martyr. Or Thoreau might refuse to "hear that he was dead" because it's impossible to believe, or comprehend, that Brown is dead—not because the shock of the news can't be absorbed but because anyone as alive in action, principle, and spirit as he was cannot have died for all the life in him.

It may be that Brown survives indefinitely into an extended future (though he was hanged) in just the way the life of a meteor or of a Schubert Sonata outlasts the microscopically small, clocked interval of its entry into, and departure from, the world. My most recent contact (two weeks ago) with a Schubert Sonata, in one sense ended when my CD player stopped, and I paused before moving on. Yet I know simultaneously that the music has not ceased but extends sempiternally. Taking the long view, we might say that John Brown's origin is as old and dateless as Old Testament prophets or angels, and that his life extends forward from his hanging to our time and into an indeterminate beyond. The eloquence of his life outlasts the interval between his census-recorded life-and-death in much the same way as the radiance of a meteor outlasts the momentary flash of its light or the echoing rebound of a Sonata outlasts my most recent hearing.

Life and death are anomalous. They follow no single law of determination. My recording of Sonata D946 has stopped playing but that does not determine that it is not still alive—as ever. The gloaming shifts imperceptibly toward night but that does determine that the day is not still alive—as ever. As I stride out to the backyard from the kitchen, the threshold of my door belongs to the beckoning outside, but that does not determine that the threshold does not also belong to the inside of the house. The anomalous location of thresholds may matter less than the anomalous extent of the life of a Schubert Sonata, and both may matter less than the anomaly of Brown's death. He was hung yet perhaps, we hear, he is not definitively dead.

Thoreau calls tidal creatures belonging to sea and to land and to neither and both "anomalous creatures."[34] Something anomalous escapes a law or pattern of expected and well-defined action or status. It belongs only problematically to them. As Thoreau has it, Brown is anomalous

---

[33] *Essays*, "The Last Days of John Brown," p. 428
[34] *Cape Cod*, p. 81.

ontologically. There's something deeply problematic about whether his hanging gives or takes life. A medic's rule-bound conventions for determining the place and time of his death are not absolutely determinative; he belongs to an anomalous wild.

Daniel Webster miserably failed to survive his death. His vote for a strengthened fugitive slave law was his noose. He died even though censustakers found him living a year later. For a previously admired Northern Senator to promote a law that strengthened the powers of slavers to roam the New England countryside marked his moral death.[35] On pain of arrest, the law forced citizens of Concord and Boston to assist in the capture of escaped slaves. In 1850 Theodore Parker preached in Boston that Webster "takes back his [previous anti-slavery] words and comes himself to be slavery's slave."[36] Webster is an anomaly, a slave, despite appearances. Webster died despite appearances.

In 1852, on the occasion of Webster's physiological departure, Parker asks if he can now mourn the man who two years earlier had signed the hated bill. He answers that he cannot. Webster *died two years earlier*.[37] John Greenleaf Whittier reinforced the point: "When faith is lost, when honor dies, the man is dead!"[38] Webster dies when he disavows his antislavery position, not in a coroner's verdict. Despite hanging, John Brown lives on. When faith is secure and honor alive, the man is alive. Long after clerks stamp him "dead," John Brown lives.

7.

If we credit Plato, to abandon the thought of death is to abandon philosophy. Courts list the living and dead, but those records do not reveal who really lives and dies. Thoreau cites the inscription, *Memento mori!*—Think of your death!—worrying that we hear this only in a "groveling" sense.[39] We grovel before death rather than seek that angle—"the influx of a better thought"—from which life defeats death.[40] In order to die you must first have lived, and among the villagers or politicians, who is truly alive? An exultant life

---

[35] Both Thoreau and Bronson Alcott allude to gunshots in the woods signaling recapturing, killing or terrorizing a man, woman, or child on the way to Canada.
[36] See Edward J. Renehan, Jr., *The Secret Six, The True Tale of the Men who Conspired with John Brown* (Columbia: University of South Carolina Press, 1997), p. 47.
[37] Ibid. p. 48.
[38] Ibid.
[39] *Essays*, "A Plea," p. 414.
[40] *Walden*, "Spring," p. 303 [para 19].

passes through death to add *more* to life. If, as Thoreau claims "we've wholly forgotten how to die", it's because we've forgotten how to live.[41] We abandon life by letting death be merely life that is "rotted or sloughed off."[42] We die each day we fail to live, and each day we live death has failed. Some will have death determined only by medics or census-takers. Others will have death determined by loss of character or honor or exuberant vitality. Brown's hanging does not kill but amplifies his character, radiance and honor. Thoreau "fails to hear" that Brown is dead—because he lives.[43] Kierkegaard suggests that Socrates escapes death at the moment of sentencing.[44] At that moment his character is fixed beyond corrosion or decay. He cannot lose integrity through threats of death; it has no grip. Thoreau sees Brown's hanging against the martyrdom of Socrates as well as of Christ.

Cultures keep moral moments alive. They keep persons of great character alive through their display in texts or theater, in reveries passed on by kin or community. Such moments fuel worthy aspirations and are fulfilled in deeds and dispositions. Ideals of character, action, or bearing provide tacit or explicit models to measure life's worth in frankness or honor, courage or great kindness, dedication to justice or to the needs of kin. These pictures of worth get embedded as inescapable parts of lived reality. An ideal, or set of them is sustained through our praising judgments, and through our continued affirmations in concert with others. Aversions play a role, too. Dispraise or mocking distance keeps the unworthy at bay, indirectly reinforcing the worthy counterpart. We affirm and dispraise in concert, a fact hidden by a North-Atlantic ideological regime valorizing autonomy. However, "No man is an Island," and no woman either. We grow up in families, neighborhoods, tribes, and collectivities that shape us even as we learn to step out on our own. Convictions grow amidst parents, neighbors, friends, and adopted next-of-kin. And some, like Thoreau, might become, as an adopted next-of-kin, our conscience. Exemplars are found and maintained through depiction, song, and direct face-to-face exchange. In contact, we soak in their traits, bearing, and deeds. John Brown is an exemplar for Thoreau, and perhaps through praise, he becomes one for us. Thoreau says, in effect, "*Here is Life! Behold!*"

As an animated physiology, Brown ceases with his hanging; yet his story, his life, his ensoulment does not stop there. In the words of the Civil War camp song, Thoreau keeps him from "amoulderin' in his grave"—keeps

---

[41] "A Plea," p. 414.
[42] "A Plea," p. 435.
[43] "Last Days," p. 428.
[44] See *Fear and Trembling*, p. 141.

him from diminishing to wood shavings.⁴⁵ Beyond physiology, humans enter a cultural life that links sisters, mothers, brothers, friends, teachers, mayors, musicians, whose souls richly mix and are receptively porous to each other in the moment and over time. And we enter the abundance of Plato, Shakespeare, Christ, the Buddha, and endless others, an abundance that continues indefinitely past the demise of a discrete physiology. This exchange, flowing over indefinitely expanding time and space, constitutes what we can call "infinite culture." It shapes what it is to be among the living.

Taking Thoreau rowing, seeking wild apples, or defending John Brown as signs of his being alive, we can see this "becoming alive" at three overlapping levels of resolution. First, he exercises poetic capacities of reception and transformation at the level of perception. A splinter appears as a spar. Second, he exercises moral capacities of perception, deed, and character in styles of living that carry life beyond the confines of its merely physiological expression. If he risks bodily harm or social acceptability for an ideal then he shows that character can trump physiological-only or conformist-only considerations. And at a third level of resolution, his "becoming alive" is marked by his exercise of hermeneutical, interpretive, and expressive capacities, engaging, altering, and reproducing, the culture he inherits and inhabits.

Powers of cultural articulation let us articulate and reproduce our inherited poetic and moral surround, passed on in texts, folklore, and endless conversation that we in turn pass on. We receive and dispatch ways of understanding comportment toward kin, strangers, and those exemplary characters we praise and admire, as they live out their place under the sun. It is in this context of cultural transmission that we encounter Thoreau's powers of imaginative translation, his capacity for lyric transfigurations of others that in turn transfigure our own imaginations. Ktaadn becomes an outpost of the gods. Fuller's remains become relics. John Brown becomes a meteor. These are radical rejuvenations and amplifications of otherwise commonplace perceptions of Ktaadn, Fuller, and Brown. These uncommon perceptions save them from archival dustbins. Ortega calls these efforts "essays in intellectual love," essays that effect "salvations."⁴⁶

Effecting "salvations" through poetic translation incurs risks. We are asked to believe not only that Fuller's bones are in communion with the sea,

---

⁴⁵ The shavings from creating mouldings were "moulderings."
⁴⁶ Ortega calls his *Meditations on Quixote* "essays in intellectual love." As he puts it, "[these essays] ... have no informative value whatever; they are not summaries, either—they are rather what a humanist of the seventeenth century would have called 'salvations.'" See my discussion in *Lost Intimacy in Western Thought: Personal Philosophy from Thoreau to Cavell* (New York: Continuum, 2009).

but that the bulk of villagers and citizens who have entered the census tables in and about Concord have not yet learned to walk, let alone learned to live or die. Do these enigmatic pronouncements destroy Thoreau's credibility? Or do they snap us awake, alert us to the anomalous zones in which life-and-death play? For Thoreau, these startling reformulations are neither passing fancy nor conceptual tinkering.

One way or another, Thoreau's poetic translations move us into reality, into contacts that amplify and transfigure one register of reality to become its successor. With the right touch, such change will seem mysteriously inevitable. Thoreau drops us into ignorance about what it is to walk or to live or die. He floats the strange reality that even Washington and Franklin have neither lived nor died. Their life-and-death is no more than a *mechanical tick*. As Thoreau wryly puts it, they merely "ran down like a clock"; they "were let off with out dying." Released from the ranks, "they were merely missing one day."[47] Or so it appears under the light that is the meteor John Brown.

---

[47] "A Plea" p. 414.

12

Souls in Infinite Culture

Behold! I tell you a mystery. We shall not all sleep, but we shall all be changed, in a moment, in the twinkling of an eye, at the last trumpet.
—1 Corinthians 151–2

He is more alive than ever he was ... He has earned immortality.
—"The Last Days of John Brown"[1]

1.

Thoreau achieves resurrection for John Brown. Along with Emerson and a few others, he meets Brown for an evening some months before the raid on Harper's Ferry. Later, after his civilly certified death, Thoreau delivers John Brown transfigured. Brown would be ill-served by having the interval of his life recorded only in the clerk's notes registering his birth and burial, or if he is a meteor, as Thoreau proposes, in the astronomer's timing of the few seconds of its flash. A photographic plate can't pick up the extended cultural impact of a meteor, nor can it catch the meteor that is John Brown. The interval of Thoreau's beholding is much longer, for it is repeated again and again, with each reading generation, like my hearing and rehearing of a late Schubert's sonata. As portents, meteors are as timeless as John Brown is timeless. Now a full century and a half later he is revived yet again—as a portent.

Thoreau notes the dates Brown leaves Concord, his battle at Harper's Ferry, his mounting the gallows and his burial in North Elba. But in a deep sense these dates do not answer whether Brown is living or dead. As a philosopher, Thoreau wonders how one can die if one has never lived, and how one can live if one's death does not echo through the tissues of one's life, making it add to, rather than deplete, that life. He says Washington and Franklin did not really die, for their passing failed to speak, failed to echo back through their life and on to inspire others. Unlike the deaths of Socrates or Christ or Brown, theirs were not deaths died for something of monumental importance.

Brown dies for freedom, his death speaks for it, enriching the life devoted to it. "It seems," Thoreau writes, "as if no man had ever died in America

---

[1] *Essays*, "The Last Days of John Brown," p. 428.

before, for "in order to die you must first have lived."[2] From a plateau like that beneath Ktaadn's cloud-shrouded place of the gods, the place of creation, a census-keeper's tally of life and death dwindles precipitously in significance. An apotheosis brings John Brown into view, and diminishes Franklin and Washington. As we've heard, their deaths are no more than a mechanical tick. As Thoreau slyly puts it, they merely "ran down like a clock"; they "were let off with out dying." Released from service, "they were merely missing one day."[3] From the summit of Ktaadn where gods forge worlds, these were minor deaths, or no deaths at all. "No temple's veil was rent," Thoreau protests, "only a hole dug somewhere."[4]

Why should a veil be rent? Well, we want to learn something, not only from a life, but from a death. Thoreau finds no shattering revelation in commonplace demise. Brown's death rends a veil; it conveys—is—a revelation, an apocalypse. To die on a gallows for the best of things throws light back on life, affirmatively. To listen to Brown's words from jail, Thoreau says, is to hear a new testament, and he confronts his countrymen with scathing irony, "You don't know your testament when you see it."[5]

2.

Thoreau installs a standard for life-and-death that will seem harsh and ungenerous to those many thousands who hope to have lived, and hope that their deaths are fitting and instructive, despite being mundane or unheroic. Thoreau tells us that only one who fully lives can really die, and only one who really dies can have fully lived. For Thoreau, Brown is not just one of a number who share the widely distributed characteristic of fully living (and dying). He embodies a measure—an impossible, or at least extravagant measure—of living.

John Brown is an exemplar by means of whom we know an excellence, and without whom we would be ignorant. Everest is not only an *example* of high alpine terrain; it is *exemplary*, the *measure*, of snowcapped majesty. Brown is not simply an *example* of moral heroism, any more than the "yard stick" at the Bureau of Standards is simply an example of something a yard long. He is the final measure of what heroism will be. Thoreau drives this measure up and out of reach. In this apotheosis, Brown rises to a select

---

[2] "A Plea," p. 414.
[3] Ibid.
[4] Ibid.
[5] Ibid.

company that includes Socrates and Christ and but one or two others. For ordinary mortals aspiring to virtue or excellence, this standard might seem useless or brutally dismissive. Thoreau is disheartening and candid: "Only a half dozen or so have died [hence lived] since the world began."[6]

I am sticking to the idea that for Thoreau, Brown is a measure, an exemplar of moral heroism. I am not asking whether, all things considered, John Brown is a good man, or whether his actions are justifiable. Were I to pursue it, the matter of justification would entail asking if our moral landscape can accommodate apparent "moral terrorists," as it were; and asking if Brown might be less a terrorist than a prematurely enlisted Union Army officer (he jumped the gun); and asking if he is a reincarnation of the farmers and villagers of Concord who opened fire on those surely legitimate defenders of civic order and the law, the British Army; and asking if his action was one in a sequence of earlier battles, a tactical response, say, to the slavers' sack of Lawrence, Kansas.

I set aside issues of justification in favor of seeking intelligibility. I ask how Thoreau's position can be intelligible in a charitable reconstruction of his words. I ask why, in general, we should pay attention to men or women held up as exemplary when they install a unrealizable standard. Why valorize moral virtue (in the life of Brown or Socrates or in exemplary walking) when this deflates those with less heroic capacities or aspirations? Well, a standard hopelessly out of reach still pushes us somewhere beyond an uninspired merely *passable* life (or death).

To give leeway to a higher requirement can pull us out of complacency and that can be ecstasy. A glimpse of the best makes the merely passable no longer the only game in town. Excellence unattainable by most can be exultingly inspiring. Listening to a performer I could never become, I learn something special about musical depth. Thoreau sets a measure of valor at the highest notch. To complain that it seems too high sounds like sour grapes or resentment. From this angle, an exemplar does not give us a specific goal to attain but gives us a new light altering the landscape. Perhaps a lofty anti-slavery oration makes slavery less possible than it was. The world after Brown is not the same as the world before Brown. He does not give us the specific telos of our action but casts his light over the space in which our specific actions will occur. Those who graze in a good-enough, passable pasture will find Brown mad, a fanatic, a fantasy-driven killer, subject to delusions of grandeur, and irresponsible, threatening all civil order. Thoreau based his assessment of Brown on first-hand acquaintance. Some months

[6] Ibid.

before Harper's Ferry, Brown had approached both Thoreau and Emerson for funds—without being terribly specific about his plans.

Talking with him over dinner, both men were impressed by Brown's demeanor, courage, and character. In their view—and they were sharp observers of character—it was no fanatic or bungler that they faced. Through his apotheosis, Thoreau saves Brown from the abuse he otherwise attracts, and saves some in Concord (and its surrounds) from indifference to his testament. And Thoreau's writing stiffens the spirit of Abolitionists.

Our ideals of full living are many and varied. We may fail at the demands John Brown exacts, and if Thoreau's practice sets the bar, we may also fail at truly walking. We can nevertheless sharpen our sensibilities in the light of their lives. And there's more than one standard to pit against the complacency of only passable living. Brown pitches a demand at apocalyptic intensity. But we need not choose between the life of Brown and the way of quiet desperation. More gentle calls come from "Walking," "Wild Apples," and *Walden*. There's a paradise in the taste of a December apple, picked some months after freezing when its fermentation makes it the favorite of the gods. We can exalt in knowing wild apples, and that can be achievement enough.

3.

When Henry's brother died of lockjaw, Henry nearly died with him. It was as if their physiologies were porous, letting a moment of disease pass from one to the other. Henry took on all the symptoms of John's disease. Their souls, too, became porous. John's death entered Henry's spirit, both killing part of him and bringing alive an impulse to write an account of their time together.[7] This resuscitation of John's spirit came out in *A Week*. Later still, Thoreau takes in John Brown's spirit, and sends it out in writing. Reversing directionality, John Thoreau and John Brown enter Henry's spirit through the porous membrane that is his soul, and transform it. Henry suffers Brown's affliction, and having allowed it entry, keeps it from death, writing "A Plea for Captain John Brown," and for his burial, "The Last Days of John Brown." Brown's spirit enters Henry's and is blessed. Writing becomes consecration.

---

[7] See Wai-Chee Dimock's path-breaking discussion. A somatic-psychic border is porous within any single person, but also between persons and across time. Henry's body is porous to John's, and his psychic borders are porous, receiving the *Gita* that then links humankind globally and through time from the *Gita* to Gandhi, to King, and to endless others: "Global Civil Society: Thoreau on Three Continents," *Through Other Continents: American Literature Across Deep Time* (Princeton, NJ: Princeton University Press, 2006), pp. 7–22.

As Thoreau puts it, Brown is a transcendentalist in virtue of transcending garden-variety goodness. He risks his life escorting a dozen hunted strangers to a Canadian freedom through hostile and armed territory. He pursues a heroic vocation. He would bring captives from captivity. He aroused a dread among the Missourians through whose territory he passed, Thoreau said, for it was known they confronted a man who would not be taken. Later, as news of Harper's Ferry traveled north, Brown became a meteor, an Angel of Light, a portent and taste of apocalypse ahead.[8] "He has a spark of divinity in him," Thoreau says, and attests, "Of all the men who were my contemporaries, it seemed to me that John Brown was the only one who had not died."[9] Crito offers Socrates an escape from certain execution. A Kansas fighter, Silas Soule, offers Brown an escape, which he refuses. Like Socrates, Brown secures "immortal life." Thoreau would save Brown as Paul would save Jesus and as Plato would save Socrates. Each figure inhabits a field of spirit, a porous place of mutual openness, spread temporally forward and back, and spatially in every direction. Saving words arc in this place, to receive saving words, reanimate them, and pass on their salvations to endless unknown others. Souls take in, give back.

4.

We are biological and cultural creatures that exercise power and undergo powerlessness in the reception and reproduction of second nature—cultural spirit. We live in—and suffer under—lasting institutions that surpass physiological inheritance: music, politics, and schooling; ways of burial, birth, and war; of painting, poetry, and sports; of raising kids and marrying them; of writing out lives. These forms of life are supra-personal—institutional—and *intensely* personal. They inform the persons we are, our second natures. A culture's practices and varied exemplars take residence as an inheritance that we in turn distribute. Thoreau is invaded by his brother's suffering in a physiological transmission of symptoms, brother to brother. Biologically, John had lockjaw, Henry didn't, one survives and the other doesn't. It's also true that Henry enters a new somatic-psychic configuration (call it Henry-J, or John-H) that translates forward in the cultural words of *A Week on the Concord*, and translates still further afield as *A Week* finds living breath in my classroom.

Perhaps in his present incarnations as *A Week*, *Walden*, and "Civil Disobedience" (or "Resistance"), Thoreau is as robust as he ever was. To

---

[8] "A Plea," p. 416.
[9] "Last Days," p. 428.

acknowledge the liveliness of Thoreau, or Henry-John, confirms the efficacy of cumulative generations of cultural reproduction, and confirms porous boundaries between Henry and *A Week,* between *A Week* and us, and between us and those to come. We are porous and reciprocally dependent. When I shut down a gate to you, I kill part of you and part of myself. If enough souls shut down to a style of music, that style dies, ceases to be translated into ever-new life. If I shut down to the brothers-Thoreau, part of *A Week* will die. If collectively we die to the spirit of *A Week,* culturally we die a small (or large) death.

Imagine that *A Week* goes unread and dies, and after it "Resistance to Civil Government" and *Walden.* Henry will have suffered a death and a dimension of global interconnectedness will have died, as well. The death of "Resistance" or "Disobedience" will take with it a part of Gandhi and Martin Luther King, and lessen the punch of the idea and practice of resistance that underlie parts of American and post-colonial Indian history. Conversely, Thoreau and Gandhi survive as "Civil Disobedience" is attentively read. We live and die in solitude but also collectively.

Reliving Thoreau's "Resistance" or *A Week on the Concord* resuscitates part of cultural life that stretches back to Thoreau's Concord, and rebounds forward through Gandhi and King and rebounds backward to resuscitate some of the oldest writing on the globe. Thoreau reaches back to the *Gita* and over to Greece and Aeschylus and then forward to Milton who in turn reaches back to Biblical time and space. *A Week* relives a river trip a mere century and a half ago and also relives passages on death and war that Thoreau culls and transmutes from the *Bhagavad-Gita.* We might think of carbon radiating from an ancient bone, still sending out powerful signals from a distant past, say the past of the *Gita,* and the more recent past of *A Week.*

The image of radiation from a shard of ancient life predicts steady disintegration of signal. Yet some cultural artifacts or texts seem to show only expanding signal strength. Like storms gathering in mid-ocean, their energy grows with a force far exceeding their initial impulses. Or perhaps growing cultural dispersion is like the spread of an ancient species of forest life, a broadcast marked by multiple advances and declines, adaptations and transmutations. The *Gita* alive in the woods outside Concord is not exactly the *Gita* in third-century Bombay or in nineteenth-century London. Despite endless translations (and occasional mistranslations), "A Plea for Captain John Brown" and "Slavery in Massachusetts" amplify our natures—our second natures. These essays only gain strength as we hear beneath their surface Aeschylus, the Book of Joel, or the *Gita,* resonances that confirm infinite culture.

The weight of Thoreau's writing starts with his effort, but the distribution of its weight relies on others. We might hazard that his hopes are requited. If not everywhere, he has his attentive circle of readers keeping him alive, in France and Russia as well as Singapore and Concord. The day after Brown's death, no doubt under immunological stress, Thoreau caught the cold that would kill him, by coroner's accounts. By other accounts, he was just beginning his career.

5.

Cultural events spring out of their underlying material contexts. Catgut and varnish, wood and steel, are the material underlay for the sweet sound of a violin. But the spread of a new concerto heard around the globe is a transmission that springs free from a plane of catgut and steel.[10] John's material life-and-death (and his spirit) can spring into Henry's. The spirit of the *Gita*, a material book, can pass into the spirit of *A Week*. As we read *A Week*, we absorb a Henry animated by John and the *Gita*. Who knows the boundless material underlay of the *Gita* or Henry or John? For *A Week on the Concord*, we need at least lumber, paper, water, and pencils—and the institutions of publishing and libraries—and then cultural ceremonies of schooling in history and verse, and ears that can hear, all of which allow spirit to spring free.

The powers of bodily expressiveness begin with an underlay of physiology and bodily mobility, but these bodily—not to forget vocal—expressions spring free, say in an Anthony Hopkins cinematic performance that conveys feeling, rhythm, emotion, mood, intensity, inspiration, and so much more, a presence rooted in, but not reducible to, a material underlay. The powers of subtle poetic expressiveness begin with an underlay of intelligible words but can spring free in the eloquence of a Thoreau. His remark that he had not heard of John Brown's death is a crucial moment in the raising of Brown— from physiological extinction to spiritual perdurance. A spirit plays on the surface of an expressive body and voice, and a spirit plays on the surface of a prose and poetry penned from Concord.

---

[10] "There are in fact many materialisms, a whole zoo of species. There is perhaps only one species [I'd endorse]: I might call it simple, or perhaps common-sense, or perhaps pre-ontological materialism. Whatever exists in our cosmos is material, or at least has a material basis. [That is to say], whatever exists, however 'ethereal' or 'spiritual' it appears, has a material basis, and it could be undercut or destroyed by damaging or disorganizing some matter." Charles Taylor, "Descombes' Critique of Cognitivism," *Inquiry, An Interdisciplinary Journal of Philosophy* (47:3): 211.

We let powers at play in the words of the texts speak to us as our own—powers of mood, intensity, pitch, and particulars—where they transform and transfigure. Through openness to eloquence we achieve openness to otherness, to the other as our own, and ourselves in the other. And more directly, we find the spirit of Thoreau renewed in his evocation and consecration of the spirit of Ktaadn, of wild apples or lilies, of Fuller's bones and John Brown's death. And that keeps us alive.

Addenda

On "translation"

In the last paragraph of "The Last Days of John Brown," Thoreau figures the day of his death as the day of his "translation"—as if Brown's words and actions now begin lengthy translation, perhaps from an earthly to a heavenly text, but surely from his words and actions into words that Thoreau and others will offer to ensure he has not spoken in vain. Thus Brown is translated from the gallows to new life, and to an indefinitely extending life. In a different instance of translation, the old body is buried in North Elba, yet a new body appears translated to canvas, one painted by Thomas Hovenden nearly three decades later, ca. 1884, now hung in the Philadelphia Museum of Art. Thoreau foretells this cultural translation days before Brown's demise, predicting that the likeness of Brown will appear as an "ornament in some future national gallery" (final paragraph, "A Plea"). The man's spirit was also translated through its rendering by James Redpath (*Echoes of Harper's Ferry*, 1860), and later by W. E. B. Du Bois (*John Brown*, 1909), and Russell Banks (*Cloudsplitter: A Novel*, 1998).

The Burns case and before

In the Shadrach case (1851), the rescue of a purported slave from the Boston courthouse was successful: a group of free Blacks stormed the courtroom, taking the guards by surprise, grabbed Shadrach, and fled through a large supportive crowd to a waiting carriage. In the Sims case (1851), a rescue failed. Guards were prepared this time and in great enough number to keep a large crowd from breaking into the courthouse. Sims was returned to Georgia where his "master" gave him a near-fatal public whipping—as a lesson to would-be-rescuers in the north.[11] Burns was kidnapped (or

---

[11] This failed rescue and the subsequent Burns trial are recounted in Garrison's *Liberator* and in Austin Willey's *Portland Inquirer,* regularly, May 25–June 5, 1854.

arrested) on Wednesday, May 24, 1854. Friday, free blacks and white abolitions met separately to plan his rescue. Theodore Parker, Wendell Phillips, Thomas Wentworth Higginson, and others voted that night to muster a confrontation the next morning. Their black counterparts, who had been meeting separately, had already come to the streets to storm the courthouse. The attempted rescue that night became an improvised but concerted effort. There were enough guards within to repel them. Burns was tried under increased guard on May 27–31. The verdict was delayed so that Federal and Boston military and civic authorities had time to orchestrate a show of force. The verdict was delivered on June 2. The militias dressed Burns in silk and brightly colored pantaloons for a showy and humiliating walk to the ship for delivery South.

On Victor Hugo's plea

Victor Hugo wrote a plea for Brown's life from his Guernsey exile. It was dated December 2, 1859, the day Brown was hung, and was widely published in Europe and America:

> Politically speaking, the murder of John Brown would be an irreparable mistake. It would create in the Union a latent fissure that would in the long run break it. Brown's suffering might strengthen slavery in Virginia, but it would upend all American democracy. You save your shame, but you kill your glory. Morally speaking, it seems a part of the human light would put itself out, that the very notion of justice and injustice would hide itself in darkness, on that day where one would see the assassination of Emancipation by Liberty itself.
>
> [...] Let America know and ponder on this: there is something more frightening than Cain killing Abel, and that is Washington killing Spartacus.[12]

On the complex unity of Thoreau's production

Thoreau ends his last essay, "Wild Apples," with a long quote from the Old Testament Book of Joel that cites the Lord's dissatisfaction with his people and the consequent destruction by plague of all orchards, including life-giving apple orchards. Thoreau's citation of the destructiveness of the Lord should be linked to the presumption, quite common in the years leading up

---

[12] Victor Hugo, "Letter to *The London News* regarding John Brown," (1859), reprinted in James Redpath, *Echoes of Harper's Ferry* (Boston: Thayer and Eldridge, 1860), pp. 102ff.

to the Civil War, that the coming bloodshed would be God's vengeance on a sinful slave-holding people.

Thoreau is happy to move effortlessly from Hindu to Greek to Hebraic to Christian divinities. Just above, before these addenda, I recounted Thoreau's Dionysian joy in drinking a frozen, thawed, and fermented apple. Innocent, pagan, Dionysian delight precedes God's wrath—but surely not as *punishment* for pleasure. Jehovah's wrath, for Thoreau, is reserved for slavery and all those who permit it. It's a credit to Thoreau's genius that unlike the writing of *Walden*, which filled nearly a decade (1844–54), his eloquent political essays are started and completed in a matter of weeks in the heat of unrelenting political skirmishes.

If we pair "Slavery in Massachusetts" with "Wild Apples" we find a chiasmus, a crossing of opposites recurrent in Thoreau's writing. The fundamental movement of "Slavery in Massachusetts" is dark disillusionment with the stench of slavery's corruption—yet it ends with the hope of the lily. The fundamental movement of "Wild Apples" is gentle celebration of the land and its fruits (even though orchards are sadly replacing the wild)—yet it ends with the disillusioned wrath of God.[13]

If we are on the verge of apocalypse, and perhaps always on the verge, what will be revealed? For Thoreau, at least, I sense it will be something like the rhythms of an endless creation worth praising, where perishing heralds resuscitation and life heralds perishing. This interplay of heaven and hell is as central to Thoreau as his fundamental impulse of love for the world, the affirming and preserving impulse that lets his political writings implicate the preservation of human character and freedom and also the preservation of the expressive animation of nature. Simultaneously, this impulse lets Thoreau's evocations of nature implicate the preservation of character and freedom among the creatures, human and otherwise, who traverse and inhabit it.

Transcendentalism

A group of Concord intellectuals called themselves "transcendentalists" in tribute to what they knew of Kant's "transcendental philosophy." But the banner meant many things.[14] When Thoreau calls John Brown a "true transcendentalist," he means someone who transcends moral mediocrity. On the other hand, "The Transcendental Club" of Boston saw itself following

---

[13] The impetus to work out the interplay between "John Brown" and "Wild Apples" comes from Clark West.

[14] See Furtak's entry, "Thoreau" in *The Stanford Encyclopedia of Philosophy*.

the spirit of Kant and his Romantic and Idealistic successors. Frederick Hedge returned from Germany afire with Kant, Herder, Fichte, Schiller, Coleridge, and others, who offered a lofty moral philosophy that stressed, in Kant's phrase, "mankind's exit from its self-incurred immaturity."[15] Allied with imagination, reason could provide intuitions (notions not derived directly from worldly experience), resembling Kant's regulative ideals like God or Freedom. Many transcendentalists were Ex-Unitarian Ministers who endorsed the new biblical criticism from Germany. The search for the historical Jesus yielded a fully human moral exemplar who transcended moral mediocrity. They endorsed an active, world-shaping mind, energized by the productive imagination, closely linked to Kant's idea of artistic genius. Kant had denied cognitive access to the thing-in-itself. Decoupled from accountability to it, imagination and poetry were set free.[16] Thoreau writes, "The boundaries of the actual are no more fixed and rigid than the elasticity of our imagination."[17] The imagination stretches our apprehension of "the actual", permitting transformation—for "the actual" is not fixed through time and place, but changes, ahead and behind our perceptions of it. In Cavell's moral perfectionism, imagination clears a path to the less imperfect persons we can be. The boundaries of my actuality are elastic. Imagination shows us that we are never beyond reproach; so we imagine an improved self that we then strive to make actual.[18] Thoreau thought philosophy should be devoted to the care of the unfinished self. His imagination takes him to Concord's jail; his transfiguring experience travels transcendentally to suffuse the imaginations of Gandhi and King (and countless others through their conveyances)—thus remaking the actual world.

---

[15] See Kant's "*What is Enlightenment?*" in Louis White Beck, *Kant on History* (New York: Bobbs Merrill, 1963).
[16] See Phillip Gura, *American Transcendentalism: a History* (New York: Hill and Wang, 2007).
[17] *Journal*, Vol. V, May 31, 1853, p. 203.
[18] See Cavell, *Cities of Words: Pedagogical Letters on a Register of the Moral Life* (Cambridge, MA: Harvard University Press, 2008), and *Conditions Handsome and Unhandsome* (Chicago, IL: University of Chicago Press, 1990).

13

Currents of Time

That afternoon the dream of the toads sang through the elms by Little River.
　　　　　　　　　　　　　　　　　　　　—*Journal*, October 26, 1853

For a philosopher there is more grass growing in the valleys of silliness than up on the barren heights of cleverness.
　　　　　　　　　　　　　　　　　　　　—Wittgenstein[1]

Let's return to Thoreau's first book, *A Week on the Concord and Merrimack Rivers*. Here we take up many of the themes that have emerged in our earlier excursions, now discovered flowing in the prose of *A Week*. The journey recounted is lyrical and fanciful and down-to-earth all at once. It exposes Thoreau's talent for "dreaming awake" of cranberry skiffs and other wonders (if not directly of toads) and shows him absolutely abjuring philosophical cleverness-with-abstractions. He pursues instead what the villagers would certainly call foolishness—grown men off for a week (in actuality, it was two weeks) for no purpose a citizen could possibly fathom.

To find poetry, philosophy, and salvation in radiant particulars is what one scholar wryly calls "descendentalism."[2] *A Week* provides shifting words, places, prospects, and bits of creation: schools of fish, a cranberry bobbing in a marsh. Tracing an upward ascent toward Kantian regulative (and transcendental) Ideas, or toward his "transcendent" preconditions for knowing, risks lifting us to weightless theoretical abstraction. Thoreau would leave our feet on the ground, or have us feel a skiff slide with sustaining rivers. *Walden* takes God from on high down to the pond, to its surfaces and depths. Thoreau finds God "culminating in the present moment"[3] most characteristically, the moment of contact with marvelous particulars. However suspicious of church-faith he might be, he could write: "My profession is to be always on the alert to find God in nature—to know his lurking places."[4] God might lurk in the dream or snore of a toad or in excursions in the valley of foolishness. Thoreau attends to flowing, shimmering things—the touch of

---

[1] Epigraphs: October 26, 1853, p. 453. Wittgenstein, *Culture and Value*, Peter Winch (trans.) (Chicago: University of Chicago Press, 1980), 80e.
[2] Porte, pp. xiii, xiv, 10, 140.
[3] *Walden*, "Where I lived," p. 95 [para 20].
[4] *Journal*, September 7, 1851.

a river's shad and weeds, its waves and winds, its oaks and cranberries—even its cruel histories (think of Hannah Duston's bloody capture and bloody escape).

1.

I take up, for the most part, only the prelude to *A Week*, all of eight pages, titled "Concord River," and move at a gently rowing pace. John died in Henry's arms. An undercurrent in this writing is an ache for salvation, or communion with the departed—the absent. Mourning and commemoration of things embedded in the wider cycles of creation go hand in hand. Thoreau mourns while exulting with rivers, their fish, oaks, and meadows. This communion is what we now know (from our earlier ventures) both as "impersonal mourning" and "sympathy with intelligence"—openings to revelations, instances of perceptual *Philia*.[5] High above rivers, he savors a view from Mt. Greylock, and then from Mt. Washington, the northern-most point of his journey. But he begins locally, by the so familiar yet so marvelous banks of the river that winds through the village.

After a number of poetic invocations, the prelude begins like this:

> The Musketaquid, or Grass-ground River, though probably as old as the Nile or Euphrates, did not begin to have a place in civilized history until the fame of its grassy meadows and its fish attracted settlers out of England in 1635, when it received the other but kindred name of CONCORD from the first plantation on its banks, which appears to have been commenced in a spirit of peace and harmony. It will be Grass-ground River as long as grass grows and water runs here; it will be Concord River only while men lead peaceable lives on its banks.[6]

On the arrival of English settlers, the river gains a new name transferred from the name of the village. The town appears to have been "commenced in a spirit of peace and harmony." But how peaceable were the English newcomers? Did the town *earn* its name? The gentle hint is "No," for Thoreau immediately adds, "To an extinct race it was grass-ground, where they hunted and fished." The first inhabitants may be extinct, but Thoreau has them *appear* as he honors their history and words. In the first line of his

---

[5] See Malcolm Clemens Young, *The Spiritual Journal of Henry David Thoreau* (Macon, GA: Mercer, 2009), Ch. 5, "Seeing as Communion."
[6] *Week*, p. 5.

prelude, he gives us not the Commonwealth's name for this meadowy river, but *their* name.

The English took over the river and naming rights, baptizing Musketaquid, "Concord River." The place is settled by English eager to farm, to fish, and to pray—a people who will push out the long-standing tenants. The village is baptized "Concord," and in the same breath, "The 12th Church of Christ." Thoreau tells us that he relies on the records of "old Johnson," the region's first historian or bard. This is *Christian* "concord or harmony"—so called. It is not *Indian* peace or serenity. The advance of the Massachusetts plantation, we're told, is "Wonder Working Providence." Thoreau repeats this phrase from "old Johnson" deadpan. He doesn't believe it for an instant.

Within the first leaves of the book we learn that the river is not unto itself alone, but belongs to a larger waterway, one tributary among others all leading to the sea. We can see the river in a pedestrian way as belonging just to the environs of Concord, but Thoreau wants to expand our attention. He leads us elsewhere, down to the Merrimack, an attenuated stream that stretches north to disappear in the snowy heights of Agiocochook, Mt. Washington, and then descends many miles south to be swallowed in the vast Atlantic. Thoreau leads us also to an attenuated elsewhere in time, even back to the Nile—not to mention bringing us back in time to those earlier associates of the Meadow River, those dwellers who called it Musketaquid.

It flows as a network, a reticulation. Part meadow, part river, its broad marshland forms an amphibious, anomalous zone, especially in spring floods. There we find birds of the air belong also to water, brothers who belong to both land and water, a dory painted blue above water line and green below, to mark belonging to sky, water, and marsh. All flow with and against currents of water and wind.

Anomalous, amphibious zones embrace flow and movement. They are neither here nor there, both this and that, zones for outlaws and wanderers. In Thoreau's posthumous *Cape Cod*, they are the zones of scampering crabs, half of the sea, half of the sands, anxiously and sideways inhabiting that changeling zone where walking one belongs to the curling, rippling advancing flood, and also to the wet-dry terra firma—only momentarily awash, while the beach gently hisses as waters advance and retreat.[7]

Concord River is well stocked with shad and alewives. Johnson observes that salmon would be present too, but for the downstream falls that are too high to leap. Soon the brothers will encounter the settlers' hand-built falls upon the Merrimack, made to drive mills. These dams, as Henry observes, will halt the upward flow of fish in their attempted transcendence from

---

[7] *Cape Cod*, p. 81.

below—until they *too* become extinct. Fish and non-fish, Europeans and First Peoples, inhabit anomalous zones between water and rock, death and life.

2.

In and about Concord, river and town, we might hope for an eponymous harmony-in-the-making. Some years after writing "Concord River," as the Civil War approaches, Thoreau glimpses a scaled-down heaven in a lily rising inconspicuously from a malodorous swamp. He suffers the stench of a fugitive slave bill that welcomes slave catchers to roam his woods, draining them of heaven—but for this miraculous lily.[8] On earlier days, he finds harmony-in-the-making. In pure fun, he scampers across snow.

> I saw a fox ... making across to the hills on my left. As the snow lay five inches deep, he made but slow progress, but it was no impediment to me. So yielding to the instinct of the chase, I ... bounded away, snuffing the air like a ... hound.[9]

He has a knack for finding numberless heaven-filled ecstasies. Thoreau nods toward paradise in *A Week*, but also acknowledges hell.

Writing from the gentle flow of the river we hear of the gradual unsettling of the first residents and feel not only the vitality of his excursion companion, but also the sense of John Thoreau's death. Inscribed in the book's dedication is his plea, or prayer, "Be Thou my muse, my Brother." Then, there is a horror by no means masked or washed over. In the "Thursday" chapter of *A Week* we learn of apocalyptic events near the spot where the Concord flows into the Merrimack.

Thoreau tells of murders in Haverhill and some miles north. The events of 1697 swirling around Hannah Duston are as bloodcurdling as Goya's black painting, *Cronos Devouring his Children*. Perhaps the rivers form an anomalous region where paradise is lost, and any shred of paradise regained is dark—and our precise place, somewhere between loss and gain, is to be questioned at every bend.

The brothers reach the headwaters of the Merrimack, climb the slopes of Mt. Washington, and make their downstream run. They row and sail swiftly, wind and current to their advantage, sweeping back toward the inflow of the Concord. Haverhill is just past the turn up to Concord. A lifetime after the

---

[8] *Essays*, "Slavery."
[9] *Journal*, January 30, 1841.

founding of Concord in 1697, and one hundred and thirty years before the river trip, the town becomes stained in blood. Thoreau coolly inserts these events, interrupting his account of homecoming. Hannah Duston, a settler, is dragged from her home by a small band of Indians. They lead her out toward the river, and dash the brains of her nursing infant against an apple tree—thus, the end of Eden. We switch anxiously between a pristine then a bloody river, between burdens of guilt and hopes for redemption.

Duston is brought several miles up the Merrimack. She is under watch that night by only a remnant of the group. As they sleep she kills and scalps them, children included—a second end of Eden. She steals their canoe, paddling frantically down the very Merrimack the brothers are now plying, the very Merrimack that will welcome the Concord's inflow that will bring them home—that marvelous tributary spreading out into gentle marsh land, welcoming "gulls wheeling overhead" and "ducks by the hundreds," halfway to heaven.[10]

The Meadow River, or Musketaquid, became "Concord" as the plantation extended its prerogatives. The legacy might have been honored and in place. Then scholars and visitors would gather Thoreau's spirit in the good village of *Meadow* or *Grass-ground*. Instead, we have *Concord* Village on *Concord* River, well past paradise. The river survives apparently indifferent to names. The reality of waters transcends any name, though it takes "transcendental" poets to whisper that secret. It is they who word the world, in ways that show that words are not all, and are never finished.

Thoreau offers transcendence of the cruel or banal toward a paradise regained, landing us in the ordinary, among diurnal things appearing and reappearing. Immanence is in stride with transcendence and transcendence is anchored in everydayness. Walkers or pilgrims are knee-deep in marshes and swamp lilies and don't transcend muck. Skiffs ease out of land-bound restraints but the boat stays earth-bound, even as its image may be found, as one gazes in waters, in the *heavens*. The brothers assume the rhythms of water—not quite the plodding of pilgrim's feet. Thoreau-style transcendentalism must have poets with oars, and also with wings, affording rhythms and looks of the sky. Thoreau gives us bounteous things here and now that reveal a reach beyond banal here and now.

Village schoolteachers at the time, the brothers take to the river to escape the humdrum of weekly business and the worst of prose, to row and climb free, to abide in clouds that give infinite prospects. This graceful communion among meadows and fish has a dark underlay: John's death, extinct peoples, Hannah Duston. It would be understatement, but still to the point, to speak,

[10] *Week*, p. 7.

with Cora Diamond of "the difficulty of reality."[11] We are bi-focal and tri-focal creatures in a world focused now this way, now that. It's anomalous—heaven, hell, and much in between.

3.

In "Concord River," we find Thoreau's characteristic eye bringing us instantaneously elsewhere (though never out of this world):

> Many waves are there agitated by the wind, keeping nature fresh, the spray blowing in your face, reeds and rushes waving; ducks by the hundred, all uneasy in the surf, in the raw wind, just ready to rise, and now going off with a clatter and a whistling like riggers straight for Labrador, flying against the stiff gale with reefed wings, or else circling round first, with all their paddles briskly moving, just over the surf, to reconnoiter you before they leave these parts; gulls wheeling overhead, muskrats swimming for dear life, wet and cold, with no fire to warm them by that you know of, their labored homes rising here and there like haystacks; and countless mice and moles and winged titmice along the sunny, windy shore; cranberries tossed on the waves and heaving up on the beach, their little red skiffs beating about among the alders;—such healthy natural tumult as proves the last day is not yet at hand.[12]

Such words—such things—beckon continually beyond even as they plunge us into the evident wonder, risk, and allure of the simple: the *cranberry is a skiff* fitted out for sailing.

We listen to the mobile, transforming flow of Thoreau's words. The wind is not just disturbing the waters, it is "keeping nature fresh." We are allowed to participate in the world's renewal, "spray blowing in your face." The muskrats don't just paddle, but "swim for dear life." We hear a life that is dear, bounteous, and dangerous simultaneously, a shape-shifting flow, for better and worse.

There are ducks, not just sitting or stuffed or bobbing, but "ducks by the hundred, all uneasy in the surf, in the raw wind, just ready to rise." They're ready in their uneasiness to see something elsewhere—and rise toward it. In beholding this, we also are "uneasy in the surf" and ready to rise. Words translate us aloft. The ducks are "now going off with a clatter and a

---

[11] Stanley Cavell, Cora Diamond, John McDowell, Ian Hacking, and Cary Wolfe, *Philosophy and Animal Life* (New York: Columbia University Press, 2008).
[12] *Week*, p. 7.

whistling like riggers straight for Labrador, flying against the stiff gale with reefed wings." All gaps between sailors in rigging and ducks wheeling aloft are closed. Any gaps between *my* viewing and *ducks-viewed* are closed, too. There is a single arcing ascent, a kind of union and loss of self—an ecstasy. The ascending ducks are "like riggers straight for Labrador," and we are high up in the yards of a sailing ship. This is the place, Melville warns, where Platonism becomes tempting.[13] It can be both bracingly ecstatic and mortally imprudent to go aloft, to scan, to dream. We need befitting *reverie* and befitting *grip* on the mast.

The flock of hundreds might "circle round first, with all their paddles briskly moving, just over the surf, to reconnoiter you before they leave these parts." Or, having reconsidered, they settle down again on the waters of the marsh. Gulls don't just fly, but are "wheeling," even as the river and its words wheel on and on, the moving waters holding the image of moving birds.

Thoreau gives us "countless mice and moles and winged titmice," letting a repeated *"mmm"* hum us forward in translatability, with "mice" next to winged "titmice." It is *we* who acquire wings, as both *sounds* and *species* fly by in passing perceptions. Our muskrats are "wet and cold, with no fire to warm them by." Thoreau adds *sotto voce*—"so far as we know." Perhaps, this is an offhand, but serious question: What do we in fact know of the other, of each other? What cold or fire lies in their homes? Muskrats swim "for dear life," haunted by dangers, real or imagined, hurrying to a familiar haven, "their labored homes rising here and there like haystacks." There is a time for safe harbor.

Cranberries are cranberries, of course, but not only that. The poet's eye, the translator's eye, finds them "tossed on the waves and heaving up on the beach, their little red skiffs beating about among the alders."[14] They may sail through the chop as if in heaven—or be tossed up on the beach as wrecks. Perhaps, other skiffs are "beating about" on the way to Labrador, or beating their way up the Merrimack toward Agiocochook, "Home of the Great Spirit." These skiffs journeying outward are also skiffs seeking safe harbor by an alder. They are also just cranberries rising and falling, bobbing, on wavelets on the edge of a watery meadow. Across the breeze-swept marshes, in travels here and there, Thoreau finds "such healthy natural tumult [as] proves the last day is not yet at hand."[15] And why not add, "Let us therefore cast off the hour of darkness and put on the garments of light."[16]

---

[13] *Moby Dick*, many editions, Ch. 35, "The Mast Head."
[14] In sailing jargon, to aim, or "tack" into the wind, is to "beat" into the wind.
[15] *Week*, p. 7.
[16] Romans 13.12, KJV: "The night is far spent, the day is at hand: let us therefore cast off the works of darkness, and let us put on the armor of light."

Here we have religion. These images and words paradoxically release us from bondage by tying us back into an overflowing, unfinished reality, a Creation. *Religio*, on one etymological reconstruction, is a re-sewing of torn ligaments, and thus a repair that reanimates what had become the broken movements of routine and quiet desperation. It aims to suture and to staunch inescapable pain. On this view, religion has less to do with purifying creeds or beliefs than effecting repairs that let life course through previously broken bodies and spirits. Life is reanimated through exposure to the transforming radiance of things. We are transformed as things are transformed under the poet's attentive eye.

The writing articulates life at once philosophical, religious, and literary-poetic. It is a life of walking, seeing, tasting, hearing in imagination-drenched immersions. We sense a way of taking up with the world and of being happy to be of it. Yet seeking life and serenity can miserably fail. Will the emphasis fall on despair or exultation, on confidence or self-doubt, on loss or return? Reality is difficult and gives us *reasons* for both.[17] Perhaps which way we tilt is a matter of refined perception, striking (or refusing) a balance. Thoreau is startled into life and delight and invites us along. With Isaiah, he will "go out in joy" where "mountains and hills will burst into song ... and all the trees of the field will clap their hands."[18] This is miles from Galileo, who manages to bury nature in a whirl of colorless atoms and soundless mechanical parts.

Wheeling gulls and red cranberry skiffs assure Thoreau (and us) that "*the last day is not yet at hand.*" "The end of the *world* is not yet," he writes in his *Journal*. There, he reflects on poetry: "The sun climbs to the zenith daily high over all literature and science ... the sun of poetry and of each new child born into the planet has never been ... brought nearer by a telescope. So it will be to the end of time. The end of the world is not yet."[19]

Poetry encompasses all living knowledge and literature; it delivers worlds as fresh and new as a newborn child. In poetry worlds are born again, Thoreau tells us, just as the sun rises each day. This truth will be made not a whit stronger by appeal to a telescope (or to Newton, or to sciences of the brain).[20] There is ample time, accordingly, for receiving the world,

---

[17] See "Difficult Reality," in Stanley Cavell, Cora Diamond, John McDowell, Ian Hacking, and Cary Wolfe, *Philosophy and Animal Life* (New York: Columbia University Press, 2008).

[18] Isaiah 55.12.

[19] *Journal*, April 2, 1852.

[20] For the interplay of disciplined science and poetic perceptions see Laura Dassow Walls, *The Passage to Cosmos: Alexander von Humbolt and the Shaping of America* (Chicago: University of Chicago Press, 2009), p. 5; *Seeing New Worlds: Henry David Thoreau and Nineteenth-Century Natural Science* (Madison: University of Wisconsin Press, 1995), and Cora Diamond, "Knowing Tornadoes and Other Things," *New Literary History* 22, No.4 (1991).

articulating it for others, enjoying it (such as we may). Wallace Stevens declares, "The search for reality is as momentous as the search for God."[21] Reality *sought* is as wondrous and terrible as the poets foretell.

4.

As we've insisted, "transcendentalism" is a term of limited cataloging convenience. If Thoreau is tucked in this drawer, it would be in recognition of his walking and writing practices, each the inside of the other, each "transcending" itself to inhabit the other. In writing, he evokes lively meanings from an object of attention (a cranberry), giving it birth and renewal in an act that annuls its dullness—transcends it. Then, in walking anew in the world, he brings a cranberry back from birth to inhere in the immanence from which he began—a bounteous particular, now seen better and better seen.

Particulars that are poetically rendered occupy amphibious, anomalous zones. In their liveliness, they break through regions, districts, matrixes, and boundaries. A cranberry is a fruit, is itself and is *also* a rigged sailing ship—and a little red *skiff*. Amphibious, anomalous zones lie where the truncated meanings of the prosaic lap over ever extending or transcending meanings that each ordinary thing (or congeries of things) contains.

Birds high above waters and above grasses create an axis that extends down to reeds and alewives, riverbed fish, and pebbled bottoms. They radiate surface-up / surface-down on a *vertical* axis. Singularities also radiate *sideways, transversally*. Concord River becomes one of many tributaries, as if any given site were a nodal point in a skein of unfolding strands. Particulars radiate *temporally* forward and back. The Musketaquid-Concord belongs with the Euphrates and Nile—timeless rivers attaining a kind of eternity through backward-looking constructed identities.[22]

In considering Thoreau's scientific discipline, Laura Walls contrasts "bottom-up," Thoreauvian empirical holism with "top-down," non-Thoreauvian rationalist holism.[23] As I see it, in his field work Thoreau sometimes seeks a holistic overview and sometimes is content just to map a little corner of things.

---

[21] Stevens, "An Ordinary Evening in New Haven," *Collected Poems* (New York: Vintage, 1990), p. 465. See Joel Porte's discussion of Thoreau's faith and its affinities with Wallace Stevens' poem in *Consciousness and Culture: Emerson and Thoreau Reviewed* (New Haven: Yale University Press, 2004), p. 465.

[22] *Week*, p. 7.

[23] Walls, *Seeing New Worlds: Henry David Thoreau and Nineteenth-Century Natural Science* (Madison: University of Wisconsin Press, 1995), pp. 60–93.

The little map is often built up from glimpses from *here and now* that hang together in gestalts. He's like a biological illustrator who wants to get the details of little things exact. Although he appreciated big-picture holistic stories like Darwin's, he wasn't obsessed with over-arching theory. And I suspect he knew that the ideal of a *single*, timeless map, the mother of all maps, is an illusion as chimerical as "the view from nowhere." In any case, as we've seen time and again, anything like a Thoreauvian disciplined epistemology or search for knowledge plays second fiddle to readiness for unknowing and amazement. It plays second fiddle to the "Sympathy with Intelligence" that would allow him to be overtaken by a most unscientific absorption *in* and ecstatic reverence *for* the things of creation, an unknowing requisite to redemption.

I'd avoid calling Thoreau a transcendentalist because he anchors his thought in the diurnal and immanent, as these radiate pasts, futures, heights, or depths.[24] Interdependence among things of land, river, and sky (alders, shad, or gulls) creates affinity among things. Each affords the poet's eye more than a biological or Newtonian location. They convey bounteousness and lack, fulfillment and despair, skill and terrible flailing. Muskrats swim for dear life, cranberries beat upwind, and thunder forbiddingly roars. And Thoreau gives us the "not yet" of a world. It is not caged into its present forms. He's free to anticipate and find the next morning's delights.

5.

Thoreau's lyrical eye and voice give us John Brown, the martyr for abolition, whom Thoreau calls the only true transcendentalist. Perhaps, Brown had a poet's eye for truths not yet of the world. A traveler or pilgrim constantly encounters things not yet. As a writer and traveler, Thoreau puts himself in the way of new things that his poetic eye and ear can take in. Poetic reception and rendition are not elitist prerogatives. Thoreau's neighbors are neither near-saints nor wild insurrectionists, nor by ordinary standards, poets. Nonetheless, in Thoreau's reverie they work poetically and live transcendentally.

> You shall see rude and sturdy, experienced and wise men, keeping their castles, or teaming up their summer's wood, or chopping alone in the woods; men fuller of talk and rare adventure in the sun and wind and rain, than a chestnut is of meat, who were out not only in '75 and 1812,

---

[24] See Furtak's *Stanford Encyclopedia of Philosophy* "Thoreau" entry on the ambiguity of Thoreau's relation to "transcendentalism."

but have been out every day of their lives; greater men than Homer, or Chaucer, or Shakespeare, only they never got time to say so; they never took to the way of writing. Look at their fields, and imagine what they might write, if ever they should put pen to paper. Or what have they not written on the face of the earth already, clearing, and burning, and scratching, and harrowing, and plowing, and sub soiling, in and in, and out and out, and over and over, again and again, erasing what they had already written for want of parchment.[25]

Thoreau had a healthy respect, even love, for men of the field, and I would not exclude women. Think of the alluring, scantily clad lass on the slopes of Mt. Greylock, with whom he imagines spending some (lusty?) days.[26] The positive and continuing role Thoreau assumed as a companion to Emerson's wife and a support to the household, the shock of his loss of a marriage bid, and his evident "domesticity" and "gender blurring" living by the pond are topics recently under fascinating and overdue discussion. Apart from women, this reputed curmudgeon could write on "Friday" of *A Week*,

> I pass along the streets of our village of Concord on the day of our annual Cattle-Show, when it usually happens that the leaves of the elms and buttonwoods begin first to strew the ground under the breath of the October wind, the lively spirits in their sap seem to mount as high as any plow-boy's let loose that day; This [is an] autumnal festival, when men are gathered in crowds in the streets as regularly and by as natural a law as the leaves cluster and rustle by the wayside ... I love these sons of earth, every mother's son of them, with their great hearty hearts rushing tumultuously in herds from spectacle to spectacle, as if fearful lest there should not be time between sun and sun to see them all, and the sun does not wait more than in haying time.[27]

6.

To sense things of the moment is to sense their eternity. We are given the good news that "We need pray for no higher heaven than the pure senses

---

[25] *Week*, p. 8.
[26] *Week*, p. 182. And see, for example, Laura Dassow Walls, "*Walden* as Feminist Manifesto," *ISLE: Interdisciplinary Studies in Literature and Environment* 1.1 (1993): 137–44. Her essay is also in *Walden, Civil Disobedience, and Other Writings*, William Rossi (ed.) (New York: W. W. Norton, 2008), pp. 521–7.
[27] *Week*, p. 358.

can furnish ... "May we not see God?"²⁸ The past, future, and the eternal saturate things of the moment. In "Concord River," after giving us muskrats desperately swimming, and noting that "the end of the world is not quite at hand," Thoreau writes of the divine: "As yesterday and the historical ages are past, as the work of to-day is present, so some flitting perspectives and demi-experiences of the life that is in nature are in time veritably future, or rather outside to time, perennial, young, divine, in the wind and rain which never die."²⁹

His prelude to *A Week* ends with a meditation on the river's easy gait:

> I had often stood on the banks of the Concord, watching the lapse of the current, an emblem of all progress, following the same law with the system, with time, and all that is made; the weeds at the bottom gently bending down the stream, shaken by the watery wind, still planted where their seeds had sunk, but ere long to die and go down likewise.³⁰

These last words—"ere long to die and go down likewise"—close out his thoughts on moving forward. But the river in flow, that purported emblem of progress, slows to a stop well short of tragedy. Paradoxically, speaking of inescapable death occurs in tones ringing with affirmation of all life.

There is death. But Thoreau also takes a vantage "outside to time, perennial, young, divine." Flow is anomalously in "the ephemeral here and now" and also in "the lastingly out-of-time," as our temporal perspectives become so *indistinct* in the deep past or deep future or deep present as to seem virtually *timeless*. Paradise, after all, is lastingly out of time yet in today's meadow. In the last words of "Concord River," Thoreau turns to the particular as the portal to meaning in time (and out of it). He yields himself to the river, ready to be carried downstream and elsewhere, in serene being with time:

> the shining pebbles, not yet anxious to better their condition, the chips and weeds, and occasional logs and stems of trees that floated past, fulfilling their fate, were objects of singular interest to me, and at last I resolved to launch myself on its bosom and float whither it would bear me.³¹

---

[28] *Week*, p. 382. Consider *Walden*, "Where I lived": "God culminates in the present moment," p. 95.
[29] *Week*, p. 8. See Ch. 4, p. 120, on music.
[30] *Week*, p. 12.
[31] "Concord River," final sentence.

14

Grounding Poetry

Human forms of feeling, objects of human attraction, our reactions constituted in art, are as universal and necessary, as revelatory of the world, as the forms of the laws of physics. This is the writer's faith ...
—Stanley Cavell

A serious and good philosophical work could be written consisting entirely of jokes.
—Wittgenstein

[F]ind at least a line ... that starts to sing. Sometimes even one word is enough to open a window on a new view of the world.
—Mihaly Csikszentmihalyi[1]

1.

What have poets to do with philosophers? What do both have to do with the sort of personal narrative that we find in Thoreau's *Walden*, or *A Week on the Concord*? Can Thoreau's writing be simultaneously philosophical, poetic, and autobiographical? As they become part of deadening chatter or routine, words can begin to sound like administrative or legal protocols. A poet undoes the hardening of words, returning new life to them as they roll out in phrases and sentences, and so the world is reanimated. Through poetic evocation, Thoreau loosens the grip of routine-only perceptions of Concord River—the shallow view that Concord River is only a place on a map. He amplifies the life of the river by extending the name backward in time. "Concord River" becomes a suggestive extension of "Musketaquid." This gives the river lively historical depth. In *Cape Cod*, he loosens the sands and the dunes back toward a fuller history. He calls it an arm of New France. A name-shift poetically stretches our sense of time and place.

These transfigurations are relayed in first-personal narration. Despite obvious departures from strict personal history, Thoreau verges on autobiography, extending a canon that would feature Montaigne's *Essays*, Rousseau's

---

[1] Epigraphs: *Senses*, p. 102; Norman Malcolm, Ludwig Wittgenstein: A Memoir (Oxford: Oxford University Press, 2001), p. 28; Mihaly Csikszentmihalyi, *Flow* (New York: HarperCollins), p. 131.

Reveries, and Kierkegaard's *The Point of View of my Work as an Author*. To acknowledge this canon means setting aside a long-standing Western presumption that philosophy's vaunted *reason* must have an inherent *quarrel* with poetry, the personal, or the spiritual. When philosophy splits off in Plato and others from the deeper history of poetry, drama, and religion, it denies its roots in tragedy, myth, music, "intoxications," and irrational passion. *Philosophy is not poetry!*

2.

Stanley Cavell's brilliant and difficult *The Senses of Walden* counts Thoreau as a first-rate philosopher who belongs to an alternative canon where reason is not at odds with a religious and poetic sensibility.[2] He presents Thoreau implicitly working out Kantian themes, often in directions Kant himself would disapprove of. Cavell makes Thoreau more Kantian than we would have thought, and stretches a Kantian perspective to include more than we would have thought possible.

Thoreau characterizes the world as "answering to our conceptions," which is to make an uncontroversially Kantian point.[3] That Thoreau intimates a "transcendental deduction" of the "thing-in-itself" is a *surprise*, a stretch—a "deduction" Kant didn't provide, but "should have," as Cavell puts it.[4] Kant's "thing-in-itself" can clarify Thoreau's wedding of objective research and response to alluring presences, as I'll show later. Here's another surprise from Cavell:

> our images ... of dawn and day and night, of lower and higher, ... of freezing and melting and moulting, of birds and squirrels and snakes and frogs, of houses and bodies of water and words, ... are as *a priori* as our other forms of knowledge of the world.[5]

Images of birds and moulting, of water and dawn, give us the vital *presence* of things in the world. And they're *a priori*, available before the poet works them up in a revelation of reality.

Only because *prior* images gather to prepare our reception of Thoreau's poetic witness are we convinced—*if* we are—of the sublimity, of the revelation, delivered in the reflection of distant hills in the surface of the

---

[2] Branka Arsić's *Bird Relics* gives the most compelling account of Cavell's reading I know, pp. 253, 260, 268, 314, 327. She takes Thoreau to *resist* Kant, rather than stretch him.
[3] *Walden*, p. 97.
[4] *Senses*, p. 104.
[5] Cavell, *Senses of Walden*, p. 101.

pond. The reflection tells us "how intimate heaven is with earth."[6] Then there's a reverie of multiple reflections delivered as Thoreau kneels by the edge of Walden, almost in prayer.[7] He finds his face looking up from still waters, and finds it next to the pond's Maker's, as if the three—Thoreau, the Pond, and its Maker—were in communion, in intimate dialogue.[8] The sublimity is not read off as bare-bones observation from the canvas of experience, nor from the watery surface of the pond. It arrives from imagination's resources, resources that await activation from elsewhere in moments of marvel. The reflected allure of distant hills bursts in on us as if self-evident in its glory, just awaiting a powerful recollection, right now. It's not *a posteriori* registration of empirical data. There is magic in reflecting waters.[9] It's as if we were discovering something that had been sleeping deep in the soul, and is now suddenly being brought to full life. The wonderful constellation of watery reflections of my face and the face of a Maker, and perhaps fish below, seems to speak from eternity, and to carry the eternity of a just-now-perceived poetical necessity.

3.

A good string of images—say, part of a reverie from Thoreau—can reveal reality exactly as closely and correctly as the report a good field biologist files after scouring a meadow. There's a structure to good poetic deliveries that lies hidden, just as there's a structure to good field-work deliveries that lies hidden (to non-scientists). Hidden structures, once seen, give necessity and impact to good poetic delivery. Finding them is excavating the hidden grammar of images and showing how they can be revelatory of the world.

If I read "fish-fish-fish" and refuse the conclusion that I've encountered nonsense, I have to imagine a context that allows that string of words to grab hold and deliver. "Fish fish fish" might be *"Fish! ... Fish! ... Fish!"*—orders uttered at the start of a fishing contest. Or it might be the *glee* of fishermen finally discovering a well-stocked pool. Or "fish fish fish" might be a language instructor repeating the word "fish" for non-English speakers working on pronunciation. Once we have the context, a segment of a shared way of life, there's a necessity in the way the words grip and reveal reality. On hearing

---

[6] *Journal*, August 31, 1851.
[7] *Walden*, "The Ponds" pp. 186–7. I consider this passage in detail, section 4, below.
[8] Ibid.
[9] As we noted above, Lucretius also has us contemplate the heavens in a shallow puddle: *De Rerum Natura*, Bk 4, p. 92.

the words, we "get it" with the certitude of hearing "2+2 = 4" or "That's a Great Heron!"

The hidden structure of a string of words (for example, "fish-fish-fish") comes out with finding a proper context. And there's also a matter beyond cultural context (*where* the words are uttered, and *why*). We can call it discovering hidden grammar. I can take "fish ... fish ... fish" to be a perfectly formed sentence, despite appearances. It's a concise way of saying, "Look: there are *fish who go after other finny creatures*—fish who fish fish." To hear the sentence is to hear the tacit but powerful grammatical necessities of a well-formed English sentence. Once we get the hang of it, we can take a more challenging word-string, initially nonsense. We can hear "fish ... fish ... fish ... fish ... fish" as a single well-formed sentence. It says that there are fish who go after other finny creatures who themselves go after finny creatures. A set of apparent nonsense words or images makes sense, grabs onto reality in a revelation, once we grasp its hidden a priori structures.

Think of the hidden grammar in a brief, single-sentence reverie Thoreau provides. It's a thought we considered earlier, an apparently casual but deeply *enigmatic* aside. Thoreau writes, "All intelligences awake in the morning." If I'm unprepared for this, then I might be tempted to skim on. But knowing Thoreau's genius, I might pause to let sense assemble (if it will). I begin to hear this aside in several ways, finding alternative grammars and contexts that will give these words impact or point. I let them play. "All intelligences awake in the morning" might say:

a) "All intelligent *people* awaken to (or are awakened by) the morning"
b) "All intelligence, whether of persons or of trees, whether of trout or stars, awakens with dawn"
c) "All secret messages—spy craft, "intelligence"—awaken the alert listener"
d) "Dawn brings all shining beings alive to bless us with news"

Each reading requires a rather different structural underlay to make it work as the revelation it is. There is not one uniquely correct way to hear these words, but that doesn't mean that one or another, or even all of these, aren't *bone fide* revelation. There's no uniquely correct way to hear "fish-fish-fish," but that doesn't mean we can't find structures that animate those words and let them sing and deliver the realities they can. Hidden grammars lie under the poetic thought that "All intelligences awake in the morning." Once I start unveiling them, I realize that imagination is stronger than I might have thought. It delivers reports as strong as the detective's report, or the field biologist's. Bringing them into view is giving poetry the grounding it has and revels in.

4.

I mentioned a few pages back the charming reverie that places Thoreau prayer-like at the edge of the pond and finds his face reflected therein. It deserves more attention. It starts casually:

> Why, here is Walden, the same woodland lake that I discovered so many years ago; … it is the same liquid joy and happiness to itself and its Maker, ay, and it may be to me. It is the work of a brave man surely, … He rounded this water with his hand, deepened and clarified it in his thought, and in his will bequeathed it to Concord. I see by its face that it is visited by the same reflection; and I can almost say, Walden, is it you?[10]

What could prepare us to countenance this? We're given a pond that draws in (and enjoys) a joy to herself, a "liquid joy" that is also her Maker's. It's also a joy offered to the supplicant from Concord at pond's edge. "Liquid joy and happiness" flows through Maker and pond and pilgrim—a miraculous three-become-one.

In his earliest essay, Thoreau had asked if it weren't true that joy is the condition of life.[11] Here it is the condition even of the life of the Maker. All being drinks from its cup. It is a grateful remembrance of times past. Joy holds memories from earlier years when the pond's surface also faithfully reflected her Marker and the face of the youth at her edge. Identities are reciprocally constituted in looks of joyous regard. What better image of contentment or heaven than the "liquid joy and happiness" we're given here? It draws a pilgrim, a pond, and its Maker to mutual embrace. In a moment of yearning, or almost disbelieving intimacy, Thoreau whispers, "Walden, is it you?"

If the moment clicks, it clicks. As it settles in, it reminds me of listening wide-eyed, as Thoreau recounted the reverie of the dreaming frog, a reverie not unlike the Walden scenario, but now in a whimsical vein, with a moment of self-doubt thrown in. The frog looks toward the heavens and receives its many visions. Recovering, he wonders if perhaps he has gone mad.

> The frog had eyed the heavens from his marsh, until his mind was filled with visions, & he saw more than belongs to this fenny earth—He mistrusted [feared] that he was become a dreamer & visionary—leaping across the swamp to his fellow. What was his joy & consolation to find that he too had seen the same sights in the heavens—he too had dreamed the same dreams[12]

---

[10] "Ponds," p. 187.
[11] *Essays*, "The Natural History of Massachusetts," p. 22.
[12] *Journal*, May 21, 1851, pp. 207–8.

These are delightful and instructive vignettes, but I don't want to lose touch with the thread of meta-level tests that improvise a tentative *grounding* of such reverie in reality. The dreaming frog gives us a clue about how grounding might start. I feel the earth rumble north of the Bay, and question my sanity. I call up a neighbor. She reassures me: an earthquake just hit!

Images can shock us awake to what's real. But are such shocks sufficient for grounding? Kant means to *demonstrate* the ubiquity and force of causality in the world. Thoreau has no rigorous arguments made to deliver the eloquence of the world, or the sort of wonders dreaming frogs might report. Instead, he shows us—sings to us, kids us into hearing—the unmistakable eloquence of the pond or the frog. Reveries, poetic evocations, humorous asides, and parables perform a magnificent service. New worlds shower upon us, each invites our inhabitation—or reminds us that we *already* inhabit them.

5.

Thoreau follows Kant in praising the *productive powers of imagination*.[13] There are moments of *conviction* as Thoreau gives us the shimmering image of a Maker. When an array of images *works*, we're convinced that things *must be* as they're depicted. We are prepared for conviction by *prior* images of water and skies and frogs or toads looking skyward—what Cavell called *a priori* images, images "as *a priori* as our other forms of knowledge of the world." Just as *a priori* categories (like causality, plurality, or possibility) precede and underwrite the botanist's knowledge of the world, so *a priori images* precede and underwrite the poet's knowledge of the world. A capacity to be taken by the allure of a pond's Maker or the magic of reflecting waters rests on a concatenation of *a priori* images: pond, Maker, reflections, waters, a thing's shimmer or allure. These images, Cavell may be saying, saturate the domains of imaginative perception the way causality (and other categories) saturate a scientific report of the breakup of ice in spring.

Revelations come upon us with *poetic necessity*. The mark of our being in the neighborhood of revelation is our listening wide-eyed, and enraptured— we're told that frogs eye the heavens and we (half?) believe it.[14] Consider what a contemporary psychologist says about learning to read or hear words or images.

---

[13] Immanuel Kant, *Critique of Pure Reason*, Norman Kemp Smith (trans.), A 100-2; A 118.
[14] *Journal*, May 21, 1851, pp. 207-8.

> The first time children realize that the expression "having Grandma for dinner" could mean either as a guest or as a dish, it will be somewhat puzzling, as will a phrase like "a frog in the throat." In fact, breaking the ordered expectations about the meaning of words can be mildly traumatic at first, but in no time at all children catch on.[15]

Breaking ordered expectations of words can be traumatic for children but also the opening to revelation once they "get it." Just so, adult expectations are traumatized by the disorder of speaking of dreaming frogs, but that disorder can also open toward revelation. The world is richer for having dreaming frogs.

Befitting reveries perform double service. They deliver new worlds, and excite second-order investigations (or groundings) of the perceptions they induce. Unlike routine research reports, poetic renditions trigger a search for groundings: Why say, "a frog in the throat," or "the sound of frogs dreaming"? Alert readers listen for clues, for veiled but rooted necessities. (Do frogs dream because they snore?) Alert readers are happy to excavate for the hidden grammar that allows "*fish fish*" to be a full sentence rather than nonsense.

In our excursion called "Child of the Mist" we tarried with this evocative line: "*... eternity remains. I would drink deeper; fish in the sky, whose bottom is pebbly with stars.*" If my ears and eyes are tuned, I will have a flash of recognition at "fish in the sky," and another as I see a watery bottom "pebbly with stars." These flashes deliver the underpinnings to the perceptions given by those lines. I will be excavating what grounding these images *have*, giving them the best grounding possible.

This intuitive process—endlessly inventing and testing conjectures with others—is the best grounding possible. To ground them is to root them in what is given, and as Wittgenstein says, "*What is given is forms of life.*"[16] Conversational exchange is a pervasive form of life. The images we seek to ground find an embeddedness in forms of life, forms of reality and of practices than which nothing deeper is given—or needed. Together images and practices, grammar and contexts, all moving in a flow of life, provide the best grounding we can have for judgments, assessments, and reveries closing in on realities.[17] When fish appear in the stars, or a frog has visions and finds that his neighbors do too, these reveries are grounded (if they are)

---

[15] Milaly Csikszentmihayi, *Flow* (New York: HarperCollins, 2009), p. 130.
[16] Ludwig Wittgenstein, *Philosophical Investigations* (Oxford: Blackwell, 3rd edn, 2001), Iixi, p. 226.
[17] Lee Braver, *Groundless Grounds: A Study of Wittgenstein and Heidegger* (Cambridge, MA: MIT Press, 2012), pp. 35-7 and throughout.

by checking ways of life, and checking *Thoreau's* way of poetic-philosophical life, and the emergence of lyrical images from it. And they are grounded by noting the role of images, and of schemas of interrelated images, in shaping it. Does Thoreau succeed? The burden lies in our assessments and negotiations and improvisations reading him. And the burden lies in our reading Cavell and in our reading others who shed light. And it lies in testing (again and again) one's own *cumulative* readings against the experience of reading *this* Thoreau reverie—yet once more. We hope "fish in the sky" becomes more and more an inescapable revelation.[18]

Conviction comes to rest not on detached argument or clinical analysis, but on the convincingness of what Wittgenstein calls conspicuous representations—akin to what I've called "befitting reveries."[19] Philosophical elaboration and amplification—moving toward grounding or toward the loss of all anchors—is letting stories release further stories, and release a hidden grammar to images. If these 'second-order' amplifications are successful, they sharpen a reverie's detail and direction, and also ground it—or *fail*. Instead of the commendation "befitting," we may find the reverie to be unfit, that it ill becomes the life it was meant to excite and to serve.

Hearing that trees are moulting, or that frogs are dreaming, we can ask how these composite images work, in language or life. We seek background preparations that make just these words—moulting trees, dreaming frogs—pleasingly befitting in just *this* context (or that). Our questioning may confirm that a word or phrase is unhappy or useless. It idles or falls flat, like empty noise. But our probing amplifications may reverse this tide. Unbidden, a reality *accosts* us through images delivered befittingly. When poetic words work, they snap us awake—bring us to life.

6.

Thoreau offers us words, phrases, and sentences that conjure the conditions of their utterance. In sensing these contextual and grammatical and life-form conditions, we come to see, or hear, as Cavell puts it, that

> Human forms of feeling, objects of human attraction, our reactions constituted in art, are as universal and necessary, as revelatory of the world, as the forms of the laws of physics. This is the writer's

---

[18] As Charles Taylor puts it, "the power to make us resonate builds through a whole constellation, before erupting (as it may) in a single word or phrase." Taylor, *A Secular Age*, p. 760.

[19] On "conspicuous representations," see PI #122.

faith—confidence that what we are accustomed to call, say, the "connotations" of words, the most evanescent of the shadows that they cast, are as available between us as their "denotations."[20]

Feelings, art, and poetry are revelatory of the world. The faculty of *understanding*, Kant holds, prepares us for factual knowledge by providing the relevant *a priori* categories, say, causality. The faculty of *imagination*, I propose, prepares us for reception of resonance, presence, or eloquence—to be encountered, say, in the deeply wise eyes of a child, or in Thoreau seeing a Maker's reflection in the waters of Walden Pond. Seeing God in local waters is a moment of wonder, glistening with poetic-religious inevitability or necessity. We step back, and exclaim, "Yes! That's how it must be!" That reality, *given just then*, is as powerful and real as the physicist's reality delivered in impressive equations.

Cavell and Thoreau refuse to take images as in every case second best to bits of raw factual knowledge. The legitimacy of both is secured by a reliance on *a priori* structures and cultural forms of life. The probity of our contacts with the world via images is exactly on a par with the probity of our contact through observational and scientific reports. Each can misfire, and each can reach target.

7.

There is another angle to consider regarding the excavation of hidden image-structures. In Thoreau's case, as Cavell insists, each word conjures the very thing that is uttered. Each thing in the flow of his writing speaks. An utterance flows from the writer's voice or pen, and equally flows from the expressive density of things. Eloquence can be stripped of things, just as it can be stripped of words. Things can morph into diminished objects gleaned for strict knowledge. Or they can resound in their full eloquence through the magic of poetic retrieval and rendition.

Things of expressive density word what they are. This amplifies Thoreau's striking claim in *Walden* that things speak in their own language, a language without metaphor.[21] Cavell speaks dramatically of "the writer's attempt to register within the writing of the word the entire language from which a word is woven."[22] Words resonate with other words in expanding circles that come to encompass entire languages and entire forms of life that undergird

---

[20] *Senses*, p. 102.
[21] *Walden*, "Sounds," p. 108 [para 1].
[22] *Senses*, p. 102.

them. Radiant things become grounded as they become apparent participants in mutually constitutive weaves of relationality.

Thoreau encounters one thing, then another, and evokes the expanding nexus of their relationships, their speaking to each other "without metaphor." Thus Concord River—both the mobile site of life, and also the words of *A Week*—finds its ground among relations among eloquent things. Musketaquid and alder are linked to ever-expanding networks—alders giving refuge to cranberries, Meadow River flowing down to the maw of the sea. Each thing and word is caught up *en route* in an ecology of living-and-dying, in what Wittgenstein called the "stream or flow of life" and its "natural history."[23]

8.

In testifying to experience, the poet speaks first-personally in linking things and words. This brings philosophy to autobiography, for in weighing testimony we need to sense who speaks, from what place, with what authority, with what credibility. In *A Week* Thoreau establishes his concrete location and movements, or a persuasive semblance of these. That shows us where he stands with regard to his words and the things he words. This gives his words the weight they have—the best grounding we have—and should be all we need. Of course we always want more and stronger authority. We want to believe, as Cavell puts it, that philosophers are "in possession of an authority that goes beyond what they are able to articulate out of their own experience and practice and wit on each occasion of being stopped to think."[24]

Thoreau gives weight to the translation of a "mere" muskrat into a muskrat "swimming for dear life," who aims for "the warmth of a fire." My success in sensing grounds depends on the credibility of his testimony, and on the emerging reticulated support of my standing with them. In an idiom we've used before, we find a reverie befitting—or not, a description convincing—or not. The "bottom line" is not a stock, standard-issue literal attachment of timeless name to unwavering thing. This is a fantasy of a

---

[23] For "flow of life," see David Stern, *Wittgenstein on Mind and Language* (Oxford: Oxford University Press, 1996), pp. 186ff. For "natural history," see Wittgenstein's *Philosophical Investigations* (London: Blackwell, 3rd edn, 2001), entries 25 and 415: "What we are supplying are really remarks on the natural history of human beings."

[24] "Reflections on Wallace Stevens at Mount Holyoke," *Artists, Intellectuals, and World War II: The Pontigny Encounters at Mount Holyoke College, 1942–1944*, Christopher Benfey and Karen Remmler (eds) (Amherst: University of Massachusetts Press, 2006).

one-to-one correspondence or perfect fit. The bottom line is whether and how we buy into the force of our words in their inter-animations—our own and Thoreau's—and whether and how we accept our immersions in, and exposures to their cognate things and worlds. The bottom line is whether we sense their felt-weight settle down after ongoing conversational negotiations of that weight and life.

9.

We are conversational creatures with bottom-line capacities for communicative mutuality. We talk and weigh out our credibility with each other, talk and weigh out our contacts with the world, and with ourselves—and suffer the loss of credibility and contact, too. Listening and speaking, getting confidence in the weight of our words (and the weight of our worlds)—our standing with them—is a shared venture, a community trust. As Thoreau puts it, "We get the language with which to describe our various lives out of a common mint."[25]

Early in *Walden*, in "Sounds," Thoreau speaks of things and Nature speaking "without metaphor."[26] He doesn't immediately fill in his meaning, but I'd fill in by saying that the violin speaks to the cello without metaphor, and the wind speaks to the waves without metaphor. We might leap to the conclusion that Thoreau thinks that nature speaks literally. But all speech is not *either* figural *or* literal. The figural-literal contrast often has no grasp. When I complain of a stabbing pain in my forehead I'd not be using an ornamental metaphor; but I needn't insist that the stabbing is literal. We start as children immersed in an anomalous shifting surround.[27] We swim in an unfolding world that is just too shifting, and our verbal tracking of it just too improvisatory, to yield anything like a stable and all-purpose center, on the one hand (called "the literal"), and on the other, a periphery (called "the metaphoric)."

We think there is a stark "either/or" that we must doggedly face. We just have to gird up our loins and decide which way a piece of speech goes, to the metaphor bin, or to the literal one. And there's the corollary that if we're out

---

[25] Thoreau, Letter to Wiley, April 26, 1857, *Correspondence*, p. 478.
[26] *Walden*, "Sounds," p. 108 [para 1].
[27] "On the Origin of Language" finds Rousseau saying that figurative meaning *precedes* the literal. I'm happy to see pride of place taken away from "the literal." But I wouldn't valorize the metaphoric as always its opposite. The child just doesn't have the relevant contrast in control. What she thinks is no doubt neither literal nor figural. Even for adults the contrast in many cases will turn out to be idle.

to corner truth, as Thoreau is, we have to opt for the *literal*. But we should resist. When the cello speaks back to the horn, or the waves murmur to the breeze, or my forehead suffers a stabbing pain, we are not wandering among ornamental figures where truth has no grip. But if it's true that my pain is stabbing or that the violin speaks, this is not the land of the woodenly literal, either. And when dreams speak, is their speech literal, metaphorical, or neither? Do we even understand our question?

Donald Davidson opens an essay on metaphor boldly: "Metaphor is the dream work of language."[28] That seems on target. But to say "language performs dream work"—the saying of it—will have transformative effect (or not) quite *apart* from whether I can place that remark as literal, figural, or neither. "The dream work of language" is as brilliant and befitting a reverie as Thoreau's reverie of dreaming toads. The reveries ring true. The literal-figural contrast is neither exhaustive nor always effective. It's not a reliable life buoy to cling to. Waves lap the edge of the sands, but their lapping is neither literal nor figural.

Our first utterances are inevitably articulations of what William Day calls "a sudden aspectual vision."[29] But to be non-literal is not in every case to be figural or metaphoric. We negotiate, case by case, how to take a literal-figural contrast, and just as importantly, *whether to grant it at all*—on what basis, and for what purpose. To debate whether saying "the waves lap the shore" is literal or figural presumes that the literal–figural contrast is always in play. It isn't. Thoreau announces that Nature speaks without metaphor, but we can now see that it doesn't follow that Nature speaks *literally*. Nature might speak as the waves speak, neither metaphorically nor literally. The robin sings to the robin and it sings to us without metaphor—we can leave it at that.

We begin life exercising prodigious translation and decoding abilities that continue to grow into adulthood and age. We happen on a poem of Emily Dickinson, or a page from *Finnegans Wake*, or Thoreau's *A Week*. We live to decipher the weight and meaning of words and things that bud and burgeon in ever-more-intricate, enticing, and terrifying figurations—and all too often, fall back into fine phrases and chatter, not worth hearing, cold, like jokes gone stale. Of course, the commonplace literal and prosaic will flourish worthily and powerfully in stretches of scientific, bureaucratic, and practical discourse and attendant life. But in full lives neither the prosaic nor the figural, as commonly construed, are dispensable. There's a place for befitting poetic reverie, and for catching a mood in a newly minted phrase.

---

[28] "What Metaphors Mean," *Critical Inquiry*, 5 (1) (1978): 31–47.
[29] See William Day, "On Wanting to Say Something: Aspect Blindness and Language," in William Day and Victor Krebs, *Seeing Wittgenstein Anew* (Cambridge: Cambridge University Press, 2010), p. 212.

10.

Words like "death," "love," "attachment," "adventure," and "friend" can become hardened, reduced to appearances in pro-forma utterance. Discovering their life is rediscovering the life of the things they bespeak. Strings of words like "the freedom of rivers," or "an ache for salvation," may also become empty or pro-forma, and plead for new life. Reading Thoreau is a communicative venture that ends on good days in a release toward new life in words and the lives of things. We save both language and things from cold storage.

My way of writing on "Concord River" will succeed as words and their resonances overlap holistically in a network of reinforcement and support. Things and meanings inhabit something like an anomalous zone. Thoreau lets a cranberry become a skiff. I absorb and stand by his inter-animation of skiff and cranberry. Or perhaps I dismiss these words as humor or "mere metaphor" or "a pretty turn of phrase" (Ha! Cranberries become skiffs!).

Words stand or fall as Thoreau's and my credibility in wording them stands or falls—as intelligibility stands or falls in writing of muskrats swimming for dear life toward a hut with no warming fire. "[A] Joke or dream or metaphor can, like a picture or a bump on the head, make us appreciate some fact."[30] And jokes, dreams, and bumps can misfire. It's no doubt true that "understanding a metaphor is as much a creative endeavor as making a metaphor, *and as little guided by rules.*"[31] But without rules, how to we know we're on safe ground in interpreting Thoreau's poetic improvisations?

Authority will rest in mutual trust as I offer something (a cranberry skiff) as possessing importance and as you take that offering in good faith, and weigh the invitation to honor a "cranberry skiff" collaboratively with me (and with others) in extended dialogs tending toward embrace of Thoreau and his rendering.

Here is Cavell on grasping the weight and authority of words:

> [It's] a matter of our sharing routes of interest and feeling, modes of response, senses of humor and of significance and of fulfillment, of what is outrageous, of what is similar to what else, what a rebuke, what forgiveness … all the whirl of organism Wittgenstein calls 'forms of life.' Human speech and activity, sanity and community, rest upon nothing more, but nothing less, than this. It is a vision as simple as it is difficult, and as difficult as it is (and because it is) terrifying.[32]

---

[30] Donald Davidson, "What Metaphors Mean," *Critical Inquiry*, 5 (1) (1978): 31–47.
[31] Ibid. (my emphasis).
[32] Cavell, "The Availability of Wittgenstein's Later Philosophy," *Must We Mean What We Say?, Updated Edition* (Cambridge: Cambridge University Press, 2002), p. 52.

11.

Thoreau offers John Brown as a martyr, marking his death as a breakthrough to glory. Unlike Washington or Franklin, he died for something; Franklin and Washington merely "went missing." Weighing the authority and accuracy of these words of praise, as Thoreau fixes them to glorious ideals—weighing their capacity to be poetically and philosophically grounded—resembles weighing Thoreau's remark that only a few have learned "the art of walking," or that "Concord River" is perhaps only a temporary replacement of the name "Musketaquid" ("Concord" will be withdrawn, he avers, when concord has fully disappeared). Will we find it credible that Cape Cod's marriage to New England dissolves a previous marriage to France? Should we acknowledge that it was once New France? Grounding is a matter of *testing* for grounds, and trading in hunches—not hitting rock bottom with a shout.[33]

Our footing in improvising the sense and weight of an improvised poetic utterance is at risk, swept by the ebb and flow of currents of conversation that threaten (or reform or affirm) our sense of the eloquence of things and our words. But nothing here signals an evitable defeat or *debilitating* uncertainty. Such footing carries its sense of cautious certitude, when it does, with the same flair as my cautious sense of certitude that crabs belong to the sea *and* to the land, or that my back door threshold belongs to the inside *and* to the outside of the house. Aspectual knowledge, so often appearing poetically or paradoxically, *shifts*. And our sense of certitude likewise shifts as we weigh a Thoreau reverie for authority and accuracy.

We ask whether the threshold is inside *or* outside, or whether the crab is in the sea *or* on land, or whether Thoreau *really* sees fish in the heavens, or whether his frog *really* dreams. The questions are fine, but we get no once-for-all answers. Answers get negotiated (and renegotiated) case-by-case, instance-by-instance. Yet we are not put tragically or foolishly at risk in asking or having no hope for sure-fire all-purpose resolutions. My footing is not necessarily at risk as I stand amidst the advance and retreat of the tide. Nothing about being caught in its anomalous flow forebodes inevitable failure. Balance has its own instincts and moments of surety. Acknowledging that crabs and thresholds inhabit anomalous zones is recognizing their mobile dance. And accepting this increases their lively intelligibility and allure. It's a net gain. Walking meditations both release poetic imagination

---

[33] For gaining a sense of a position through conversations that intimate rather than arguments that coerce, see the discussion of Taylor's *A Secular Age* by James K. Smith, *How (Not) to Be Secular*, p. 120. And for philosophy as exploring a position aesthetically rather than demonstrating it as a matter of logic alone, see Alva Noë, *Varieties of Presence*, p. 126.

and bring us down to earth. This grounding of the poetic is robustly relational and improvisational—as when I viscerally know I am on terra firma (or not) as waves rush at my shins.

12.

I promised to explore the value of considering Kant's "thing-in-itself" in perceptions of presence and aspects. This famous (and infamous) notion can facilitate understanding the easy shifts we make between seeing the world as the biologist does when, for writing her report, she strips it of poetic presence and allure—and then seeing the world as the poet does, when she brings out the full glory of presence even as "hard facts" remain.

Kant says we cannot have knowledge of "the thing-in-itself." If knowledge is all that matters, this restriction on knowledge makes "the thing-in-itself" interesting merely as a fact about knowledge—its outer boundary. But this unavailability of knowledge might signal a most interesting and perhaps even urgent existential reminder of finitude in knowing. It reminds us that struggles to know will be unending, that there will always be something further beyond presently available knowledge to taunt us, humble us, with its inaccessibility. To acknowledge that completeness is unavailable is not just a neutral fact to take in. It carries a moral, anti-promethean, existential reminder of finitude.

There is a further insight opened to us with accepting the unknowability of the thing-in-itself. Lack of full knowledge leaves open other modes of access to the world. Knowledge is not our sole access. Imagination animated by lively images provides an equally powerful access. If I am struck by the wonder of sunset, being impressed by it is not a matter of knowing it. And if I sense my neighbor's anger at the noise floating over the fence that divides us, access to that presence overflows the confines of strict knowledge. I access the anger or love of another by means that don't stop with strict cognitive observation.

Cavell takes the "thing-in-itself" as registering the finitude of human knowing, and, more provocatively, as showing that our fundamental relation to the world is not one of knowing.[34] Anger or love can give us reliable access the world.[35] Of course either can distort reality too. But the anger of outrage

---

[34] Thoreau's concept of "neighbor" or "neighboring" can be read as our being always "next to the world"—not fully *in* it. Being "next to" can be a non-knowing mode of access to the world. See Cavell, *Senses,* p. 102.

[35] See Furtak's *Stanford Encyclopedia of Philosophy* entry, "Thoreau."

gives us access to evil (when it is there) and the love of a child can give us the loveliness of the child (when it is there). Going sideways to Cavell's account, let's say that the "thing-in-itself" is a "placeholder" for our capacity to see something—and the reciprocal capacity of the world to present something—under multiple aspects ranging well beyond what's given as an object of knowledge-only. There is something I know (the sun descends to the left of that pine). But if I wince at the piercing light, an aspect of sunset arrives that is irreducible to an "object for observational-knowing only." Appeals to "the thing-in-itself" make room for acknowledging that the sun going down can be a moment of meteorological interest, of wincing pain, or of infinite beauty. Moments of awe or beauty or pain are moments when knowledge evaporates or rests on the shelf.

We fancy (we don't *know*) that an infinite beauty resides hidden but waiting to appear from a reservoir of unanticipated revelations, a reservoir that we clumsily call "the thing-in-itself." The 'elusiveness' of the "thing-in-itself" is analogous to what Ryle called the "'systematic elusiveness of the 'I.'"[36] We accept "the I" as a source of speech and agency, even as it lies unknown just behind specific instances of action or speech. Behind the utterance "I want toast" is the elusive "I" that utters the public request. Similarly, the "object" we clumsily call "the thing-in-itself" lies behind any specific delivery of an object or presence. Strict knowing and measurement satisfy our meteorological interests, yet sunset can enflame or subdue. The clumsily-called "thing-in-itself" cradles a wide associative aspectual field. For example, sunsets can strike us as subtle, overwhelming, or depressing as well as plain wondrous. Although we do not know the thing-in-itself—it is unobservable, we have no data about it—we nevertheless can be struck, overtaken, enchanted, by emanations from it. And let's face it, the sun that Newton triangulates is none other than the sun full of enchantments and life.

Let's say that Thoreau's writing grounds something like Kant's "thing-in-itself." There are not two objects, one in appearance, the other unknowable and "behind" it. There is one object that holds a number of aspects, available sequentially or simultaneously. First is the aspect that affords observational knowledge: the sun sets just to the left of the oak. However, a sun known observationally or meteorologically is partially eclipsed when the same sun gives me something more, or other. It might appear as an indistinct blur of orange, or a force whose allure sweeps me away, or whose melancholy deflates my hopes for an unchanging serenity. In any case, these aspects belong as much to the sun as its meteorological aspects. A storm's fury, a desert's quiet, a wind's roar are aspects of storms, deserts, or winds—aspects as real as

---

[36] Gilbert Ryle, *The Concept of Mind* (Chicago, IL: University of Chicago Press, 2000).

their meteorological features. A locus of attention can deliver both an object of knowledge and a presence that is not directly observed but immediately sensed. To give a poetic elaboration of being struck by a sunset's wonder is to offer conditions for that occasion. It is to offer part of a "deduction of the thing-in-itself"—an acknowledgment and thoughtful elaboration of a source of eloquence (as well as of stripped-down objecthood).

In wonder, the mind does not need to stop at information (of this or that); it's not part of a fact-gathering mission. It may be triggered by facts or prompt us to get more, but wonder is also a response whose legitimacy can stand on its own. It can travel apart from an itch to explain this or that. Wonder (or devastation, or delight) is absorbed, its effects, undergone. Here is Emily Dickinson again:

> And then a plank in reason, broke,
> And I dropped down and down
> —And hit a world at every plunge,
> And finished knowing—then—[37]

The mind and heart leave off prying for more data, for better explanations, for more knowing. They are patient with rain or a slant of sun. Mind and heart are stopped here and now, finished with knowing, or knowing why. But there's no despair. There's room for delight in being stopped short in wonder.

Dickinson finds "a plank in reason break"—she falls and falls. But having finished knowing, gripped in the fearful immediacy of an utter absence of "grounds of reason," or knowing why, she nevertheless finds worlds remain. Worlds without justifying grounds, we might say—though we've seen there are subtle ways to ground poetic response from within new worlds. What escapes grounding is worlds-entire, forms of life entire.

13.

One can "finish knowing" and still fall in love, plunge into dread, or slip into grief or delight. Each "fall" or "plunge" or "slip" can eventuate in the revelation of things in a world, things with which we can have communion or sympathy. Each interruption of her fall, each world-encounter, shows up as a way of being in the world, a way of being that begins despite groundlessness, despite the death of grounded knowing. Thoreau is not writing to get objective certainties, but to brace a soul, to embrace a 'grounding' through conversations with others, through 'trying out' our intuitions and

---

[37] Dickinson, "280" lines 17–20.

convictions in an enterprise relying on trust and mutual acknowledgment. He articulates a different moment than giddy falling—as Dickinson's "plank of reason breaks." A moment of unknowing revelation of presence has its marvelous securities. She hit a *world* at every plunge. Why not a wondrous world?

We remember Thoreau's testament in "Walking"—"The highest we can attain to is not Knowledge but Sympathy with Intelligence."[38] Our highest, most fulfilling attunement to the world comes when we are alert for local "Intelligence," as radiant things give radiant news of love, dread, grief, or delight—from this alder or that rock, or from this grand vista. Only an attentive sympathy and affinity with such news can deliver us to sustaining worlds, where knowledge-as-data, or knowledge-as-explanation, no longer are sole access to the speaker's podium. Then there is time to hear new life in enjoyment of perceptual communion.

Thoreau does not hold the hyper-Romantic view that twentieth-century style scientific knowledge necessarily kills poetic evocation, or inevitably leads to an objectified self, empty of life. Our universities shift financial resources away from poetry and the humanities toward vocational–professional training and scientific enterprise. This threatens the survival of poetry in the humanities. Yet Thoreau (and many others) attest to the possibility of a warm *compatibility and mutuality* here. The worlds unveiled by a poetic-religious sensibility need not battle the worlds uncovered by a disciplined science. Poetry reveals and celebrates endless wonders, including wonders that science unveils. Thoreau resists any tilt toward the primacy of the scientifically factual and theoretical. Science and poetry are not in a zero-sum game, a gain to one signaling a loss to the other. Nevertheless, in a wide swath of high- and middle-brow culture, and in the administrative-business social order, not to say the academy, the primacy of the scientific, technical, and utilitarian is presumed. Poetry is consigned to the side-streets of entertainment, intensely private pursuit, or cocktail party polish.

14.

The retrieval of the poetic, as I envisage it, is not a nostalgic wish for different, enchanted times. It embodies a realism of the locally poetic that resists the ever-encroaching claims to Empire by regimens of science and technology, or cold common sense, regimens deaf to the value of reverie, poetry, music, or the elusive and radiant presence of the world—its capacity

---

[38] *Essays*, p. 172.

to deliver fear, delight, or wonder, for instance. In the academic world, a retrieval of the poetic would be resistance to the hegemony of just-the-facts research, of varieties of critical unmasking or of vanguard theory that undermines or trivializes the felt-weight of words and things and our experiences with them.

Thoreau is one of an impressive phalanx to announce the loss of enchanted worlds. One thinks of Marx and Heidegger, Blake, Rousseau, and Wordsworth, and notable environmentalists from Thoreau to the present day.[39] Of course the very forces of disenchantment that strip the world, human society, and the person down to their mechanical parts, also underwrite advances that improve quality of life. I think of medical technology and air transportation. But accepting a Galilean world of atoms and computer chips does not rule out an adjunct world of enchantments. Neither needs to claim hegemony. My alders can be thirsty and yearn for spring while I unstintingly know and admire their cellular biology. There is no problem loving a lily while loving the elegance of its fit in an ecological niche—or just *knowing* its fit. Thoreau knew both ways of seeing and absorbing, and saw no need to choose. When we're served cappuccino and a croissant, we're not forced to choose one over the other. But one, in the moment, may exert more appeal.

> [I]n my account of this bream I cannot go a hair's breadth beyond the … miracle of its existence. I can only think of precious jewels, of music, poetry, beauty, and the mystery of life. I only see the bream in its orbit, as I see a star, but I care not to measure its distance or weight. The bream, appreciated, floats in the pond as the centre of the system, another image of God.[40]

Thoreau relished warm moments of actual *convergence* of sympathetic openness to presence, on the one hand, and on the other, disciplined knowledge of objects and their properties. Knowing the meteorology of tornadoes does not preclude being awed by their power. Dickinson has us stopped (in wonder, in surprise, in terror) by a world after knowledge is finished. Thoreau has us relish his naming innumerable fish while he longs to become them in their liquid darting.

---

[39] See, among others, Lawrence Buell, *The Environmental Imagination: Thoreau, Nature Writing, and the Formation of American Culture* (Cambridge, MA: Harvard University Press, 1996).
[40] *Journal*, November 30, 1858.

15

Face of the River

Stupid kindness ... [is]as beautiful and powerless as dew
—Vassily Grossman[1]

Levinas is witness to the Shoah; Thoreau is witness to a river, a pond. They might converse about witness and sympathetic first person address especially in moments of pain or abandonment. They might also converse on answerability to a call from a particular other in distress. An influential continental philosopher, Levinas was in the thick of philosophical conversations in Paris between the world wars. He was captured as the Nazis invaded France and sent to a work camp. Though a Jew, because he was in military uniform when captured, he was not deported to a death camp.[2] His writing career resumed after the war, when his works gained increasing acclaim. It is partly chance that brings me to imagine Thoreau and Levinas in conversation. Lyman Mower, a colleague, had seen connections between these writers I could not have imagined. The chance to imagine what this encounter could tell us became irresistible.[3] Along the way I discovered how an ethics happy with parables could be helpful in wrestling with the enigmas of loss and catastrophe.

One befitting parable or half-fiction that Levinas presents has a woman just freed from captivity in a Nazi camp. Suddenly she spots her former torturer. With a rock in her hand, and no one to stop her, she nevertheless foregoes killing this now helpless tormentor. Like Dostoevsky's fable of the Grand Inquisitor, Levinas recounts a troubling parable of the hair's-breadth separating humanity and barbarity. The nagging inconclusiveness of these

---

[1] Vassily Grossman, *Life and Fate*, Robert Chandler (trans.) (New York: Harper and Row, 1985), p. 409. Grossmann writes, "This kindness, this stupid kindness, is what is most truly human in a human being. It is what sets man apart ... But, as I lost faith in good, I began to lose faith even in kindness. It seemed as beautiful and powerless as dew." Levinas says to an interviewer, "To understand this universe, you should read Vassily Grossman." See *Is it Righteous to Be? Interviews with Emmanuel Levinas*, Jill Robbins (ed.) (Stanford: Stanford University Press, 2001) pp. 89, 218.
[2] One did not have to be in a "death camp" to die in "work camps" of malnutrition and brutal work regimes. Some estimates put the number of deaths in camps near Fallinspostel where Levinas was interred in the 30,000s.
[3] Alfred I. Tauber acknowledges a debt to Levinas, in *Henry David Thoreau and the Moral Agency of Knowing* (Berkeley: University of California Press, 2001), pp. xi, 231. See also Diane Perpich, *The Ethics of Emmanuel Levinas* (Stanford: Stanford University Press, 2008), Ch. 5.

parables recapitulates what Thoreau presents as an enigmatic union of the fathomable and the unfathomable in our walks through paradise and hell.

1.

In a classical view, ethics is what makes for a good and fulfilling life. Hilary Putnam begins an account of Jewish ethics with the rabbi's tale of God's routine: good works in the morning, study in the afternoon, sporting with whales in the evening.[4] This is an ideal life. There are no warriors, battles, or punishments, and it leaves no carbon imprint, time to consumer, or alienating labor. Thoreau sported with fish and woodchucks, and rowed for fun with his brother. He was a voracious reader and note-taker, absorbing the *Bhagavad-Gita*, as well as Greek, Latin, and modern classics.[5] He writes that his books "are the only oracles which are not decayed." If the face of a book is a timeless oracle, perhaps a human face is, too. For good works, he escorted fleeing slaves traveling north to Canada and gave a night in jail for justice, writing "Resistance to Civil Government," a primer for Gandhi and Martin Luther King.

Levinas was devoted to study and writing that culminated in a raft of books. His good works did not stop with writing or with teaching in his Jewish community. Can we picture him "sporting with whales"? Well, he does have a place for simple enjoyments: food, air, light, sleep, the sun on one's back.[6] "To live is to take pleasure in life."[7] Yet "sporting with whales" seems to raise pleasure far out of each. The biblical leviathan was not a bathtub pet. The Voice from the Whirlwind mocks Job, reminding him that he is utterly incapable of sporting with Leviathan. "But embracing the impossible responsively and responsibly is precisely what Levinas also claims is our most pressing vocation."[8] This image of mighty wrestling might also suggest that we are never to rest assured—as if we know what is possible and what is not, especially in our ethical lives. We should press imagination to the limit, imagining, for instance, a mercy and benevolence that by normal accounts would be impossible.

---

[4] Hilary Putnam, "Jewish Ethics?" *The Blackwell Companion to Religious Ethics* (London: Blackwell, 2005), pp. 159–75.

[5] Thoreau: "the adventurous student will always study classics ... They are the only oracles which are not decayed." *Walden*, "Reading," p. 98 [para 3].

[6] See John Sallis, "Levinas and the Elemental," *Radicalizing Levinas*, Atterton and Calarco (eds) (Albany: SUNY Press, 2010), p. 90.

[7] *Totality and Infinity*, Alphonso Lingis (trans.) (Pittsburgh, PA: Duquesne University Press, 1969), p. 115.

[8] Jim Hatley (private correspondence).

Witness to the ethical—to my ties to the other, to the ties that the other exacts from me—is occasioned often enough when we are powerless to save the one crying for help. Thoreau was helpless holding his brother—writhing, dying, in his arms. He bears veiled witness to that pain and that friendship (and so much more) in *A Week on the Concord*. For his part, Levinas is witness to the millions lost in the Shoah, and witness to his helplessness to rescue his family and others. Injustice and unspeakable loss leave visceral wounds. Yet despite desolation, each finds unexpected moments of joy and delight. It is a bitter truth that one cannot leave the Shoah behind. Thankfully, that is not the only reality Levinas inhabits. John Thoreau's violent death and the hanging of John Brown leave bitter tastes. Yet Thoreau took unrestrained delight in others and animals, in meadows and swift waters, and Levinas took delight in the pleasures of conversation and teaching.

Both Thoreau and Levinas have us hear the address of the world, especially as it calls us to caring responsibility. We speak or act as the world speaks to and acts on us—with demands and invitations. As we mature, our responses become subtle. Listening to a difficult reality soon enough brings us to philosophy, the search for illumination through conversation with others. Mower reminds us that

> [Philosophy] begins in dialogue, and this connection can only be characterized as ethical. The call and response of dialogue is the best everyday, practical example of how ethics seeps into life.[9]

We are rational, political, language-using, and tool-wielding animals, and also conversing animals. We inherit and inhabit practices of articulation and address. We take up such practices making them our own, and can witness to demands that intrude from outside habitual practices—as in artistic inspiration or ethical revelation. In dialogue we negotiate meanings in ongoing passionate and measured disputes, in acclamations and condemnations, invitations and declarations that shape and establish (or diminish) our connections with others—our humanity.

For Levinas the ethical call to responsibility is primal. There is nothing deeper. In human activity and passivity, all that springs as significant and telling flows from our response to relational address. Nothing lies beneath it—not objects, Gods, force fields, or language—not knowers, actors, beliefs or doctrines. As my colleague puts it, "Relationship goes all the way down." He goes on:

---

[9] Lyman Mower initiated this conversation joining Levinas and Thoreau.

This is Levinas' theory of the subject, a subject that emerges in response to a call from beyond itself. Thoreau, too, sees himself in relationship to other people, animals, and events in such a way that their demands upon him are partially constitutive of who he is.

A moral claim emerges from an unknown source and disrupts a world. For Thoreau, a meadow or river addresses alert sensibility. He finds himself bearing lyrical witness to its wonder, raising the hearty sense that it's there to be celebrated and preserved.

2.

Thoreau and Levinas will converse across seas, languages, and times. For Levinas, ethics is primarily responsibility. We are given no rest from its call. His is a hyperbolic or "insomniac" responsibility focused on the ethical prohibition, "Do not Kill!" The command accosts us, intervenes, takes over. It demands submission. It does not recommend principles or virtues. It does not appeal to conscience or an edict of God. It bursts from nowhere, or at most, from the epiphany of a face stripped of power. He is unique among contemporary ethicists in taking the claims of responsibility or of prohibition of injustice to be an experiential deliverance, an epiphany or *Augenblick*, striking like a clap of thunder.

This eccentric position can be misconstrued. One critic writes,

> If I understand an obligation, if it is a universal and intelligible principle, then I have made it mine, one of my projects, something I have appropriated and made my own, and so not an obligation at all, but another piece of my freedom, another good idea I have and want to pursue. If I do not understand an obligation, then it is arbitrary; and then I am unable to distinguish among obligations, to distinguish, say, the command that Yahweh gave to Abraham ('that Isaac die') from the command issued to the Nazi guards ('that the Jews die')[10]

Yet for Levinas, obligation is an event, not an intelligible universal principle. And obligation is never one of my projects—it comes to me, I don't advance it—nor is it a good idea that I endorse. Obligation seizes; I don't seize it. And we have plenty of obligations we do not (fully) understand, and that does not make them arbitrary. I have an impulse to protect my child. It's not arbitrary. And how could I understand that obligation beyond saying, "I have it! I'm

---

[10] John D. Caputo, *Against Ethics* (Bloomington: Indiana University Press, 1993), pp. 8–9.

human, after all!" In *Fear and Trembling*, to correct the record, Kierkegaard distinguishes Yahweh's command to Abraham from a Nazi's command to kill. Unlike a Nazi *vis a vis* a Jew, Abraham must love Isaac every minute; and he must know he will get Isaac back.[11]

When Thoreau deals not with meadows or hawks but with humans, response to ethical prohibitions is experiential and primal, too. Think of his prophetic defense of John Brown, about to be hanged for his anti-slavery raid on the arsenal at Harper's Ferry. How could one understand the evil of slavery in terms of ... *something else*? An appeal to abstract right will seem alien next to the outcry, "He's human! Slavery is repulsive, disgusting!" Abstract rights and principles rely for their authority on primal revulsions at cruelties and desecrations.

At times we give witness to the ethical when there is nothing to be done, when we are powerless to save the one crying for help. Thoreau was helpless holding his brother—writhing, dying, in his arms. For his part, Levinas is witness to the millions lost in the Shoah, and witness to his helplessness to save his family and others. Such unspeakable loss leaves visceral wounds. One cannot leave the Shoah or the death of a beloved brother behind, but their bitter tastes do not dominate. Thoreau took unrestrained delight in neighbors and animals, in meadows and swift waters. Levinas took delight in the pleasures of conversation and teaching.

In addition to emphatic prohibitions against killing, desecrating the dead, or silencing voices of protest, there are soft-spoken invitations and solicitations. To cherish children, hearth, and place, attentive to the fragility of each, is to respond to their native solicitations. In the 1970s, Carol Gilligan contrasted an ethics of personal care with an ethics of impersonal rules and strict obligations or rights.[12] Levinas and Thoreau anticipate this move to extend ethics toward attentive care. This extension brings two corollaries. Caring response can be aesthetic and ethical, and the recipient of care need not be a person.[13] A beautiful old violin or magnolia bush calls for response in the register of aesthetic delight as well as in the ethical register of preservative care. Ethicists speak of the heritage value of an old house or an irreplaceable landscape or an art object.[14] Here the aesthetic and ethical are interwoven, and attentive care is not directed at a person. Thoreau gives

---

[11] See my discussions of Abraham, *Knights of Faith*, pp. 82–9, and in *Selves in Discord and Resolve* (London: Routledge, 1996), Chs. 4, 5.
[12] See Carol Gilligan, *In a Different Voice* (Cambridge, MA: Harvard University Press, 1982).
[13] See Ch. 6.
[14] As Kant saw, the serenity of stars can speak to a viewer's self-worth. Inversely, clouding a sky with smog can erase moral self-worth.

moral attention to living things, trees or hawks, and to non-living things, rivers and morning mists.

3.

An experiential ethics rests on perceptions, on hearing, seeing, or being disgusted. A demand or invitation is encountered in *striking, immediate events*—it is certainly *not* derived from propositions proposed as a theory any rational mind should accept.[15] As one reaches to protect a child, one might think, "she's about to fall, about to be harmed." But this is not to advance or act on a principle ("Always treat children well"). The stress is not on deferring to or acting on a moral maxim but on valuing this child, on seeing this cruelty, on hearing this call. Yet often one's situation is not simple. We can be face to face with something we know demands (or invites) ethical response yet be baffled. What is called for can seem bafflingly elusive or opaque. Sometimes the difficulty can be tragic and leave us stunned. In any case, helpful rules can seem to lose grip. The ethical path can seem dark. Jim Hatley puts this eloquently:

> The Tzadik (righteous one, or saint) is not on a straightforward path, for the other's approach requires a storm-tossed and creative wisdom lying beyond the automatic or anonymous application of principles to particulars. In fact a wisdom is demanded that at times utterly befuddles the rational straightforwardness of principles. This discernment, this wisdom, might be Temimuth, an aversion to the idol, an aversion to the miscategorization of the infinite as merely finite.[16]

Not all issues of affliction are open to solution through rational negotiation or adjudication. The Book of Job teaches that ill-fortune may overwhelm our understanding, and just as clearly, good-fortune can baffle all understanding. For Thoreau, and for Levinas as he enters the spirit of Dostoevsky, Grossman, or Torah, we're taught that we are blessed by new worlds, beyond principles or understanding.

---

[15] Hilary Putnam removes Levinas from the tradition of ethics-as-legislation / justification and aligns him with Cavell's account of ethics as becoming my next and better self: *Jewish Ethics as a Guide to Life* (Bloomington, IN: Indiana University Press, 2008), p. 72. See also Diane Perpich, "Getting down to cases," *Essays on Levinas and Law*, Desmond Manderson (ed.) (London: Palgrave, 2009), pp. 21–38. For morality as vision, see Patrick Stokes, *Kierkegaard's Mirrors* (London: Palgrave, 2010), reviewed in my *Excursions with Kierkegaard* (Bloomsbury, 2012).

[16] Personal communication. See James Hatley, *Suffering Witness: The Quandary of Responsibility After the Irreparable* (Albany: SUNY Press, 2000).

Here is a parable of responsibility from Levinas, a moment of ethics that fails to yield simple directives. She had barely been freed when by happenstance or a dark pull of the place, this woman, a Russian, returned to the site of her Nazi imprisonment. (This is a paraphrase.[17]) She revisits the cells of her captivity and torment. Russian soldiers, her liberators, are at hand as she recognizes one of her German captors, now himself captive, humiliated and afraid. He is in dirty rags, bent under the indignity of hauling out excrement and putrefying corpses. He is weak.

She stoops to draw up a brick and brings it up under her jacket. He does not deserve to live! Justice will be mine! She has strength, seething anger, and a taste for vengeance. A quick blow to the temple will do it. What stands between her and a righteous killing? Nothing! Who would blame her? Yet as if against her will, she finds her hand not on the brick but on a morsel of bread, a scrap she had saved for herself.—In a whisper, "Here, take this!" She lifts the scrap gently to his lips. Later she is ashamed, almost as if she had been again defiled. Through sleepless nights, she rehearses her humiliation. She was a fool not to kill him. Worse, she was tender.

When Levinas privileges ethics, he is privileging a prophetic biblical stance, full of mysterious justice and the surprise of *surplus* goodness or mercy. To contemporary students of ethics, this is unfamiliar territory. He is not providing a principle of absolute altruism or commending a principle of forgiveness. Like many biblical parables, the story projects unsettling oppositions that resist summation. We have a tale of mercy; vengeance, set aside. Then we see shattered confusion, a woman deranged by pain. Pathetically, she identifies with her oppressor. Then she disavows her act. The tale seems suddenly weightless, without traction. There's nothing for a Kantian, Utilitarian, Virtue-ethicist, or Divine-command theorist to latch on to.[18] It's useless to anyone immersed in the Law of Nations or Victim's Rights or Transitional Justice. Yet the tale has palpable ethical resonance.

The story belongs to a biblical time before ethics meant Aristotle or Kant. It rings of Dostoevsky's "Grand Inquisitor," and of Kierkegaard's retelling

---

[17] Levinas takes this story from Vasily Grossman, *Fate and Life*, Robert Chandler (trans.) (New York: Harper and Row, 1985), and reports to an interviewer, "To understand this universe, you should read Vassily Grossman." See *Is it Righteous to Be?*, Jill Robbins (ed.) ((Stanford: Stanford University Press, 2001), p. 39. The story is discussed by Michael Morgan, *Discovering Levinas* (Cambridge: Cambridge University Press, 2007), pp. 1–15. Compare Acts 16.23-34: The prisoners had been flogged; the doors are opened. Paul doesn't flee, that the prison-guard not be slain for dereliction.

[18] See Michael L. Morgan *Discovering Levinas* (Cambridge: Cambridge University Press, 2007). Morgan helpfully places Levinas in dialogue with Nagel, Rawls, and Korsgaard. However, Levinas would resist abandoning ethical "felt-necessity" for theories of rules and deliberation.

the Abraham–Isaac story. It rises from the underground, revealing things disturbingly beyond our grasp, even as we are grasped.[19] Such good/bad dreams don't give us a hierarchy of goods or a ranked list of prohibitions. We interpret the scene as we might a nightmare or a miracle. Such tales stretch ethical imagination rather than deliver closure or judgment or rules of thumb. In retelling his story of the woman, Levinas speaks as an Old Testament prophet might.[20] But prophets aren't in the same boat with Aristotle, Hume, or Kant.

4.

Thoreau recounts a horrific occasion on the Merrimack. In 1697 Hannah Duston plummets downriver by canoe toward Haverhill, fleeing Abenaki tribesmen who might discover her escape. Beneath its thwarts lie the bloody scalps of her captors and their children, proof of her heroics. Marauders took her from her home up the Merrimack after splattering the brains of her nursing child against a tree.

The stories of the brick-wielding woman and of Hannah Duston are intractable. At first blush, the Levinasian tale commends mercy and benevolence; vengeance is set aside. Yet at second blush we think, "She's a fool to back down. She says as much herself!" Which is right? At first blush Thoreau's tale commends bravery, ingenuity, and survival against great odds. At second blush, we see she is no less bloodthirsty than her captors—a tragedy that leaves everyone stained. We want conviction: the woman with a brick is correct—or incorrect; Hannah Duston can be vindicated—or can't. Ethics gives answers, doesn't it?

Here are hauntingly powerful ethical questions but no answers. Ethical hopes are raised (the presence of unconditional benevolence or heroic courage). Raised only to be dashed. The woman with bread calls herself a fool; absolute benevolence could hardly be universally applicable. Paralysis sets in. We're left in silence, in an abyss of ethical kinetics. Perhaps we should think of these as "what if" thought experiments meant to expand moral imagination rather than give practical answers. Imagination can expand possibilities that undermine conviction. What if God told Abraham to take Isaac to the mountain? What if God spies Moses and thinks of killing

---

[19] See Kierkegaard, "The Joy of it: That the Weaker you become, the Stronger God becomes in you," in *Christian Discourses*, Howard V. and Edna Hong (trans.) (Princeton, NJ: Princeton University Press, 1997).

[20] Lyman Mower finds Thoreau fascinated with the prophetic demands of Jesus, Joel, and Isaiah.

him?[21] Such thought experiments or gripping reveries raise convictions—God couldn't do that!—only to destroy them. God did do that! The stories undermine dogmatic conviction.

The quasi-biblical story of a woman with a brick exposes the field of ethics but we cannot strive to emulate her conduct. Her mercy and generosity, her rejection of vengeance, in just those circumstances, is not the educated response of a habitually virtuous woman. It's hardly intelligible that citizens could be trained in responsiveness to gratuitous good. "Stupid good," or "Stupid Magnificence" appears in the Whirlwind's Voice in the Book of Job. We witness the delivery of sublime seascapes, night, Leviathan, snow, without rationale. Such gifts found the requisite world from which both forensic arguments and further epiphanies and demands can emerge. The story of the woman implants the possibility of gratuitous ethical good.

In the near-biblical story of a woman with bread, Levinas invites us to countenance a kind of lawless, gratuitous goodness (the flip side of gratuitous evil). It intervenes unbidden and unwanted, a kind of eucatastrophe, a good ending beyond all expectation and with hardly any rationale. Ethics must "start" with a rogue or "stupid" goodness, Levinas thinks, refusing any handbooks of *what to do when* or of *what trumps what*. There's no recourse to "Be merciful!" or "Obey the moral Law!"; to "Promote the greatest happiness!" or "Do no evil"; to "Justice first," or "Love thy neighbor." Parables or stories from Kafka, Tolstoy, Kierkegaard, and endless others seem to capture a sense of unknowing, of not knowing one's way about, of being without recourse to Reason or an articulate Ethics. It's a witness to imponderables where simple orientation and forensic justification break down.

5.

We can suppose an implicit scale of ethical importance and urgency. At one end we find indifference, inattention, not to mention violence in varying degrees; at the other end we have the vivid sense of one's answerability for the life of another. As the woman does, we can find ourselves lost in the midst of a "stupid kindness, as beautiful and powerless as dew."[22] (Powerless: radical receptivity is far from rational self-assertion.) Or we can find ourselves in the less radical receptivity at play in less dramatic encounters—say the address of an alluring melody or of a book waiting to be read.

---

[21] Exodus 4.24.
[22] See Robbins (ed.), *Is it Righteous to Be?* pp. 217f, and Michael Morgan, *Discovering Levinas*, p. 8.

For Thoreau, things of the earth speak, but he does not allow just any or every rock or crow, at any time at all, to corner his answerability. Such unmonitored absolute receptivity would overload ethical sensibility, jamming reception and stalling action. John Brown overrides the call of the woodlot. Levinas can grant a family cat, or a great aunt's shawl, prerogative to call on his answerability, when a more prominent face of another is not pressing. Both can say, "Be attentive, do not discard, or harm!" Letting cocks crow and rocks speak, claiming our attention, will not dilute the urgency—when apt—of responding to the human face. This is not a zero sum game. From Thoreau we sense the possibility of answerability to this patch of garden, to this nocturnal creature, to this alpine setting. Attending to the rocky shoal just now receiving the advance of the sea might seem only an aesthetic orientation, yet the latent presence of the ethical becomes clear if the shoal is washed by oil, flaring ethical outrage. If the shoal is part of creation, its befouling is also a desecration. More than economic and aesthetic value is at stake.

Thoreau is not alone in inviting us to acknowledge the call of a distant mountain or near by birds. Biblically, in words that still resonate, the sea has the face of the deep, and heavens look down with heavenly face. Virgil has stones weep.[23] Why is Levinas cautious in spreading the facing relation to cats or fine furniture? We can't look to see if a snake or an oak or a stone has a face. Nor can we just stipulate the scope of facing relations. Thoreau's vision of things-that-call-for-preservation might lure Levinas to his orbit, where one can see the face of a river. The preciousness of a swallow's flight or the face of a child elicits preservative care for the swallow or child, and also for the world in which it abides. A gardener's responsible, caring attention to earth and its yield belongs to the domain of ethical response.

Consider an extraordinary passage where Levinas bears witness to the capacity of a delightful dog to provide care for human others.

> There were seventy of us in a ... unit for Jewish prisoners of war ... The French uniform still protected us from Hitlerian violence. But the other men, called free, who had dealings with us and gave us work ... stripped us of our human skin. We were subhuman, no longer part of the world ... And then a wandering dog entered our lives. One day he came to meet

---

[23] William Day brought me to Aeneas contemplating a portrait of war and a world where "things weep"—I'd say, "where even stones weep." Aeneas' "Lacrimae rerum" is indeed "tears of things." But neither of the two great recent translations let things weep. Robert Fagles: "The world is a world of tears, and the burdens of mortality touch the heart." Robert Fitzgerald: "They weep here \ For how the world goes, and our life that passes \ Touches their hearts." A face weeps, and a face in a painting weeps, a willow weeps, and skies and stones will weep at our folly.

this rabble as we returned under guard from work. He survived in some wild patch in the region of the camp. But we called him Bobby, an exotic name, as one does with a cherished dog. He would appear at morning assembly and was waiting for us as we returned, jumping up and down and barking in delight. For him, there was no doubt that we were men.[24]

This second Levinasian story, rather different from the woman with bread, suggests relations that are preparation for the demand not to harm. Bobby's delight is contagious. In the bleakest of circumstances that would seem to have defeated all care, an unexpected camp pet solicits and draws out a care among those who have come close to abandoning it. Prisoners find their willingness and capacity to care restored. The pet's bounding greeting is not a face declaring, "*Do not kill!*" but a face of enabling hospitality that supplements an ethics of prohibition. From a different angle, the prisoners for the first time are treated non-instrumentally, even as Kantian ends-in-themselves. Bobby is a gift to the desolate, a life-giving nourishment, almost food. He leads those bereft of humanity back into it. He is God's intermediary, bringing prisoners back into their skins.

6.

Thoreau bears witness to Concord River, its capacity to speak, to call on our moral responsiveness. As one scholar suggests, Thoreau is a "descendentalist," letting elevated ideals descend to bob and weave immanently, by and within the river's ebb and flow.[25] Poetry and philosophy are voiced from vibrantly animated occasions—poetic-transcendent-immanent, temporal-atemporal, tributary-oceanic—each carrying untold possibilities, not excluding seeing God.

> in the heavens there are rivers of stars and milky ways. There are rivers of rock on the surface and rivers of ore in the bowels of the earth. And thoughts flow and circulate, and seasons lapse as tributaries of the current year.[26]

Thoreau's living faith is grounded in what particulars can voice. He would see wondrous occasions shine sideways or transversally, backward and

---

[24] Levinas, *Difficult Freedom*, Sean Hand (trans.) (Baltimore: Johns Hopkins University Press, 1990), p. 152. Levinas calls Bobby "the last Kantian in Nazi Germany"—he treats the prisoners as ends-in-themselves.
[25] See Porte, *Consciousness and Culture,* and Addenda, "Transcendentalism," Ch. 12.
[26] Undated notes, 1837–47.

forward in time, up toward heaven and down toward the dark of a river bottom. He believed we have not yet begun to see, hear, and taste the things of the world in their inter-animations—not yet sensed that our salvation lies in translating ourselves into the poetry of the world. Radiant particulars strike as a day's river travel brings us its shad and weeds, wavelets and winds, its dams and bargemen, its alders and cranberries, its apple trees and histories of good and evil.

Levinas testifies to a call bringing me to a quick regard for this other person. Thoreau testifies to an alert regard for the human and non-human. Rocks and scudding clouds have voice to sing, demand or cajole. The shad or melons can seem so familiar and everyday as to remain underwhelming. But they also can harbor a dimension that is wondrous, and in some lights strange, bewildering, or unsettling. This oscillation of opposites, from the mundane to the radiant, can make the shad, melons, or cranberries of signal, eloquent importance. Thoreau lets this neighborly (while uncanny) resonance emerge from the endless particulars of our worlds.

The story of the woman dropping her brick depicts a double transfiguration. The ex-tormentor is seen in his need (obscuring his earlier sadism). She is seen in her benevolence and forgiveness (obscuring her need for revenge). Just so, the shad are transformed even as Thoreau is transformed in attending them.

7.

The first inhabitants knew it as "Musketaquid." Now the brothers will row down to the Merrimack, then up to the source high in the snow-dusted mountains.

> Compared with the other tributaries of the Merrimack, it appears to have been properly named Musketaquid, or Meadow River, by the Indians. For the most part, it creeps through broad meadows, adorned with scattered oaks, where the cranberry is found in abundance, covering the ground like a mossbed.[27]

Within the first leaves of the book we learn that the river is not unto itself alone but belongs to a larger waterway, one tributary among others. We can see it in a pedestrian way as belonging only to the environs of Concord, but Thoreau wants to expand our attention. He leads us down to the Merrimack, an attenuated river stretching north to the snowy heights of Agiocochook,

[27] *Week*, p. 9.

Mt. Washington, and then descends south to be swallowed by the Atlantic.[28] And he leads us to an attenuated temporal elsewhere, back to the Nile (as he suggests in "Concord's" first sentence)—not to mention back to earlier associates of the oak-adorned Meadow River, who called it Musketaquid.

The Concord flows as a network of strands, a tributary that is part meadow, part river. Meadow and river are intermixed, especially in spring floods, forming a broad marshland, an anomalous zone. The birds of the air belong also to water. The brothers belong to both land and water, their sturdy dory painted blue above water line and green below. It belongs to sky, water, and marsh. These flow with and against meadowed currents of water and wind. Thoreau gives us particulars that resonate in ever-expanding relational networks.

Anomalous, amphibious zones are zones of flow and movement, neither here nor there, zones for outlaws and nomads. In Thoreau's *Cape Cod* they are the zones of scampering crabs half of the sea, half of the sands, anxiously and sideways inhabiting that changeling zone where in walking one belongs to the rippling flood inundating the sands, and to wet-dry terra firma only momentarily awash, the beach sounding gentle hisses as waters advance and retreat.[29]

Concord River, we're told, is well stocked with shad and alwifes. Salmon would be present too, but for the downstream industrial dams too precipitous to leap. As Henry observes, these barriers stop the upward flow of fish in transcendence from below, until they too become extinct. Fish and non-fish inhabit anomalous zones between life and death. Our ethical worlds shift between heaven and hell. Too easily we become awash in an ethical no man's land where persons pass in a fog, indifferent to the other's face, to care and delight, and exchanges becoming only mechanical or violent.

8.

Here, again, is a moment of redemptive writing from *A Week on the Concord*. It calls out a renewal of hope and delight amidst danger, far from clinical observation. Its cadences are recapitulations of earlier walks and reveries, a penultimate, lyrical reckoning, as it were.

> Many waves are there agitated by the wind, keeping nature fresh, the spray blowing in your face, reeds and rushes waving; ducks by the

---

[28] Ephesians 3.18 calls us to regard the "breadth, and length, and height, and depth" of the divine. Compare lines from Psalms and from the Whirlwind in the Book of Job.
[29] See *Cape Cod*, p. 81.

> hundred, all uneasy in the surf, in the raw wind, just ready to rise, and now going off with a clatter and a whistling like riggers straight for Labrador, flying against the stiff gale with reefed wings, or else circling round first, with all their paddles briskly moving, just over the surf, to reconnoitre you before they leave these parts; gulls wheeling overhead, muskrats swimming for dear life, wet and cold, with no fire to warm them by that you know of, their labored homes rising here and there like haystacks; and countless mice and moles and winged titmice along the sunny, windy shore; cranberries tossed on the waves and heaving up on the beach, their little red skiffs beating about among the alders;—such healthy natural tumult as proves the last day is not yet at hand.[30]

Such description sustains a here-and-now that rebukes the routine dullness of so much perception. It is an unabashed celebration of more-than-Newtonian excess, opening to an indefinitely extending, beckoning otherness of wonder, risk, allure, and invitation (if not demand). It is as if we are told simple parables of "stupid goodness, as beautiful and powerless as dew," glance by glance—word by skimming word.

We have ethics as care as first philosophy in a poetic witness to the face of the River—ethics narrated in tiny parables, etched in the moment, fleetingly in the watery instant. Such slaughter-scored memory is for the moment supervened in a celebration of the many fruits of uncanny goodness.

The wind is "keeping nature fresh", renewing it and renewing us through its touch, "spray blowing in your face." Muskrats "swim for dear life," for life is simultaneously dear, bounteous, and dangerous, an amorphous, shape-shifting place for better and worse. We have "ducks by the hundred, all uneasy in the surf, in the raw wind, just ready to rise", ready in their uneasiness to rise toward something higher. We too are "uneasy in the surf" ready to rise. They're "now going off with a clatter and a whistling like riggers straight for Labrador, flying against the stiff gale with reefed wings." There's no gap between sail-riggers and ducks wheeling aloft, nor between where we are and where they are, joined in a single arcing ascent, in a kind of ecstasy. The flock might "circle round first, with all their paddles briskly moving, just over the surf, to reconnoiter you before they leave these parts." Or having reconsidered, settle down again. In any case, they commune with us.

Gulls are "wheeling," even as the river and its words wheel on and on. Our muskrats are "wet and cold, with no fire to warm them by." Thoreau adds sotto voce "so far as we know"—a rather offhand way to ask what we in fact know of the other, or each other, or of the unfoldings before us. They swim

---

[30] *Week*, p. 7.

"for dear life," hurrying in fright to the secure haven of "their labored homes rising here and there like haystacks." Home is the place of mutual hospitality.[31] Cranberries are cranberries, but not only that as the poet's eye finds them "tossed on the waves and heaving up on the beach, their little red skiffs beating about among the alders". They may sail through the chop as if in heaven. Or be tossed up on the beach as wrecks. Perhaps some are "beating about" to windward up the Merrimack toward Agiocochook, "Home of the Great Spirit," even while they are also skiffs seeking safe harbor by an alder, and are also just cranberries rising and falling, bobbing on wavelets on the edge of a watery meadow, an edge of the Concord.

This is the active face of the river, each wrinkle, each crease, a familiar trail calling out our attention—calling for our concern in matters of life and death, safety and danger, adventure and shipwreck. It is not uttering prohibitions, yet is nevertheless a face calling for our attentive concern—an ethical concern. Looking out across the wind-swept marshes, Thoreau finds "such healthy natural tumult [as] proves the last day is not yet at hand."[32] He might have added the Pauline invocation, "Let us therefore cast off the works of darkness, and let us put on the armor of light."[33] Looking back, having Thoreau in stride with Levinas allows us to shorten the distance between the claims of the face of a river, and of the face of a stranger.

Levinas and Thoreau solidify the sense that we are claimed by persons and often by non-persons, quite apart from our having access to a general theory that fixes value or specifies ways to legitimate our felt-sense of particular ethical claims. There is no reason to believe that a Levinasian ethics diminishes the need for a Thoreauvian attention to the expanse of creation. Attention to rivers, stars, woodlots, mountains, need not muffle our alertness to the call of the human face. At last, there is a faith in possibilities that open before us, an absolute faith, beyond any estimation of probabilities of its fulfillment. It is a faith in inexplicable, gratuitous good.

---

[31] See Bob Plant, *Wittgenstein and Levinas* (London: Routledge, 2005).
[32] *Week*, p. 7.
[33] Romans 13.12, KJV. Carson Webb points out that the KJV's use of "armor" fits nicely with Thoreau's allusion to tumult. He adds that Paul writes "of the armor of light" with the expectation that the last day is *indeed* at hand—not, as Thoreau has it, "not yet at hand" (personal correspondence).

Closing Thoughts

[That philosophers who have] grudgingly come to accept the pertinence of Kierkegaard and Nietzsche persist in turning deaf ears to Thoreau strikes me ... as soul-boggling and heartbreaking.
　　　　　　　　　　　　　　　　　　　　　　—Stanley Cavell[1]

From the banks of the Concord we have endless miniatures of vibrant life. From the slopes of Ktaadn, Washington, Greylock, and the diminutive Wachusett we attain more sweeping prospects. From an even greater, satellite height, the surface of earth can present the mobile expressiveness of a face, each wrinkle, fold, and pore, each eye and ear, traced by multiple crossings and paths on varied surface—these are sites to attend to, sites that call, one by one, with insistence, query, or serenity.

Descending from satellite or Greylock we enter Thoreau's most familiar close-up immersions—the details of meadows or burrows, moist, living facts, the finning creatures of a river or pond, the crazed echoing cry of a loon, the swimming of desperate muskrats. We find wonder, sometimes terror, sometimes a wry surprise, and often laughter. We are stopped, impressed, and so often silenced. Thoreau witnesses to joys and delights among ephemeral things, each porous to a wider world laterally, and to deeper worlds vertically and temporally. Serenity and delight are not always the order of the day. But even through declines, deaths, or catastrophes, Thoreau gives no quarter to despair.

We inhabit a changeling reality with a rich spectrum of demands, invitations, fertile gaps, innuendo, warnings, attacks, and consolations. It can elicit, or call out for response, for an address in return. We can respond to a demand for instance, with counter demands, or to an invitation with refusal or stalling. Sometimes we condemn what reality invites us to see and respond to; at other times the invitation is a blessing, we are blessed by what we behold. We bless things that appear in moments of illumination and they bless us; we curse appalling injustice, and are cursed by it. As often we resign in mild disgust. Thoreau refuses to close off ever-surprising address from the next thing to be encountered, speaking in whatever register from its living density.

In medieval lore, changelings were elves or trolls placed in human care in an infant exchange conducted in secret. A human newborn was stolen,

---

[1] Furtak et al., *Thoreau's Importance*, p. 235.

and an elf child was clandestinely put in its place. The strange child raised by humans thus was anomalous, and had unnervingly mysterious powers and provenance. Our realities are of uncertain provenance and possessed of strange and wonderful, anomalous presence.

It is a difficult, changeling reality we inhabit, and far from univocal. Social and political worlds, family and individual ones, can be dispiriting, tragic, painful enough to challenge any shallow and naive predilection for delight we might harbor. Thoreau will not yield to sustained sadness or anger. He reminds us that we are placed in a wider creation. As important, he reminds us that existence itself is a miracle, reflected in the wonder of seashores, riverbanks, gliding hawks, or thunder-rent air. Anomalous, changeling realities call for poetic recounting, for renditions that give marvelous echo to those particular things that elicit our attentive care.

Closing Images, Reveries, Prayers

Journal

I feel a sad cheer when I hear these lofty strains, because there must be something in me as lofty that hears. But ah, I hear them but rarely! Does it not rather hear me? ... God must be very rich, who, for the turning of a pivot, can pour out such melody on me ... So much hope had slumbered. There are in music such strains as far surpass any faith in the loftiness of man's destiny. He must be very sad before he can comprehend them. The clear, liquid notes from the morning fields beyond seem to come through a vale of sadness to man, which gives all music a plaintive air. It hath caught a higher pace than any virtue I know.[1]

Walden

Nature puts no question and answers none which we mortals ask. She has long ago taken her resolution. "O Prince, our eyes contemplate with admiration and transmit to the soul the wonderful and varied spectacle of this universe. The night veils without doubt a part of this glorious creation; but day comes to reveal to us this great work, which extends from earth even into the plains of the ether." Then to my morning work.[2]

Journal

Shall we not have sympathy with the muskrat which gnaws its third leg off, not as pitying its sufferings, but through our kindred mortality, appreciating its majestic pains and its heroic virtue? Are we not made its brothers by fate? For whom are psalms sung and mass said, if not for worthies as these? When I hear the church organ peal, or feel the trembling tones of the bass viol, I see in imagination the musquash gnawing off his leg, I offer up a note that his affliction may

---

[1] *Journal*, 1, pp. 361f.
[2] "The Pond in Winter" p. 273 [para 1]. Cramer gives the quote as Thoreau's translation of Langlois' French edition of the *Harivansa, ou Histoire de la Famille de Hari* 2:361.

be sanctified to each and all of us. Prayer and praise fitly follow such exploits. I look round for majestic pains and pleasures. They have our sympathy, both in their joys and their pains. When I think of the tragedies which are constantly permitted in the course of all animal life, they make the plaintive strain of the universal harp which elevates us above the trivial. When I think of the muskrat gnawing off his leg it is as the plectrum on the harp or the bow upon the viol, drawing forth a majestic strain or psalm, which immeasurably dignifies our common fate. Even as the worthies of mankind are said to recommend human life having lived it, so I could not spare the example of the muskrat.[3]

A Week

If I am not I, who will be?[4]

Autumnal Tints

Why, it takes a sharp-shooter to bring down even trivial game ... ; he must take very particular aim, and know what he is aiming at... And so it is with him that shoots at beauty; though he wait till sky falls, he will not bag any if he does not already know its seasons and haunts, and the color of its wing,— if he has not dreamed of it, so that he can *anticipate* it; then indeed he flushes it at every step ... He prays for it, and often sacrifices ... After due and long preparation, schooling his eye and hand, dreaming awake and asleep, ... he goes out ... and *therefore* gets them. He had them half way into his bag when he started.[5]

Walden

The volatile truth of our words should continually betray the inadequacy of the residual statement. Their truth is instantly translated; its literal monument alone remains.[6] I cannot exaggerate enough to lay even the foundation of a true expression. Who that has heard a strain of music has feared then lest he should speak extravagantly any more forever?[7]

[3] *Journal*, VI, pp. 98–9, February 5, 1854.
[4] *Week*, p. 156.
[5] *Essays*, p. 156.
[6] *Walden*, "Conclusion," p. 316 [para 6].
[7] *Walden*, "Conclusion," p. 315 [para 6].

Closing Passions

We have become secular people, partial people; we no longer believe in, much less live in the interpenetration of the natural and the supernatural: we have lost that sense of mystery that creates ceremony, that reveals to us the garden of the world we live in. In our loss of that sense of mystery, we have lost what galvanizes us against sloth, prevents our souls from growing woolly and fungous ... Blind to the seasons' gifts, numb to nature ... careless of ourselves and of others, bored alike by damnation and salvation, we become graceless by inaction. It is one (one) aim of poetry to recover that sense of mystery, to beckon us from sloth.

—Kelly Jolley, *Stony Lonesome*[1]

1.

Here's a plaque from the foot of Mt. Washington. Thoreau would not have seen it.

> CAUTION: The appalling and needless loss of life on this mountain has been due largely to the failure of robust trampers to realize that wintry storms of incredible violence occur at times even during the summer months. Rocks become ice-coated, freezing fog blinds and suffocates, winds of hurricane force exhaust the tramper, and when he stops to rest, a temperature below freezing completes the tragedy. If you are experiencing difficulty, abandon your climb! The highest wind velocities ever recorded were attained on Mt. Washington. Since the worst is yet to come, turn back without shame, before it's too late.[2]

Stanley Cavell would call this passionate speech. What makes it passionate is the way it gets under my skin; it invades my psyche in the area of my shames and prides and fears. Cavell would say that it "improvises in the disorder of my desires." Should I go on up the trail, not yet icy—or turn back? That might seem like a straightforward practical question to be settled by experts— perhaps I should consult a guide. Yet it's not hard to imagine that this CAUTION could bring me into Dante's dark woods, a place where the troubled soul is

---

[1] *Stony Lonesome*, p. 65.
[2] *Appalachian Mountain Club White Mountain Guide*, 1976 edn (Boston: AMC Books, 1976), p. 3.

exposed, where a simple caution drifts toward a sort of life-crisis: how do I handle this challenge—who will I be, or become, in meeting, or fleeing it?[3]

The CAUTION *might* make me fear for my soul. Although I often use "self" and "soul" interchangeably, it's instructive to see care for the soul moving in different terrain than care for the self. The self is self-assertive, makes its way in the world by undertaking executive initiatives, has critical and rational drives, and a will to take charge of life and master its obstructions. Care for the soul will be something else again. To care for or value the soul is to value the self's deepest passion, and "passion" is a yielding, a suffering, as much as a doing. We "give way" to our passions, let *them* lead *us*. The heart is not the center of mastery, rationality, and self-assertion. To yield to and care for passions of the heart is often to yield to the unfathomable and untamed, the irresolvable or intractable—the realm of conflicting shadows. David Rothenberg captures the risks of allowing the soul latitude. "There is something dangerous about the grooves that capture the soul. They pull us in and there is no escape."[4]

Why should the trailhead CAUTION strike me as an address to my *soul*? If it were merely an innocuous traffic advisory—"Bump ahead!"—it would be a practical piece of information that my prudent, rational, calculating mind ought to take account of. But the CAUTION seems to elicit darkness and danger, fear of a grotesque and needless end to my life. It invades my less-than-rational passion for the unknown and forbidden, challenging prudence with the thrill and allure of edgy or extreme adventure.

For many, keeping safe and alive is not the only value. Life and death can present a dangerous symphony of thrills, falls, threats, and vast vistas—matters of passion and the soul—and they dare us to join. Perhaps this CAUTION reminds me to reel in my romantic taste for adventure and remember my finitude, curb my passion for heroics. But if the majestic and sublime can be supremely indifferent to my well-being, despite the self's will-to-mastery, which should win out, the appeal to the self's desire to keep in control or the soul's desire to be swept away? The CAUTION poses the question without answering it. Its surface intervention is a warning against recklessness. It might also activate exactly the desire for recklessness that brings a climber to the mountain base.

Let me propose that this CAUTION can be read as a sharp reminder of a finitude that I've abandoned, or neglected that might instill a piety before the power of mountain storms, ice, and killing temperatures. If so, the reminder is addressed to the soul in an idiom that is not *solely* secular. The sacred puts the exclusively executive self at risk.

---

[3] Dante begins *The Divine Comedy* finding himself midway in his life in a dark wood.
[4] David Rothenberg, *Sudden Music: Improvisation, Sound, Nature* (Athens, GA: University of Georgia Press, 2002), p. 123.

2.

I inhabit a typical secular university. Despite my invocations of the sacred or the soul, I doubt I'll be called before academic inquisitors. If I were, the indiscretion would be my trespass on private property, my invasion of a space inviolable, the space of religious sensibility or passion or piety (or its lack). The secular assumption is that my students have the privilege to protect their souls (empty or full) from intrusion. The charge against me would be that in speaking of the soul and piety and finitude I breach the self-protective walls of secularity. I'm asking my students to suspend their privileged insularity from the sacred (or the regions of the soul). After all, the university has an overridingly secular calling it wishes to transmit to students under its wing: seek simple knowledge, transmit it, increase it, master skills of critique. Its calling does not include transformation or agitation or humbling of selves or souls. I hoodwink those over whom I hold inordinate power by touching on gods, prophecy, piety, not just in an abstract theoretical way, but in letting reverence and prophecy touch down in the class. The realities of hubris, piety, the sacred or demonic, redemption or sin, may well enter as my voice and my texts speak and bespeak these realities emergent in reading this CAUTION aloud. That makes my classroom a temporary haven for pious souls, not executive secular selves. It intrudes illegitimately on the privacy of innocent listeners—*this* one, in the second row.

If I were asked collegially what piety and soul were doing in a secular classroom, I could ask in return why we should stick with a valorization of the secular that is offended by any whiff of piety? Perhaps the piety-evoking text is what passes for a fully secular trailhead CAUTION. I didn't hold a church service or make students kneel. Why, in this age of moral dark woods, is questioning the limits of the executive self a violation of the aims of the humanities?

Literature, philosophy, art, religion, and music are portals to all things human. There's truth in the reticence, patience, and listening of piety. It's a relief from relentless self-assertive critique. In teaching, I move quite naturally from a mountain-base CAUTION or a quasi-religious poem of Emily Dickinson to contemplative activities (reading, writing, thinking) that are focused on texts tilted toward the religious.[5] Is it harmful to hear these words as prophecy: "*The Worst is Yet To Come! Turn Back without Shame!*"— *Apocalypse* at hand.

---

[5] See my "Preservative Care: Saving Intimate Voice in the Humanities," in *Lost Intimacy in American Thought: Recovering Personal Philosophy from Thoreau to Cavell* (New York: Continuum, 2009).

3.

A prolific man of letters and gripping philosopher, Stanley Cavell takes "passionate utterance" to be a key to a place where the soul is at stake. Passionate utterances are "invitations to improvisation in the disorder of desire."[6] He doesn't cite a CAUTION posted at trailheads in White Mountains National Forest. That's my piece of "found art" that sets us improvising on mortality and hubris, shame and self-assertion, piety and impiety. Cavell gives us examples of passionate speech and advances a view of "redemptive writing" and "redemptive reading"—as if souls could be saved in the reading and writing of philosophy and literature.[7] Cavell writes of redemptions literature can provide from a prestigious Ivy League university, not from a school of theology.

Looking back, we can find witness to "passionate speech" from the start of his long career—witness to the plight of a soul in dark woods. Here he quotes Jean Giraudoux in the epigraph to a signal 1962 article, "The Availability of the Philosophy of the Later Wittgenstein":

> Epochs are in accord with themselves only if the crowd comes into these radiant confessionals which are the theaters or the arenas, and as much as possible ... to listen to its own confessions of cowardice and sacrifice, of hate and passion ... For there is no theatre which is not prophecy. Not this false divination which gives names and dates, but true prophecy, that which reveals to men these surprising truths: that the living must live, that the living must die, that autumn must follow summer, spring follow winter, that there are four elements, that there is happiness, that there are innumerable miseries, that life is a reality, that it is a dream, that man lives in peace, that man lives on blood; in short, those things they will never know.[8]

---

[6] Cavell introduces "passionate utterance" roughly forty years later as an extension of what John Austin called "performative utterance" (*How to do things with words*, 1955). See "Passionate and Performative Utterance," *Contending with Stanley Cavell*, Russell B. Goodman (ed.) (Oxford: Oxford University Press, 2005), Ch. 10, esp. pp. 192–3. "A performative utterance is an offer of participation in the order of law. And perhaps we can say: A passionate utterance is an invitation to improvisation in the disorders of desire."

[7] See Cavell, *Little Did I Know: Excerpts from Memory* (Stanford: Stanford University Press, 2010). See also William Day, "A Soteriology of Reading: Cavell's Excerpts from Memory," *Stanley Cavell, Literature, and Criticism*, Andrew Taylor (ed.) (Manchester: Manchester University Press, 2011).

[8] "The Availability" is reprinted in *Must We Mean What We Say: A Book of Essays* (Cambridge: Cambridge University Press, 1976), Ch. 2. It helps to reread this early '62 essay as an invitation to read *Philosophical Investigations* in an existential and theological light.

Can philosophers devoted to rational analysis make anything of this? The words seem maddeningly sermonic or hysterical—if acceptable, then certainly as poetry, and certainly not as levelheaded philosophy. Cavell published these in the most rhetoric- and poetry-averse of philosophical journals. I must say that reading those lines in the 1960s was a promising and bracing breath of fresh air.

Academic philosophers in the mainstream have disowned passionate speech and the passions. We have classes in how to think critically but none in how to feel attentively, classes in rational decision theory but none in responsible and varied passions. Many read *Genesis* as botched evolutionary biology. But this is like saying that ballet is a botched way of running for a bus. Is our blindness to the varied registers of biblical narration, ballet and biology a matter of retarded logic or stunted passions? Seeing better and feeling with more subtlety can yield metamorphosis of spirit toward the good. Of course, the worst of passions and imaginings can be—must be— deflated by rational critique. But defeating the worst is not attaining the best. Nor is it making the better or the best intelligible, or alluring.

The great novels of Henry James or George Eliot (among many others) show conversational and emotional exchange—rather mild passions— effecting change in persons and desires. We arrive, at least imaginatively, at a more tempered, modulated, and less imprisoning or explosive, set of passions. Here is George Eliot, redeeming us not from sin but from a certain blindness.

> That element of tragedy which lies in the very fact of frequency, has not yet wrought itself into the coarse emotion of mankind; and perhaps our frames could hardly bear much of it. If we had a keen vision and feeling of all ordinary human life, it would be like hearing the grass grow and the squirrel's heart beat, and we should die of that roar which lies on the other side of silence. As it is, the quickest of us walk about well wadded with stupidity.[9]

She raises unanswered and unanswerable but inexpugnable questions.[10] Is it tragic that our rhythms, our periods of inhalation and exhalation, are poorly adjusted to the rhythms of the seas, seasons, or stars—or tragic that our breathing is manic relative to the slow breathing of oaks or the leisurely drift of clouds? Is it *tragic* that the stride of our walks is outmatched by the timeless and immeasurable stride of mountains? Should our frequency be

---

[9] *Middlemarch*, Ch. 20. She senses a danger in close contact with the otherness of things.
[10] Biblical ethics often is delivered in narratives that, like a Kafka parable, raise the most profound questions while refusing satisfying answers.

more akin to the heartbeat of hummingbirds? How fast, or slow is our dance? Eliot's words bring us to think on first and last things, the traditionally hallowed ground of the sacred. Her words remind us that dull vision or numbness toward ordinary human life is imprisoning. Salvation is better seeing, imagining, and feeling. If we let ourselves open to a revelation of "quite ordinary" reality, we'd die on the spot from the sublime roar. She reminds us that ethics can tell us how to restrain the bad, and as importantly, perhaps more importantly, it can tell us what might release the good—as a more imaginative vision of the "frequency" of life might.

4.

"Passionate utterance," as Cavell has it, is speech neither purely descriptive nor the ceremonial or quasi-legal domain of performative utterance. To say, "freezing fog blinds and suffocates" might be construed as simply fact-stating. But at a trailhead it's a screaming CAUTION, informative but also pleading and warning, urgently uttered from the heart, meant to impact my heart. It's meant to burn into the "tramper's" soul, instill imaginative empathy with another tramper, one caught in mortal tragedy. It improvises pleadingly in the disorder of my desires.[11] It does not alter the social world, say as a promise does. It has none of the force of a ranger's shout at close quarters: "Evacuate!" If I head back rather than continue, it's due to its elegant improvisation, not to overt threat or coercion.

Similarly, Giraudoux leads me to consider that my desires are disordered and distort my knowledge. I know and don't want to know that I'm cowardly, or will die, or that there is misery, or that man lives on blood. Passionate utterance invokes the shifting shapes of passion and desire, of imagination and sensibility, prompting the responsiveness Kierkegaard calls our subjectivity. Arcing words in passionate utterance lift us—or they might leave us indifferent. They live or die as we receive or refuse them, as we hear their redemptive register or not, find them saving or banal: "No man is an Island ..."—"the readiness is all ..."—"Let it be!"—"Ain't I a woman?"—"the unexamined life is not ..."—"I have a dream ..."

---

[11] We learn promises (a paradigmatic performative as Austin introduces the term) first as making and marking a "promising bond" to parents and siblings, for instance. As a child grows and reconfigures herself, one part of "the self" can make promises to another: say one vows or promises oneself to be a better violinist or listener. Cavell puts it epigrammatically: "the 'having' of a self is being the other to one's self, calling upon it with the words of others." Cavell, *Philosophical Passages, Wittgenstein, Emerson, Austin, Derrida* (Hoboken, NJ: Wiley-Blackwell, 1995), p. 102.

The power of these words is analogous to the power of aesthetic judgments. I hear Hamlet's "Let it be!" or Donne's "No man is an Island" or Sojourner Truth's "Ain't I a woman?" and am moved to reiterations, with critical and furthering comment, carrying the words forward in my own voice. These words (and mine) spread exponentially, broadening their echo spatially and temporally over an ever-widening community. They are proposed, invitational, intimate universals. They are life-lines; they will either hold, or not; we grab them or not.

If philosophy links to passions, commitments, desires as I undergo these—if it invokes passionate speech that can improvise in my soul—then philosophy will not be just a series of lawyer-like arguments, or analyses of social contracts, or debates about sense and reference. The inherited exemplars of this wider sort of writing would include Rousseau's *Reveries of a Solitary Walker*, Kierkegaard's *The Point of View of my Work as an Author*, Montaigne's *Essays*, and closer to home, nearly everything in Emerson or Thoreau, not to mention large tracts of Dickinson, Melville, and William James. Philosophy needs passion and song, for it is, after all, a love story. Love of wisdom means attention to the fine texture of lives, and love of a form of life suited to oneself and to others, in the light of the good, in the light of a love and life one can affirm. We find these truths affirmed over and over in Thoreau's *Walden, A Week on the Concord*, or "Walking."

5.

Here is W. G. Sebald bearing down squarely on literature and redemption:

> Why can I not get such episodes out of my mind? Why, when I take the S-Bahn toward Stuttgart city center, do I think every time we reach Feuersee Station that the fires are still blazing above us, and since the terrors of the last war years, even though we have rebuilt our surroundings so wonderfully well, we have been living in a kind of underground zone? Why did it seem to the traveler on a winter night ... that the network of lights [from the new administrative complex] glittered in the darkness like a constellation of stars spreading all over the world, so that these Stuttgart stars are visible not only in the cities of Europe, the boulevards of Beverly Hills and Buenos Aires, but wherever columns of trucks with their cargoes of refugees move along the dusty roads, obviously never stopping, in the zones of devastation that are always spreading somewhere, in the Sudan, Kosovo, Eritrea, or Afghanistan? So what is literature good for? Am I, Hölderlin asked

himself, to fare like the thousands who in their springtime days lived in both foreboding and love, but were seized by the avenging Fates on a drunken day, secretly and silently betrayed, to do penance in the dark of an all too sober realm where wild confusion prevails in the treacherous light, where they count slow time in frost and drought, and man still praises immortality in sighs alone? The synoptic view across the barrier of death presented by the poet ... is both overshadowed and illuminated, however, by the memory of those to whom the greatest injustice was done. There are many forms of writing; only in literature, however, can there be an attempt at restitution over and above the mere recital of facts, and over and above scholarship.[12]

In times of mass death, in Haiti, Rwanda, or Auschwitz, and of the sorts Sebald so effectively chronicles, what is literature or philosophy? Can teaching literature or philosophy or religion help? Can a soul be bared in settings that deny souls? At an entirely different level of questioning, after the extinctions that have befallen Germans and Rwandans and Jews and so many others, how is human being to go on? For if atrocities gut the landscape of German or Rwandan or Jewish souls, what possibility is left for reviving *future* Jewish or Rwandan or German souls?

6.

Henry James ends a story with a writer confessing:

> We work in the dark—we do what we can; we give what we have. Our doubt is our passion and our passion is our task. The rest is the madness of art.[13]

We work in the dark when we read certain passages from Thoreau, say his loping in train with a fox, or sensing gods laugh at Spaulding's Farm. Half of the dark is sensing what he senses, and the other half is not knowing whether it can illuminate our own dark woods—not knowing how much the passion of these words will rearrange *our* passions—if they do, and to what effect. We submit, I suppose, to the madness, the slight mitigation, of art.

Here are befitting closing lines from T. S. Eliot, *Four Quartets*:

---

[12] Sebald, *Campo Santo*, "An Attempt at Restitution" (New York: Modern Library, 2005).
[13] James, "The Middle Years," 1893, *The Tales of Henry James*, Edward Wagenknecht (ed.) (New York: Frederick Ungar, 1984).

> And what there is to conquer
> By strength and submission, has already been discovered
> Once or twice, or several times, by men whom one cannot hope
> To emulate—but there is no competition—
> There is only the fight to recover what has been lost
> And found and lost again and again: and now, under conditions
> That seem unpropitious. But perhaps neither gain nor loss.
> For us, there is only the trying. The rest is not our business.[14]

But I would rather end on an upbeat, Thoreauvian note. There are moments in writing that invoke passion and presence, when interpretation does not "go all the way down," where there is precisely no space between words and their impacts, where presence leaps from the page the way wonders leap from the world. And with no space for interpretation, there is enormous room for love of the world, for ongoing revelation, for suspension of doubts. Here is a taste of brie, or a wince at sudden light, or the flight of an ethereal hawk. Thoreau gives us these. We know then that not all meaning is textual or discursive. At such times interpretation, and certainly abstract discourse, miss the grounding tenors of life.

Early on Thoreau remarks pointedly,

> We fancy that this din of religion, literature, and philosophy vibrates through the universe, and is as catholic a sound as the creaking of the earth's axle; but if a man sleep soundly, he will forget it all between sunset and dawn.[15]

But he doesn't forget this "din of religion, literature, and philosophy" *for good*, and what he forgets is no trivial set of throwaways.

The mind is cleared to make room for the next day's awakenings. Sleep is preparation for reawakening. Reawakening is releasing the poet's unclouded lyrical eye. Glaring noontime styles of representation and analysis, or those that take flight at dusk, muffle the eloquent presence that originally calls philosophy, poetry, and religion into being. The morning "intellect of the poet [keeps] in advance of the glare of philosophy."[16] Yet in mysterious ways even din and glare can harbor dormant sparks that in time awaken passionate perception: "our philosophy hears the cock crow in every barn-yard within our horizon. There is something about it that is a newer testament,—the gospel according to this moment."[17]

---

[14] T. S. Eliot, *Four Quartets* (New York: Houghton Mifflin, 1971).
[15] *Essays*, "The Natural History of New England," p. 23.
[16] *Week*, p. 61.
[17] "Walking," p. 254 [para 82].

Chronology

1817 Born July 12 in Concord, Massachusetts.
1833–7 Harvard College.
1837 Teaches a few weeks at Concord Center School.
1838–41 Opens private school in Concord with John Thoreau.
1839 Travels up the Concord and Merrimack rivers with his brother John.
1840 First poems and essays in *The Dial*.
1841–3 Lives with Ralph Waldo Emerson and his family in Concord.
1842 John dies violently of lockjaw; Little Waldo dies days later; Henry collapses; he publishes "Natural History of Massachusetts."
1843 "Walk to Wachusett" and "A Winter Walk" published; tutors William Emerson's children on Staten Island.
1845 Builds and moves into cabin on Walden Pond.
1846 Leaves the pond for short trip to Maine and climb up Mt. Ktaahdin; spends a night in jail for refusing to pay tax protesting the invasion of Mexico.
1847–8 Lives off and on in Emerson household while Ralph Waldo lectures in England.
1848 Lecturing career begins; publishes "Ktaadn and the Maine Woods."
1849 Publishes *A Week on the Concord and Merrimack Rivers* and "Resistance to Civil Government."
1850 Travels to Cape Cod; then to Fire Island seeking Margaret Fuller's remains.
1851 Gives lecture, "Walking, or the Wild."
1853 Travels again to Maine.
1854 Publishes *Walden* and "Slavery in Massachusetts."
1855 Travels again to Cape Cod; publishes portions of "Cape Cod."
1856 Takes surveying job in New Jersey.
1857 Travels to Cape Cod yet again and to Maine woods; publishes "Chesuncook."
1858 Travels to the White Mountains.
1859 Gives "Autumnal Tints" lecture in Worcester. Begins writing *Wild Fruits*; delivers "A Plea for Captain John Brown."
1860 Gives lecture "Wild Apples" in Concord, and "The Succession of Forest Trees". In early December catches the cold that becomes bronchitis, severely weakening him. Last lecture, "Autumnal Tints," given in Connecticut.

1861 Works on *Wild Fruits* and *The Dispersion of Seeds;* travels to Minnesota for his health.
1862 Knowing he is dying, sends off "Autumnal Tints," "Life without Principle," "Walking," and "Wild Apples to *The Atlantic Monthly*.
May 6: Dies in Concord, Massachusetts.

Works Cited

Alcott, Bronson. *The Journals of Bronson Alcott*, edited by Odell Shepard. Boston: Little Brown, 1938.
Arendt, Hannah. *Love and Saint Augustine*, edited and with an interpretive essay by Joanna Vechiarelli and Judith Chelius Stark. Chicago and London: University of Chicago Press, 1999.
Arsić, Branka. *Bird Relics: Grief and Vitalism in Thoreau*. Cambridge, MA: Harvard University Press, 2015.
Arsić, Branka, ed. *American Impersonal: Essays with Sharon Cameron*. New York: Bloomsbury, 2014.
Arsić, Branka. "What Music Shall we Have? Thoreau on the Aesthetics and Politics of Listening," in *American Impersonal: Essays with Sharon Cameron*, edited by Branka Arsić. New York: Bloomsbury, 2014.
Arsić, Branka. "Magical Life: Thoreau and Benjamin on Nature in Mourning," London Graduate School, recording http://backdoorbroadcasting.net/2012/05/branka-Arsic?-memorial-life-thoreau-and-benjamin-on-nature-in-mourning/
Bachelard, Pierre. *Poetics of Reverie, Childhood, Language, and the Cosmos*. Boston: Beacon Press, 1971.
Bates, Stanley. "Stanley Cavell and Ethics," in *Stanley Cavell*, edited by Richard Eldridge. Cambridge: Cambridge University Press, 2003.
Bernasconi, Robert. *Rereading Levinas*, edited by Bernasconi and Critchley. Bloomington: Indiana University Press, 1991.
Bernstein, J. M. *The Fate of Art*. Unversity Press: Penn State Press, 1992
Braver, Lee. *Groundless Grounds: a study of Wittgenstein and Heidegger*. Cambridge, MA: MIT Press, 2012.
Buell, Lawrence. *The Environmental Imagination: Thoreau, Nature Writing, and the Formation of American Culture*. Cambridge, MA: Harvard University Press, 1996.
Bugbee, Henry. *The Inward Morning: A Philosophical Exploration in Journal Form*, Foreword by Alasdair MacIntyre, Introduction by Edward F. Mooney. Athens, GA: University of Georgia Press, 1999.
Cafaro, Philip. *Thoreau's Living Ethics: Walden and the Pursuit of Virtue*. Athens, GA: University of Georgia Press, 2004.
Calarco, Matthew. "Faced by Animals," in *Radicalizing Levinas*, edited by Peter Atterton and Matthew Calarco, 113–33. New York: SUNY, 2010.
Cameron, Sharon. *Writing Nature: Henry Thoreau's Journal*. Chicago: University of Chicago Press, 1985.
Caputo, John D. *Against Ethics*. Bloomington: Indiana University Press, 1993.
Cavell, Stanley. *Cities of Words, Pedagogical Letters on a Register of the Moral Life*. Cambridge, MA: Harvard University Press, 2008.

Cavell, Stanley. *The Claim to Reason*. Oxford: Oxford University Press, 1979
Cavell, Stanley. *Conditions Handsome and Unhandsome*. Chicago: University of Chicago Press, 1990.
Cavell, Stanley. *Little Did I Know, Excerpts from Memory*. Stanford: Stanford University Press 2010.
Cavell, Stanley. *Philosophical Passages, Wittgenstein, Emerson, Austin, Derrida*. New York: Wiley-Blackwell, 1995.
Cavell, Stanley. *Philosophy the Day after Tomorrow*, Cambridge, MA: Harvard University Press, 2005
Cavell Stanley. "Reflections on Wallace Stevens at Mount Holyoke," in *Artists, Intellectuals, and World War II: The Pontigny Encounters at Mount Holyoke College, 1942–1944*, edited by Christopher Benfey and Karen Remmler. Amherst, MA: University Massachusetts Press, 2006.
Cavell Stanley. "The Division of Talent." *Critical Inquiry* 11.4 (June 1985): 519–38.
Cavell Stanley. *The Senses of Walden*. New York: Viking Press, 1972.
Cavell, Stanley, Cora Diamond, John McDowell, Ian Hacking, and Cary Wolfe. *Philosophy and Animal Life*. New York: Columbia University Press, 2008.
Coetzee, J. M. *Elizabeth Costello*. New York: Penguin Books, 2004.
Conway, Dan. "Answering the Call of the Wild: Walking with Bugbee and Thoreau," in *Wilderness and the Heart: Henry Bugbee's Philosophy of Place, Presence, and Memory*, edited by Edward F. Mooney, Foreword by Alasdair MacIntyre, 3–17. Athens, GA: University of Georgia Press, 1999.
Crane, Gregg D. *Race, Citizenship, and Law in American Literature*. Cambridge: Cambridge University Press, 2002.
Crary, Alice. *Beyond Moral Judgment*. Cambridge, MA: Harvard University Press, 2007.
Csikszentmihalyi, Mihaly. *Flow*. New York: Harper Collins, 2009.
Davidson, Donald. "What Metaphors Mean." *Critical Inquiry* 5 (1) (1978)
Day, William. "Aspect Blindness and Language," in *Seeing Wittgenstein Anew: New Essays on Aspect-Seeing*, edited by William Day and Victor J. Krebs, 204–24. Cambridge: Cambridge University Press, 2010.
Day, William. "A Soteriology of Reading: Cavell's Excerpts from Memory," in *Stanley Cavell: Philosophy, Literature, and Criticism,* edited by James Loxley and Andrew Taylor, 76–91. Manchester: Manchester University Press, 2011.
Diamond, Cora. "Knowing Tornadoes and Other Things." *New Literary History* 22.4 (Autumn, 1991): 1001–15.
Diamond, Cora, Cavell, Stanley, John McDowell, Ian Hacking, and Cary Wolfe. *Philosophy and Animal Life*. New York: Columbia University Press, 2008.
Dickinson, Emily. *The Complete Poems of Emily Dickinson*, edited by Thomas H. Johnson. Boston: Little, Brown, and Company, 1960.
Dimock, Wai-Chee. "Global Civil Society: Thoreau on Three Continents," in *Through Other Continents: American Literature across Deep Time*. Princeton: Princeton University Press, 2006.

Dimock, Wai-Chee. Thoreau on animal sounds. Available from https://www.youtube.com/watch?v=i8nN8azvabs
Eliot, T. S. *Four Quartets*. New York: Houghton Mifflin, 1971.
Emerson, Ralph Waldo. *Early Lectures: 1838–1842*. Cambridge, MA: Harvard University Press, 1972.
Fingarette, Herbert. "The Meaning of Law in the Book of Job," in *Revisions: Changing Perspectives in Moral Philosophy*, edited by Stanley Hauerwas and Alasdair MacIntyre. London: University of Notre Dame Press, 1983.
Foltz, Bruce V. *The Noetics of Nature: Environmental Philosophy and the Holy Beauty of the Visible*. New York: Fordham University Press, 2014.
Friedlander, Eli. *Walter Benjamin, A Philosophical Portrait*, 147–50. Cambridge, MA: Harvard University Press, 2012.
Friedlander, Paul. *Plato, an Introduction*. Princeton: Princeton University Press, 1958.
Furtak, Rick Anthony. "Skepticism and Perceptual Faith: Henry David Thoreau and Stanley Cavell on Seeing and Believing." *Transactions of the Charles S. Peirce Society*, 43 (3) (2007): 542–61.
Furtak, Rick Anthony. "The Value of Being: On Appreciating the Beauty of the World," in *Thoreau's Importance for Philosophy*, edited by Furtak, Ellsworth and Reid, 112–26. New York: Fordham University Press, 2012.
Furtak, Rick Anthony, Jonathon Ellsworth, and James D. Reid, eds. *Thoreau's Importance for Philosophy*. New York: Fordham University Press, 2012.
Furtak, Rick Anthony, Jonathon Ellsworth, and James D. Reid, eds. "Henry David Thoreau," in *The Stanford Encyclopedia of Philosophy*. Stanford: Stanford University Press.
Garber, Frederick. *Thoreau's Redemptive Imagination*. New York: New York University Press, 1977.
Garrison, William Lloyd, ed. *The Liberator*, xxx. 1854.
Gilligan, Carol. *In a Different Voice: Psychological Theory and Women's Development*. Cambridge, MA: Harvard University Press, 1982.
Glatzner, Nahum, ed. *Dimensions of Job*. New York: Schocken, 1969.
Griffiths, Paul J. *Intellectual Appetite*. Washington, DC: Catholic University of America Press, 2009.
Gros, Frédéric. *A Philosophy of Walking*. London: Verso, 2014.
Grossman, Vasily. *Fate and Life*, translated by Robert Chandler: Harper and Row, 1985.
Grouw, Katrina van. *The Unfeathered Bird*. Princeton: Princeton University Press, 2013.
Gura, Phillip. *American Transcendentalism: A History*. New York: Hill and Wang, 2007.
Hadot, Pierre. *Philosophy as a Way of Life*. London: Blackwell: 1995.
Hadot, Pierre. "There are Nowadays Professors of Philosophy, but not Philosophers." Translated by Aaron Simmons. *Journal of Speculative Philosophy* 19 (3) (2005).

Hampshire, Stuart. *Morality and Pessimism*. Cambridge: Cambridge University Press, 1972.
Harrison, Robert Pogue. *The Dominion of the Dead*. Chicago: University of Chicago Press, 2003.
Harrison, Robert Pogue. *Forests: The Shadow of Civilization*. Chicago: University of Chicago Press, 1992.
Harrison, Robert Pogue. *Gardens: An Essay on the Human Condition*. Chicago: University of Chicago Press, 2008.
Hatley, James. *Suffering Witness: The Quandary of Responsibility After the Irreparable*. New York: SUNY Press, 2000.
Hocking, Ernst. *Gifford Lectures*. 1941 (unpublished).
Hodder, Alan D. *Thoreau's Ecstatic Vision*. New Haven, CT: Yale, 2001.
Hodder, Alan D. "Asian Influences," in *The Oxford Handbook of Transcendentalism*, edited by Joel Myerson, Sandra Harbert Petrulionis, Laura Dassow Walls. Oxford: Oxford University Press, 2010.
Hugo, Victor. "Letter to the *London News* regarding John Brown," 1859.
James, Henry. "The Middle Years," in *The Tales of Henry James*, edited by Edward Wagenknecht. Frederick Ungar, 1984.
Jolley, Kelly. *Stony Lonesome*. Auburn AL: New Plains Press, 2014.
Kant, Immanuel. *Critique of Pure Reason*, translated by Norman Kemp Smith. New York: St. Martin's, 1965.
Kant, Immanuel. "Conjectures on the Beginning of History"; "What is Enlightenment?," in *Kant on History*, edited by Louis White Beck. Indianapolis: Bobbs Merrill, 1963.
Kierkegaard, Søren. *Christian Discourses*, translated by Howard V. and Edna Hong. Princeton: Princeton University Press, 1997.
Kierkegaard, Søren. *Fear and Trembling*, trans. Alastair Hannay. New York: Penguin Books, 1985.
Kierkegaard, Søren. *Papers and Journals, A Selection*, edited and translated Alastair Hannay. New York: Penguin Books, 1996 [9 July 1837].
Larmore, Charles. *The Romantic Legacy*. Columbia: Columbia University Press 1996.
Levinas. *Difficult Freedom*, translated by Sean Hand, 152. Maryland: John Hopkins, 1990.
Levinas. *Is it Righteous to Be? Interviews with Emmanuel Levinas*, edited by Jill Robbins. Stanford: Stanford University Press, 2001.
Levinas. *Time and The Other*, translated by Richard A. Cohen. Pittsburg: Duquesne University Press, 1990.
Levinas. *Totality and Infinity*, translated by Alphonso Lingis. Pittsburg: Duquesne University Press, 1969.
Lilley, James D. "Being Singularly Impersonal: Jonathan Edwards and the Aesthetics of Consent," in *American Impersonal: Essays with Sharon Cameron*, edited by Branka Arsić. New York: Bloomsbury, 2014.

Llewelyn, John. "Am I obsessed by Bobby? (Humanism of the Other Animal)," in *Rereading Levinas*, edited by Bernasconi and Critchley, Ch. 4. Bloomington: Indiana University Press, 1991.

Lovibond, Sabina. *Ethical Formation*. Cambridge, MA: Harvard University Press, 2002.

Lucretius. *De Rerum Natura*, trans. Frank O. Copley. New York: W. W. Norton, 2011.

Mahoney, Brendan. "The Echoes of Walden: Reading Thoreau's Inverted Scripture through Cavell." *The Concord Saunterer: A Journal of Thoreau Studies* 21 (2013).

Manderson, Desmond, ed. *Essays on Levinas and Law*. Basingstoke: Palgrave, 2009.

Martin, Wayne M. "Conscience and Confession in Rousseau's Naturalistic Moral Psychology." Available from privatewww.essex.ac.uk/~wmartin/MartinRousseauPaper.pdf

McGregor, Robert Kuhn. "Henry David Thoreau: The Asian Thread," in *Thoreau's Importance for Philosophy*, edited by Rick Anthony Furtak, Jonathon Ellsworth, and James D. Reid. New York: Fordham University Press, 2012.

Melville, Herman. *Moby Dick*. New York: Penguin Books, 1992.

Menand, Louis. "Pulp's Big Moment," *The New Yorker*, January 5, 2015.

Moi, Toril. "'They Practice Their Trades in Different Worlds': Concepts in Post-structuralism and Ordinary Language Philosophy." *New Literary History* 40.4 (Autumn, 2009): 801–24.

Mooney, Edward F. *Knights of Faith and Resignation: Reading Kierkegaard's "Fear and Trembling."* New York: SUNY Press, 1991.

Mooney, Edward F. *Lost Intimacy in American Thought: Recovering Personal Philosophy from Thoreau to Cavell*. New York: Continuum, 2009.

Mooney, Edward F. *On Søren Kierkegaard: Dialogue, Polemic, Lost Intimacy, and Time*. Hampshire: Ashgate, 2007.

Mooney, Edward F. *Kierkegaard's Repetition and Philosophical Crumbs*, ed., intro. and notes, translated by Marilyn Piety. Oxford: Oxford University Press, 2009.

Mooney, Edward F. "Heidegger on Poetic Thinking." Available from https://edmooneyblog.wordpress.com/2014/12/17/heidegger-on-poetic-thinking/

Morgan, Michael L. *Discovering Levinas*. Cambridge: Cambridge University Press, 2007.

Mulhall, Steven. *The Wounded Animal: J. M. Coetzee & the Difficulty of Reality in Literature & Philosophy*. Princeton: Princeton University Press, 2009.

Nannay, Bence. "Narrative Pictures," in *The Journal of Aesthetics and Art Criticism*. New Jersey: Wiley-Blackwell, 2009.

Nietzsche, Friedrich. "Why I am a Destiny," in *Ecce Homo*, translated by Duncan Large. Oxford: Oxford University Press, 2007.

Nietzsche, Friedrich. *Thus Spoke Zarathustra*, translated by Graham Parkes. Oxford: Oxford University Press, 2005.

Nietzsche, Friedrich. "Schopenhauer as Educator," in *Untimely Meditations*, edited by Daniel Breazeale, translated by R. G. Hollingdale. Cambridge: Cambridge University Press, 1997.

Nightingale, Andrea. "Auto-Hagiography: Augustine, Thoreau." *Arion* (Fall 2008): 111–48

Noë, Alva. *Varieties of Presence*. Cambridge, MA: Harvard University Press, 2012.

Ortega y Gassett, Jose. *Meditations on Quixote*, translated Evelyn Rugg and Diego Marin. Urbana: University of Illinois Press, 2000.

Oswald, Alice. *Memorial, An Excavation of the Iliad*. London: Faber & Faber, 2011.

Perpich, Diane. *The Ethics of Emmanuel Levinas*. Stanford: Stanford University Press, 2008.

Perpich, Diane. "Getting down to Cases: Can a Levinasian Ethics Generate Norms," in *Essays on Levinas and Law*, edited by Desmond Manderson, 21–38. Basingstoke: Palgrave, 2009.

Plant, Bob. *Wittgenstein and Levinas*. New York: Routledge, 2005.

Porte, Joel. *Consciousness and Culture: Emerson and Thoreau Reviewed*. New Haven: Yale University Press, 2004.

Postnock, Ross. "'Don't think, but look!': W. G. Sebald, Wittgenstein, and Cosmopolitan Poverty." *Representations* 112 (1) (Fall 2010): 112–39.

Primack, Richard B. and Abraham J. Miller-Rushing. "Uncovering, Collecting, and Analyzing Records to Investigate the Ecological Impacts of Climate Change: A Template from Thoreau's Concord." *BioScience* 62.2 (2012): 170–81.

Redpath, James. *Echoes of Harper's Ferry*. Boston: Thayer and Eldridge, 1860.

Rose, Gillian. *Love's Work*. New York: Schocken, 1997.

Rothenberg, David. *Sudden Music: Improvisation, Sound, Nature*. Athens, GA: University of Georgia Press, 2002.

Rousseau, Jean-Jacques. *Reveries of the Solitary Walker*, translated by Peter French. New York: Penguin Books, 1974.

Rousseau, Jean-Jacques. *On the Origin of Language*. Chicago: University of Chicago, 1966.

Ruehl, Robert Michael. "Preservative Care and Becoming Feral: Thoreau's Religious Perspective in *A Week on the Concord and Merrimack Rivers*." *Concord Saunterer* 21, (2013): 77 XX.

Sallis, John. "Levinas and the Elemental," in *Radicalizing Levinas*, edited by Atterton and Calarco. New York: SUNY Press, 2010.

Sebald, W. G. "An Attempt at Restitution" in *Campo Santo*. New York: Modern Library, 2005.

Smith, James K. A. *How (Not) to Be Secular*. Grand Rapids: Wm. B. Eerdmans Publishing Company, 2014.

Steiner, George. *Real Presences*. Chicago: University of Chicago Press, 1989.

Stern, David. *Wittgenstein on Mind and Language*. Oxford: Oxford University Press, 1996.

Stevens, Wallace. "An Ordinary Evening in New Haven," in *Collected Poems*. New York: Vintage, 1990.

Tauber, Alfred. *Henry David Thoreau and the Moral Agency of Knowing*. Berkeley: University of California Press, 2001.

Taylor, Charles. *A Secular Age*. Cambridge, MA: Harvard University Press, 2009.

Taylor, Charles. *Dilemmas and Connections*. Cambridge, MA: Harvard University Press, 2011.

Taylor, Charles. "Descombes' Critique of Cognitivism." *Inquiry, An Interdisciplinary Journal of Philosophy* 47:3: 211

Thoreau, Henry David. *The Correspondence of Henry David Thoreau*, edited by Walter Harding and Carl Bode. New York: New York University Press, 1958.

Thoreau, Henry David. *Cape Cod*. Boston: Thomas Y. Crowell Company, 1961.

Thoreau, Henry David. *The Journal of Henry D. Thoreau*, edited by Bradford Torey and Francis H. Allen, Vols I–XIV. New York: Dover Publications, 1962.

Thoreau, Henry David. *The Maine Woods*, edited by Joseph J. Moldenhauer. Princeton: Princeton University Press, 1972.

Thoreau, Henry David. *A Week on the Concord and Merrimack Rivers*, edited by Carl F. Hove, William L. Howarth, and Elizabeth Hall Witherell. Princeton: Princeton University Press, 1980.

Thoreau, Henry David. *Journal of Henry D. Thoreau*, Vols I–VIII, edited by John C. Broderick, Robert Sattlemeyer, and Elizabeth Hall Witherell. Princeton: Princeton University Press, 1981–2008.

Thoreau, Henry David. *Collected Essays and Poems of Thoreau*, edited by Elizabeth Hall Witherell. New York: Library of America, 2001.

Thoreau, Henry David. *Walden: or Life in the Woods*, edited by Jeffrey Cramer. New Haven: Yale University Press, 2004.

Thoreau, Henry David. *The Correspondence of Henry D Thoreau*, Vol. 1, 1834–48, edited by Robert N. Hudspeth. Princeton: Princeton University Press, 2013.

Thorson, Robert M. *Walden's Shore: Henry David Thoreau and Nineteenth-Century Science*. Cambridge, MA: Harvard University Press, 2014.

Walls, Laura Dassow. *Seeing New Worlds: Henry David Thoreau and Nineteenth-Century Natural Science*. Madison: University of Wisconsin Press, 1995.

Walls, Laura Dassow. *The Passage to Cosmos: Alexander von Humboldt and the Shaping of America*. Chicago: University of Chicago Press, 2010.

Walls, Laura Dassow. "*Walden* as Feminist Manifesto," in *Walden, Civil Disobedience, and Other Writings*, edited by William Rossi. New York: W. W. Norton, 2008.

Wasianski. *Kant's Last Years*, quoted in W. R. Washington Sullivan, *Morality as a Religion*. Charleston, SC: BiblioBazaar, 2007 [orig. 1898].

Webb, Carson. *Attunements to the Good Life: Religious Joy and the Critique of Eudaemonism in the Writings of Søren Kierkegaard*, Ph.D. Dissertation. Syracuse University, 2014.

Westfall, Joseph. *The Kierkegaardian Author: Authorship and Performance in Kierkegaard's Literary and Dramatic Criticism*. Berlin: Walter de Gruyter, 2007.

Wettstein, Howard. *The Significance of Religious Experience*. Oxford: Oxford University Press, 2012.

Willey, Austin, ed. Maine's *Portland Inquiry*, June 1, 1854.

Williams, Rowan. *The Edge of Words: God and the Habits of Language*. New York: Bloomsbury, 2014.

Wittgenstein, Ludwig. *Culture and Value*, trans Peter Winch. Chicago: University of Chicago Press, 1980.

Wittgenstein, Ludwig. *Philosophical Investigations*, 3rd edn. Oxford: Wiley-Blackwell, 2001.

Wittgenstein, Ludwig. *Tractatus Logicus Philosophicus*. London: Routledge, 1974.

Young, Malcolm Clemens. *The Spiritual Journey of Henry David Thoreau*. Macon, GA: Mercer University Press, 2009.

Zamir, Tzachi. *Acts: Theater, Philosophy, and the Performing Self*. Michigan: University of Michigan, 2014.

Zamir, Tzachi. "Talking Trees." *New Literary History* 42 (2011): 439–453

Credits

The following are heavily revised versions of material that first appeared as follows:

Ch. 2. "Thoreau Mourning Turtle Doves: An Amble through Concord and beyond," *Zeteo, Journal of Interdisciplinary Writing*, Fall 2012.

Ch. 4. "Reflections from Concord," in *The Human Place in the Natural World: Essays on Creation and Creatureliness,* edited by Benson, Treanor and Wirtzba. New York: Fordham University Press, 2015.

Ch. 6. "Thoreau's Wild Ethics," *The Concord Saunterer*, Fall 2012, Ch. 6,

Ch. 7. "Van Grouw's *The Unfeathered Bird*: Picked Bones, Plucked Hens, Plumed Skeletons." *Zeteo, Journal of Interdisciplinary Writing*, August 2013.

Chs. 9, 10. "Wonder and Affliction: A Dionysian World," in *Thoreau's Importance for Philosophy*, edited by Rick Anthony Furtak et. al. New York: Fordham University Press, 2012

Chs. 11, 12. "Translations: John Brown, Apples, Lilies" in *Lost Intimacy in American Thought: Recovering Personal Philosophy from Thoreau to Cavell*. New York: Continuum, 2009.

Chs. 13, 14. " 'Concord River': Living Transcendentally on Currents of Time." *ISLE, Journal of the International Society for Literature and the Environment*, 2013.

Ch. 15. "Witness to the Face of the River: Thinking with Levinas and Thoreau", (with Lyman Mower), in *Faces of Nature: Levinasian Ethics and Environmental Philosophy*, edited by William Edelglass, Chris Diehm, and Jim Hatley. Pittsburgh, PA: Duquesne University Press, 2012.

Closing Passions. "Passionate Speech in Dark Woods of a Life: Academic Practice in a Post-Secular Age." *Listening: A Journal of Religion and Culture*, 2011.

Index

a priori images 204, 208, 211
Abenaki, (cf. Native American) 230
abolitionism 102, 172–3, 182, 200
Abraham 88n. 17, 161, 226–7, 230
academic xiii, 13, 32, 34, 60–1, 69, 97, 98, 160ff., 221, 245, 247
Achilles 137
activism xiii, 26, 43, 106, 108
Aeschylus 139, 184
aesthetic xiv, 36, 42, 76–7, 95, 105, 109, 113, 123, 144, 157, 227, 232, 249, 255
affection 67, 166
affinity 138, 143, 148, 151, 153, 155, 200, 220
affliction 3, 18, 29, 77, 125, 136ff., 141, 154, 158, 163, 170, 182, 228, 241
Alcott, Bronson 126, 175
angels 55, 116–17, 127, 129, 136, 174
anomalous reality (zone) 25, 41, 73, 82–3, 86–7, 93–4, 116, 120, 126, 131, 141, 174ff., 178, 193–4, 196, 199, 202, 213, 215–16, 235, 240
Apocalypse 173, 180, 183, 188, 245
Apollonian 138–9
apples (frozen) 98, 136, 138–9, 143
Arendt, Hannah 73
Aristotle 31–2n. 32, 115, 161, 229–30
arrowheads, flint-chips 31, 116
Arsić, Branka 17n. 1, 23n. 14, 28, 31, 36n. 45, 38n. 6, 75n. 35, 87, 97n. 2, 116, 120n. 6, 133n. 33, 140n. 29, 204n. 2
askesis xv, 37–8, 97
aspirations 25, 62, 100, 107, 153, 176, 181
attention 14, 41, 54, 70, 84, 94, 98, 103, 108–9, 124, 181, 193, 199, 219, 228, 231–2, 234, 237, 249
attunement 7, 12, 72, 125, 144, 147–8, 151, 220
Augustine 63, 99
aura 7, 10
Aurelius 136, 154
Auschwitz 250
Austen, Jane 101
authority (of words) 13, 105n. 19, 212, 215–16, 227
autonomy 192

Bach, J. S. xiv, 52
Banks, Russell 186
Basho 34
Bates, Stanley 98, 105, 161–3
beauty xiii, 3, 8, 11, 20–1, 34, 40, 42, 45, 61, 65, 70–1, 76, 82, 84, 88, 92, 107, 109, 115, 120, 141n. 34, 144–5, 149–50, 173n. 32, 218, 221, 242
behold 10, 31, 33, 60, 76, 95, 106, 139n. 20, 100, 153, 167ff., 176, 179, 196, 239
Beiser, Fred 136
benevolence 224, 230, 234
Berry, Wendell 108
better thoughts 2, 91, 94, 105, 107, 152
bird relics 116
Birth of Tragedy (Nietzsche) 76, 88n. 18, 136, 137n
Blake, Harrison 20, 22, 38n. 7, 73
Blake, William 221
body (cf. corpse) xiv, 18, 36–7, 38, 41, 46, 51–2, 63, 66, 75–6, 90, 106–7, 109, 113, 115, 117, 133, 135, 137, 140–1, 149, 152, 157–8, 168, 171, 182n. 7, 185–6

bones xiv, 3, 30n. 28, 75, 90, 106–7, 108, 111–13, 115–17, 140–1, 148, 152, 158–9, 167, 169–73, 177, 186
Book of Job 77, 79, 87, 93, 95, 102, 224, 228, 231, 235n. 28
Book of Joel 184, 187, 230n. 19
Boston Massacre 173
bounteous 5, 59, 69, 73, 126, 166, 169–70, 195–6, 199–200, 236
Bristlecone Pine 19–20, 25, 32, 36, 41
Brown, Andrew 129
Brown, John 4, 13, 23, 43, 60, 72, 75, 100, 102–3, 106, 135, 138, 142, 160n. 39, 161, 165–88, 200, 216, 225, 227, 232
Brown, Lucy xiii, 24, 119–21, 125
Buber, Martin 99
Buddha 177
Bugbee, Henry 3n. 9, 27n. 19, 108, 168
Burk, Edmund 169
Burns, Anthony 46, 72, 142, 159, 165, 172–3, 186–7

Cafaro, Philip 61
Cameron, Sharon 4, 10, 63n. 7, 97n. 2, 123n. 9
Cape Cod 26, 30, 87, 89–90, 103, 106, 135, 162, 193, 203, 235
Cape Cod 61–2, 91, 102, 216
care 3, 30, 34, 86, 97, 105–6, 108–9, 165, 189, 227, 232–3, 235–6, 239–40, 244
Carlyle, Thomas 98, 161
Cartesian (Descartes) xiv, 66–7, 70, 76, 155
Cavell, Stanley 4, 26, 34, 35n. 41, 98n. 3, 99, 104, 105n. 20, 107, 124, 140n. 30, 141n. 35, 149, 151, 153–4, 163, 189, 204, 208, 210–12, 215, 217–18, 243, 246–8
changeling 193, 235, 239–40

child of the mist 3, 6, 19, 24–5, 27, 36, 39, 41, 48, 52, 119–33, 209
Christ, Christian xv, 26, 38, 51, 103, 139–40, 152, 159, 165, 173, 176–7, 179, 181, 188
civil disobedience (cf. *Resistance to Civil Government*) 19–20, 30, 43, 47n. 44, 60, 103, 106, 138, 162, 165, 183–4, 224
Civil War 43, 72, 74, 98, 102, 142, 160, 166, 176, 188, 194
clothes 4n. 11–12, 116–17
coffin 95, 142
Coleridge, Samuel xv, 189
commemoration 77–8, 90, 106–7, 162
communicative mutuality 213
communion 11, 38, 41, 50, 52–3, 71, 75, 88, 125–6, 141, 143–4, 148–50, 159, 161, 166–8, 172, 177, 192, 195, 205, 219–20
Concord, Mass xiii, 13, 17, 21, 23, 26–7, 33, 38, 39, 43, 51, 55, 75, 89–90, 95, 107, 103, 116, 137–8, 140–1, 152, 159–60, 175, 178–9, 181–2, 184–5, 188–9, 192–5, 201–2, 207, 234
Concord River 4, 60–2, 192–5, 199, 203, 212, 216, 233, 235, 237, 239
consciousness xiv, 66, 76, 100, 136, 151
corpse 28–30, 41, 75, 91, 115–16, 135, 140, 229
Corsa, Andrew 32n. 32
Crary, Alice 153n. 19
Creation 30, 32, 53, 59–61, 66–7, 69, 75–8, 88, 137, 143–4, 150, 155, 160, 166–7, 169, 180, 188, 191–2, 198, 200, 232, 237, 240–1
Csikszentnihalyi, Mihali 68n. 13, 209
Cynics 98

Dante 99, 101, 244

Davidson, Donald 214–15
dawn 10, 28, 46, 51, 53–4, 57, 72, 74, 94–5, 160, 167, 170–1, 204, 222, 251
Day, William 140n. 30, 214, 232n. 23, 246n. 7
death xiii, 18, 20, 22–5, 28–9, 31, 41, 45, 72–8, 84–7, 90–1, 94, 99–100, 108, 113, 115–16, 119–26, 128–30, 137–45, 165, 167, 169–70, 172–6, 178–82, 184–6, 194–5, 202, 215–16, 225, 227, 235, 237, 239, 244, 250
death camp 239
death of God 67
Descartes xiv, 62, 66
descendentalism 191, 233
desolation 21, 81, 87, 98, 122, 172, 225
desperation 37, 140, 163, 170, 182, 198
detachment 7, 49, 71, 149n.
Dewey, John 105
Dial, The 89, 139
Diamond, Cora 158, 162, 196
Dickinson, Emily 28, 71, 101, 172, 214, 219–21, 245, 249
difficult reality *see* Cora Diamond
Dillard, Annie 108
Dimock, Wai-Chee 18n. 5, 87n. 14, 139n. 25, 182n. 7
Diogenes 38, 60, 98
Dionysian (Dionysius) 4, 135, 137–9, 152, 188
disenchantment 32, 148, 221
Divinity 60, 65, 76–7, 143, 145, 155, 183
domesticity 106, 162, 201
Donne, John 249
Dostoevsky, Feodor 91n. 23, 157n. 32, 223, 228–9
Douglass, Frederick 23, 160n. 39
dream 4–5, 19, 26, 47–8, 52, 55–7, 62, 71, 92–5, 122, 125–6, 128, 130, 132, 145, 157, 170, 191, 197, 207–10, 214–16, 230, 242, 246, 248
dreaming-awake 5, 145, 170, 191, 242
dreaming toads (frogs) 95, 191, 208, 210, 214
Du Bois, W. E. B. 186
dualism xiv, 66, 76
Duston., Hannah 139, 194–5, 230

Eaton, William 31n. 31
ecology 6, 43, 81, 212
Eden 195
elegy 18, 27, 108
Eliot, George 26, 247–8
Eliot, T. S. 250
Emerson, "little Waldo" xiii, 22, 86, 108, 119, 138, 142
Emerson, Ralph Waldo xiv, 26, 35, 47n. 44, 63, 71, 89, 99, 105, 107–8, 136, 151n. 11, 163, 179, 182, 201, 249
empiricist 144, 147
enchantment 32–3, 49, 51–2, 112, 148, 218, 221
Enlightenment 62, 66, 189n. 15
environmental virtue 97, 108
epiphany 76, 226
episodic philosophy 3, 10, 29, 34, 82, 157
epistemology 67, 70, 200
ethics 3, 37, 97–110, 223–31, 233, 236–7, 247n. 10, 248
evil 23, 29, 76–7, 86, 102, 144, 149, 218, 227, 231, 234
evocation 35, 77, 101, 117, 153, 156–7, 158, 165–6, 186, 188, 203, 220
executive self 244–5
exemplars 44, 99, 160, 176–7, 180–1, 183, 189, 249
exhilaration 106
expressive xiv, 3, 115–16, 136, 150–1, 177, 185, 188, 211, 239

expressive bones xiv, 3, 111–17
exuberance 34, 36, 79, 98, 140, 160

fables 56, 57, 87, 91
face 4–5, 19, 97, 127–8, 143, 176, 196, 201, 205, 224, 226, 228, 232–3, 235–6, 239
Fear and Trembling (Kierkegaard) 88, 160n. 39, 169n. 19, 176n. 44, 227
Fichte, Johann 189
fidelity 107, 93
Fingarette, Herbert 92n. 27
Finnegans Wake 214
Fire Island xiv, 74, 89–91, 100, 141
fishing 82–3, 130–3, 205
forgiveness 215, 229, 234
forms of life (flow of life) 156, 183, 209, 211, 212n. 23, 215, 219,
Forster, E. M. 153
Franklin, Benjamin 23, 178–80, 216
Freud, Sigmund 105
frogs (cf. toads) 6, 44, 65, 132, 157, 171, 204, 208–10
frugality 102
Fuller, Margaret 30, 74–5, 85, 89–91, 100, 107, 135, 137–8, 140–3, 148, 150, 152, 159–60, 167, 169, 171, 177, 186
Furtak, Rick 2n. 7, 11n. 35, 21n. 10, 68n. 15, 124n. 10, 140n. 30, 153, 159n. 38, 173n. 32, 188n. 14, 239n. 1

Galileo 30, 32, 51, 53, 66, 198
Gandhi 19, 43, 103, 182n. 7, 184, 189, 224
Garrison, William Lloyd 172, 186n. 11
genius 18, 40, 42, 44, 53–4, 89, 110, 141n. 34, 150, 188–9, 206
Gilligan, Carol 109, 227
Giraudoux, Jean 246, 248
Gita (cf. *Vedas*) xv, 28, 38n. 6, 51, 60, 98, 168, 182n. 7, 184–5, 224

God, godly, gods 6, 10, 12, 14, 20, 23, 27, 40–4, 48, 50–3, 55–6, 60, 65, 67, 71–2, 76–7, 86, 88, 93, 102–3, 109, 117, 128–9, 136n. 9, 139, 143–4, 152, 155–7, 166, 168–70, 177, 180, 182, 188–9, 191, 199, 202, 211, 221, 224–6, 230–1, 233, 241, 245, 250
Goethe xiv, xv, 60, 110
Goya 194
grammar 205–6, 209–10
Grand Inquisitor (Dostoevsky) 223, 229
gratitude 14, 71, 73–4, 77, 79, 87–8, 106, 108, 140, 162
gratuitous good 231, 237
Great Hall (at Spaulding's) 55–6, 128
Great Moral Philosophy 99, 104–5, 163
grief, grieving ix, 22–5, 27–32, 36, 60, 73, 76, 93–4, 121, 123–4, 139, 141, 152, 167, 219–20,
Griffith, Paul 69–70
Grossmann, Vasily 223n. 1, 228–9
grounding poetry 6, 206, 208–12, 216–19, 251

Hadot, Pierre 26, 60, 61n. 3, 104, 108, 144n. 44
Hamlet 32, 47n. 45, 60, 135–7, 139, 152, 157–8, 249
Harper's Ferry 103, 166, 171–2, 179, 182–3, 186, 227
Harrison, Robert Pogue 99, 162n. 47
Hatley, James 224n. 8, 228
Hegel, G. W. 105, 161
Heidegger, Martin 54n. 72, 99, 104–3, 130, 149n. 7, 221
Higginson, Thomas Wentworth 172, 187
holism 199
Homer 51, 60, 76n. 38, 139, 201
Hopkins, Anthony 185
hospitality 152–3, 233

Hovenden, Thomas 186
Howe, Julia Ward 173
Hugo, Victor 103, 187
humanities xiv, 34, 220, 245
Hume, D. 230

Iliad 76, 136,
illuminations 51, 61, 66–7, 93, 108, 225, 239
images xv, 105, 113, 131–2, 154, 156–7, 198, 204–6, 208–11, 217, 241
imagination 5–6, 22, 25, 41, 52, 65, 78, 90–1, 99, 107, 109, 112–13, 122–3, 125, 129, 143–4, 144, 150, 153n. 19, 177, 189, 198, 206, 208, 211, 216–17, 224, 230, 248
immortality 31, 84, 104, 137, 142, 171, 250
impersonal grief (mourning) 23–5, 28–31, 36, 63, 73, 94–5, 97n. 2, 123–4, 163, 167, 192
independence 61–2, 74, 97, 101
indifference 31n. 32, 86, 94, 123, 149, 182, 231
innocence 28, 35, 48, 62, 85–6, 92, 94, 122, 124, 126, 139n. 23
instinct 14, 42, 62, 92, 99, 138, 155–6, 160, 166, 194, 216
intelligence (intelligences) 3, 8–11, 27, 34, 47–57, 61–2, 66, 69–71, 93, 126, 143, 161, 192, 200, 206, 220
interpretation 5n. 11, 13, 251

James, Henry 157n. 32, 247, 250
James, William 26, 98–9, 249
Jewish (Jewish ethics) 152, 224, 232, 250
Job, Book of 77, 79, 86–7, 92–5, 101–2, 224, 228, 231, 235n. 28
Jolley, Kelly 243
Joy xvi, 21, 32, 35–6, 39, 42, 48, 54, 60, 63, 72, 74, 79, 84, 87–8, 90, 92, 95n. 32, 121, 125, 132, 138–9, 145, 158, 162, 173, 188, 198, 207, 225, 239, 242
justice, injustice xiii, 20–1, 25, 46, 76–7, 86–7, 93, 95, 101, 103, 109, 120n. 6, 124, 152, 165, 171, 176, 187, 224–6, 229, 231, 239, 250

Kafka, Franz 231, 247n. 10
Kant, Immanuel 4, 9, 42n. 24, 98, 100, 115, 122, 136, 142–5, 147, 155–7, 169, 188–9, 191, 204, 208, 211, 217–18, 227n. 14, 229–30, 233
Kerouac, Jack 42n. 21
Kierkegaard, Søren xiv, 12, 34n. 39, 61, 67, 88, 98, 104–5, 126, 136, 141, 159–61, 163, 169n. 19, 176, 204, 227–31, 239, 248–9
King Lear 34, 136
King, Martin Luther 19, 43, 103, 184, 224
knowledge 5, 7–13, 24, 27, 34, 40, 47–50, 56, 61, 67–71, 115, 122, 124–6, 129, 198, 200, 208, 211, 217–21, 245, 248
Krishna and Arguna 98

lamentation 24, 121, 139
language 4, 5n. 11, 47, 54, 74, 155–6, 171, 205, 210–15, 225
language (dream-work of) 214–15
Levinas, Emmanuel 4, 97, 100, 136n. 8, 223–37
life xiv–xv, 2, 7, 10–11, 14, 23–5, 27–30, 33, 37, 39–44, 48–9, 51–2, 54, 60–6, 70–8, 81, 85–92, 97–110, 116, 122–30, 135–43, 148–53, 156–63, 165–8, 171–88, 196–200, 202–3, 205–15, 218–21, 224–5, 231–51

lily 7, 14, 17–18, 21, 35, 53, 110, 137, 142, 166, 172–3, 188, 194, 221
literal-figurative (cf. reverie) 212–14, 242
loons 3, 7–8, 46, 50, 239
love xiii, 7–9, 18, 25–6, 28, 34–6, 42, 46–7, 54, 61, 67–8, 70–4, 85, 93, 101, 104, 121–4 138, 140, 144, 149, 152–4, 165–6, 170, 177, 188, 201, 215, 217–20, 227, 249–51
Lucretius xv, 51, 129

magnanimity 61–2, 64, 74, 97, 101, 162
Mahometan 152
market values 14, 37, 51, 67, 69
Martin, Wayne 147n. 2
Marx, Karl 32, 105, 163, 221
meditation (walking meditation) xiii, 3, 5, 38, 61, 87–8, 104, 168, 177n. 46, 202, 216
melancholy 17–18, 86, 90, 124, 158, 218
Melville, Herman 75n. 34, 213, 249
mercy 224, 229–31
metamorphosis 76, 137, 141, 143, 171, 247
Mexico 22, 43–4, 103, 159, 165
Milton, John 60, 168, 184
Moby Dick (Melville) 75n. 34, 99, 197n. 13
Momento Mori 132
Montaigne, Michael de xiv, 154, 203, 249
moods xvi, 7, 13, 22, 40, 87, 100, 139, 155
moral perfectionism 105, 107, 109, 189
Moses 49, 230
Mt Greylock 1n. 2, 75, 88, 106, 142, 192, 201, 239
Mt Ktaadn 2, 48, 62, 88–9, 102, 105–4, 138–9, 161, 166–7, 170–3, 177, 180, 186, 239

Mt. Thoreau 20
Mt Washington 20, 88, 192–4, 235, 239, 243–4
mourning 3, 18, 28n. 22, 30–3, 38, 74–8, 84, 93–4, 123–4, 158, 167, 192
Mower, Lyman 39, 136n. 8, 149n. 7, 223, 225
Mozart, W. A. 6, 115
music (music box) xiii, xv–xvi, 11–13, 20, 35, 36n. 46, 42, 46, 52–3, 55–6, 64, 73, 78, 81, 120, 123, 133, 137–40, 166, 170, 174, 177, 181, 183–4, 204, 220–1, 241–2, 245
Musketaquid 62, 192–3, 195, 199, 203, 212, 216, 234–5
muskrat (musquach) 22, 64, 74, 82, 110, 196–7, 202, 212, 215, 236, 239, 242–3
mystery 2, 65, 100, 127, 131, 221, 243
myth 52, 71, 103–4, 135, 139n. 23, 154–5, 204

Nagel, Thomas xv
narrative 3, 33, 78, 94, 105–6, 112–13, 148–9, 154, 157, 162, 203, 247n. 10
Native Americans 43, 47, 102
natural history 43, 61, 103, 112, 147, 21–2
naturalist xiii, xv, 6–8, 19, 47
nature xiv–xv, 6–8, 12, 18, 23
Nazis 223, 226–7, 229, 233n. 24
necessity (poetic) 131, 163, 205, 208, 211, 229n. 18
Newton, Isaac, Newtonian 198, 200, 218, 236
Nietzsche, Friedrich 34, 48, 55, 67, 71, 76, 88, 98–9, 105, 110, 126, 135–8, 159, 161, 163, 239
Nightingale, Andrea 38n. 5, 99
Noe, Alva 10n. 30, 216n. 33
Nussbaum, Martha 99, 101

Index 271

Oedipus 136-7
Oikeiosis 147, 149
Ortega y Gassett 177
outrage 1, 21-3, 63, 72, 86, 108, 139, 152-3, 160, 163, 215, 217, 227, 232

Packer, Barbara 151n. 11
parable 208, 223-4, 229, 231, 236, 247n. 10
paradise xiii, 7, 18, 21, 41, 45-6, 49, 55-6, 59-60, 84-5, 129, 137, 139, 142, 172, 182, 194-5, 202, 224
Parker, Theodore 175, 187
particulars 41, 54, 59, 64, 73, 88, 101, 113, 124, 172, 186, 191, 199, 228, 233-5
Pascal, Blaise 104
passionate speech 34, 77, 149n. 4, 153-4, 225, 243, 246-51
Paul (Pauline) 74, 76, 183, 229n. 17, 237
perception xiii, 3, 5-6, 10, 14, 37, 40-2, 55-6, 81, 88, 106-7, 123, 126, 140, 143-50, 152, 167, 177, 189, 197-8, 203, 208-9, 217, 228, 236, 251
perceptual affiliation 61, 143, 147-8
performatives 170, 246n. 6, 248
Philia 61, 143, 149, 152-3, 192
Phillips, Wendell 187
Philosophical Investigations (Wittgenstein) 115, 147n. 1, 157, 212n. 23
philosophy xiv-xv, 3-4, 26, 34n. 37, 35, 38, 47, 57, 76, 81, 87, 98, 104-5, 122, 127, 130, 139, 141, 154, 156-62, 168, 175, 188-9, 191, 204, 212, 216n. 33, 225, 233, 236, 245-7, 249-51
Pierce, Charles 99
piety 244-6

pilgrimage 38-9, 41, 45, 56, 61, 66, 76, 104, 106, 162, 169
Plato 31, 71, 98, 104, 139, 161, 175, 177, 183, 204
plenitude 39-40, 70, 95, 121, 131, 133
porous souls 4, 18n. 5, 177, 182-5, 239
Porte, Joel 144n. 44, 199n. 21
prayer 38, 61, 88, 128, 132, 194, 205, 207, 241
presence 3, 7-15, 46, 50, 52-3, 63-8, 70, 72-3, 77, 108, 127, 148, 150-1, 153, 160, 168, 170, 185, 204, 211, 216n. 33, 217-21, 230, 232, 240, 251
present moment 3, 6, 26, 45, 105, 131, 137, 155n. 25, 191, 202, 221, 239, 251
preservative care 3, 106, 108-9, 227, 232, 245n. 5
principles 100-3, 106, 162, 226-8
prohibitions 42, 98, 101, 227, 230, 237
prophetic 23, 47, 61, 66, 107, 227, 229-30
Proust, Marcel 157n. 32
Putnam, Hilary 224, 228n. 15

radiance 13-14, 41, 49, 51, 53, 70-1, 73, 76, 84, 143, 158, 167, 174, 176, 198
reality, changeling 193, 235, 239-40
rebirth 40, 45, 56n. 81, 75-6, 124, 126, 137-9, 150, 169
redemption 66, 101, 103, 140, 195, 200, 245, 249
Redpath, James 186-7
regulative ideals 189, 191
relics 75, 90-1, 107, 116, 152, 158, 170, 177
religion, religious xiv-xv, 41, 43, 81, 87-8, 97, 99, 104, 198, 204, 245, 250-1

Rembrandt 115
representations 13, 91, 157n. 31, 210n. 19, 251
Resistance to Civil Government 19, 30, 46, 60, 103, 106, 155, 160n. 39, 162, 183–4, 224
resonance xiv, 13, 35n. 44, 49, 76, 66, 143, 155n. 25
responsibility 56, 161, 225–6, 229
revelations 9, 31, 33–4, 40, 49, 87, 97, 105, 144, 192, 208, 218
reverie (befitting) xiii, 4–6, 9, 12–15, 19–20, 34, 48–51, 55–7, 60, 65, 71, 78, 83–4, 88, 90–4, 104, 120–1, 122–32, 142–3, 149n. 4, 150, 155–8, 167, 170, 176, 197, 200, 205–10, 212, 214, 216, 220, 231, 235
rights 42, 81, 101, 109, 124, 157, 162, 193, 227, 229
Rilke, Ranier Maria 88
Romantic 32, 51, 117, 122–3, 161n. 43, 189, 220, 244
Rorty, Richard 99
Rothenberg, David 244
Rousseau, Jean Jacques 147n. 2, 150–1, 154, 155n. 25, 157, 170, 203, 213n. 27, 221, 249
Royce, Josiah 99
rules 54, 100, 109, 215, 227–30
Rwanda 250

Sartre, J.-P. 61, 105
saunter 45, 55–6, 102, 168–9, 171, 173
Schiller, Friedrich von 189
Schopenhauer, Arthur 98–9
Schubert, Franz xiv, 90, 94, 151, 174, 179
science xiv, 7–9, 11, 40, 51, 53, 66, 104, 198, 220
Sebald, W. E. 34n. 38, 101, 249–50
second intention 128
serenity 9, 55, 72–4, 87, 98, 100–1, 105, 120n. 5, 121, 124, 158, 163, 165–7, 193, 198, 218, 227n. 14, 239
Shadrach case 186
Shakespeare 47, 177, 201
Shoah 18, 223, 225, 227
Silenus 137, 142
simplicity 61–2, 74, 97, 101, 103
Sims case 186
skeleton 3, 113, 115
slave catchers 21, 59, 85, 93, 144, 173, 194
slavery (anti-slavery) 18–19, 21, 23, 41, 43, 61, 97, 103, 108, 142, 152, 159–60, 161, 172, 175, 181, 187–8, 227
Slavery in Massachusetts 17, 23, 106, 136, 142, 160n. 39, 162, 165, 172, 184, 188
Snyder Gary 20
Socrates 31, 38, 47–8, 70, 98, 108, 136, 154, 176, 179, 181, 183
solitude 29n. 27, 39, 51n. 60, 92, 196, 108, 171, 184
song 13, 24, 33–4, 46–7, 52, 53–4, 61, 67, 70, 77–8, 92, 94–5, 115, 121, 126–30, 149, 157, 165–6, 169, 171, 173n. 32, 176, 198, 249
Spartacus 103, 187
Spaulding's Farm 6, 48, 50–2, 55–6, 126, 128–9, 250
Spring 5, 22, 24, 28, 30, 54, 98, 73, 84, 92, 109, 116, 121–3, 125, 140, 165, 167, 171, 173, 185, 193, 208, 221, 225, 235, 240, 250
Staretz Silouan 173
Stevens, Wallace 104n. 19, 199, 228
stone fruit (stones weep) 31, 93, 116, 232
subjectivity 100, 151n. 10, 158, 161
sublime (grand, petite) xiii, 5, 48, 61, 76, 88–9, 91, 93, 95, 102, 122n. 8, 124, 136, 144, 168–71, 231, 244, 248

Sumner, Charles 141
surprise xiii, 2–3, 11, 13, 34, 41, 47, 49, 108, 149, 155, 157, 186, 204, 221, 229, 239
swamp 2, 17, 24, 84–6, 66, 132, 137, 139–40, 142, 173, 194–5, 207
sympathy (with intelligence) xiii, 3, 8–12, 27, 34, 47–54, 56, 61–2, 64–74, 93–4, 101, 106, 125–6, 143, 152, 161, 192, 200, 219–20, 241–2

Tauber, Alfred 239n. 1
Taylor, Charles 67n. 12, 100–3, 185n. 10, 210n. 18, 216n. 35
theology 10, 51, 140n.
thing-in-itself 217–19
Thoreau, John xiii, 18, 22, 24–5, 27, 31, 41, 64, 73, 85–7, 93–4, 116, 120–1, 126, 128, 137–40, 182, 184–5, 192, 194–5, 225
time xv–xvi, 14, 25, 30, 39, 41, 46, 60, 68, 78, 82, 91, 104n. 19, 126, 130–1, 167, 175, 177, 179, 184, 189, 193, 198, 200, 202, 212, 229, 234, 247
toad (cf. frog) 28, 81, 85, 95, 169, 191, 208, 214
Tolstoy, Leo 231
Torah 228
Transcendental Club 19, 188
transcendental deduction 155, 204, 219
transcendentalism 188, 199–200
transfiguration 86, 108, 141, 171, 173, 177, 203
translation 170, 177–8, 184, 186, 212, 230, 232n. 23
trust 2, 14, 48–9, 61–2, 64, 74, 97, 101, 132, 207, 213, 215, 220
truth (truths) 5, 32, 40, 57, 62–3, 79, 87, 91–2, 157, 198, 200, 214, 225, 242, 245–6, 249
Truth, Sojourner 249

Underground Railroad 43, 60, 103
Unitarians 189
unknowing 8–9, 34, 47–50, 56, 69, 71, 73, 98, 125–6, 200, 220, 231
utilitarianism 68, 100, 220, 229

van Grouw, Katerina 111–17
Vedas 10, 51, 70
vengeance 188, 229–31
Virgil 93, 232
virtue 18, 61–2, 64, 67, 74, 97–8, 100–4, 108–9, 162, 181, 226, 229, 241
Voice of God 77, 93, 95, 156, 224

Walden 2, 5–7, 10, 17, 26–31, 35, 51, 61–2, 72, 85, 89–93, 98–9, 106, 117, 125, 129–30, 138, 162, 182–4, 188, 191, 203, 213, 249
Walden Pond xiii–xvi, 54, 66, 76, 103, 106, 157, 162, 165–7, 205, 207, 211
Walking xvi, 6–7, 9, 11, 24, 27, 38–50, 53, 59, 71, 106, 124–5, 128, 138–9, 165, 220, 249
walking 1–2, 5, 37, 38–50, 66, 74, 78, 88, 127, 142, 152, 168, 181–2, 198–9, 216, 235
Walls, Laura Dassow 198–9, 201
Washington, George 23, 161, 178–80, 203, 216
Webb, Carson 88n. 17, 237n. 33
Webb, Steve 141n. 32
Webster, Daniel 172, 175
Week on the Concord and Merrimack xvi, 4, 18, 21–2, 26–7, 31, 62, 76, 93, 98, 106, 136, 139–40, 142–4, 183–4, 192–202, 203, 212, 235, 242, 249
weeping stones 93, 116, 232
whales 224
White Mountains 27, 142, 246
Whittier, John Greenleaf 175

Wild Apples xvi, 32, 106, 152, 162, 166–9, 182, 187–8
Wittgenstein, Ludwig 34, 105, 115, 127n. 20, 155–7, 209–10, 212, 231
wonder 3, 9–14, 24, 34, 39, 48–9, 53–5, 61, 68, 70–1, 77, 87, 102, 104–5, 108, 111, 115–16, 120–1, 125–8, 131, 133, 137, 139, 143–4, 150, 152–9, 165–70, 191, 196, 208, 211, 217, 221, 239–41, 251

Wordsworth, William 221

Yahweh 49, 226–7
Yogi, yogin xiii, xv, 37–8, 103
Yosemite 47n. 44, 97

Zamir, Tzaki 29n. 26, 151n. 10
Zeus 170
Zossima, Father (Dostoevsky) 91n. 23

www.ingramcontent.com/pod-product-compliance
Lightning Source LLC
Chambersburg PA
CBHW071808300426
44116CB00009B/1235